AN UNNECESSARY MAN:
The Life of Apollon Grigor'ev

WAYNE DOWLER

An Unnecessary Man:
The Life of
Apollon Grigor'ev

UNIVERSITY OF TORONTO PRESS
Toronto Buffalo London

© University of Toronto Press Incorporated 1995
Toronto Buffalo London
Printed in Canada

ISBN 0-8020-0712-0

Printed on acid-free paper

Canadian Cataloguing in Publication Data

Dowler, Wayne, 1945–
An unnecessary man : The Life of Apollon Grigor'ev

Includes index.
ISBN 0-8020-0712-0

1. Grigor'ev, Apollon Aleksandrovich, 1822–1864 –
Biography. 2. Authors, Russian – 19th century –
Biography. 3. Critics – Russia – Biography.
I. Title.

PG3337.G72Z66 1995   891.78'309   C95-930608-0

University of Toronto Press
acknowledges the financial assistance
to its publishing program of the
Canada Council and the
Ontario Arts Council.

This book has been published
with the help of a grant from the
Canadian Federation of Humanities,
using funds provided by the
Social Sciences and Humanities
Research Council of Canada.

Contents

Preface

Many people have contributed to the making of this book. I wish to thank in particular my colleague at Scarborough College, Jane Abray, not only for reading the manuscript with such care and making a host of valuable suggestions for its improvement, but also for being such a true and supportive friend. I am deeply indebted as well to Joseph Frank of Stanford University and Gleb Žekulin of the University of Toronto, both of whom read the manuscript in its later stages and gave me excellent advice about how to make it better, in addition to providing the encouragement that I needed to finish it. None of the above people can be held responsible for those places in the book where I persisted in the error of my ways in spite of their best efforts. Thanks are also due to John Parry for his intelligent editing of the manuscript and to my colleague Arthur Sheps for some timely help. Finally, I want to recall the dear memory of Leonard Schapiro, with whom on many occasions I discussed Russian intellectual history in general and Apollon Grigor'ev in particular, and without whose knowledge and concern I would be much the poorer today.

The dates are all rendered in the old style unless indicated as new style (n.s.). The Julian calendar lagged behind the Gregorian by twelve days in the nineteenth century, and by thirteen in the twentieth. A slightly modified Library of Congress transliteration system is used in the book.

AN UNNECESSARY MAN:
The Life of Apollon Grigor'ev

Introduction

Apollon Grigor'ev's time has come again, as he knew it would. The failure of Marxian ideology in the post-industrial world has sparked a reorientation of thought in the region of the former Soviet Union away from the tradition of left political radicalism, which helped to legitimize communism, and towards a search for a new legitimacy in the non-radical intellectual sources and traditions of the pre-Revolutionary past. The dissolution of the Soviet Union and the loss of a Soviet identity have turned Russians away from the universalistic claims of socialism to a renewed emphasis on nation and nationality.

Grigor'ev was the best of the non-radical literary critics in the nineteenth century and arguably the greatest of all of Russia's critics in the century. Like almost all Russian critics, he went beyond literary concerns in his critical works and developed a comprehensive view of Russia and the world. He rejected the universalism and rationalism of much of the western thought that animated intellectual debate in Russia. He advocated, in their place, an aesthetic appreciation of the world, based on the concrete realities of particular peoples and nations, with their distinctive cultures and histories. Listen today to the more moderate among Russian conservative nationalists and hear the voice of Apollon Grigor'ev. Listen in particular to Alexander Solzhenitsyn's views on the nation in his 'Letter to the Soviet Leaders' and other writings or to his ideas about art in the 'Nobel Prize Lecture' and hear again the voice of Apollon Grigor'ev.[1] He is a profound and attractive source for contemporary conservative nationalism in Russia and is set to become one of its most potent inspirations.

Grigor'ev would not himself have been surprised to learn that his ideas have regained currency. He recognized that intellectual and spiritual tendencies move in unpredictable cycles and that his idealist way of understanding reality had become 'unnecessary' even in his own time. In the face of the materialism, positivism, and scientism that swept up the Russian intelligentsia in the years following the Crimean War and of the 'nihilism' that they produced, Grigor'ev adopted the persona of the 'unnecessary man' and often signed his articles 'One of the Unnecessary People.' Grigor'ev distinguished carefully between the unnecessary (*nenuzhnyi*) and the superfluous (*izlishnii*) man. The latter was a moral, humble, and weary individual who suffered from the 'incommensurability of his means with his aspirations.' The former was simply unnecessary because the 'need for him had gone.' But, Grigor'ev continued, 'Life is a strangely mysterious business: it contains the principle of irony and is in some ways a two-faced Janus ...' One can in good conscience fight for what appears to be necessary, but life will sometimes suddenly and quite unexpectedly do an about-face and declare the apparently unnecessary necessary once again.[2]

Grigor'ev's admirers, too, recognized that certain historical periods were inhospitable to his ideas. In May 1918, the poet Alexander Blok was scheduled to speak to the students of the School of Journalism in Moscow about Grigor'ev. When Blok arrived for the lecture, he announced that he was going to talk instead about the Roman conspirator Catiline. Grigor'ev's times, he explained to his listeners, were out of harmony with their own 'winged and threatening hour of history,' and Grigor'ev did 'not resonate' in the contemporary environment.[3]

In spite of his reluctance to make Grigor'ev the principal subject of his talk, Blok considered it 'important for me now to say a few words about the writer.' In 1846, he began, the great writer Nikolai Gogol' had published his notorious *Selected Passages from Correspondence with Friends* (Vybrannye mesta iz perepiski s druz'iami). Tainted by the suspect approval of the tsarist authorities, the book was known by reputation to the public, but its pages were seldom read. Most knew it only through the critic Vissarion Belinskii's famous 'Letter to Gogol'.' That letter, Blok complained, interpreted Gogol's book one-sidedly and judged it unfairly. Sadly, all who read Belinskii believed him. 'But among those "all," one was excepted: the young Apollon Grigor'ev appreciated at once what "ardent spiritual matters" the content of the book comprised.'

Grigor'ev also, in 1848, wrote a letter to Gogol', which, Blok contended, was no less substantial than Belinskii's, which had often been published as a separate brochure. 'It would be no sin,' Blok declared, 'likewise to publish Grigor'ev's letter to Gogol'.' Blok confessed to a bias against Belinskii. Were he a dispassionate literary historian, he said, he could perhaps evaluate the man objectively, 'but while I search fervently in the books of life, present (in both meanings) [*nastoiashchaia* also means 'real'] life and not the past, I cannot forgive Belinskii; I shout, "Shame on Belinskii!"'

For all his greatness, Blok explained, Belinskii committed a great sin against Gogol'. More than any other thinker, Belinskii gave the shove that set members of the Russian intelligentsia tumbling down the stairs of Westernism, bumping their heads painfully on every step, and 'most of all on the last step, the Russian revolution of 1917–1918.' And Blok prophesied the rebirth of Grigor'ev's view. Read Gogol''s book, he urged, with Westernizing blinkers removed, and discover much that is new: 'Finally, open, along with Gogol', his faithful interpreter, Apollon Grigor'ev, and be convinced that the time has come to stop passing over a completely original Russian configuration of the soul which opens up new vistas. He is obscure and confusing, but behind that obscurity and muddle, if you take the time to scrutinize them, new ways of looking at life will be revealed to you.'4

At the end of the twentieth century, it is hard to disagree with Blok. There can be little doubt that time and again, Grigor'ev's thoughts about art and culture, philosophy, history, and ideology have been borne out against those of his opponents, and many of his judgments are now the commonplaces of students of Russian history and literature.

After the consolidation of the Bolshevik Revolution, Grigor'ev was treated as unnecessary in Russia. Russian scholars did not completely ignore him; rather they accommodated him where they could do so and dismissed him where they could not. But with the recent disintegration of that ideological stranglehold – the origins of which Blok, perhaps unfairly, attributed to Belinskii – life's irony has displayed its other face. As Russians retrieve the great variety of their past in a less mediated form, the unnecessary man will no longer be unnecessary and will indeed reveal, at least to some, 'new ways of looking at life.'

In an obituary in a journal not well disposed to the critic's ideas, the anonymous author conceded that Grigor'ev had been highly 'valued by Russia's most gifted writers.'5 And so he was. Bemused, frustrated, and angry as they often were with him, writers of the stature of Fedor Dostoevskii, Afanasii Fet, Alexander Ostrovskii, and Ivan Turgenev, along with other important cultural figures such as the composer Alexander Serov and the great actor Ivan Gorbunov, deeply respected (feared, in Turgenev's case) his judgments and loved the man. More than a decade after Grigor'ev's death, Ia.P. Polonskii, who had experienced both the friendship and the enmity of the critic, urged Ostrovskii, who knew Grigor'ev so well, to base a character in one of his plays on him: 'As a personality, Grigor'ev merits the brush of a great artist; truly, he was purely Russian by nature – a kind of elemental thinker, impossible in any Western country.'[6]

This book cannot pretend to such artistry. Its perspective is that of the historian of ideas and culture and not of the artist or literary historian or critic. Grigor'ev's work is too often known only through the criticism of his opponents. His reputation is still deeply coloured by the hostility and ridicule heaped on his writings by radical and liberal critics of his day. Thanks to them, he is known to many as inconsistent, unfocused, obscure, difficult to read. And so he is little read. His idealist and, at bottom, religious view of the world has, as he foresaw, made him almost perennially out of season in the intellectual mainstream.

There are, of course, many approaches to the writing of biography. After much thought, I decided to write a traditional study of Grigor'ev. Though undeserved, his relative obscurity is a fact that needs to be addressed and remedied before other biographical methods can be effectively applied, as I hope they will be, to his life and work. For the most part, I have traced Grigor'ev's thought chronologically, as it developed, rather than organizing it around either some grand scheme or smaller themes within the life's work. In order to allow readers to judge for themselves whether Grigor'ev's detractors are right about his writings, I have set out a number of his major critical articles at length. This biography, therefore, aspires to do no more than to make the life and thought of Apollon Grigor'ev as transparent to readers as possible, so that they too can know and judge this man, who, according to the novelist and aesthete Konstantin Leont'ev, 'not only resembled a Russian but was *the thing in itself*.'[7]

PART ONE
Romantic Idealist

1

A Feverish Imagination
1822–1842

I was raised meanly and without joy.

Ivan Turgenev, *Diary of a Superfluous Man*

On 22 July 1822, Apollon Alexandrovich was christened in the parish church of St John the Divine in Moscow. He had been born six days earlier, near the Tver' Gate, in the home of his godmother, a widowed towns-woman, Anna Stepanovna Shchekoldina. His parents were not married.[1] Ten years earlier another 'child of the heart,' Alexander I. Herzen, had been baptized in the same church. Herzen and Grigor'ev never met and were always spiritually distanced by what Grigor'ev called Herzen's 'cyni-cal atheism.' But the profoundly aesthetic appreciation of life that charac-terized their mature thought linked the two men, and their illegitimate births and the coincidence of their place of christening symbolized from the beginning their lasting affinities.

Two days after the christening, Apollon was admitted to the Imperial Moscow Foundling Home as child no. 2,714. Though his father, Titular Counsellor Alexander Ivanovich Grigor'ev, belonged to the hereditary nobility, his son was registered, because he was illegitimate, in the petty-burgher estate (*meshchanstvo*). Later, Apollon achieved personal nobility by way of promotion onto the Table of Ranks upon graduating from Mos-cow University. His lowly origins, however, fostered in him a profound sense of social inferiority that tormented him as a young man. In later years, he professed an amused contempt for privilege and exaggerated his own spiritual closeness to the people.

The child's parents soon put right the accident of his birth by marrying, on 26 January 1823. Four months later, Alexander Ivanovich, now recog-nized as Apollon's legal father, assumed full parental rights over his son.

The boy's mother was Tatiana Andreevna, daughter of a serf who had been coachman in the Grigor'ev household. The new family took up residence in the home of Apollon's godmother, where in November was born a second son, Nikolai, who lived less than a month.[2]

Alexander Ivanovich was proud of his status as a hereditary noble; but it was not a distinction of long standing. His father, Ivan Grigor'evich, had achieved the honour only in 1803. The patriarch of the Grigor'ev family died long before his grandson's birth, but Apollon was deeply affected by the dominant image of his grandfather. He likened him to the despotic Stepan Mikhailovich Bagrov, the patriarch of Sergei Aksakov's *The Family Chronicle* (Semeinaia khronika).[3] Born in 1762 in the provinces, Ivan Grigor'evich arrived in Moscow at the age of fifteen, according to family legend, on foot and wearing the shorn sheepskin coat of the peasant. He began his service career as a scribe in a branch of the Moscow provincial administration and advanced steadily up the Table of Ranks until in 1803 the family name was inscribed in the Genealogical Book of the Nobility of Moscow Province.[4]

With ennoblement came the right to own land with serfs, and Ivan Grigor'evich bought a small estate in Vladimir Province. On first arriving in Moscow, he had moved into the house of his uncle, the archpriest of the local parish. Apollon later rested his thin claim that he was descended from the clergy on that distant relative. Ivan Grigor'evich remained in his uncle's home for more than a decade. There he married Marina Nikolaevna, a freed household serf, and there were born their first two children, Alexander (1787) and Ekaterina (1788). His rising fortunes enabled him in 1790 to buy a large urban property consisting of two houses. Two more children, Alexandra (1800) and Nikolai (1804), were born there. The family prospered until the autumn of 1812, when the fires that followed the French occupation of Moscow severely damaged the property. It was subdivided, and part was sold. The family's fortunes never recovered from the blow.[5]

Ivan Grigor'evich's success in state service was of little interest to Apollon. What captivated him about his grandfather was the reputed robustness of his character. Grandfather Grigor'ev was said to have been personally acquainted with Nikolai Novikov, one of the most prominent Freemasons of the reign of Catherine II, and was probably himself a Mason. The family story was told that Ivan Grigor'evich had hastily to destroy the books given to him by Novikov after the latter's arrest was ordered by Catherine. Grandfather was well-read, especially in religious literature, and had collected a large library. When Apollon was eleven, the library was moved from the estate in the country to the Grigor'ev house in Moscow. He recalled with shame that he trampled with childish spite on the expensive leather bindings of the books, which, neglected, were if not stolen by the servants, then nibbled by the mice.

Like his grandfather, Apollon, as a very young man, almost certainly joined a Masonic lodge in Moscow, and he would seem to have maintained at least occasional contacts with Freemasonry throughout his life. He took great pride in his grandfather's independence of mind and spirit, which had made the old man bold, again according to family legend, even in conversation with bishops. Apollon later emulated his boldness in his own fierce independence from the literary camps in Russia and paid a heavy price for his audacity. In his autobiography, the first instalment of which appeared in 1862, Grigor'ev recounted that at one time he believed that there was 'some sort of secret link between my soul and my grandfather's, some sort of metempsychosis that was not really metempsychosis but a solidarity of souls.' He claimed that his grandfather had at critical moments in his life appeared in his dreams. At one time, he confessed, he even used to sit in view of his grandfather's former house, years after his death, waiting for the old man's return and counting on him to solve his problems.[6]

Ivan Grigor'evich's temerity towards his peers was readily transformed into tyranny in his family relations. The harsh patriarchy of traditional Russian life ruled the Grigor'ev household. Domestic life with Ivan Grigor'evich was a misery of material excess, despotism, piety, and quarrels. The spirit of his eldest son – Apollon's father, Alexander Ivanovich – was permanently deformed by the terror that he experienced during his father's tyrannical outbursts. As an adult, Alexander Ivanovich, too, indulged in savage, irrational explosions, usually directed against the servants. It was, Grigor'ev wrote, 'something physiological, a toll paid to something congenital, something completely mad and furious, something whose onslaughts I myself sometimes felt, under different provocations, of course, and to which I, too, gave myself up like a beast.'[7] Not surprisingly, Alexander Ivanovich grew up self-effacing and chameleon-like in society, while at the same time exercising a petty tyranny over subordinates and the weak. Grigor'ev claimed to have despised his father 'from the moment I first became conscious,' despite brief periods of reconciliation with him. He saw in him only crude egoism and cynical heartlessness, masquerading as the highest morality. A weak man, 'he would have been my slave forever had it pleased me,' Apollon complained of his father.[8] The servant of Mammon, he was, his son wrote condescendingly, a 'wholly banal and carnal man: transcendent longings and transcendent lyricism were completely incomprehensible to him.'[9]

Others did not share the son's harsh assessment of Alexander Ivanovich. Afanasii Fet, who was to become one of Russia's leading lyric poets, boarded in the Grigor'ev household while he was attending university. He formed an almost filial affection for Alexander Ivanovich and continued to visit him long after he left the university. In his memoirs, Fet took Apollon to task for judging and treating his father, who had denied him nothing, so shabbily.[10]

For all his son's contempt for his failings, Alexander Ivanovich had asserted his own independence at least once. He had been the beneficiary of a rather grand education at the Nobles' Pension of Moscow University. On entering state service in 1809, he began to forge a brilliant career as a provincial secretary to the Senate. His advance ended abruptly in 1818, however, when he took to drinking heavily. In December of that year he secured a leave of absence that stretched into more than two years. When he returned to service early in 1822, it was to an inferior career path in the Moscow city magistracy.

The real story of what happened in 1818 has been lost. According to family legend, Alexander Ivanovich had fallen in love with Apollon's future mother, Tatiana Andreevna, in that year. But she was a serf, and his parents forbade him to marry her. Brokenhearted, he had fallen into dissipation and lethargy. The legend is not, however, fully accurate. Ivan Grigor'evich had been dead for several years by 1818.[11] His wife, Marina Nikolaevna, was herself a former serf. Though Russian mothers traditionally possessed a moral right to approve or not their sons' choice of bride, it would have been difficult for Alexander Ivanovich's mother to thwart the determined wishes of her eldest son. More probably, Tatiana Andreevna, for reasons of her own, initially refused him. She was by far the stronger personality of the two; Fet testified that Alexander Ivanovich was in marriage 'dogmatically [as a matter of course] subordinated' to his wife.[12] Whether the conception of Apollon was the result of a moment's release of the young couple's pent-up passion or of calculation cannot be known.

Tatiana Andreevna, though literate, had little education. She accompanied her reading with a loud whispering sound. She was acknowledged by family friends to be clever, holding opinions on a wide range of topics, but eccentric, sometimes expressing her thoughts boldly and quite unexpectedly to complete strangers. In 1827, she bore a third child, a daughter, who also died within weeks of her birth. Hard on the baby's death, the mother was afflicted with a strange illness that stayed with her until her own death twenty-five years later. Each month for several days she experienced a psychological transformation. She grew self-obsessed and raged at a fate that she believed had cheated her and at a husband who she claimed had failed her. In the grip of those spells, she lost all sense of proportion and stormed at the servants. During the attacks, her eyes clouded, yellow spots appeared on her face, and an 'ominous smile' hovered on her lips.[13] This second self, which acknowledged no restraint, must have provided her some relief from the grief over her children's deaths that she seemed otherwise unable to express. In good health, she exercised a thorough domestic tyranny, dominating her husband and the servants and doting on her son, whom she spoiled and cosseted beyond even contemporary Russian standards.

This strained and unhealthy ménage was from time to time augmented by an assortment of relatives. There was Apollon's grandmother, Marina Nikolaevna, an unassuming and religious woman who had outlived her husband's despotism. For most of the year, she lived on the country estate, which the two sons had made over to her in order to support her and their sisters.[14] A great-uncle came for a while, when Apollon was ten, to share an upstairs room with the boy. Deeply religious, he read sacred works and prayed constantly, soon contriving even to die while at prayer. Deeply superstitious as well as religious, he terrified Apollon with tales of witches and living corpses. Apollon's favourite visitor was his oldest aunt, Ekaterina Ivanovna, a spinster 'from pride,' who remembered as a lost Arcadia the past glories of her father's home before the fires of 1812.[15] There was a great-aunt who was given to seeing visions and who conducted that most independent of the traditional activities of Russian women, a thriving folk-medicine practice in the neighbourhood. There was Uncle Nikolai, who shamed Apollon at age thirteen into dressing himself instead of being dressed by a servant.[16]

By the time he grew up, Grigor'ev had formed a dismal opinion of the traditional Russian family. For Russians, he maintained, the family was always a 'wicked step-mother' and never a 'mother.'[17] Whether his view was forged in his own experience or determined by the patriarchal image of the family in Russian folktales and literature is hard to tell. No sound basis for a conventional biography of Grigor'ev as a child exists; most of what is known comes from his autobiographical *My Literary and Moral Wanderings* (Moi literaturnye i nravstvennye skital'chestva), the first part of which was published in 1862 and the unfinished remainder in 1864, or from occasional remarks in his letters. There were no siblings to confirm Grigor'ev's memories or to remember matters differently, no surviving letters or diaries of parents, other relatives, or servants, and, until he went to the university at sixteen, no memoirs by friends. What survives of his childhood is what Grigor′ev himself selected as significant.

By the time he wrote *My Literary and Moral Wanderings*, childhood memoirs had become a literary genre in Russia. Alexander Herzen had recently published *My Past and Thoughts* (Byloe i dumy), which had included a lengthy section about his childhood, and Lev Tolstoi had written his *Childhood* (Detstvo) and *Youth* (Iunost′). Grigor′ev was writing his own memoirs with those precedents in mind, and their conventions almost certainly influenced both what he remembered about his family and the way he remembered it.

Even more crucial in determining the content and form of Grigor′ev's childhood recollections was the fundamental premise of his own literary critical theory. Grigor′ev believed that individuals, ideas, or cultural artefacts were above all else organic products of a specific time and place. They were typical of their age, and their examination illuminated the entire era in which they were produced. In *Wanderings*, Grigor′ev portrayed himself as the 'son of a particular era,' as 'typical' of an epoch. He went on to assert that he did not intend to 'write an autobiography, but a history of my impressions,' and only of those impressions that 'broadly characterize the times.'[18] His memoirs were therefore a highly self-conscious exploration of his childhood in search of the sources of both his own and Russia's cultural and moral biography since his birth forty years earlier.

Apollon's earliest memory was of a house near the Tver′ Gate where he lived, after leaving his godmother's, until he was five. It was a multi-dwelling building that belonged to an Old Believer merchant, Ignatii Ivanovich Kazin. Apart from the Grigor′evs, twenty-six persons were in residence. The house left him with happy memories of a bustle and excitement that contrasted sharply with the boredom and routine of his later childhood homes. Years afterward, Nikolai Strakhov, one of his nearest collaborators in his last years, recalled that Grigor′ev liked best of all to live in a small room in a small tavern crowded with Russian people. There, amid the turmoil, he would contentedly write.[19]

In 1827, the family moved to the southeastern part of the Zamoskvorech′e district of Moscow. The area lay south of the Moscow River, within walking distance of the old city centre. It was itself an old district, with winding streets of mainly wooden houses and generously dotted with the onion domes of the parish churches. The principal inhabitants were merchants, denizens of the 'dark kingdom' of A.N. Ostrovskii's plays of the 1850s, whose patriarchal mores set the tone of local life. Later, Grigor′ev was to see in them the light and the hope for a culturally autonomous Russia. Apart from the merchants, the district had become popular with lesser government officials, who lived there in significant numbers.

Grigor'ev attributed most of his later attitudes to life and art to his childhood in the Zamoskvorech'e. Not even Ostrovskii, he contended, had captured the poetical side of the district. There in the house that his family rented on the Bolvanovka, Grigor'ev's 'semi-conscious childhood began, that is, the childhood whose impressions formed and retained some meaning.'[20] The house, significantly, was out of harmony with its surroundings. It and its twin next door were both owned by a gentry family. 'Noble' as were its 'pretensions,' the house looked shabby and neglected in the street of well-kept merchants' homes. From the locked yard, Apollon looked out onto the back streets into a forbidden world of the festive dances of factory workers, lovers' trysts, the group fist-fights that traditionally enlivened village life and now gave spice to the existence of the urban poor, and other, less violent popular games. Those colourful scenes of licence and uninhibited pleasure and pain formed the heart of his later 'democratic' aesthetic. Inside the house, he was inundated with toys that bored him.[21]

Life in the Bolvanovka was spoiled for him, he recalled, by the onset of his mother's illness and the advent of Latin. According to custom, the upbringing of Russian boys was left in the hands of women during the first five or six years of their childhood, after which they were handed over to the tutelage of men. His mother had already taught Apollon his ABCs, but his formal education began when a tutor was hired in November 1827. Sergei Ivanovich Lebedev was a seminarian and medical student, who, after graduating, was to take a post as a country doctor in the Tambov district.[22] An unimaginative teacher, like most of his kind in those days, his method was to set assignments for rote learning and subsequent drill. He was Grigor'ev's first contact with the seminarians, a breed with which he was later to have little patience.[23] Along with F.M. Dostoevskii, he came to hold their training in the seminary responsible for the narrow dogmatism of the nihilist leadership in the 1860s.

At first, learning was a torment for Grigor'ev. He sat at his studies for hours but did not work. He memorized lessons, then recited them badly, often intentionally so. Arithmetic provoked tears. Until he was twelve, learning was crammed into him: Latin, Russian language and literature, even some mathematics, and, thanks to a resident French tutor-companion (*diad'ka*), an excellent knowledge of French. The tutor remained with the family until 1838, when, while drunk, he fell down the stairs leading from the mansard and died of his injuries. Apollon's natural intelligence and curiosity eventually overcame his obstinacy and laziness and the shortcomings of contemporary pedagogy; from age twelve, his love of learning, which was to make him, by common assent, one of the best-read men of letters in Russia, blossomed. But he did not forget the agonies of boredom that he had suffered over his rote lessons. He was himself a teacher for many years and also served briefly as tutor of the teenaged son of Prince Trubetskoi. A reluctant, but skilled and often inspiring teacher, Grigor'ev rejected in his own classroom the rote learning still recommended in the school system long after his tutor had inflicted it on him.

Routine and confinement governed the household. The day began at seven, when, until the age of thirteen, Grigor'ev was dressed by his nanny. After reciting his prayers in Latin and Russian, he joined his parents for a vast cup of heavily sugared tea. While he drank it, his mother combed his hair for him, a morning ritual that she continued until he ran away to St Petersburg as a young man. In times of her illness, Apollon lived in fear that the comb would dig unexpectedly and painfully into his scalp. Grigor'ev's later image of the dual nature of women, who combined love and cruelty, must have owed a great deal to those sessions. The combing done, she often took Apollon into her bed for a while. When he escaped his mother, he sought out Sergei Ivanovich in his room. The tutor assigned a lesson or two before departing for the university. Alexander Ivanovich, too, went off to his duties, leaving Apollon to stew over the lessons while his mother nagged the servants.

At one o'clock, Sergei Ivanovich returned, and the assigned lessons had to be recited. Instruction ended at two, when Alexander Ivanovich got back from the office. Then dinner was served, a large and splendid meal – a 'divine service,' as Grigor'ev recalled. Studies or, if required, additional repetitions of the morning's lessons resumed until tea before six. Later, there was the family supper, and then, from nine to ten, while the servants ate, Sergei Ivanovich read novels aloud in the dining-room while Apollon lay listening on a rug in the hallway. At ten, he was sent to bed, and the reading was adjourned to his parents' bedroom. Through the thin partition, or crouched in the hall by the bedroom door, Apollon could go on attending to whichever romantic or gothic novel had currently captured their fancy.[24]

Those overheard readings fuelled in Grigor'ev an already feverish imagination. Though his parents saved the more lurid bits for late-night reading, the son lay awake to hear them or, failing that, surreptitiously read them himself the next day while at his lessons. Pretending to grapple with arithmetic or Latin, Apollon often composed romantic tales of his own, of which he was invariably the hero.[25]

Such early literary impressions of exotic locales, striking images, and heated emotions were reinforced by other powerful stimulants. The witches and living corpses of great-uncle's world of superstition were inhabitants also of the servants' imaginative landscape. The servants had all recently been moved to Moscow from the countryside, and they regaled Apollon with the folk superstitions and, eventually more important, the popular tales, legends, and songs of Russia. When he was fourteen, the supernatural stories in which his childhood psyche was steeped combined with a reading of E.T.A. Hoffmann's fantastic tales to upset his nerves. He could not sleep at night but lay awake in the grip of 'that sweetly soothing, sickly tormenting mood, that sensitivity to the fantastic, that nearness of another, strange world.'[26] His nerves later became more robust, but the other, strange world remained near to him. Once, many years later, when Strakhov refused to advise him on a particular matter, Grigor'ev turned to the walls of the room and invoked the spirits behind them to guide him.

As a child, Grigor'ev was on good terms with the servants; later he recognized the distortions introduced into their relations by serfdom. Whenever in one of their frenzies his parents threatened a servant with punishment, Apollon howled in the servant's defence. His closeness to the servants fortified his 'peasant's heart,' in which throughout his life beat a love for this 'new, good, intelligent, and *broadminded* people with their sprees, hard drinking, and prodigious dissipation' and inspired his democratic and progressive conception of nationality.[27]

But Apollon learned more from the servants than Russian folklore, a rich vocabulary of profanities and obscenities, and demotic leanings. The servants' hall also awoke in him his earliest sexual stirrings. The ribald stories told by Vasilii the coachman were probably common fare for Russian boys of the time. But the proximity of the servants in an overcrowded and over-regulated household exacted a toll. Ten at night, Grigor'ev remembered, was 'the canonical hour, the hour when the whole household went to sleep *de jure* and when *de facto* the most complete debauch of every sort of lechery, drunkenness and perversion began.'[28] The language seems exaggerated, but the powerful impression left is unmistakable. When he was a little older, Apollon abetted his own manservant, Ivan, in visiting his mistress by letting him out of the locked house after vespers and readmitting him before matins.[29]

Grigor'ev wrote his memoirs under the still-fresh impression of Herzen's *My Past and Thoughts*. Herzen discussed at length the effect of the servants' hall on children and concluded that it 'had no really bad influences upon me at all,' though he 'picked up coarse expressions and bad manners.'[30] Rightly or wrongly, Grigor'ev did not share that conclusion. The early arousal of his sexual instincts, he believed, had unleashed his youthful fantasies about women. When he was seven, the daughter of a country neighbour visited for a week. She was eleven and pretty. They hid together, sat in the same chair together, and whenever she was near, a 'prickling and sweet, sparkling sensation' crept over his body. For a while, she was the heroine of his romantic compositions. From that time on, he felt 'something strange' when close to women.[31] Years later, he confided to a female friend that 'a strongly passionate relationship with a woman is as necessary to me as is water to a fish.'[32]

In an autobiographical story written in the 1840s, Grigor'ev revealed that from the age of twelve he ached for living experience but was constantly denied it. Only his sexual longings were real. In the cloistered and fetid atmosphere of his parents' home, there were no models for a natural life and natural relations with people. Instead of observing living people, he turned in childhood to images drawn from the best and worst of European romantic novels and popular histories. Those images were heroic, idealistic, self-sacrificing. Relations between men and women were exalted and noble, in the spirit of romantic love, but charged as well with a mysterious and clandestine power. He became a dreamer and, possessed by the heroic and idealistic phantoms of European literature, felt useless and deprived. Finally he accepted his ineffectiveness and even came to believe that everyone around him was superior to him. He became, he concluded, two people: one who strove for freedom, another who subordinated freedom to suffering.[33] The sports of the streets and the high fences, locked gates, parental control, and routine of home; the romantic ideal in books and the reality of his sexual desires; love and sex; suffering and freedom – these were the secret poles of his life in the Zamoskvorech'e. 'Cunning,' Grigor'ev recalled, 'the slave's weapon, developed in me early, and I always made out that I understood nothing indecent.'[34] In the memoirs, his personal experience of the disjuncture of the ideal from the real thanks to the 'phantoms' of European literature served as a symbol for the alienation of a whole generation of Russian intellectuals from their native reality and their belief in Western superiority.

Apollon's tutor, Sergei Ivanovich, contributed as well to his pupil's early, heightened awareness of women. Though harsh toward seminarians as a group, Grigor'ev declared a preference for the Moscow over the St Petersburg variant and harboured a warm spot in his heart for his first teacher. He described him as not a 'true' but a 'sentimental romantic,' who wrote bad poetry and doggedly pursued a series of uninspired love affairs about which Apollon's father gratuitously offered both advice and ridicule. Undeterred, Sergei Ivanovich spent whole evenings in his room with Apollon, recounting the progress of his affairs.

On other evenings, the tutor's friends from the university gathered in his room. The universities in the 1830s were still quaking in the aftershocks of the Decembrist conspiracy of 1825.[35] Sergei Ivanovich's friends were intimidated and cautious. But hearing them converse, Apollon could sense their enthusiasm for the poems of A.S. Pushkin and A.I. Polezhaev or the novels of A.A. Bestuzhev-Marlinskii. During those conversations, he also learned of another kind of student: 'Even in sober moments, how they told each other tales about those others, the comrades who were terrifying to them, who devoted themselves head and heart to Schellingism, to the point of moral intoxication, or who devoted their whole life to their raging passions.'[36] Awareness of those others must have been a goad to Apollon's second self, which longed for freedom.

In 1830 or 1831, Alexander Ivanovich bought a house on the Malaia Polianka, in the southwestern part of the Zamoskvorech'e district. It was a wooden structure built over a stone basement, in which were located the servants' quarters. The public rooms were on the ground floor, along with the master bedroom. Up a narrow staircase was a mansard, divided equally into two identical bedrooms. One was Apollon's; the other, after the untimely death of his French companion, was occupied by Afanasii Fet. Like the previous house, this one was enclosed by a high fence, and its great wooden gate was kept locked. Even the small wicket gate in the great gate was kept on the bolt. By that time, Alexander Ivanovich was sufficiently important in the magistracy to be regularly bribed, as his father had been before him. Fet remembered the feed for the horses and milch cow that was provided free and the frequent deliveries of provisions and supplies for which no one ever paid.[37]

With the financial means in hand to give their son the best education available, Apollon's parents set about the delicate task of attaining it. Since Apollon had been registered at birth in the *meshchanstvo*, he was subject to military service in the ranks – a dire fate in pre-reform Russia. Strings were pulled, and on 4 May 1833 a Moscow magistrate issued Apollon a certificate of discharge from the petty-burgher estate, on condition that within a specified period of time he graduate with a university degree.[38] Toward the end of 1832, Sergei Ivanovich had himself graduated and resigned his duties as Grigor'ev's tutor. I.D. Beliaev, a prominent professor of Russian juris-prudence, undertook to prepare Grigor'ev for the university entrance examinations.

In 1838, Apollon triumphantly passed the examinations and in August was admitted to the Law Faculty of Moscow University. At sixteen, he was chubby, grey-eyed, and fair-haired, a 'model of modesty and restraint,' as Fet, who met him at that time, noted.[39] Exceptionally intelligent, already well-read in the classics of European literature, and keenly attuned to con-temporary literary trends, Apollon had also studied piano with one of Moscow's better teachers and become an accomplished musician. Long after his death, his friends remembered him as a youth of sixteen seated at the piano playing excerpts from his favourite opera, Giacomo Meyerbeer's *Robert the Devil*, while dramatically, some thought pedantically, annotat-ing the music as he played.[40] He was so able in French that he had just com-pleted a Russian translation of Shakespeare's *King Lear* from a French version.

In choosing to study the law, Apollon was probably pleasing his parents rather than following his own desires. But not all of the prescribed courses for the law degree, especially in the early years of the program, were taken in the Law Faculty. In the first year, for example, students read the theory of literature (rhetoric), theology (moral and dogmatic), Latin, and Greek, as well as two courses in the Law Faculty, and in the second year they pur-sued, along with three courses within the faculty, Russian history, universal history, and logic.[41] Among Grigor'ev's professors were T.I. Granovskii, one of the leading Westernizers; M.P. Pogodin and S.P. Shevyrev, who were associated with the conservative nationalist doctrine called 'official nationality,' which upheld autocracy, Orthodoxy, and nationality as the essence of the Russian being; and, within the Faculty of Law, N.I. Krylov and P.G. Redkin, who were at the time deeply influenced by Hegel.

The rector of the university, Count S.G. Stroganov, and most members of the faculty, regarded Grigor'ev as their most promising student and hoped to prepare him for the professoriate. So good was he that Stroganov began to fear for him in the suspicious climate of Nicholas I's Russia. Once, after Grigor'ev had demonstrated to the count that he was indeed the author of a particularly fine legal judgment written in French, Stroganov told him, 'Vous faites trop parler de vous; il faut vous effacer.'[42] Krylov was especially taken with Grigor'ev, often invited him to his home, and later helped him to get work at the university. Grigor'ev met all the expectations placed in him by scoring a perfect grade of 5 in every course that he took over four years and winning the gold medal on graduating in 1842.[43]

While at the university, Apollon formed a deep and abiding attachment to M.P. Pogodin, who held the chair of Russian history. Pogodin was a liberated serf, an enthusiastic Russian nationalist with strong Slavophile connections, and, from 1840, editor of the monthly journal *Moskvitianin* (The Muscovite). His reputation for miserliness was later earned, but he had first acquired it unfairly when he dared to grumble about having to support the genius of N.V. Gogol' by housing and feeding him for an extended period at considerable personal expense. Gogol''s aristocratic and better-heeled friends, who might otherwise have had to assume the burden of genius themselves, not surprisingly judged the socially inferior Pogodin reprehensible in his reluctance. Pogodin was abstemious in his spending, which is hardly surprising in light of his humble beginnings, but there were many financial demands made on him. Over many years, Pogodin patronized and at times financially supported a number of young writers. Several of them deeply respected him and were grateful for his counsel. To Apollon, who secretly (later openly) despised his father, Pogodin assumed the role not only of mentor, but also of surrogate parent and even confessor. For years to come, he was Grigor'ev's stern conscience, who scolded, cajoled, and threatened this ward of whom he despaired but could never bring himself to abandon completely. Grigor'ev rebelled against Pogodin, tormented him, and at times raged at him but loved and respected him always and regarded him as his guide on all historical and political questions.

In the early 1840s, Moscow University was still engulfed by the two great 'waves,' as Grigor'ev was later to call them, in philosophy and literature that dominated the days of his youth and formed his mature outlook. The first was idealism, which 'swept before it all who could think,' and the second was romanticism, which 'swept before it all who could feel.'[44] After the vogue of Schelling that had so thrilled and shocked the generation of students to which Apollon's tutor had belonged, the university was by the end of the 1830s increasingly the philosophical domain of Hegel. Professors Krylov and Redkin were two notable advocates of Hegelianism who approached the study of the law and legal history through a Hegelian lens. Their best student, Grigor'ev, was caught up in their enthusiasm and became an ardent student of Hegel. Early in his university studies he had taught himself German in only six months, at first in order to enjoy Goethe and Schiller in the original, but then to plough through Schelling and as much of Hegel as he could get his hands on. He chattered so much about his idol that on one occasion his servant Ivan attracted his attention outside the theatre after a performance by shouting 'Hegel's carriage!' over the heads of the crowd.

Grigor'ev was not only the kind of brilliant student whose remarks were written down by his classmates, he was also genuinely popular. Since Hegel dominated the intellectual landscape of students at the time, Grigor'ev, the adept, naturally emerged as the leader of a circle. The group met on most Sunday afternoons either at the Grigor'ev house or at the home of K.D. Kavelin. In addition to Grigor'ev and Kavelin, the future legal historian and liberal theorist, the circle boasted a brilliant coterie of soon-to-be writers, publicists, and activists. The best known were the poets A.A. Fet and Ia.P. Polonskii, the historian S.M. Solov'ev, and the Slavophile publicists and activists I.S. Aksakov and Prince A.V. Cherkasskii.

The meetings, though idealist in philosophical spirit, ranged well beyond a Hegelian framework. Two surviving documents suggest that the level of philosophical discussion in the group was not very sophisticated. The first is the earliest known manuscript by Grigor'ev. It was written in October 1840 and entitled 'Fragments from the Chronicle of a Spirit' (Otryvki iz letopisi dukha). Consisting of eleven rather disjointed syllogisms about God, perfectibility, and human striving, it was very much the work of a young believer confronted for the first time with the possibility of his own unbelief.[45] The second is a letter to Grigor'ev from N.M. Orlov, the son of one of the Decembrists and a member of the circle. It, too, is a series of syllogisms that sets out to accomplish the signally non-Hegelian task of demonstrating the existence of God mathematically, a subject the group had recently discussed.[46] Juvenile as they were, the discussions were ardently pursued. Urged on by one another, the members of the group not only honed their debating skills but acquired a wide and enduring training in German idealist philosophy.

Years later, Fet maintained that in all their arguments and conversations 'there was not the least hint of any social questions. Only the abstract and general arose as, for example, to understand how Hegel viewed the relationship of reason and being.'[47] If the two documents above were truly representative, then Fet was right. Grigor'ev's circle probably did devote much of its time to 'futile chasing and demonstrating of the tail of the Absolute.' But the historical interests of Solov'ev and Kavelin, the legal studies of several members, and the enthusiasm of Fet, Grigor'ev, and Polonskii for contemporary Russian poets and critics, including Belinskii, must at times have turned the conversation away from the purely philosophical and to the exigencies of Russian life. Though there is no evidence that the members of the group took any interest in Fourierism or other socialist tendencies, they were not entirely oblivious to certain aspects of leading French social thought – at least some of them, for example, had read the works of Georges Sand. (*Simon*, Sand's first attempt at incorporating socialist ideas in fiction, was published in 1836, and *Le compagnon du tour de France*, a much more successful effort, appeared in 1840. Her works were openly discussed in Russian journals of the day.)

What is certain is that the circle's members did not perceive themselves to be critics of contemporary Russian life or advocates of a defined social point of view. But the jibe by A.V. Novosil'tsev, one member, that Moscow University was built on three ideas – the prison, the barracks, and the cattle yard – and that certain university officials were cattle drovers, had an edge that suggests that not every exchange over the sweet tea with slices of lemon and kalatch was confined to the unfolding of the World Spirit, as Fet would have us believe.[48]

If Grigor'ev imbibed philosophical idealism in university lectures and the stimulation of his circle, he absorbed literary romanticism in the intimacy of home and friendship. Fet, who was studying literature at the university and had previously been living in Pogodin's pension, moved into the Grigor'evs' mansard in January 1839. Though vastly different personalities, Fet and Grigor'ev became fast friends. Perhaps it was their character differences that gave the relationship a sadistic tinge. Fet, the stronger of the two, both physically and psychologically, would torment Apollon by twisting his arm behind him and cruelly squeezing his fingers. Fet was worldly and wise, the opposite of the cosseted Apollon. Alexander Blok called Fet Grigor'ev's 'demon-tempter,' from whom he first learned his taste for tobacco, song, and the ways of the gypsies.[49]

Love of poetry was their strongest bond. Fet had been in the habit of writing his poems in an old notebook. Shortly after his arrival, a new, yellow notebook appeared, and in it, neatly transcribed in Grigor'ev's hand, were Fet's poems. Grigor'ev himself was at the time writing lyrical verses, which he often declaimed. One included the lines, 'O my native land / Land of my fathers, once more I behold you.' When Fet, not surprisingly, criticized them, Grigor'ev, in despair, wrote a poem that began agonizingly, 'I'm not a poet, alas, God help me!' (Ia ne poet, o, Bozhe moi!).[50]

Fet fondly described the cloistered Grigor'ev household as the cradle of his intellectual being. The family routine had changed little since earlier days. Now Grigor'ev got up each day at about 7:30 a.m., dressed and went to the piano in the hall to awaken his parents with a sonata. At 8:00 a.m., Alexander Ivanovich, in warm sweater and skull cap, and Tatiana Andreevna, in dressing gown and frilly nightcap, came out to the dining-room and drank tea. Fet was sent a mug of tea in his room. While drinking her tea, Grigor'ev's mother, as before, combed her son's hair. In his autobiographical story 'One of the Many' (Odin iz mnogikh) of the mid-1840s, Grigor'ev remembered those sessions with horror. His mother was by this time frequently in the grip of her chronic illness. He remembered her pale suffering face, her feverish eyes, and her pathological malice. His father cautiously offered a dish to her, and if it were not just right she could not resist making a cruel remark. As she harped at the father, she never grasped the effect on the son, who could think of nothing else but escape.[51] When tea was finished, Alexander Ivanovich, in reddish wig and uniform dresscoat, and Apollon, in student uniform and peaked cap, walked across the bridge and through the Alexander Garden below the Kremlin, where they parted, the son to the university, the father to his office.

At 2:00 p.m. the coachman picked up Apollon at the university; Alexander Ivanovich usually walked home. At 3:00 p.m. the whole family, along with Fet, ate a sumptuous dinner, following which the parents napped and the two friends did lessons or read. At 8:00 p.m., there was tea; next came more reading, and bed. On religious holidays, father and son attended mass.[52] Apollon was never permitted to go out alone. His servant, Ivan, dogged his footsteps, and wherever he was in the evening the coach was in the courtyard or just around a corner. Polonskii reported that Apollon always made his excuses at 9:00 p.m. and left for home.[53]

In the midst of this routine, Fet challenged Grigor'ev to think again about the mass of novels and poems he had heard and overheard as a child and to reassess his literary tastes and values. In turn, he was himself challenged by Grigor'ev's growing critical powers. When Fet arrived in the Grigor'ev household, Apollon's idol was Lamartine, whose verses Fet found impossibly prosaic. He persuaded Grigor'ev to take an interest in Victor Hugo.[54] Later, Grigor'ev remembered the pleasure that he got from Hugo's historical novels and from the adventures of Alexandre Dumas. Walter Scott made little impression on him, and he remained indifferent to Scott even as an adult. He judged *Anne of Geierstein*, *Kenilworth*, and *The Talisman* weak and found Scott's Cromwell and Louis XI to be pale shadows beside Hugo's versions. He also preferred Donizetti's *Lucia di Lammermoor* to Scott's *Bride of Lammermoor*.[55] In poetry, Lamartine gave way in his affections to Goethe and Schiller, to whom Fet also introduced him. Heine fascinated them both. Soon the two friends were reading Byron together. In Russian literature, M.Iu. Lermontov's *Hero of Our Time* (Geroi nashego vremeni) made a powerful impression on them, as did for a time the poetry of Benediktov.[56]

Romanticism was also sweeping through the theatres of Moscow. Grigor'ev's parents always encouraged their son in any pursuits that they believed to be improving and generously gave him the means to attend the theatre and opera, provided that Fet accompanied him. The friends often saw, on the stage of the Bolshoi Theatre, the great Russian tragic actor P.S. Mochalov, who came to typify for Grigor'ev the Russian romantic era and whose performances haunted him for the rest of his life. M.S. Shchepkin was also acting in Moscow at that time, and the brilliant stage career of P.M. Sadovskii was just beginning. A.S. Griboedov's *Woe from Wit* (Gore ot uma) played in Moscow every year from 1830 to 1845; Gogol''s *The Government Inspector* (Revizor) was staged annually between 1836 and 1845; Schiller's *The Robbers* (Die Räuber) had the longest run, playing every year from 1829 to 1845. Shakespeare's *King Lear* and *Hamlet* also had annual runs throughout much of the period; in 1838, there was a production of *The Merry Wives of Windsor*, and in 1841 *Romeo and Juliet*, in a translation by the future editor of *Russkii vestnik* (The Russian Messenger), M.N. Katkov, was performed.[57] At the Malyi Theatre, the two friends could enjoy the 'lighter fare' of French drama. They also grew to love the opera, especially the works of Meyerbeer. Grigor'ev's first love was the theatre, and he spent much of his career as a theatre critic. He once seriously considered becoming a provincial actor and as a critic retained a special fondness for provincial theatre. He frequently took part later in life in amateur theatrical productions. The establishment of a truly professional national Russian theatre was long one of his most cherished hopes.

Fet once recorded in verse that in their student days 'Hegel himself could not prevent' Grigor'ev from falling in love. Elsewhere, he claimed that 'in those years I did not court women,' whereas Grigor'ev was always 'in love, again in love.'[58] The identity of most of the women of Grigor'ev's dreams is not known. They must have themselves been unaware of his passion; his love almost always went undeclared. An exception was Lisa, one of his parents' godchildren, who, as Apollon suddenly noticed on her name day, had become a woman. No sooner had he fallen in love with her than her father announced her betrothal to an officer, a 'citizen of substance.' At the wedding, an unhappy Grigor'ev, in his role as best man, had to hold the wedding crown, with its garland of flowers, over the bride's head. During the ball afterward, she asked to dance with Fet, who was also in attendance, and forthwith declared her love for him. Later that day, she confessed her passion for Fet to Grigor'ev, who, by now overwhelmed, poured out his own feelings for her.[59] The mingling of the sublime and the sexual sides of woman's love that he had intuited as a child had by now entered his consciousness. In an autobiographical tale of the 1840s, he wrote of a woman he saw in church who reminded him of Mary Magdalene at the foot of the cross. The 'rapturous memories of her appearance' overcame the spiritual apathy that was tormenting him and enabled him to pray.[60]

Religious sensibility lay at the centre of Grigor'ev's outlook throughout his life. He early perceived the centrality of suffering in human life. Ia.P. Polonskii recalled that once during their student years Grigor'ev asked him, 'Do you doubt?' 'Yes,' answered Polonskii. 'And do you suffer?' 'No,' said Polonskii. 'Then you are stupid,' Grigor'ev replied.[61] Religious questions continued to haunt him after he graduated. At the end of 1842, he reported to S.M. Solov'ev, who was visiting Paris, that he was reading all the books in the library on mysticism, especially the works of Jakob Boehme. He was particularly intrigued by the ideas of Louis-Eugène-Marie Bautain, a French writer of the 1830s who combined Rousseauesque notions of simplicity with a mystical search for God and the infinite in the mortal and finite. Grigor'ev concluded, however, that mysticism was as far from the truth of Christ as pantheism. Worship of the internal world of man left the soul as empty as did worship of the external world. The real attraction of Christianity for him was its ordinariness and universal accessibility.[62] Fet remembered his friend's wild swings of mood at this time, from the despair of atheism to moments of extreme asceticism in which he prayed before the icons, the hot wax of a candle flowing over his fervently clenched fingers. Fet was himself as susceptible to spiritual despair as Grigor'ev. As late as 1844, Pogodin recorded in his diary a visit from Fet and Grigor'ev, who were both suffering the agonies of religious doubt.[63]

Once Grigor'ev wrote sardonically that since Russians were a 'rather ignorant and coarsely primitive people,' they were incapable of distinguishing a mere idea from real life. 'Once a particular current [veianie] sets our heads spinning, then they really start to spin.'[64] Whether those lines accurately characterized Russians or not, they were true of their author in his youth. As he left the university for adult life, his head was spinning with ideas and his soul with doubts, with the 'phantoms' of his childhood reading which so far were almost the only life he knew.

2

Thinking and Feeling
1842–1847

Sometimes a person loves suffering terribly,
to distraction, and that's a fact.

Fedor Dostoevskii, *Notes from Underground*

Grigor'ev was about to exchange his sheltered life in Moscow for the temptations of St Petersburg. In the capital, he had for the first time to fend for himself among the ambitious and unscrupulous who peopled its streets in numbers larger than anywhere else in the empire. Hard and bitter as the experience was, St Petersburg gave him the taste of real life for which he had longed. He also gained valuable experience as a journalist and editor, tested his poetic powers, and dabbled in the forbidden waters of Freemasonry and socialism. In St Petersburg, a number of the European 'phantoms' of his youthful reading had left the page to roam the streets and hold forth in drawing-rooms and taverns. Grigor'ev's encounter with them excited and confused him. In grappling with many of the burning questions of the day, he was able as well to explore the many answers proposed by others. Though in the end he dismissed most of them, the experience ultimately served to clarify his view of Russia and the West and set him off on his own distinctive course.

When he graduated in 1842, Grigor'ev had gone to work in the library of Moscow University. His mentor, Professor Krylov, in whose home he was by this time a frequent guest, took it upon himself, however, to secure a more suitable position for his protégé. When the secretary of the university council retired, Grigor'ev was invited to apply for the post and won it in a close ballot held among the members of the council.[1] In September 1843, he took the oath of state service, and early in October he was granted the rank of collegiate secretary. His parents were delighted by their son's promising career prospects, but their joy was short-lived. By the beginning of March 1844, he had run away to St Petersburg, the first of several flights at times of crisis in his life.

Grigor'ev's intimacy with the Krylovs had led to an introduction to the Korshes, one of the more interesting families of Moscow society. Mme Korsh's husband had died young, leaving her alone to raise her children, a son and three daughters. Herself a woman of strong and independent character, whom Grigor'ev acknowledged to have been an important formative influence on him, she had furnished her daughters with a modern, progressive education. There were two still at home when Grigor'ev met them. Both young women, whom Fet swore he had never seen dressed in anything other than white gowns, had grown up to be professed disciples of Georges Sand, whose doctrine of the 'liberation of the heart' they fervently espoused.

Grigor'ev fell, with characteristic desperation, in love with the older daughter, Antonina, late in 1843. The progress of his love was recorded in 'Pages from the Manuscript of a Wandering Sophist,' an odd document that purported to be a diary but was probably written as a continuous whole.[2] The most striking aspect of the affair was that at no time did Grigor'ev declare his feelings although he believed that Antonina had divined them. Her younger sister Lidiia guessed all and made herself his confidante.

Shame and false pride prevented Grigor'ev from speaking out. Though he had graduated from the university and taken a position in government service, almost nothing had changed in his domestic life. Each day his mother subjected him to a session of haircombing; whenever he went out, a manservant dogged his steps. It seems not to have occurred to him that he should keep his salary, which he dutifully turned over to his parents. They were apparently unaware that a young man needed spending money and returned him nothing from his earnings. He began to give lessons on the side to earn pocket money but had to borrow heavily as well. Thus he launched early on a lifetime of indebtedness. Apollon's feelings about his parents were too complex to permit him to express his outrage to them. Instead, he raged against the constraints imposed on him to his uncle Nikolai. But Nikolai had earned the disapproval of Apollon's parents by marrying an attractive woman much younger and richer than he and had forfeited his influence on his brother and sister-in-law.

His father's pusillanimous social attitudes particularly enraged and humiliated Apollon. In a letter of 1846 to his father, he explained why he had run away to St Petersburg. He recalled in particular, the time when his fellow student and social equal, K.D. Kavelin, the future historian, first visited the Grigor'ev household. Apollon's father pointedly came out into the hallway to thank Kavelin for befriending his son.[3] The force of his humiliation even after the passage of several years was palpable in the letter. In the aristocratic ethos of Moscow in the 1840s, Grigor'ev, like others of modest, and in his case questionable, social origins, felt and was made to feel deeply his inherent inferiority. In 'Pages from the Manuscript of a Wandering Sophist' (Listki iz rukopisi skitaiushchegosia sofista), Grigor'ev deplored his birthright: 'Had I been born an Aristocrat, I would have been a perfect Egmont from Goethe – but as it is I am only despised and irksome for not being an Aristocrat.'[4]

Reminded on all sides of the deficiency of his birth and oppressed by his infantile familial relationships, Grigor'ev found that even youth could not buoy up his confidence. So when that very same Kavelin, who was just completing his master's degree and was about to be appointed to a teaching post in the Law Faculty, emerged as a suitor of Antonina, Grigor'ev felt like a child compared to his self-confident and independent rival. In agonized silence, he watched the relationship grow.[5] From hiding in St Petersburg he later wrote, 'In Moscow there awaits me only *humiliation* – and better suicide than humiliation in the eyes of the only woman I sincerely love ...'[6]

The problems of his personal life began to affect his work as secretary to the university council. Its routine nature poorly suited his temperament in any event. He started to plot an escape from family despotism, bureaucratic routine, and humiliation in love. At first he planned to apply for a teaching post in Siberia. In order to prevent his father from finding out through his colleagues about his application, he decided to seek the post through St Petersburg. On 25 February 1844, he asked the rector of the university for a leave of absence in order to conduct some business in the capital. A few days later, he astonished Fet by confiding that he had got some money from a Masonic lodge and was departing for St Petersburg by coach the next day. He asked his old friend to see him off and then to return home to inform his parents of his flight. At three the next afternoon Grigor'ev departed. He had little luggage; his mother controlled his shirts and underwear, and he could not ask for more than a single item at a time without arousing suspicion. Fet dutifully performed the melancholy task. In spite of anger and grief at their son's betrayal, his parents despatched Ivan, the servant, to the address in St Petersburg where Grigor'ev had told Fet he could be found. Ivan took with him shirts, toilet items, and several hundred rubles.[7]

Though Grigor'ev continued until as late as October 1845 to talk about going to teach in Siberia, he did not apply for a position there. Instead he requested an extension of his leave of absence from the university and within days of his arrival applied for a service position in St Petersburg. By June 1844, his friend S.M. Solov'ev, Moscow University's most brilliant young historian, had replaced him as secretary of the university council. At first employed in the Office of Heraldry, Grigor'ev transferred in December to a more prestigious position in one of the departments of the Senate.

The deficiencies that Grigor'ev had revealed as secretary to council soon disqualified him from his new position as well. He clearly was not cut out for state service. By June 1845 the overseer of his department reported to the Ministry of Justice that Grigor'ev was not happy in his work and was often absent, purportedly from ill-health. When, however, a doctor was sent around to his lodgings to attend to him he was not at home. In July he was relieved of his duties in the Senate and transferred back to the Office of Heraldry. He never reported for duty there and finally won permission to retire from state service on the grounds of poor health in December 1845.[8] In justification of his decision to leave the service, he wrote to Pogodin that he could not continue because 'the service kills' and any human being who was truly alive would be 'ashamed to waste half a day doing the work of a machine.'[9]

His professors had singled him out for an academic career when he was still a student. Now, without visible means of support, Grigor'ev had to endure a campaign by his parents, probably with the connivance of Pogodin and Krylov, to lure him home with the promise of a professorship at the university. He refused. Since his graduation, he had formed some harsh views about his alma mater. He wrote to Pogodin that apart from Davydov, Shevyrev, Granovskii, Solov'ev and Pogodin himself, the faculty was 'a herd of cattle' enslaved by Western science, whose sterile teaching had demoralized him as a student. He particularly rounded on the Law Faculty as 'stupid, cynical and vulgar'. A 'fanatic' such as he could do nothing there.[10] It is not apparent, then, why he applied at that time for permission to sit the master's examination in criminal law at St Petersburg University. It was probably only a feint to deflect the barrage of demands from home that he present himself in Moscow forthwith for an academic career. Many years later he pointed out that he was temperamentally unsuited to be a scholar because his was the kind of mind that knew something about everything but nothing through and through.[11]

Grigor'ev resisted returning to Moscow not only because of the 'humiliation' that awaited him there but because a more alluring prospect beckoned him in the capital. He had not only escaped from domestic tyranny and unrequited love at home, but also had fled to a world of licence and a more vital literary life. He had at last escaped the fences and locked gates of his childhood. He went to St Petersburg, he wrote, driven by an 'unquenchable thirst for life.'[12] On the one hand, it was a thirst for writing. Grigor'ev's first published poems had in fact appeared in *Moskvitianin* (The Muscovite) in 1843, before he left Moscow. Now, in June 1844, he published his first poem in a St Petersburg journal, *Repertuar i Panteon* (Repertoire and Pantheon), and his verses appeared regularly there in subsequent issues. Shortly after he left the service, he wrote enthusiastically to Pogodin about the progress of his literary career. He pointed out that he had already published part of a novel in *Repertuar i Panteon*, was preparing a major translation of Béranger's songs, and was working on other translations from French and German. He also reported that he was writing a drama in verse.[13]

On the other hand, his thirst was for all the temptations of life in the capital. Grigor'ev blamed his dissipated existence there on his depressed state of mind. He pointed out that bouts of sadness and ennui had afflicted him since the age of fourteen but had assailed him more often in St Petersburg. He could escape them, he convinced himself, only by diving into the 'pool of the capital's attractions of all sorts,' where he 'frequently forgot his human dignity.'[14] The acquired taste for dissipation as an antidote to ennui became a chronic need to which he catered throughout his life.

Grigor'ev's literary connection with *Repertuar i Panteon* brought him into friendly relations with its editor V.S. Mezhevich. This man, whom he called 'one of the too few noble people that I know,' had previously edited St Petersburg's police gazette and since retained close ties with police authorities. In the fall of 1845, Grigor'ev moved into the editor's home. According to the gossips, he formed a close but platonic relationship with Mezhevich's wife, to whom he used to confide all his secrets. He found in this plump, round-faced blonde a similarity to Ophelia and used to sit on a bench at her feet and recite to her passages from *Hamlet*. His no-doubt ironic identification with the Danish prince in these years was intended to signal his own doubts and uncertainties; and his sitting at the feet of a woman symbolized his belief, profoundly influenced by Georges Sand, in the moral centrality of women.[15]

Rumours about Grigor'ev's behaviour must have been rife back in Moscow. Pogodin wrote demanding an explanation. In order to quell the stories, Mezhevich himself wrote to Pogodin to assure him that the tales were slander. He added that since moving in, Grigor'ev had won the respect of the household and was working conscientiously at his writing and translating.[16] He neglected to add, however, what a frequent visitor to evening gatherings at his home noted: at those events, Grigor'ev spoke ardently and intelligently, but only until midway through dinner; before the cigars, he was already incoherent with drink.[17]

A few months later, Grigor'ev was once again explaining to his parents that the rumours still circulating in Moscow that he was drinking heavily and even had suffered a head injury were false. He was, he claimed, as 'healthy, lively and sober as always'.[18] The truth remained far otherwise. His relationship with a certain Konstantin Solomonovich Milanovskii, under whose spell he had fallen in Moscow, especially helped to undermine his moral balance. Milanovskii, before dropping out of the university, had been a classmate of Fet's. Fet described him as intelligent, a known Mason, and a cheat in matters of money. Later, V.G. Belinskii threw Milanovskii out of his circle for his fraudulent dealings. Grigor'ev must have disobeyed his parents' prohibition on associating with Milanovskii; in a letter of 1846, he apologized to them for being blinded by the man, who caused him, he admitted, to behave badly toward them.[19]

Scarcely had Grigor'ev arrived in St Petersburg when, as years later he wrote to Pogodin, he met the 'devil' in the form of Milanovskii on the Nevskii Prospekt. Soon he was again under his pernicious influence. Milanovskii must have played on Grigor'ev's feelings of guilt about abandoning his parents and his dissolute life in the capital. He encouraged the dissipation in order to secure his hold on the young man. One memoirist of the period called Grigor'ev the archpriest of that 'thief' (Milanovskii), who absolved him from every excess.[20] By his own admission, Grigor'ev foolishly assumed a debt of Milanovskii's and ended by paying dearly for his lapse in judgment. By mid-1846, he had recognized his friend for the 'scoundrel' that he was and claimed to have escaped his influence. Milanovskii, he soberly reported, had harmed him only materially but had not destroyed his reputation.

Like all government servants in the 1840s, Grigor'ev had had to sign a declaration that he 'did not belong to any Masonic lodge or to any secret society either inside the empire or outside it' and undertake 'in future not to belong to any such organizations or to have any relations with them.'[21] But Grigor'ev had already had contact with Masonic bodies in Moscow and almost certainly had formed a link with the Masons when he arrived in St Petersburg.[22] His association with Milanovskii was further evidence of those ties. In his stories and poems as well, there were frequent references to the Masons and their influence on the spiritual and intellectual development of Russia.

In addition to contributing poems and stories to *Repertuar i Panteon*, Grigor'ev began to write for the journal in 1845 a series of letters about Russian drama and the Russian stage. Those letters initiated for him a continuing and lively lifelong connection with the theatre. They were particularly hard on drama critics in Russia and on actors for their disdain for the tastes of the masses. Grigor'ev's harsh words about the contemporary theatre in Russia attracted the attention of the Third Section, the political police. The last straw for the police came in January 1846, when Grigor'ev wrote what purported to be a review of a fictional provincial performance of *Hamlet* but was in fact a review of a real performance, with the great actor V.I. Karatygin in the leading role. Grigor'ev was an admirer of Karatygin in almost every role he played except Hamlet. His ridicule of the performance, prompted L.V. Dubel't of the Third Section to complain to the director of the Imperial Theatres, A.M. Gedeonov, that an actor such as Karatygin, who enjoyed the confidence of the tsar, merited greater respect from journalists. He followed the matter up by notifying the editor of *Repertuar i Panteon*, Mezhevich, that in all cultural matters criticism should be confined within strict limits.[23]

In February 1846, the budding critic published a little book, *Stikhotvoreniia Apollona Grigor'eva* (The Poems of Apollon Grigor'ev), in which were collected many of the items that had already appeared in print, along with some new ones and translations of a series of what turned out to be Masonic works. The book, in an edition of fifty copies, was intended to be his final act in St Petersburg, a city with which he had become thoroughly disillusioned. As he later wrote, he was 'infuriated by the baseness' around him in the capital.[24] He punctuated his distaste by writing a bitter poem, 'Farewell to Petersburg' (Proshchanie s Peterburgom), on leaving at the end of February. The poem began 'Farewell cold and passionless / Magnificent city of slaves / Barracks, bordellos and palaces' and went on to condemn its mean tsarist service and petty vanity, its bureaucrats and pretension to stand on the same cultural level as western Europe.[25] But on arriving in Moscow he found nothing to do there, apart from writing a few poems. Discouraged, he soon returned to hated St Petersburg.

There he continued to publish poetry in *Repertuar i Panteon* as well as regularly contributing to it a theatre column, the last instalment of which appeared in December 1846. More important, he was also acquiring a new skill as effective editor of the journal. With his reputation now sufficiently well established, he was able to publish in other journals as well. Several of his poems appeared in *Biblioteka dlia chteniia* (Library for Reading), and his translation of Sophocles' *Antigone* came out in *Otechestvennye zapiski*

(Notes of the Fatherland). He also contributed a number of articles to *Finskii vestnik* (The Finnish Messenger) on the question that was increasingly to occupy him – the relationship between literature and nationality. Troubled as was his St Petersburg apprenticeship, it nevertheless prepared him broadly for the rigorous life of the writer in the censored world of Russian literature.

A rich and varied intellectual life bubbled beneath the crust of censorship in the Russia of the 1840s. Much of the attention of historians of the period has focused on the Slavophile versus Westernizer controversy. The Slavophiles, led by K. S. Akasakov, A.S. Khomiakov, and I.V. Kireevskii, stressed the cultural, political, and social distinctiveness of Russia in comparison with western Europe. According to them, the spiritual mission of the West, which had been completed in the philosophy of Hegel, had been to develop the rational side of human nature. Western rationalism had its roots in the rationalism and legal formalism of classical Rome. The religious expression of rationalism in the West was the authority of the papacy, which the Slavophiles associated philosophically with the principle of necessity. Protestantism represented a reaction against papal authority and an excessive assertion of the spiritual autonomy of the individual, which the Slavophiles associated with the principle of unrestricted freedom. The social expressions of Western rationalism were economic individualism, the rights of man, and heavy reliance on law and contractual legal relationships in order to bind together an atomized society through external constraint. Russian life, said the Slavophiles, was grounded in Orthodoxy, which brought together reason, on the one hand, and faith and intuition, on the other. Russia's mission was to reconcile faith and reason and to strike a perfect balance between freedom and necessity. The principle of Orthodoxy was *sobornost'* (communalism), which brought the members of society together not through the external constraint of the law but through internal moral commitment to social cohesion – in a word, through love. The external manifestations of *sobornost'* in the nation's life were the peasant commune and the people's apolitical nature. Politics was the burden of the autocrat; morality, the refuge of the land.

Whereas the Slavophiles espoused a coherent, if controversial, doctrine, the Westernizers represented a wide variety of views. V.G. Belinskii, for example, passed through a number of stages in his short life, from adherence to Schelling's aesthetics, through a conservative period, when, under the influence of Hegel's dictum that the real is rational, he reconciled himself to the bureaucratic regime of Nicholas I, and on to utopian-socialist ideas, which by the end of his life had been modified into a variety of left-liberalism. A.I. Herzen was more consistent than his friend Belinskii. During the 1840s he was influenced primarily by French utopian socialist thought. After his emigration to the West and the experience of the 'failed' revolutions of 1848, he turned to the Russian peasant commune as the best hope of socialism. The embrace of Westernism was wide. At one extreme was the anarchism of M.A. Bakunin; at the other the cautious liberalism of the historian T.N. Granovskii or his young followers K.D. Kavelin and B.N. Chicherin, founders of the legal school of Russian history.

The focus on the divide between Slavophilism and Westernism has served well to illuminate an essential and continuing aspect of Russian intellectual discourse in the middle decades of the nineteenth century. But it has also promoted a tendency in the literature to suppose that when, at the end of 1844, the Slavophile Konstantin Aksakov dramatically leapt from his carriage in a Moscow street to embrace the Westernizer Alexander Herzen on the pavement and announce in tears that they could never again see one another in friendship, a fundamental divide was established, to which all Russian intellectuals felt compelled to conform. In fact, the Slavophile–Westernizer split was at the time more a source of gossip and amusement for most contemporaries than an occasion for soul-searching, and only a few experienced the need to choose sides.

Both Slavophilism and Westernism were the products of Western thought, and neither had deep roots in native Russian tradition. There was, however, a fundamental difference between the two groups. What distinguished all the Westernizers from the Slavophiles was the emphasis they placed on social rather than ethical solutions to social problems. Grigor'ev's nemesis in love, Konstantin Kavelin, expressed the difference best many years later in his response to F.M. Dostoevskii's famous Pushkin speech of 1880. In a public letter to Dostoevskii, he asked:

Which is more important, which is more of the essence, which should be put in the forefront – personal moral improvement or the elaboration and perfection of the conditions under which man lives in society? Some say: Strive for inner, spiritual, moral truth, come to love it with all your soul, and the perfect social life will take shape of itself. Others retort: Make social life, the social conditions, as nearly perfect as possible; then individuals will quite naturally and automatically be steered onto the path of virtue, of moral growth and perfection.[26]

Grigor'ev was well aware of the issues that were increasingly dividing Slavophiles and Westernizers and even satirized some of them in his writings. The tension between the ethical and social approaches to society's problems, which divided them, was already apparent in his St Petersburg writings and was to become the central dichotomy of his thought. But the matters that most closely concerned him early in his career were related rather to questions of individualism and the personality that flowed out of his personal experiences than to Slavophile–Westernizer debates. He readily maintained personal and professional relationships, as did many of his contemporaries, with adherents of both camps.

For Grigor'ev in this period, feelings of personal isolation in society, a divided sense of self, and relationships with women became points of departure from which he tried to work outward in his writing to broader psychological and social issues. Enlightenment thinkers had firmly placed individualism, personality, and the nature of happiness on the modern intellectual agenda, matters with which the romantics became obsessed. From childhood, Grigor'ev had been steeped, as had his whole generation, in the literature of romanticism with its stress on individual striving and fulfilment through love. Schiller's ideal of the *schöne Seele* – the beautiful soul, raised to the sublime through the pure love of and for an ideal woman – had been reinforced in the idealist philosophy of Fichte and Schelling. In the latter, the Absolute could be attained only through love. By the 1840s, however, the beautiful soul had discovered a rival in the beautiful body. Enfantin and his Saint-Simonist followers in France had, through the doctrine of the 'rehabilitation of the flesh,' asserted the centrality of sexuality in love. In her novels and by her example, Georges Sand campaigned for the 'rehabilitation of the heart' and before the beginning of the 1840s was a bright beacon for the autonomy of women in love. The principal theme of her early novels and stories was the liberation of women from the control of spouses, social class, convention, and economic necessity. Grigor'ev's early writings were concerned primarily with these matters of the personality and the heart and with the education of women with a view to making them fit to capitalize on their new liberty.

Even before he left Moscow for St Petersburg, Grigor'ev's earlier enthusiasm for Hegel was waning. When he now read, 'Was ist wirklich ist vernünftig,' he wrote to Solov'ev in 1842, he could not help smiling. The reference was, of course, to Belinskii's 'conservative reconciliation with reality' into which M. Bakunin had bullied him in the late 1830s on the basis of Hegel's much misunderstood dictum, 'What is real is rational.' On its authority, Belinskii for a couple of years embraced Russian autocracy as necessary. Grigor'ev was here expressing an anti-Hegelianism that he was to formulate fully a few years later, as well as a lifelong distaste for schools of thought and systems of belief. He stood alone, he continued in his letter to Solov'ev, 'completely alone,' with his eternal sufferings 'concealed from all.'[27]

In reality, Grigor'ev was very far from hiding his sufferings from everyone. He made them the subject of his stories and poems, which he was all too happy to publish. Most of the stories were thinly veiled autobiography, with scarcely a thought for hiding the identity of the characters. Over the years his love poetry was invariably inspired by women with whom he was actually in love. In the 1840s there were two. His earliest published poems were the result of his feelings for his 'godsister,' Lisa, the woman who declared her feelings for Fet at the wedding ball after her marriage to another man. But most of the pieces in these years were inspired by Antonina Korsh.

The earliest poems were intensely personal. They were in the manner of the Heine school, which Grigor'ev characterized as 'morbid.' The features of that school, according to Grigor'ev, were a near-absence of the typical and its replacement with an excess of the particular and of the accidental in expression. A good example was Grigor'ev's first published poem 'E.S.R.' The subject was the poet's self and the effect on him of Lisa, the woman of his passions. His soul was not redeemed and the Absolute attained, as Schiller would have had it, by his love for Lisa but was instead tied to the earth by her physical attraction. 'I will be bound to the earth / By earthly passion. / Your image stands between me and eternity.'[28]

Antonina Korsh, whose courtship by and marriage to Kavelin threw him into despair, was the principal goad to his muse in these years. 'You were born to torment me / With your affectionately cold conversation / And your free constraint,' he wrote.[29] Characteristic of the feverish intensity of feeling in the early poems was 'The Spell' (Obaianie). It began, 'You have never given me / The insane joy of suffering / But over me reigns the spell / of some unfathomable power in you.'[30] The phrase 'the insane joy of suffering' was later to impress Belinskii with its madness,[31] but the conjunction of emotional opposites, and especially the linkage of happiness and suffering, was to remain a constant in Grigor'ev's thought. It was a psychological insight that he shared with F.M. Dostoevskii, and one of a number of mutual perceptions that later accounted for the extraordinary attraction of the two men for each other.

At the centre of Grigor'ev's philosophical outlook throughout his life was the conviction, derived primarily from Schelling but also from Herder, that the general was accessible only through the particular. He clearly articulated that theme as a philosophical principle only in the late 1850s, but it was already a working assumption of his poetry and fictional prose in the 1840s. The original emphasis on the particular or personal remained in his writings, but increasingly he sought to push out from the personal experience of the narrative 'I' into the significance of that experience for the world outside. This method culminated, as we have already seen, in his autobiography written in the early 1860s.

A good early example of this approach was his treatment of his own failed relationship with Antonina Korsh, which served as a point of departure for an examination of what was soon to be called the 'woman question' in Russia. In light of the Korsh sisters' obsession with Georges Sand's views on the question, as well as the impact that Sand had made on the reading public in Russia, it is not surprising that Grigor'ev, too, approached the subject through Sand's works. Grigor'ev, like Sand, was the product of a socially 'mixed' marriage (Sand herself just missed an illegitimate birth by a month) and perhaps felt for her a special affinity. Her attack on the societal strictures of class and marriage – the main subject of her early works – was of particular relevance to him. But Grigor'ev's Sandist views about women and the social structures that blocked their equality with men were common in Russian literature at the time. They found their best-known expression in Herzen's *Who Is to Blame?* (Kto vinovat?) but were ably expressed in a number of other works, most notably A.V. Druzhinin's *Polinka Saks* and several of A.F. Pisemskii's stories and novels.

In a number of poems dedicated 'To Lavinia' (K Lavinii), Grigor'ev sympathized with the eponymous heroine of a Georges Sand story who earned public opprobrium first by being abandoned by her husband and then by declining to return to him when he realized his error in deserting her. Sand's moral was that public opinion was always prejudiced and unjust toward women. Grigor'ev agreed and concluded in one of the poems that the happiness of ideal love is impossible under the 'dull axe' of public opinion.[32] Sand's Lavinia believed that since human feelings were transient and dreams and passions fleeting, happiness was elusive and impermanent. In another poem dedicated to her, Grigor'ev concurred. Neither the poet nor she expected anything from fate. 'And so long as we do not believe in happiness / We will know only condemnation / And upholding in proud battle the sacred right to be condemned / We do not beg heaven for respite / And expect nothing from fate.'[33] It is difficult to gauge the sincerity of Grigor'ev's feminist views in these years. These works were, at least in part, merely jealous reproaches to Antonina for her own safe choice of Kavelin over him but were also blows in the 'proud battle' against the social subordination of women.

In 'A Woman' (Zhenshchina), Grigor'ev portrayed women as enmeshed in 'the lie of a fantastic dream' and asked, 'Why and by whom was she, this child of a fantastic dream, so falsely created?' And he concluded that it is society that had created her so and that wanted to believe in its false dream as it never did in reality.[34] He pursued a similar theme in 'To Lélia' (K Lelii). Lélia was the eponymous heroine of yet another of Georges Sand's novels. It, too, stressed that the fate of women was inextricably linked to questions of religion, morality, and social structure. An advocate of the emancipation of women, Lélia argued that contemporary social conditions precluded the equality of men and women. She not only rejected material motives in matters of the heart but also believed that base passions were contrary to the human aspiration to perfection. The 'pitiful impotence of physical love cannot damp down the whorling dust of her dreams.' In 'To Lélia,' Grigor'ev proclaimed the moral equality of women and men. 'I believe us to be equal ... You suffer / From an unquenchable thirst, as do I, my proud angel!'[35] In an untitled poem (Net, ne tebe idti so mnoi), Grigor'ev again found his inspiration in Sand's *Lélia*. There she had written, 'Poet, do not look into me for hidden secrets; my soul is a sister to yours.' Grigor'ev contrasted women's social inequality with men with the natural equality of their souls: 'No, it is not for you to accompany me / To the highest goal of existence / And it is not you that my soul / Has called friend and sister.' 'My path is different, my path is not yours.' And the piece concluded: 'And let me never forget / Your fateful image / I am ashamed to love a woman / And not to call her sister.'[36]

Elsewhere he satirized the fate of women in society. Alexander Pushkin's poem 'The Portrait' (Portret), with its image of a beautiful woman who passes through a conventional society like a comet, particularly intrigued him. In one of his long poems, Grigor'ev portrays a woman who, facing a life of the dullest routine, dreams that Satan, the 'eternal destroyer of woman's tranquillity,' persuades her that she is no mere star but a 'fateful comet.' In her dream, she meets the young bureaucrat of her desires who, despising women, nevertheless falls in love with her, and she with him. With his lovers' initial embrace, the poet turns to an exploration of the fateful consequences of first kisses: 'O Romeo and Juliet! You were / As young and as pure: You forgot / A whole world in a first kiss.' He accuses Shakespeare, the 'old joker,' of being a 'ruthless vampire,' who filled his young characters with love in order to suck their blood with all the greater relish.

His own heroine awakens to her own life, worse than hell with its 'braids and stockings, coffee and a stupid husband.'[37]

Perhaps because of his own painful experiences at home and his observation of the 'half Russian' Korshes, Grigor'ev had developed a strong interest in the contemporary Russian family.[38] He reported to Pogodin that he had written an article on the future of Russian family law, which unfortunately was not published and has not survived in manuscript form.[39] Grigor'ev was particularly outraged by the Slavophiles' contention that the family was the foundation of Slavic social and spiritual life. In 'Olimpii Radin,' a story in verse, Grigor'ev pointed out that in Russian folk poetry the family was, for women, only a source of suffering. The wife was, in particular, condemned to an evil fate.[40] In his satirical play in verse called 'Two Egoisms' (Dva egoizma), he depicted a certain Baskakov (a *baskak* was a Mongol tax collector) – a wandering Slavophile and obvious caricature of Konstantin Aksakov, one of the more colourful of Moscow's Slavophiles. Baskakov announces: 'The family is the Slavic principle. In my dissertation, I set out in detail how the pure idea, the Slavic idea, prevailed in the family without any admixture of other ideas.' He goes on to argue that the authority of the husband and the submissive humility of the wife were the essence of the Slavic marriage. A wife is not an object, he proclaimed, though she has no will of her own. But she is protected by laws: 'A husband can beat her but cannot kill her. He has only spiritual authority over her.'[41] We will see that Grigor'ev later expanded his view of the patriarchal Russian family and the pitiable fate of the woman in it.

Closely linked to Grigor'ev's thinking about the relationship between the sexes was the issue of egoism. In developing this theme, Grigor'ev again began from his own experience. From the distance of St Petersburg, he was able to confront the nature of his own egoism in his failed relationship with Antonina. In the long poem 'Transactions' (Videniia), he recalled at length the days in which his love for Antonina first blossomed and then withered before the triumph of his rival. He portrayed himself as defeated in love and unable to purchase happiness at any price, yet proud of his capacity to suffer.[42] In yet another poem 'To Lavinia' he characterized his love for Antonina: 'He loved you like a sick egoist ...'; later in the piece, he recognized his love as more dream than real: 'And a dream of love and a dream of a terrible suffering / Have hitherto tormented him perhaps / But as the result, I think, of endless boredom / It is time, in my opinion, to forget.'[43]

In Grigor'ev's view, true love was above all a battle of egos. It was governed by the desire of the individual personality not to be subordinated to another and could be sustained only between moral equals. He explored that theme in the story 'One of the Many' (Odin iz mnogikh). The main character, Zvanintsev, is an egoist who has completely freed himself from dependence on everything and everybody. He swears that there are no limits that he will not exceed. In order to prove his point, he declares his love for a childhood lover of his, Maria, who is married. But he is not fully convinced that he actually means what he so passionately declares. As one of his projects, Zvanintsev sets out to win for his young friend Sevskii the hand of Lidiia, daughter of the owner of a gaming house. At his second meeting with Maria, the latter confesses her love for Zvanintsev; falling ill, she dies from love three days later in a fever. Meanwhile, Zvanintsev himself falls in love with Lidiia, and she with him. But he persists with his plan to unite her with Sevskii, even though Sevskii, with his prize now in reach, has changed his mind. A further complication arises because Lidiia's father has sold her to the baron, a rich and brutal man. Trapped in a room with the baron, who wants to claim his purchase without delay, Lidiia struggles against her fate and is rescued by Zvanintsev. Lidiia and Zvanintsev recognize their equality in love and run off together. Through this improbable tale, Grigor'ev detailed a variety of egoisms in love before egoism was at last overcome through the love of equals.

One of the characters in the play, Antosha, is a portrait of Grigor'ev himself. He recalls his mother's illness, her combing of his hair, her malice, his university days, and his unhappy love. Zvanintsev gives Antosha money, which the latter refuses to take unless the former actually knows him. And so he pours out his heart to his benefactor. Soon he realizes that his salvation by Zvanintsev has become a burden and torment to himself. The proud and haughty Zvanintsev, who hides his feelings from everyone else, has so little regard for Antosha that he is unashamed to weep before him. Not his equal but Zvanintsev's slave, Antosha wonders why everyone he meets is either above or beneath him, but never his equal. He resolves the dilemma by committing suicide after leaving a note.[44] Suicide was never far from Grigor'ev's mind. He suffered deep depressions and profound melancholy, which alternated with periods of hope and activity. Whenever thoughts of death came near, he fought them off in bouts of dissipation.

The battle of egos in love was also the main subject of Grigor'ev's play *Two Egoisms*. Grigor'ev had drawn the earlier models for the egoists primarily from the works of M.Iu. Lermontov, and he now made this influence explicit. This drama in verse was essentially a reworking of Lermontov's *The Masquerade* (Maskarad). Grigor'ev even employed the same free iambics that his model had himself borrowed from Griboedov's *Woe from Wit* (Gore ot uma). In Lermontov's work (there are several versions of it, none of them definitive, and it is not clear which Grigor′ev had in mind), Arbenin is a cold egoist, contemptuous of the society around him. He is married to Nina, a beautiful, uncomplicated woman, whom he loves in a conventional way. The token of his love is a pair of bracelets that he has given to her. At a masquerade she loses one of the bracelets. It is found by the Baroness Strahl, who, her identity secure in domino, flirts with Prince Zvedich, whom Arbenin has recently saved from bankruptcy and even death. The baroness gives the bracelet to Zvedich. Arbenin first learns of the lost bracelet and then discovers that Zvedich has it. His first thought is to kill the prince, but then he tries to dishonour him by accusing him of cheating while gambling, then slapping his face and refusing to fight with him. But Arbenin is not yet satisfied, and, poisoning his wife's lemonade, he watches impassively while she dies, a victim of his proud honour. In one version (the most credible), Arbenin then learns of his wife's innocence and goes mad.

Like Arbenin, Vladimir Petrovich Stavunin, the hero of Grigor′ev's drama, is an egoist. By the time the action begins, his egoism has led him to despair and even to the contemplation of suicide. After a period of five years, Stavunin sees at a masquerade a woman with whom he was and is in love. He learns that she is now married, but not happily. Whereas Lermontov made Nina a hapless, if protesting, victim of Arbenin's pride and contemporary social mores, Grigor′ev portrayed four women, all of whom either do love or have loved Stavunin and all of whom actively participate in determining their own fates. Mar′ia Vasil′evna Donskaia returns Stavunin's love but is determined to remain loyal to her husband. She will be united with Stavunin, she declares, only in death. Elena recognizes in Stavunin a fellow sufferer. Like him, she knows the happiness that there is in suffering. She understands as well that they are afflicted by the same disease and can be cured together. But Stavunin rejects her and her cure. Vera Viazmina, too, loves Stavunin who has in the past rescued her and given her a period of happiness. Stavunin does not, however, love her but has 'toyed with her soul from boredom.' She declares herself content, however, with the moment of happiness he has given her and thanks him for the joy of torment that now sustains her. Stavunin asks her if she will give up family and the happiness that goes with it for him. She denies that the family brings happiness – it brings only chains of sympathy and love. And finally, an unnamed woman in a veil appears who turns out to be Stavunin's wife. Stavunin admits that he married her almost by accident and, unable to love her, drove her into infidelity. She asks for his forgiveness, but he denies that there is anything to forgive. It is public opinion that has punished her. He tells her that she must follow her own path because his 'is finished.' They part, reconciled but not united.

Mar'ia Vasil'evna, despised by her husband, Dmitrii, who hints to her that he knows where her heart secretly lies, is terrified by the cruelty of public opinion toward women and refuses to give in to her love or to admit it to Stavunin. Stavunin comes to visit her, ostensibly to say good-bye before leaving for the Caucasus. They talk of their past love, and while she plays and sings a song from a special evening that they shared, he poisons her lemonade. She drinks some of it, and he tells her what he has done. She thanks him for the freedom he has given her. While he begs her forgiveness she dies. He finds a doctor, then leaves, presumably to his own death.[45] 'Two Egoisms' therefore elaborated all the responses available to a woman caught in a love triangle in the of Russia of the 1840s (in addition to the passivity of Lermontov's Nina). The consequences of all of the women's responses were tragic in varying degrees. The message was Sand's: love was incompatible with the social conventions that governed the lives of men and women.

In a letter to Pogodin in which he tried to justify his portrayal of a personality such as Stavunin's, with its destructive egoism and 'consciousness of the necessity of death as the only rational outcome,' Grigor'ev gave his interpretation a religious dimension. The crisis of Stavunin and his type, of the egoists of Nicholas's Russia, was religious – a failure of Western philosophy to acknowledge God and that of the theologians to acknowledge the world. Stavunin's death arose out of a 'moment of profound asceticism, a satanic asceticism, out of knowledge without love.'[46]

In Grigor'ev's stories, the egoist was an early draft of the superfluous man, whose origins were in Pushkin's Onegin, Lermontov's Pechorin, and Griboedov's Chatskii, who came to dominate Russian literature in the 1850s. The egoist was spoiled young by life's pleasures and soon lost his taste for everything around him. He grew increasingly alienated from the conditions of society. Grigor'ev made it clear that it was not a struggle with life that created the egoist but a wrestling with vain imaginings – the 'phantoms' of his youth. Most egoists were even aware that they were the victims of phantoms but lacked the will to resist them. And so they affected a despair in which they did not quite believe. The eponymous hero of Grigor'ev's 'My Acquaintance with Vitalin' (Moe znakomstvo s Vitalinym) was such an egoist. He wanted to be a positive man but was too irritable and flighty to achieve it. He studied but was soon disillusioned by the cynical use to which others put knowledge. But in spite of his own cynicism, the summons to activity resounded in his soul. He did not believe in vice or virtue but did believe that everyone had to discover their own destiny in themselves. Everyone was responsible for fighting their own battle for life and happiness. The egoist experienced everything that life had to offer but found it all boring. He had will but could not exercise it. And so the egoist constantly deceived himself and lived in a world of lies. There was a time, Grigor'ev wrote, citing Immanuel Kant's *Religion within the Limits of Reason Alone*, when the world lay trapped in evil, but now it lay trapped in lies. Lies were not evil; they were knowledge of the good without the will to effect good.[47]

In 'Deathbed Confession' (Predsmertnaia ispoved'), Grigor'ev explored the sin of pride and its effects on his generation. The poem described the death of a young man. 'Such pride: Satan / could not be more proud than him.' His pride isolated him from other people, whom he regarded as a herd of cattle. When the author urged him to abandon his insane imaginings and live like others, the dying man smiled the smile of a serpent. He explained that from childhood he had been possessed by the idea of another existence. He noticed that humans dream of better things, that they long to break their chains and to create a whole 'new world.' He wanted to test whether that dream was empty. 'But whether truth or a dream / The cause of my day-dreaming was simple / I was created too proud / I value too highly / In myself the spark of divinity / Its divine truth / Its freedom; but it / Long ago was trampled from the age / And man from that time / Attracted by the arch serpent / Knows good and evil equally / Consciousness destroys happiness.' He saw himself as destined to introduce a new order of earthly existence. But he proved unable to produce an effect. Was he to blame, or were others? At the end, he decided that it did not matter whether he had lived in vain. 'But, one way or another, I lived.'[48]

'Deathbed Confession' provided another instance in which Grigor'ev foreshadowed some of Dostoevskii's most profound insights. The two men were not destined to meet for another fifteen years. But Grigor'ev's premonition in his poem of the God-Man, who presumes to create a new world, and his perception of consciousness as the disease of modern man laid the foundation of their future close but troubled friendship.

Grigor'ev was himself for a time as fascinated with Fourier's 'new world' as was the dying young egoist of his poem. He was even an occasional visitor at the gatherings of M. Petrashevskii whose circle avidly discussed Fourierist ideas but had long severed any connection with the *Petrashevtsy* by the time of their arrest in 1849.[49] Writing in 1930, R. Ivanov-Razumnik probably overstated the case when he maintained that in the early 1840s the two poles of Grigor'ev's intellectual existence were Freemasonry and Fou-rierism.[50] He did, however, have extensive familiarity with both. The pow-erful image of his grandfather, with his Masonic links, no doubt helped to draw Grigor'ev to Freemasonry, but it is most probable that he first approached both movements through the writings of Georges Sand. He was particularly attracted to her novel *Consuelo* (1842) and its sequel, *The Countess of Rudolstadt* (1843). Consuelo's husband in the novels, Count Albert, was a member of an order reminiscent of the Masons. As well as accepting Masonic mysticism, he also espoused many of the ideas current among French utopian socialists of the time. Among Count Albert's more prominent notions was that of the 'rehabilitation of the flesh.' He called for the equality of the physical with the spiritual life, the rehabilitation of the 'evil principle' and its unification with the 'good principle' so that love, equality, and universality would emerge as the elements of human happi-ness.

It is a measure of Grigor'ev's youthful enthusiasm for the novels that his pet name in the Korsh family circle was Count Albert. He also signed a number of his earliest published works as A. Trismegistov, another refer-ence to Count Albert, who returned from the dead (actually from a trance) in the second novel under the name Trismegist, recalling Hermes Tris-megistus, the name given by mystics to a mythical Egyptian figure, proba-bly the god Thoth, reputed author of the secrets of alchemy. In a poem, the epigraph of which was drawn from the count's apology for the 'truth of Satan,' Grigor'ev too called for the unity of the spiritual and the physical. The theme was captured in the line, 'O, believe, you are saved when you love.'[51]

Like so many of those of his contemporaries who were influenced by utopian-socialist ideas, Grigor'ev, in the fashion of the Christian socialist Pierre Leroux, tried to inject into Christianity a modern social concern. In 'An Appeal' (Vozvanie), for example, he wrote, 'Rebel, o God! – not for them / The slaves of sin, the priests of idols / But for the downtrodden and the sick ... Rebel, rebel, saviour of the world! / They have sought you out / By the path of suffering and longing / Like you they have cried out / Lämä säbächthäni more than once / And likewise they see / Your house full of merchants / And proudly rise up – and some / Have armed themselves with scourges.'[52]

Through Sand as well, Grigor'ev derived a Rousseauesque distaste for civilization, which he expressed in hostility to the city. In 'The City' (Gorod), written in 1845, he wrote ironically that he loved the city not for its buildings, palaces, and ageless granite but for the morbid suffering under its icy crust.[53] In a second poem called 'The City,' published only in 1848 but written around the same time as the first, he declared his alienation from the city. 'But I – I am alien to you, magnificent city / Neither the silent tears nor frenzied laughter / Will conceal from me your morbid depravity / Or your pathetic mocking of sacred things / Nothing about you surprises me any longer / Not your pride in shopworn scepticism / Not the caperings of a pointless day / Not the transparent mask of hypocrisy.'[54] Distaste for the civilized was not an affectation with which Grigor'ev was comfortable, however. Later, he confessed that nature affected him little, and only the artefacts of civilization could move him. Indeed, Grigor'ev's clear preference for the cultural over the natural separated him in some measure from earlier romantics.

Two other poems of the period were too radical to be printed in Russia. Instead, they first appeared in print in Herzen's émigré journal, *Kolokol* (The Bell), in 1856. Both had revolutionary overtones. The first, 'No, I was not born to beat my head' (Net, ne rozhden ia bit'sia lbom), returns to the theme of Christ as rebel against the church, and it concludes, 'And what Marat felt / Time has enabled me to understand / And were God himself an aristocrat / I would proudly curse him / But the crucified god on the cross / Was the son of the mob and a demogogue [= democrat].'[55] The second, 'When the Bells Ring in Triumph' (Kogda kolokola torzhestvenno zvuchat), referred to the republican traditions of medieval Novgorod the Great. 'Yes, it has died, the voice of the people has long ago fallen silent / Has bowed its head under the terrible tsarist knout / But the awful day will come, but freedom will sound / And the stones will utter cries / And the scattered ashes and bones of the giant / Will again unite the godly spirit in one.'[56]

Grigor'ev's direct familiarity with Fourier is apparent in the poem 'The Comet' (Kometa). It was inspired not only by Pushkin's poem 'The Portrait' but also by Fourier's theory in *Le nouveau monde* of dualism in nature and society. For Fourier, the principle of harmony in nature was represented by the orderly movement of the planets, and the destructive principle, by the erratic flight of comets. In his view, human society was a mirror of nature. It, too, contained the dual principles of harmony and destructiveness represented by planets and comets. In time, Fourier believed, comets would attain the orderliness of planets, just as the destructive elements of human society would be forged into harmony. Grigor'ev did not share Fourier's view that the comet was an evil that had to be transformed into harmony. Instead, the comet 'completes by means of struggle and testing / The goal of cleansing and the goal of self-creation.'[57]

In 1846, Grigor'ev published in a tiny edition (50 copies) a collection of his previously published poetry. *The Poems of Apollon Grigor'ev* was divided into two parts, 'Hymns' (Gimny) and 'Various Poems' (Raznye stikhotvoreniia). It received mixed reviews. An anonymous critic in *Finskii vestnik* (The Finnish Messenger) remarked that the best pieces 'achieved a moving and stern indignation.'[58] P.A. Pletnev, in *Sovremennik* (The Contemporary), was less impressed. The poems, he said, were full of the fashionable language of hyperbole but were not informed by the mystery of poetic creativity.[59] 'Ia.Ia.Ia.' (pseudonym of L. Brant) in *Severnaia pchela* (The Northern Bee) was even harsher. He judged the 'Hymns' to be caricatures. While every line was full of suffering, the reader, he complained, could not understand what the poems were actually about. All that was clear, he concluded, was that the poet was angry about something.[60]

Belinskii wrote a lengthy review of the collection in *Otechestvennye zapiski* (Notes of the Fatherland). He detected in it 'poetic sparks' but found the poetry to be of the intellect, of mind and feeling, but lacking in imagination and creativity. The poet was at his best when inspired by indignation, but the only subject he had was his own suffering. 'Mr. Grigor'ev tries to make his poetry into the apotheosis of suffering, but the reader does not sympathize with his suffering because he does not understand its cause or character, and the poet's idea is borne before us as in a kind of cloud.' Belinskii rejected the 'insane joy of suffering' as a romantic distortion of feeling and sense, which needed to be cured by the 'classicism of common sense, useful activity, and an end to the pretension to superiority over others' frail mortality.' Despite their extreme egoism, the poems aroused interest in the author's character, because 'he feels deeply and understands much.' Belinskii concluded: 'Mr. Grigor'ev can write but he needs to grasp the significance and nature of his talent ... But he is in no way a lyric poet, and by making himself the hero of his own verses, he only gets himself muddled up in vague and endless reflections and sensations.'[61] A few months later, in his 'Glance at Russian Literature in 1846,' Belinskii called Grigor'ev's volume the best of the 1846 collections. Again he spoke of flashes of genuine poetry but attributed them to the influence of Lermontov. The rest consisted of the 'dark, mystical phrases' of Grigor'ev.[62]

There was almost no contemporary comment on the stark contrast between the simple, celebratory, and reconciliatory mood of the 'Hymns' and the complex, dark, and anguished tone of the poems. Even had Grigor'ev's contemporaries recognized the source of the former, they would have been unlikely to incriminate Grigor'ev by acknowledging it. Later commentators correctly pointed to their Masonic character and attributed them to Grigor'ev's attachment to Freemasonry at the time.[63] In 1957, a Soviet scholar, B.Ia. Bukhshtab, discovered a Masonic collection published in Berlin in 1813 entitled *Volständiges Gesangbuch für Freimauern* (Complete Hymnal for Freemasons). The compilation contained all but four of Grigor'ev's 'hymns.' He concluded that since Freemasons were required by their rules to sing during their meetings and since Russian adherents had few translated hymns available, Grigor'ev's translations must have aided them immeasurably in fulfilling their vows.[64] Freemasonry was banned in Nicholas I's Russia; to conceal his source, Grigor'ev substituted the word 'brothers' each time 'Masons' appeared in the songs.

The tension between the two sections of the collected poems was deliberate. It reflected the parallel tension between the ethical and social approaches to social issues that Grigor'ev saw respectively in Freemasonry and utopian socialism. Freemasons believed in the universal brotherhood of mankind and in the aim of individual moral perfection. The movement had arrived in Russia in the mid-eighteenth century in the mystical form that it had first adopted in many of the German states. It was attractive to an upper class, among which the official religion had lost its hold since the reign of Peter the Great, and served as a semi-secular substitute for Orthodoxy. The focus on individualistic self-perfection and the inner life of the soul, already apparent in the mystical European variant, was reinforced in Russia by the suspicion of the government and, after 1815, its outright hostility. The emphasis on social service typical of many Western Freemasons was muted and later, with official repression, virtually absent in Russia. The Masonic songs translated by Grigor'ev underscored the mystical and contemplative side of Freemasonry rather than its commitment to good works. The two sections illustrated what Grigor'ev saw as the two major pulls on the personality of his day, the isolated calm of mysticism and the tumultuous clash of social idealism with reality.

Intrigued as he was by Fourierism and Freemasonry, Grigor'ev saw them as coats to try on but not to purchase. He later denied that he was ever a socialist, and he ought to be taken at his word. A letter of 1849 from A.N. Pleshcheev to S.F. Durov, one of the main and more violent conspirators in the Petrashevskii affair, suggests that if Durov knew Grigor'ev at all it was only slightly,[65] and the police in the investigation into the conspiracy in 1849 showed virtually no interest in Grigor'ev. By the time he wrote the long poem 'Olimpii Radin' in 1845, he had already repudiated Fourierism and arrived at his mature view that the ideas of utopian socialism, or of any other theory, were too narrow to deal with the ever-changing complexity of life. The hero, Olimpii Radin, had once been an advocate of the doctrines of the 'new world.' But by the end of the poem, he is convinced that the ideas of Fourier's *New World* are inadequate to settle real personal and social problems.[66]

Though Grigor'ev continued to flirt with the Freemasons for the rest of his life, he had, at least by 1847, begun to associate Freemasonry with the causes of the destructive egoism of his generation. In the character of Vasilii Imeretinov in the epistolary novelette *Another of the Many* (Drugoi iz mnogikh), Grigor'ev exploited his unfortunate relationship with Milanovskii to explore the contribution of Freemasonry, with its admixture of mysticism and humanism that brought it nearer to atheism than to Christian belief, to the growth of egoism in the nineteenth century.[67] Under the influence of Gogol', he was soon to reject Freemasonry as an insufficient ethical stimulus to the development of personality and to turn instead to Orthodoxy.

Active as he was in the literary life of the capital, Grigor'ev was still unable to make a living there. He had by now fallen seriously into debt; by the end of 1846 he was worn out by work, melancholy, and the dissipation that he enlisted as an antidote to ennui. St Petersburg continued to oppress him; his parents constantly importuned him to return home. The flight to St Petersburg had launched his literary career and provided him with valuable experience as a journal editor. But neither Freemasonry, which had funded his escape, nor Fourierism, which had, with its promise of a 'new world,' given him hope, had proven capable even of addressing the problems of the human condition that increasingly overwhelmed him.

Deeply dissatisfied with his own 'sterile sophistry,' Grigor'ev wrote early in 1847 to S.M. Solov'ev in Moscow to inquire whether the conservative journal of Pogodin, *Moskvitianin*, could guarantee him enough pages a month to assure a living. As proof of his reliability as an editor he cited his work for *Repertuar i Panteon*; as proof of his 'Orthodox and Slavic spirit,' he cited his recent articles in *Finskii vestnik*.[68] Those pieces, which had appeared anonymously, indeed suggested a renewed and growing interest on Grigor'ev's part in things Russian and Christian. Among them were reviews of books by M.M. Speranskii on Russian law, of Speranskii's translation of part of Thomas à Kempis's *On the Imitation of Christ*, and of the writings and speeches of Metropolitan Filaret of Moscow. In one of those Grigor'ev introduced the idea of the 'predatory' and 'humble' types in Russian history and literature. He traced the predatory back to the Varangians or Vikings, who were said to have founded the Russian state, and the humble to the Slavs who had invited the Varangians to come and rule over them.[69] Later these types became central to Grigor'ev's view of his nation's historical and literary development. As qualifications for employment, the articles were apparently inadequate. He heard nothing from *Moskvitianin*.

3

A Way Out of Despair
1847–1849

My business is the soul and the
durable matters of life.

Nikolai Gogol', *Selected Passages from
Correspondence with Friends*

In St Petersburg, Grigor'ev had explored in prose and poetry the fashionable intellectual and ideological trends of the day. He had concluded that the prevailing 'two egoisms,' – the universalism of the socialists and the religio-cultural nationalism of the Slavophiles – were too theoretical, divorced from reality and exclusivist. Neither was capacious enough to embrace life's complexity in its entirety; neither was able to overcome the divide between personal affirmation and social existence; and neither provided a means to turn social ideals into social realities. Grigor'ev returned to Moscow in early 1847 dissatisfied and perplexed. Soon, however, he discovered in Gogol''s notorious *Selected Passages from Correspondence with Friends* (Vybrannye mesta iz perepiski s druz'iami) affirmation of his own half-hidden doubts about egoism and confirmation of his growing preference for the ethical over the social and the concrete over the abstract in art and life.

Despite receiving no assurances of work from *Moskvitianin* (The Muscovite), Grigor'ev returned to Moscow and the parental hearth in January 1847. The resumption of his old relationships in Moscow brought him again into the Korsh family circle, with momentous consequences for the future. Sometime in the second half of 1847 he married Lidiia Korsh, the younger sister of Antonina and his earlier confidante. Solov'ev called her the worst of the sisters, 'stupid, with pretensions and a stammer.'[1] Another contemporary, however, remembered her as the 'educated and most kind maiden Lidiia Fedorovna Korsh.'[2] A surrogate love for Grigor'ev, she was salt in the still-open wounds of his hopeless love for Antonina.[3] Raised as she had been in a comfortable, Westernized household, an ardent and, it was to prove for Grigor'ev, too literal student of Georges Sand's views about women's freedom in love, Lidiia Fedorovna was poorly equipped to sympathize with her new husband's increasingly passionate Slavism[4] (of which the articles in *Finskii vestnik* [The Finnish Messenger] had been the harbinger), to cope with his ardent and mercurial nature, or to share his chronic poverty.[5] The newlyweds probably had little more in common than their love for and jealousy of Antonina.

The early years of the marriage proceeded in relative calm. A first child, Vladimir, was born early in 1849 but lived only a few days. Peter was born in January 1850, and Alexander in January 1852. Grigor'ev's immediate concern was to secure an income commensurate with his new responsibilities. On returning home, he had begun in February to contribute to *Moskovskii gorodskii listok* (Moscow City Flyer), a new daily newspaper, which survived for only a year. Fortunately for Grigor'ev, Pogodin at last took him on in October 1847 as compiler of the 'European Survey' section of *Moskvitianin*. Though the post provided him with some income, he was miserable in it from the beginning. He complained that Pogodin restricted him to contemporary news and reproached him when he translated more thoughtful articles from serious journals such as the *Revue des deux mondes*. He asked to divide the section into two and to undertake a proper survey of the countries of Europe instead of merely copying from other journals.[6] Pogodin refused. That quarrel, which ended in Grigor'ev's leaving *Moskvitianin*, was a taste of the coming stormy relations between the two men.

Even while working for *Moskvitianin*, Grigor'ev was constantly short of money. Pogodin was stingy with even the most loyal contributors, and Grigor'ev was compelled to search elsewhere for income. Soon despairing of earning enough from his literary endeavours, he decided to re-enter state service. On 1 August 1848 he was hired on a trial basis to teach civil and land law at the Aleksandrinskii Orphans' Institute in Moscow, and a year later he was confirmed in those duties permanently.[7] He had also been negotiating, at first with no success, with A.A. Kraevskii, the editor of *Otechestvennye zapiski* (Notes of the Fatherland), to publish translations, articles, and stories in that journal anonymously.[8] In June 1849, arrangements were completed, and once again he found an outlet for his passion for the theatre in a series of articles, 'Notes about the Theatre in Moscow'

(Zapiski o teatre v Moskve), that appeared regularly throughout the rest of 1849 and most of 1850. And finally he re-established relations with Pogodin early in 1850 and began once more contributing to *Moskvitianin*.

In order to piece together a living, Grigor'ev was prepared to work for any number of journals, regardless of their tendencies. When he was approached by F.A. Koni about the possibility of publishing his translation of *King Lear*, however, even he baulked, since the version had been done when he was only sixteen, and from the French. But he offered Koni translations from Musset and Goethe. In additon, he informed Koni, he was prepared, under the name of Pavel Efimovich Basistov, to write a chronicle of the Moscow theatre, similar to the one he was already doing for *Otechestvennye zapiski*, for no more than the cost of the tickets.[9] Nothing came of the offer.

Grigor'ev's return to Moscow roughly coincided with the publication of N.V. Gogol''s *Selected Passages from Correspondence with Friends*. The evidence is abundant that the reading of Gogol''s book represented a turning point in Grigor'ev's personal and intellectual development. In June 1847, he wrote to Pogodin that *Selected Passages* had revealed for him the abyss over which he stood of 'unsupported doubt, self-satisfied theories, depravity, lies and unscrupulousness.' He announced that thanks to Gogol' he now felt the inner strength to redeem himself.[10] In one of the letters that he wrote to Gogol' in the autumn of 1848, he described his own state of mind at the time he first read *Selected Passages*. He spoke of his dissoluteness, which he attributed to an early satiety in life, his consciousness of his inability to conform to the ideal, and his lack of faith and apathy of heart.

In *Selected Passages*, Gogol' strikingly revealed all of the moralism and religious propheticism that had lain, almost concealed, in his earlier works. The book was a plea for the individual and social redemptory powers of Christian understanding and love. But it also supported a hierarchical, patriarchal, and even oppressive social order that so much resembled contemporary Russia that even the writer's closest friends were outraged. The author of the *The Government Inspector* (Revizor) and *Dead Souls* (Mertvye dushi) had been idolized by liberals and radicals as the chief critic of the status quo. Now he revealed himself as its defender. The apparent reversal stunned the liberal camp. The most famous response was Belinskii's 'Letter to Gogol',' in which the dying critic passionately indicted his treason to right thinking. Belinskii's enthusiasm for his colleague had, however, always been based on misunderstanding and wishful thinking. Gogol' had been a critic not of the autocratic political and social order as such but only of abuses within it; he had not envisaged the revolutionary transformation of the society and politics of the country but their reform from within by the correction of human error and abuse through Christian example. In permitting *The Government Inspector* to play in Moscow and St Petersburg year after year, despite its trenchant criticism of official corruption, Nicholas I better understood the playwright's intentions than did Belinskii.

In the furore caused by the publication of *Selected Passages*, few grasped that Gogol' had not changed his spots. The major exception in the chorus of condemnation was Apollon Grigor'ev. In a review in *Moskovskii gorodskii listok*, Grigor'ev pointed out that the party that had placed Gogol' on a pedestal had failed to grasp that 'his way of thinking differed from theirs.' The man, he said, had not changed; rather his supporters had failed to comprehend him from the start. Building on conclusions that he had begun to form in the capital, Grigor'ev saw the cause of this failure in the disease of the age – the 'pride of the individual.' Gogol' and V.I. Odoevskii, author of *Russian Nights* (Russkie nochi), were, in Grigor'ev's opinion, the only writers to have noticed that, in spite of the demonic power of individualism, the majority still tyrannized over the individual. The reason was that in each person ruled a weak will, without a centre of gravity. That led to the sort of restless dissatisfaction and disillusionment about which the lyric poets wrote. Gogol''s book was penetrated, said Grigor'ev, by the profound idea that all people bear within them their own truth. In order to realize their truth, however, a concentration of the self was needed, a gathering of everything into the self.

Gogol', he continued, had placed the greatest emphasis in *Selected Passages* on the woman question. That was proper because at the present moment of social development the situation of women, children, and the poor was the only important issue, and the one that constituted the great historical task of Christianity. Under Gogol''s influence, Grigor'ev now abandoned the utopian-socialist solution of the declared absolute equality of women and men that he had supported in his poetry during his St Petersburg period. A woman, he maintained, could not be equal to a man even if only for physiological reasons. But he did not discard his liberal views entirely. Contemporary society, he complained, did not permit freedom of relations between the sexes. The challenge was to create a situation in which both were seen as a unity. Everyone must be a 'member of a single, indivisible whole, and in this sense we will know neither slaves nor freemen, neither the male sex nor the female.'[11]

Grigor'ev pointed out that Gogol' was above all an artist whose vocation was precious to him. When Gogol' insisted that he was not born to inaugurate a new epoch in literature and that his task was 'the soul and the durable matters of life,' it was not an expression of false modesty or a rejection of his calling. For him, as for every artist, the business of art was life. A true artist had no desire to inaugurate an epoch or stand at the head of a party.[12] The job of art was to address social issues. But their solution was not social. Instead, the solution lay in the moral development of the personality.

Grigor'ev was dissatisfied with the fragmentary nature of his assessment of *Selected Passages*. When several months later he heard a rumour that Gogol' himself had been pleased with the review, he decided to write directly to the author. During October and November 1848, he wrote to Gogol' three lengthy letters, in which he elaborated on the themes that he had first raised in the review and took up some new ones as well.

He opened the first epistle with an apologia for Belinskii's fury in his 'letter to Gogol',' which had become notorious since Grigor'ev's review. Belinskii's opposition, though fanatical, said Grigor'ev, was at least honest. The critic had understood Gogol''s significance in Russian literature, but only one-sidedly. He had worshipped the writer in a childish manner and had sought in his genius confirmation of his own 'feverishly nurtured' ideas, and then his dream had been smashed. Now he saw the man in an entirely different light; the malice, indignation, and sadness that poured from his letter flowed out of his betrayed hopes and love. Grigor'ev concluded, 'I have never sympathized with him; but I am not so bold as to indict him for his furious attacks in his letter to you which you, yourself, how well I know it, have answered with words of peace, love and humility.'[13]

The criticism of most others was, in Grigor'ev's view, harder to excuse than Belinskii's. It arose from two sources. The first was those bigots and hypocrites who, believing that only they spoke in God's name, were indignant at an outsider's voice which spoke seriously about the meaning of life. Here Grigor'ev had in mind the church hierarchy and its defenders in the camp of 'official nationality.' The second source was those 'disillusioned innovators,' the Westernizers.

Grigor'ev admitted that he, too, at first had experienced indignation like Belinskii's on reading *Selected Passages*. And, as with Belinskii, his ire arose from his worship of the author of *Dead Souls*. But soon that first impression gave way to a painful internal process, in which a great deal of his own self-love was abandoned. It was that same self-love to which all the 'offspring of our wilful age cling to as to a life raft.' *Selected Passages* had clarified everything for him, had brought him to understand that 'Christianity is the alpha and omega of any world view.' Truth, he now grasped, belonged to the few, even to one only; it was always persecuted and was on the side of the persecuted.[14] In particular, he recalled a line from Gogol''s book: 'All of us have to think how we, each in our own place, can do good ... Not without reason did God put each in the place which he now occupies.'[15] It was an easy leap from Gogol''s idea about the singular role of each individual to Herder's notion of individuals, groups, and nations, each contributing its own specific nature to the totality. The latter was to become the heart of Grigor'ev's world view.

In his second letter to Gogol', Grigor'ev turned to one of the central questions of his strivings in St Petersburg. 'Is a man responsible,' he asked, 'and in what measure is he responsible for all of his acts in general and for the inner man of the spirit in particular?'[16] He pointed out that in the novel *Who Is to Blame?* (Kto vinovat?), that 'truly brilliant, witty, and sharply paradoxical *profession de foi*,' Herzen the artist had said in artistic images what Herzen the thinker had long argued: that we are not to blame. It is the external deformities of upbringing and society in whose web we are entangled from childhood that are the culprits. If Herzen was right, it would follow that, since everything was contingent on what was given previously, there could be no escape from one's past. Humans were slaves and could not escape their servitude. All those, therefore, who longed for activity should consign themselves to inactivity. The only purpose of life for a man was to find a woman. Beyond that lay only proud suffering and silent death.[17]

All contemporary literature, Grigor'ev continued, aimed to demonstrate people's social enslavement, thus denying literature's own significance and force. Some, like the reactionary writer F. Bulgarin, saw literature as a milch-cow; others treated it as dreamy self-glorification or intellectual masturbation. The former group had no faith in the poet as prophet, as the bearer of truth. The latter assumed that if a prophet appeared, he had to speak in words of hate.

Grigor'ev denied that the individual was incapable of rising above the environment. Instead, he asserted the responsibility of individuals for their acts and the link between freedom and responsibility. In so doing he severed the last of his ties to the utopian socialists and to the whole psychology of the radical left and asserted the primacy of the ethical in social life. Good and evil resided in the soul of the individual, not in an appropriate or inappropriate social environment. In order to reinforce his point, Grigor'ev concluded the second letter with another question: 'Does one, as a man, have a right to reveal in front of others the most inner and most guarded secrets of one's soul?'[18] Merely to ask the question, he replied, was to express the cynical disregard of contemporary man for the paramount significance of our personal lives.

In the third letter, he returned to the question that had absorbed so much of his interest and the one that he had most fully addressed in his review of *Selected Passages*: the woman question. Grigor'ev denied the accusation of critics that Gogol' had nothing positive to contribute to the subject. Rather, Gogol' had shown in his book how women were enslaved by men. All of contemporary literature, Grigor'ev reiterated, was a protest on behalf of women, on the one hand, and the poor, on the other. Gogol' understood such protest as just, but rejected the means usually offered to correct the injustice. Grigor'ev insisted that Gogol' was not on the side of those who called Georges Sand a whore and defended a patriarchal order. Sand's protest bore within it both the sufferings and the aspirations of the whole era. Her thought should not be confused with the Fourierist idea that women should have 'four legal husbands and the means to satisfy carnal lust twenty times a day.' Instead, Sand showed how through egoism the most holy relations between the sexes were corrupted and that marriage all too often concealed the vilest relationships. Throughout Sand's writings, the thought shone through that marriage was holy, that women were men's partners and aids in all that was noble and great. In Sand, a woman appeared as she ought to be in Christ's kingdom – a mitigating force, important in all matters.

Grigor'ev next returned to the related subject, one of his favourites, of the family. He pointed out that family life, especially in Russia, was far from the ideal. Russian women had too narrow a view of their domestic responsibilities. The best of them believed that in running an orderly household and balancing the family budget they had attained the ideal. The upbringing of Russian women destroyed their faith in life and its benefits. It imprisoned the poor maiden in a narrow circle of daily domestic concerns and gave her no outlet for the strivings of her soul. Indeed, such outlets were deemed by society to be a danger to virtue. The result was not a woman but a child. If she happened as well to be by nature gifted and not susceptible to being completely crushed by her upbringing, she was inevitably miserable.[19] In this passage Grigor'ev was returning to an earlier theme in his work about the possibility of love only between mature equals. He was also returning to Georges Sand who, too, had lamented the inadequacies of an education and upbringing for women that ill suited them for independence. For the rest of his life, he retained his belief in the need for intellectual equality between the sexes and for an appropriate education for women.

In Gogol', Grigor'ev also found the justification for his love of the theatre. His mature passion for the Russian theatre had begun in St Petersburg when he began to write a theatre chronicle for *Repertuar i Panteon*. It was a passion that lasted his whole life. Russian drama and theatre were still in flux in the 1840s and 1850s. The previous two decades had produced very little native drama. Griboedov's *Woe from Wit* (Gore ot uma) was written in 1823 but was performed, with major cuts, only in 1831. Lermontov wrote several romantic dramas in the 1830s, but they were rarely put on. The same was true of Pushkin's romantic plays in verse, which were not written for the stage. The most successful Russian dramatists of the day wrote historical plays; those of V. Kriukovskii, N. Kukolnik, N. Polevoi, and P.M. Zotov were popular. Gogol''s *The Government Inspector* enjoyed a huge success, playing in Moscow every year from 1836 to 1845, but its realism was merely a harbinger in a sea of sentimental romanticism and vaudeville. By default much of the repertoire was dominated by foreign works.

Russian acting, too, was experiencing a period of confusion and growth. In the 1830s, the Moscow stage was dominated by P.M. Mochalov, an actor with almost no craft but blessed with an overwhelming stage presence. Relying almost entirely on inspiration, Mochalov's performances were volcanic in their volatility, long passages of mediocrity alternating with moments of true brilliance. He was, as Grigor'ev, who saw him frequently in the late 1830s and early 1840s, often pointed out, the fullest embodiment of the romantic age that gave birth to his performances – an era of protest and longing and faith in the divine origins of artistic creativity.[20] In St Petersburg the dominant acting figure was V. Karatygin, from a quite different mould than Mochalov. Karatygin was a product of the classical tradition – a great technician and master of stagecraft and self-control. Whereas Mochalov used emotion to stir his audience, Karatygin employed thoughtful characterization to probe his audience's intelligence. The best actress of the period was Vera V. Samoilova, who shared Karatygin's approach. Her brother, Vasilii, was the leading comic and vaudeville actor, and her sister, Nadezhda, was a strong comic actress as well.

Karatygin's emphasis on analysis and careful preparation of roles had its counterpart on the Moscow stage in M.S. Shchepkin. He, too, was a skilled technician, but unlike Karatygin, who employed his skills to make his characters larger than life, Shchepkin used his to create a new naturalism in his characterizations. His emphasis on realism influenced a whole generation of actors at Moscow's Malyi Theatre who formed a nucleus for the later staging of A.N. Ostrovskii's realistic dramas of the 1850s and 1860s.[21]

Equally in flux was theatre criticism. There was no lack of amateur theatre notices or of scholarly pieces, more often about the play's content than
its performance. But there were few critics who provided a comprehensive
and consistent assessment of theatre in Russia. An exception, whom
Grigor'ev regarded as an able predecessor, was V.A. Ushakov, who wrote
in *Moskovskii telegraf* (The Moscow Telegraph) in the early 1830s. Ushakov stood out because he focused on living practice rather than on theory.
He tried to judge the play as performed in terms of its truthfulness to the
life of the times of the author. Konstantin Aksakov, too, took an interest in
the whole theatre.

Grigor'ev also counted Belinskii among his teachers. Belinskii wrote a
great deal about the theatre in reviews and notices for a variety of newspapers and journals. Many of his articles were concerned with the theory of
drama, examining such questions as the delineation of the epic, tragic, and
comic or the 'objectivity' of the artist. But, like Ushakov, Belinskii was
aware of the totality of the theatre and examined each production in detail.
For him, the actor stood at the heart of the creative process in the theatre.
The author created a personage, but from a single personage the actor could
create twenty characters. The actor therefore had to be free to recreate the
author's character in concrete form. Belinskii preferred the more elemental
and unconscious approach of the romantic genius Mochalov to the studied
and calculated performances of the classicist Karatygin. But in the 1840s, he
discovered his ideal in the performances of Shchepkin, who combined
Mochalov's immediacy and naturalness with Karatygin's analysis and
stagecraft.

Perhaps most important for Grigor'ev was his colleague's distinction
between audiences in St Petersburg and those in Moscow and the kinds of
plays and styles of acting that each preferred. In the capital, Belinskii discerned an aristocratic, classicist taste, with a preference for the foreign over
the domestic. In Moscow, he detected a more democratic taste and a desire
for naturalism in acting and for Russian national drama rather than imports
– his own approach.[22]

From Belinskii's death in 1848 to the beginning of the 1860s, Grigor'ev
was his nation's leading theatre critic. Most of his colleagues focused on the
novel and short story and largely ignored the stage, whereas Grigor'ev
made a special place for the theatre. Even his début as a literary critic in
1845 had been with an article entitled 'On the Elements of Drama in Contemporary Russian Society' (Ob elementakh dramy v nyneshnem russkom
obshchestve), which appeared in *Theatre Chronicle*, a supplement to
Repertuar i Panteon. In that piece, he declared his allegiance to realism and

sided with Belinskii in stressing the democratic nature of the contemporary theatre. The proper subject of drama, he maintained, was the phenomena of everyday life; its task was to embody in concrete forms the special character of the life of a particular time and people. The theatre therefore had to broaden its reach by extending its themes to include the life of the whole nation.[23]

Though Grigor'ev lionized Mochalov, the idol of his youthful theatre experience, as a type who embodied most fully the Russian age of romanticism in the 1830s, he refused to side with Mochalov against Karatygin in the battle of the classicists and romantics in acting that Belinskii had provoked. 'We neither wish nor are able to compare these two equally great artists,' he wrote. Instead, he pointed out the 'almost insolent boldness of conception' of Karatygin in roles such as King Lear. 'Not everyone understands that with such creations of roles Karatygin is bringing about reform in art; too few artists have been able to reconcile in such a degree the highest tragedy with a simplicity, which sometimes attains to the comic.'[24]

In 1846, Grigor'ev wrote a stinging review of Karatygin as Hamlet and was rebuked by the Third Section. Yet he did not accept Belinskii's assessment of 1837 that Mochalov's characterization of Hamlet was definitive either. Great as was Mochalov's performance, Grigor'ev insisted, 'it was not Hamlet,' and his colleague had been too much influenced by the force of Mochalov's performance. In Belinskii's interpretation of the play, Grigor'ev detected too much sympathy for Hamlet's morbid personality and too little emphasis on the main hero of Shakespeare's dramas, Nemesis.[25] In a later article, Grigor'ev went so far as to maintain that Mochalov had corrupted the public's taste. In their blind enthusiasm for Mochalov, people could not separate the character from the performance. But Mochalov's age had passed, and a new type of actor was required.[26]

Grigor'ev based his thoughts about acting loosely on the work of a German philosopher, G.-T. Rotscher, *Die Kunst der dramatischen Darstellung* (The Art of Acting).[27] Rotscher argued that the actor presented an ideal individual by means of external appearance and speech. Consequently, his or her look and tone had to be capable of representing the desired ideal. Moreover, dramatic presentation succeeded only when it attained to the living or real. Quoting Rotscher, Grigor'ev maintained: 'A stage presentation imparts flesh and blood to the spiritually concrete creations of dramatic poetry, breathes life into them, gives delight to them, as living things.'[28] It was precisely this concretization of the general in the particular, which Grigor'ev had tried to achieve in his poetry, that drew him to the theatre. For him, the ideal was accessible only through the real. In a review of the actress Vera Samoilova's tour of Moscow he wrote in a convoluted style:

It is known that the ideal is formed in the soul from a number of past and present impressions and does not appear itself either from one or the other. It is true that in the human soul separate impressions, past and present, harmoniously aggregate into something whole and greater than them, taken separately, that from the past and present, so to speak, they become the future, that is, potential, having only an impalpable existence, an existence in the soul of a man – but the basis, the core of this possible existence, is real phenomena.[29]

Grigor'ev divided actors into two basic types. Some artistic natures were capable of creating whole, full characters, cutting themselves off almost entirely from their own personality. When such an artist appeared, the spectator at once knew everything about the character portrayed. From the most insignificant data, such artists created a complete and rounded image. Grigor'ev compared such actors to portraits painted by Briulov, which captured everything permanent in the subject's character and subordinated everything incidental. Grigor'ev counted among this type Sadovskii and Samoilov. The other type of actor put the stamp of his or her own personality on each character that he or she created, working by means of particular features rather than wholly. Among actors of this sort were Martynov, Mochalov, Samoilova, and Shchepkin. When the character being portrayed was very near their own personality, they created a type. Thus Mochalov was the type of Richard III but was Hamlet only partially. Generally, however, the audience was drawn to the personalities of such actors, not to the types of the characters they delineated.

Every actor had two sides. One side, said Grigor'ev, was what was given by nature. The other was what the actor did with his natural gifts. Appearance, facial characteristics, and voice were important because they helped to determine the roles that the actor could take on. But most important was the moral essence of the actor through which he or she filtered the words of the character.[30] Here again was one of the main props of Grigor'ev's criticism: artistic creativity was a moral process in which the artist passed the material that the age, or in the case of the actor the author, provided through the screen of his or her own moral sense. Such views were a foretaste of his later organic criticism.

For all the impact made on him by Gogol''s *Selected Passages*, which, he claimed, had enabled him to escape some 'profound intellectual and moral dilemmas,' Grigor'ev was still unsettled in his views. He had, it is true, clearly moved away from his earlier interest in utopian-socialist ideas and had singled out the social trend in literature best represented by Herzen's *Who Is to Blame?* as the delusion of the age. In a letter to Pogodin late in 1849, he declared that he had no affiliation to any party.[31] That situation was soon to change. Gogol''s influence, which had pulled him back from the abyss of moral and cultural despair, was conspiring with his own rapidly growing fascination with things Russian and his love for the theatre to prepare the way for his attachment to the 'young editors' of *Moskvitianin*.

PART TWO

From Young Editor to Organic Critic

4

The Leading Young Editor
1849–1855

He wants to be a gypsy, like us.

Alexander Pushkin, 'The Gypsies'

The revolutions of 1848 in western Europe caused scarcely a ripple on the surface of the Russian Empire. The arrest of the *Petrashevtsy* and the trial, mock execution, and exile of the ringleaders, among them the novelist F.M. Dostoevskii, in 1849 were only the merest echoes of the European tumult. But beneath that tranquil surface the events of 1848 did make an impression on the minds of educated Russians. On the one hand, the regime responded to the troubles in Europe by tightening censorship and further restricting travel to the West. On the other hand, the hopes of committed Russians, who had looked to the West for leadership in the struggle for liberation, were frustrated by the meagre results of liberal revolution there. Both circumstances conspired to turn Russians in upon themselves in a new tough-mindedness and self-reliance, to look to their own strengths and resources, and to adapt Western thought to them.[1] In the changed conditions after 1848, the discrepancy between the ideal and the real, the 'is' and the 'ought,' became even more pronounced, and the resulting alienation of the concerned even more acute. It was in those conditions that the Russian intelligentsia was born.

The change in attitude among thinking Russians was accompanied by the coming of age of what might be called the first echelon of a new generation of cultural activists. From ten to fifteen years younger than the Slavophiles and Westernizers and five to ten years older than the nihilists (who were to become the second echelon of the new intelligentsia), the majority of the new group were born into the petty gentry, a class long separated from the land and dependent on civil service salaries. They were urban in experience and outlook and usually well educated. Most of them followed their fathers into the bureaucracy, but a few found positions, or more commonly partial employment, in Russia's nascent cultural industry – belles-lettres, journalism, the plastic arts, and the theatre. In Turgenev's terms, they were of neither the fathers nor the children. Most were habitually impoverished, identified themselves as aesthetes, and so rejected the materialism and positivism of the nihilists, and they lived and played hard, much in the later bohemian style. Grigor'ev belonged to this first echelon of the intelligentsia, and he was soon to meet a number of his kind who came together in a group known as the 'young editors' of *Moskvitianin* (The Muscovite). In their company, he was able to combine Gogol''s idea of Christian humility with the humble type that he had himself discerned in Russian history while he was still in St Petersburg into a new definition of Russian nationality.

A typical representative of the new generation, Grigor'ev was chiefly preoccupied in these years with trying to support his growing family, which included two sons by early 1852. In May 1850, the Orphans' Institute at which he was teaching was turned into a school of the Cadet Corps, where he was not certified to teach. He was transferred along with the students of two classes to the Moscow Foundling Home and promoted to titular counsellor retroactive to April 1850. His task was to teach the students in those classes until they graduated. In anticipation of the end of his job at the Foundling Home he took on a second job, as senior teacher of law, at the First Moscow Gymnasium in March 1851. During the first half of 1851 his wife endured a debilitating and expensive illness.[2] In an effort to improve his prospects, he tried at the beginning of 1852 to enlist the support of Pogodin, S. Shevyrev, professor of Russian literature at Moscow University, and the countesses Rostopchina and Salias, both writers and contributors to *Moskvitianin*, to help him secure the post of inspector of the Moscow Third Gymnasium. But someone else was appointed.[3]

While his financial situation deteriorated and the grind of teaching drained him, Grigor'ev's marriage also began to break down. Some time in 1852 or 1853 Lidiia Fedorovna had an affair, the circumstances of which Grigor'ev later related to Turgenev, who made the story the basis of the affair of Lavretskii's wife, Varvara Pavlovna, in *A Nest of Gentlefolk* (Dvorianskoe gnezdo).[4] It is impossible to know whether Turgenev's account accurately reflected Grigor'ev's experience or feelings, but the association of the passage with his friend makes it of interest here. In the novel, Lavretskii enters Varvara Pavlovna's room in her absence and finds on the floor a carefully folded note, which he picks up and reads. The note

is from her lover, Ernest. It mocks her 'fat husband,' who was 'usually bur-
rowing around in his books,' and arranges a tryst:

Lavretsky did not immediately understand what he had read; he read it a second
time – and his head began to spin, the floor began moving under his feet like the
deck of a ship in a swell. He started crying out and sighing and weeping all at the
same moment.

He went crazy. He had trusted his wife so blindly; the possibility of deceit and
betrayal had never occurred to him ... Several minutes passed, then half an hour;
Lavretskii remained standing there, squeezing the fateful note in his hand and star-
ing senselessly at the floor; through some kind of dark whirlwind a host of pale
faces flashed before him; his heart died agonizingly within him; he seemed to be falling and falling and falling, and there was no end to it.

Varvara Pavlovna returns, and Lavretskii, fearing that he will 'tear her apart,
beat her half to death, in peasant fashion strangle her with his own hands,'
rushes from the apartment. Still he could not understand what had happened:

Bright and dark memories tore with equal anguish at his heart; suddenly he recalled
that a few days ago she had sat down with him and Ernest at the piano and sung:
'Old husband, threatening husband!' He recalled the expression on her face, the
strange brilliance in her eyes and the colour in her cheeks – and he rose from the
chair, wanting to go and say to them: 'You're not going to get away with making
fun of me!' ... Then it suddenly seemed to him that everything happening to him
was a dream, and not even a dream, but just some sort of nonsense that he could get
rid of by shaking himself or turning his head ... He turned his head and, as a hawk
drives its talons into its captive prey, so the pangs of regret cut deeper and deeper
into his heart.[5]

Lavretskii separates from his wife immediately, and time gradually heals
him. 'He was not,' Turgenev observed, 'born for suffering ...'[6] Grigor'ev
was and blamed the 'irresponsible behaviour of his wife' for the collapse of
their marriage. But Lidiia Fedorovna and he were not suited to one
another. Her family circle was an integral part of the liberal, Westernizer
tendency; Grigor'ev had just converted to an exaggerated Slavism. She had
been raised on Georges Sand's notions of freedom in love; he had recently
rejected such ideas. They quarrelled regularly, and he began to drink again
and to teach her to drink. They continued to live together for the most part
until Grigor'ev went abroad in 1857[7] but were not reunited upon his return
in 1858.

While blaming his wife for her involvement with someone else, Grigor'ev formed his own deep emotional attachment to another woman. His move to the Foundling Home had brought him into daily contact with the family of Iakov Ivanovich Vizard, who had taught French at the school and served as its supervisor of the boys' section. Iakov Ivanovich had lived in an official apartment there with his two eldest sons and two daughters. Mme Vizard operated a pension in another part of Moscow and lived there with their youngest son. Upon Vizand's death, the eldest son, Vladimir Iakovlevich, became head of the household. He had at one time been secretary to the celebrated historian T.N. Granovskii, from whom Grigor'ev had taken lectures, and Granovskii's name was revered in the Vizard household. Vladimir Iakovlevich regularly held a Sunday evening at home, and Grigor'ev, a superb conversationalist and possessor of a large library, soon became a permanent fixture in the drawing room there.

I.M. Sechenov, later one of Russia's most distinguished scientists, was a student at the time and a close friend of the middle Vizard son, Dmitrii. Sechenov remembered Grigor'ev as 'a good, intelligent and, in essence, simple man in spite of a theatrical tendency to play at being Mephistopheles.' He very much enlivened Sunday evenings at the Vizards', Sechenov remembered, with his nervous and clever speech: 'I do not know what he was in his writings, collaborating in *Moskvitianin*, but during evenings at the Vizards he was neither an enemy of the Westernizers nor an inveterate Slavophile, inclined only to the moral worth of the Russian people, and even loved to declaim certain non-radical verses of Nekrasov, often expressing surprise that he could write such charming things, given his internal makeup.'

Grigor'ev endeared himself to his student interlocutors by the fact that, though older than they by several years, he conducted himself toward them 'like a comrade, without any pretensions.'[8] Grigor'ev became the unofficial tutor in literature of one of the daughters, Leonida Iakovlevna, who was studying to be a governess. Leonida's music teacher at the time was E.S. Protopopova, an accomplished pianist who was later to marry the composer Alexander Borodin. Protopopova became Grigor'ev's confidante, and he later wrote to her a remarkable series of personal letters from Italy.

By 1852, Grigor'ev had fallen deeply in love with his pupil. She was then only sixteen or seventeen but was intelligent and talented. Very musical, Leonida Iakolevna had the additional advantages of vivacity and beauty, with her black hair and blue eyes. Many years later, her sister wrote: 'It is not surprising that Grigor'ev was attracted to her but it is surprising that he did not try to disguise his worship.'[9] Sechenov, too, remarked on

Grigor'ev's fascination: 'In her company he was always sober and made himself out to be an intelligent, rather disillusioned young man, but in young, male company appeared in his true guise, a carousing student.'[10] If Leonida noticed her teacher's love for her, she did not apparently reciprocate it. Her sister testified that Leonida, whose character was 'very reserved and prudent,' felt nothing for him.

Grigor'ev's unrequited love tormented him. Writing to Protopopova from Italy in 1857, he was still agonizing about whether she had loved him. Only Leonida could have brought him peace, he declared. Everything about her was dear to him, from her wisdom and simplicity to her apathy and coldness. He could not say, he wrote, that she was perfection, but 'she was created for him and he for her.'[11] Strong passions, he continued, were more harmful to the soul than any plague to the body. 'Nothing remains of them except the bitterness of their personal aftertaste and the everlasting poison of memories.' And he went on to blame Leonida for the debaucheries of his last months in Moscow. 'What monstrosities did I not permit myself in relation to women as if avenging myself on all for the accursed Puritan or Calvinistic purity of the one.'[12]

In light of his unhappiness and the taste for the bohemian life that he had developed in St Petersburg, it is not surprising that the other pole of his personal existence in Moscow was increasingly the taverns. He was drawn to them not only by his proven taste for strong drink but by the many gypsy performers who were the true virtuosi of Russian folk songs. Grigor'ev had for some years been interested in the performance of the Russian song. In St Petersburg he had been closely acquainted with A.E. Varlamov, the well-known singer and composer, whose songs, though not authentically folk, were written to the popular words and verses of Russian poets.[13] Inspired by a passion for gypsy music, Grigor'ev had already, through a course of self-teaching exercises, learned to play the guitar.[14] P.V. Kireevskii had published a collection of Russian folk songs in 1848, but their actual performance in educated circles was as yet almost unknown.

'In a jolly establishment near the Kamennyi most (Stone Bridge) we used to listen to Nikolka-the-Redhead, a guitarist, and Aleksei-with-the Turban, drinking vodka with kvass because our stomachs had not yet got any food in them,' T.I. Filippov, one of the young editors, recalled.[15] In a little wine cellar in Tverskaia Street, Filippov, himself a masterly performer of folk songs, discovered the guitarist and singer M.E. Sobolev, who had a silver tenor voice that was perfect for the traditional songs. After the tavern was closed to the general public, it was possible to slip into the wine cellar by the back door and there engage in noisy conversation and intoxicating song until dawn. Not for nothing did Sechenov call Grigor'ev his 'tempting serpent'; Grigor'ev, who had a key to the back door, introduced him to the wine cellar and to his numerous friends who lived in student rooms in Theatre Square.[16]

Grigor'ev prowled the taverns and back streets of Moscow in search of talented folk performers and dragooned embarrassed friends into going to listen to them.[17] He himself used to sing occasionally in the famous gypsy chorus led by I.V. Vasil'ev and passed many entire evenings at Fet's with friends, singing in his soft, vibrato voice to his own guitar accompaniment. 'In spite of a poor voice,' Fet wrote of these occasions, 'Grigor'ev gave real pleasure by the sincerity and mastery of his singing. Strictly speaking he did not sing but as if by dots marked out the musical contour of the songs.'[18]

The two poles of Grigov'ev's existence – hopeless love for Leonida and for the tavern – came together in the cycle (compiled in 1857) of poems *The Struggle* (Bor'ba), which he himself described as the best poetry of his years on *Moskvitianin*. The cycle consisted of eighteen poems. A number of them were free translations of works by the great Polish poet Adam Mickiewicz or were inspired by him. One was a free translation of a poem by Victor Hugo. Several were rooted in the Russian tradition of folk poetry. Blok, compiler of Grigor'ev's poems in 1915, felt that at least three of those – 'The evening is oppressive, the wind is howling' (Vecher dushen, veter voet), 'O, speak to me as you wish' (O, govori khot' ty so mnoi), and 'Gypsy vengerka' (Tsyganskaia vengerka) – achieved a level of true folk creativity.

Like many of Grigor'ev's earlier poems, this cycle was about a love that fate had determined could not be declared. The 'struggle' of the cycle's title was that of the poet to submit his ego to the will of fate, to accept what Grigor'ev elsewhere called the 'irony of life.' The poet did not resort in the end to facile cynicism or the consolations of abstract rationalizations. Instead, he confronted his suffering squarely and through 'struggle' achieved a certain humility that reconciled him to his condition.

The cycle opens with the poet's denial of his love for the beloved. The first piece begins: 'I do not love her, I do not love her / It is the force of habit!' He recognizes that he is unfit for her 'as Satan is unfit for paradise.' But recognition of his unworthiness does not relieve his suffering. 'God spare you, my child, from learning / How hard it is to love with such a love.' He turns to anger. 'An artful daughter of the artful Eve / You are no worse and no better than your sisters / What do you want? ... That I go completely out of my mind?' He complains of her coldness, which annihilates him; he writes of his sleepless nights. He had almost told her of his love, forgetting the stern laws of fate, then silently asked her forgiveness for his weakness. He remembers an evening with her in which all hope died, and he tries to drive away his dreams and curb his love. 'I believe in struggle and duty,' he reassures himself, and he condemns himself to uncomplaining suffering. He seeks the company of his seven-stringed guitar: 'I am ready to converse with you until dawn … Only agree with me, you sing an unsingable song.'

In 'Gypsy vengerka' (the vengerka is a Hungarian dance), Grigor'ev plumbs the very depths of his grief. It was, he wrote, 'a meteoric tavern poem about the sounds of an inconsolable despair.' It was cast ironically, but, as Fet pointed out, its current of scepticism could not extinguish its truth and beauty, and the wild revels could not conceal the happiness lost. But out of the depths of the poet's debauchery sound the first notes of reconciliation: 'Fate, you are my fate / A hard fate! / I would surely escape you / If I only had the will.' And later in the poem, he writes, 'You are my sad fate / These jokes are stupid.' And, 'Ah you, life, my life … Embrace me heart to heart! / For you it will be no sin / And let people condemn me / God will forgive me.' The poem ends with a plea that the music become ever more morbid, the sooner to burst his heart with grief.

In the closing poems of the cycle, he took leave of the beloved and recognized the justice of the sentence passed on him by fate. 'The stern court is wise, and complaining useless / I am old, like sin, and you, like joy, are young / I long ago crossed the abyss of corruption / But you are still radiant and your life is pure.' Her purity continued to shine on him like a distant star. 'But I loved you … By your purity / I was raised from the dust, with you I was pure and holy.'[19]

The Struggle affirmed Grigor'ev's sense of the inevitability of personal suffering and its role in the learning of wisdom.

Through it all, Grigor'ev continued to work. In August 1853, his duties at the Moscow Foundling Home came to an end, and by imperial order he was given a special award of 300 silver roubles for his work. He continued to teach law at the Moscow First Gymnasium. In August 1856 he received a gift of 250 roubles for distinction in service there, and in February 1857 he was promoted to the rank of collegiate assessor, effective from April 1856.[20] Though his skills as an instructor were appreciated by his superiors, Grigor'ev himself questioned the value of teaching law at the level of the gymnasium. He would have preferred to teach history and in April 1852 had travelled to St Petersburg and sat an examination that qualified him to teach it in the military school system. Only ten years later did he make use of the qualification.

Grigor'ev achieved success in teaching in spite of certain personal disadvantages which he once set out in a letter to Pogodin: an unfortunate tendency to be arrested for debt a few days in advance of receiving his salary, a 'carelessness' of dress, and an 'irrepressible love for long hair.'[21] At that time, Grigor'ev was affecting in dress what he supposed to be the traditional costume of Russian merchants, whom he had come to believe were the true bearers of Russian nationality; he could be seen roaming the halls of the school in those outfits. Fet described one of them in which Grigor'ev appeared at a party at V.P. Botkin's:

I remember that Apollon Grigor'ev came through the hall wearing a brand new black Hungarian jacket with laces, braid and chevrons, reminiscent of a boyar kaftan. On his feet were brightly polished boots with high tops cut out under the knee in a heart shape. When Grigor'ev came through the door of the salon in his turn to make his bow to the hostess, the daughter of the hostess, a little one-year old who was sitting on the parquet floor, suddenly got up and looking toward Grigor'ev bowed her head and raised her right hand to her forehead. Botkin laughed and said, 'Look, Nadia is crossing herself to Grigor'ev; she has mistaken him for a priest.'

Botkin went on to point out, Fet recorded, that though merchants did wear such boots in the eighteenth century, they had nothing to do with Russian tradition but had been a fashionable import from the West.[22]

If Grigor'ev's eccentricities of dress irked the educational authorities, so did his taste in theatre. In addition to teaching law at the school, Grigor'ev decided to direct some student plays. He appropriately chose one act from N.V. Kukolnik's patriotic drama *The Hand of the Almighty Saved the Fatherland* (Ruka vsevyshnogo otechestvo spasla), in which he himself played the national hero Kuz'ma Minin. But he also decided to produce the whole of Ostrovskii's new work, *Don't Sit in Someone Else's Sleigh* (Ne v svoi sani ne sadis'); the future actor A.A. Nil'skii, a student at the school, was awarded the leading female role. Nil'skii, whose resolve to become an actor was confirmed by the experience, recalled that the playwright himself came to the final rehearsal and brought the young thespian I.F. Gorbunov with him. The play was performed with considerable acclaim.

Indeed, it was so successful that it was entered as the School's contribution to a festival of the arts that V.I. Nazimov, curator of the school district, organized among the various gymnasiums. This time P.M. Sadovskii, one of Russia's greatest actors, attended the final dress rehearsal. On the day of the festival, the performance began, in the presence of Nazimov. The proceedings were summarily halted after the second act, and Grigor'ev and his troupe were informed that the play was unsuitable for a scholarly institution, presumably because of its robust language and honest depiction of personal relationships. Later, Grigor'ev received an official reprimand from the school authorities for selecting an inappropriate drama.[23]

Grigor'ev's salvation during these troubled years was his association with the 'young editors' of *Moskvitianin*. He described his years among them as his second youth, when a renewed faith in the soil and the people arose in his soul. 'I was reborn out of loneliness, I who for some years had led a kind of foreign existence, who had experienced someone else's passions but in no way my own – I began to search for my own personality in the depths of my soul.'[24] Most of the elements of his future 'organic criticism' were born from that search.

Moskvitianin was a monthly journal, which had been published in Moscow by Pogodin since 1841. With its advocacy of the holy trinity of Russian autocratic ideology – 'autocracy, Orthodoxy, nationality' – it was politically conservative and culturally nationalistic. Pogodin combined Slavophile belief in the exhaustion of western Europe, in Russia's political and cultural uniqueness, and in its mission to renovate the Christian world with the more official view that it was Peter the Great who had set his nation on its correct path. Whereas the Slavophiles stressed the discontinuity of Russian history beginning with Peter's Westernizing reforms Pogodin emphasized the continuity of national development. An advocate of Schelling's notion of a universal culture, Pogodin was convinced that Peter, by bringing the West to the East, had initiated a great, Russian-led cultural synthesis of universal significance. In literary criticism, Pogodin's fellow professor and regular contributor to *Moskvitianin* S.P. Shevyrev had been combating in the journal's pages the tendencies of the so-called natural school of literary criticism throughout the 1840s.[25]

About 1850 a new group formed in the editorial offices of *Moskvitianin* that was soon to challenge the supremacy of the Slavophiles as defenders of Russian nationality. The group originated in a fortuitous meeting in 1847 between A.N. Ostrovskii, a struggling dramatist, and T.I. Filippov, an aspiring philosopher and protégé of Pogodin's, in a student tavern. The young literary critic E.N. Edel'son and two poets, B.N. Almazov and L.A. Mei, soon joined forces with Ostrovskii and Filippov.

These five men formed the nucleus of a broad and diverse group, which started to attract a certain notoriety in Moscow in the late 1840s. N.V. Berg, who later counted himself among the young editors, recalled that all kinds of unlikely rumours circulated in society about them. It was said that they were 'indefatigable debauchees,' who went about most of the day dressed in peasants' sheepskin coats and blouses, despised dress coats and gloves, drank vin ordinaire by the shtoff (equal to 1.2 litres), and dined on pickles. Reputed in society to be 'trolls' who rarely crept out from their caves into 'God's light,' they had dwellings, it was whispered, that were complete strangers to the broom.[26]

Countess E.P. Rostopchina, a frequent contributor of stories to *Moskvitianin* and often a literary adviser to Pogodin, was instrumental in attaching the young editors to the journal. The countess, who shared a large stone house in Moscow with her husband, she on the ground floor and he on the top – they met only at dinner – had for some time been considering becoming the patron of a literary circle.[27] There were only two of any significance in Moscow at the time. The Slavophiles were for the most part wealthy landowners who, as Berg pointed out, kept to themselves. They were terribly serious, society regarded them with a certain irony, and the government viewed them with outright suspicion. The young editors were quite different. Far from being exclusive, their group embraced all sorts, including a number of actors; far from being aloof, they were amiably sociable. They were, perhaps, too colourful, but they were interesting and, best of all from the countess's point of view, apparently harmless politically.

She got an opportunity to establish her patronage late in 1849. During that year and into the next, Ostrovskii and some of his friends gave a series of readings of Ostrovskii's first play, *The Bankrupt* (Bankrot) in the homes of aristocrats and merchants. The actor P.M. Sadovskii, who was an intimate of the group, gave a reading at the countess's; in December 1849, Ostrovskii himself read his play at Pogodin's in the presence of Gogol', Khomiakov, Shevyrev, the great dramatic actor M.S. Shchepkin, some of the future 'young editors,' and the countess herself. She invited the dramatist and most of Pogodin's guests to an evening the following Saturday. It was the first of many such evenings at her home, with the 'young editors' as the focus of attention.[28] On those Saturdays when the countess was not available, the circle met at the home of K.A. Bulgakov, a retired Guards officer whose father was director of the Moscow postal services.

By the spring of 1851, Grigor'ev had again slipped into depression. In a letter in April, he had complained to Pogodin about the hypochondria occasioned by the hopelessness of his situation. All day he laboured at the school like a cart horse, but he could not see the value of his labours. When he arrived home, he was too tired to write. He wanted to escape but lacked the necessary connections. Once, he complained, he had enjoyed the respect of men such as Granovskii, who expected much from him, and he asked Pogodin to help him establish links with the literary world. But Pogodin was not inclined to introduce the excitable and eccentric Grigor'ev into his social circle. Once Pogodin called Grigor'ev a collaborator worth his weight in gold, a real fighter who wrote well and with feeling but who, he went on, did not know where to pick his nose and where to say his prayers. The first he did in the corner of the hallway, the second under the stairs.[29]

Fate intervened, however, to force Pogodin's hand. The teacher of Church Slavonic and Russian literature at the First Moscow Gymnasium, where Grigor'ev taught law, was Tertii Filippov, one of the founding members of the young editors. Filippov was an outstanding exception to the general neglect of the performance of folk songs in Russia. With his beautiful voice, he introduced the Russian folk song to the salons and parlours of Moscow. Invited through Filippov to a party at Ostrovskii's, Grigor'ev was said to have fallen on his knees before the young editors and begged to be counted among them when, after most of the guests had gone, Filippov performed.[30]

The 'young editors' formally came into being as a group early in 1851 when Pogodin, in an effort to revitalize a failing *Moskvitianin*, turned control of the belles-lettres and literary-criticism sections of the journal over to Ostrovskii and his companions while retaining control of the political and historical sections himself. The relationship was far from smooth and was to last only until 1854, when the young editors began to go their separate ways. Before they broke up, however, they made a major impact on the arts and criticism in Russia.

In their heyday they were a focus for an astonishing array of youthful energy and talent. The core of their circle consisted of B.N. Almazov, E.N. Edel'son, T.I. Filippov, A.A. Grigor'ev, L.A. Mei, and A.N. Ostrovskii. Around them formed a most heterogeneous and volatile group, which included the writers N.V. Berg, E.E. Drianskii, P.I. Iakushkin, A.F. Pisemskii, M.A. Stakhovich, and the Ural Cossack officer, essayist, and historian I.I. Zheleznov; the actors I.F. Gorbunov, P.A. Maksin, P.M. Sadovskii, I.E. Turchaninov, and S.V. Vasil'ev; the artists P.M. Boklevskii and N.A. Ramazanov; the musicians A.I. Diubok and N.G. Rubenshtein; a merchant, I.I. Shanin; university students; and even a shoemaker. These were the Saturday regulars.

Occasional guests included M.N. Longinov, the bibliographer and historian of literature; M.S. Shchepkin, the actor; and Prince V.A. Viazemskii.[31] On Sundays, an overlapping group met at the Grigor'ev home. Almazov, Edel'son, Filippov, and Ostrovskii were almost always there and were frequently joined by the writers A.F. Pisemskii, A.A. Potekhin, and M.A. Stakhovich, as well as the actor P.M. Sadovskii, the violinist I.K. Frishman, and K.F. Rul'e, a medical doctor and professor. An occasional guest was the Slavophile A.S. Khomiakov.[32] Another favoured meeting place was the home of the Botkins, one of the most prominent merchant families of Moscow.

P.V. Annenkov, an acute observer of the period, carefully distinguished the young editors from the Slavophiles. They were, he pointed out, often confused with one another. Indeed, they still are. The two groups, Annenkov noted, did share a distaste for the denial, which they thought characteristic of St Petersburg's literary scene, of the importance of the national way of life. They also had a shared dislike of abstract philosophizing in the area of criticism and journalism. But the young editors, in Annenkov's view, almost without exception, had the critical sense 'to discern the baselessness of certain aspects of Russian life even though they had grown up over centuries and bore the stamp of the most noble antiquity.' The Slavophiles, he added, always evaded such salutary unmaskings. The 'young editors,' like their mentor, Pogodin, brought together the Slavophile preference for Russia before Peter the Great with the Westernizers' admiration for many of the changes that that ruler had introduced. In particular, as Annenkov noted, they believed that Western science could facilitate the 'purification and strengthening of Russian nationality on its native soil.'[33]

When in 1857 Grigor'ev looked back on the 'young editors,' he identified the three principles that underlay their movement. They were art (*Iskusstvo*), democratism (*Demokratizm*), and immediacy (*Neposredstvennost'*). By 'art,' Grigor'ev meant the primacy of artistic creativity over all other aspects of mind and its inseparability from nationality. 'Democratism' was the essential unity of all strata of Russian society in the national ideal. By 'immediacy,' he referred to the direct perception of the concrete historical experience of a people of which only art was capable and the rejection of theory as a tool for the understanding of life and its organic processes. These three principles formed the basis of his mature outlook, and the rest of his career was devoted to elaborating them.

As a group, the young editors articulated a literary criticism that advocated the 'immediate' or 'spontaneous' (*neposredstvennyi*) relationship of art with Russian reality. They tried to understand what was truly national by examining the *narod* (common people) through its songs, customary laws, customs, and habits. They also sought to liberate Russian literature from foreign imitation. The young editors rejected both the accusatory literature of the so-called natural school and the Slavophiles' idealization of pre-Petrine life and condemnation of developments since Peter. They were particularly interested in music, both folk and Russian classical, and especially in its performance. At the head of their agenda stood development of a national drama and theatre. They believed that Europe had exhausted itself and that Russia, which had absorbed the best of European forms and values since the time of Peter the Great, was destined to bring new vitality and vigour to European culture.

The young editors also believed that Russian nationality was at present most clearly revealed in the plays of Ostrovskii about merchant life. Ostrovskii dealt with that subject, they believed, because the merchants as a group were culturally close to all the social levels of Russia. As Evgenii Edel'son wrote, in that class one meets 'all the forms of life and the customs worked out in our fatherland' – 'both the ancient Russian prowess experienced for whole centuries and not spoiled by any foreign influences' and the comforts of modern European life.[34] The merchant class, they believed, also used the Russian language to the full extent of its great richness. The satire in Ostrovskii's plays exposed, in their view, the falseness of merchant borrowings from the educated classes; the tension in the plays, they contended, arose from the clash between those imitations and the true merchant traditions and way of life.

Nothing could better serve to illustrate the basic ideas of the young editors and the reason for their attractiveness to Grigor'ev than Ostrovskii's own review of a story by Evgeniia Tur which appeared in the April 1850 number of *Moskvitianin*. Ostrovskii pointed out in the article that the literary and the social development of any nation were vitally linked and progressed in parallel. The moral life of a society assumed a variety of forms which provided art both with certain tasks and with certain types to depict artistically: 'These types and tasks on the one hand awaken the writer to creativity, affect him, and on the other hand provide him with prepared, worked out forms. The writer either validates the originality of any type as the highest expression of contemporary life, or weighing it against the universal human ideal, finds its definition too narrow, and the type becomes comic.'

Contemporary foreign literature, Ostrovskii continued, betrayed a preference for the individual and particular. But the distinguishing feature of Russians was their aversion for the unique and the personal, for everything egotistically separated from the universally human. That aversion gave contemporary Russian art its peculiarly accusatory character. Ostrovskii called this tendency 'the moral-social.' The more artistic the work, the more national it was, and hence the more it contained that accusatory element. Russian literature had traditionally flowed in two branches, which were now joining into a single stream. The first, heavily influenced by the foreign, ran through Lomonosov, Sumarokov, Karamzin, Batiushkov, Zhukovskii, and Pushkin; the second, comic and satirical, ran from Kantemir, through Sumarokov, Fonvizin, Kapnist, and Griboedov, and on to Gogol'. Their confluence raised Russian art to universal significance.

Art was fundamentally moral, Ostrovskii continued, but a work that consisted of moral pronouncements was not art. Rather, art consisted in the creation of living artistic forms. Art presented contemporary vices and failings in fully drawn images. Those images, in turn, prevented society from falling back into old, already condemned forms and compelled it to become more moral.[35]

Grigor'ev himself had, since his encounter with Gogol''s *Selected Passages from Correspondence with Friends* (Vybrannye mesta iz perepiski s druz'iami), been groping toward similar views. Ostrovskii's emphasis on the direct relationship between art and society, on the historical nature of literary development, on the moral nature of art in its relationship to social development, and on the concreteness of artistic forms must have come to him as a welcome clarifying vision. He became Ostrovskii's most enthusiastic supporter and made the ideas expressed in Ostrovskii's article his own. For the next five years he expanded on them and ardently advocated them in the pages of *Moskvitianin*.

In 1851 Grigor'ev became a full participant among the 'young editors' and began to contribute extensively to *Moskvitianin*. He was soon to emerge as the leading figure in the group. Most of his early contributions consisted of his 'Chronicle of the Russian Theatre' (Letopis' russkogo teatra), which was a continuation of the column he had formerly contributed to *Otechestvennye zapiski* (Notes of the Fatherland). His debut as a critic in *Moskvitianin* came in an unsigned review of P.N. Menshikov's comic drama *Prichudy* (Whims). The review affirmed the hopes that he placed in Russian drama. He reluctantly concluded that Menshikov's play lacked creativity and was only an 'intelligent but cold copy of reality.' Nevertheless, he went on, every new Russian play had to be scrutinized in the hope of finding some new aspect of Russian existence. Drama, he said, was the crowning height of poetry, 'the full and complete reflection of national life, national consciousness and national thought.'[36]

His most interesting contribution to *Moskvitianin* in 1851, however, was a review of a collection of stories called *The Comet* (Kometa). He focused in particular on a story by N. Stankevich called 'The Idealist' (Idealist). Stankevich had been one of the leading proponents of Hegelian philosophy in Russia. In his comments on the story, Grigor'ev voiced his by now fully developed antipathy for Hegelian historicism. Idealism, Grigor'ev said, was one of the diseases of his age. Idealism was a disease because it demanded from reality not what reality itself had to give but what it had in advance determined that reality ought to give. Idealism viewed all living phenomena through the distorting lens of an abstract and hence moribund preconception. The symptoms of the disease were revulsion for reality if it rebuffed the preconceived demands of our ego and a proud withdrawal into ourselves.[37] It is clear that Grigor'ev's rejection of Hegelian idealism was the culmination of his increasingly critical exploration of egoism. The path to 'organic criticism' now lay cleared before him.

Grigor'ev's first expression of what was later to be his 'organic criticism' came in the first four numbers of *Moskvitianin* for 1852. In a series of four articles entitled 'Russian Literature in 1851,' Grigor'ev for the first time clearly and fully articulated his views about Russian literature and literary criticism. The series was a milestone in his development as a literary critic. It was a first draft of his later 'organic criticism,' which clearly distinguished him from rival critical schools. In it he carved out a position that separated him from the so-called natural-school critics who dominated literary criticism in the capital. The latter had, on the authority of Gogol''s *Dead Souls* (Mertvye dushi), assumed a critical and negative attitude to almost all aspects of Russian reality. Natural-school literary critics such as I.I. Panaev, at *Sovremennik* (The Contemporary), valued literature primarily as a weapon for the realization of prescribed social aims. The natural-school critics at *Sovremennik* and *Otechestvennye zapiski* doubted the very existence of a native Russian literature and scoffed at Russian folk poetry as inartistic. While rejecting the natural school's utilitarian approach to art, Grigor'ev gave notice as well that the critical school of art-for-art's sake, exemplified in journals such as *Biblioteka dlia chteniia* (Library for Reading), which denied that art had any social value, was equally alien to him.

The review began with an examination of what Grigor'ev termed 'historical criticism.' The nineteenth century, he observed, was truly an era of historical criticism. The term had, however, recently fallen into misrepresentation and abuse. In its degraded form, it reduced artistic creativity to service to the fleeting interests of the moment; it hindered the advancement of thought by judging everything not from within the experience of real historical development but from the olympian heights of a preconceived ideal. Such a negative approach to reality had, nevertheless, once served a useful purpose.

Recently, Grigor'ev maintained, historical criticism had generated a positive side, but its adherents refused to recognize it. Borrowing from Ostrovskii's article on Evgeniia Tur, Grigor'ev argued that historical criticism, correctly understood, viewed literature as the organic product of the age and a people in conjunction with the development of its state, social, and moral concepts. Every work of literature was a living echo of the time in which it was written and a record of its concepts, beliefs, and convictions. The experience of a particular time and place was not, however, an isolated, relative phenomenon. Instead, 'in all times and places there existed something of the eternal or the immutable,' which provided a continuing yardstick for evaluation of living phenomena. Consequently, application of historical criticism to artistic works implied as well application of general aesthetic and moral laws to the life that the works depicted.[38]

Historical criticism examined relations among literary works. It compared works of art, showed the links between them, but did not extinguish the light of one in the glare of another or elevate the most recent at the expense of its predecessor. 'The task of historical criticism is to show the relative significance of all literary works in a mass, to assign to each its appropriate place as an organic, living product of life, and to verify each against the irrelative laws of creative art.'[39] Since it viewed literature as the living product of a particular social and moral milieu, it captured what was living and permanent in that milieu, played on new strings in the human soul, and so brought the new into human consciousness.

In the second article of the series, Grigor'ev pointed out that every literary era had its leading representative, who best embodied the principles of that age. In that figure the artistic and moral tasks of the age were blended. It was he who said a 'new word.' Gogol' was such a figure. Everything alive in contemporary Russian literature had its roots in him. Though Grigor'ev recognized Lermontov as a great writer, he believed at this time that the poet's 'word' was entirely negative and ultimately not very important in Russian development. Lermontov's was the protest of the individual against an oppressive reality. The protest arose not from a clear understanding of the ideal but from conditions within the diseased soul of the individual himself. Lermontov's was a 'word' without foundation, suffering without escape, thirst without satisfaction. It ended in despair and fatalism. Later, he was to revise this opinion. In Grigor'ev's view, the only remaining talented follower of the Lermontov tendency was A. Druzhinin, and in Druzhinin, he said, the tragedy of individual protest was transformed into mere meanness and caprice.

In the court of historical criticism, Grigor'ev explained in the third article, everything was judged by the fruit that it bore, no matter the artist's talent. The world view of the poet was a critical test of his or her talent. It was not entirely personal, but was derived from the time and place in which the poet lived. Genius, for all its originality, was nevertheless the lens through which was reflected the most advanced contemporary thinking, the latest true development of social concepts and convictions. While reflecting the aspirations of the age, the artist did not, however, serve them slavishly. Instead, he or she took possession of them and reconciled their contradictions through the highest principles of reason. The greater the talent, the more fully did it reflect and reconcile all the tendencies of the age.

The highest principle of reason was eternal love. On the surface, in subjecting the age to the scrutiny of the eternal moral values that lay in his or her heart, the artist appeared to be hostile to reality. Behind the hostility, however, lay a rational, not blind, love. Through the dark exterior of every work of art shone the light of an eternal ideal. The poet's world view reconciled the reader to life because it explained the meaning of life. And so a creation of true art was profoundly moral, not in the banal sense of morality that, Grigor'ev complained, saw Pushkin as immoral and could not forgive Molière for Tartuffe, but in the sense that it was a living creation. He continued, 'In the heart of a man lie simple eternal truths, and these are particularly clear to a person of true genius. For this reason, the essence of the world view of all true representatives of art is one, only the colours are different.'[40]

Grigor'ev turned in the fourth article to a detailed discussion of Gogol' and his influence. Gogol', like any true artist, was the product of his time and place. All the ideas and characters that appeared in his works were forged in the clash of his soul with the reality around him. His work was full of humour, a humour replete with the love of life and the aspiration to the ideal. Thanks to the many-sided nature of his genius, Gogol' was able to reflect the unending variety of Russian life. But he was by nature a man of passion, and the many phenomena of Russian reality that contradicted the ideal sickened him. Gogol''s main moral task had been to show that every man had become a 'rotter and milksop,' to expose the 'banality of banal man,' to remove the 'so-called virtuous man' from his pedestal, to annihilate all 'self-glorification,' and to realize *Christian consciousness* fully.[41]

The contemporary literary process, Grigor'ev avowed, was completely devoted to the analysis of the phenomena of the everyday reality of Russians that Gogol' had initiated. He divided Gogol''s followers into three camps. The first camp tried to pour the content of Lermontov's world view of personal protest into the forms of Gogol''s art. Its members discerned in Gogol' only the same protest that they had found in Lermontov and so understood only the form of Gogol'. The second camp separated Gogol''s humour from his ideal. Humour was the property only of the great artist; it was an attitude of love expressed through laughter. Those in the second camp failed to understand the nature of humour and its function in Gogol'. He gave them a new tool, the tool of analysis of everyday life. But while he looked on that life with love, they viewed it from the vantage point of personal prejudice. The result was a rash of stories that were critical of reality, but the criticism was entirely capricious. Such a literature could not be sustained for long. Readers soon found that an artist had painted reality too black, that the relatives of various landlords were not the animals the artist had made them out to be. Writers in the third camp followed Gogol''s path. They exhibited signs of true talent and independence but failed to discover any new tasks beyond those already contained in Gogol'. In the first camp, Grigor'ev placed Ivan Goncharov; in the second, Turgenev, with his *A Hunter's Sketches* (Zapiski okhotnika); and in the third Grigorovich and Pisemskii.[42]

Gogol''s 'word,' he continued, was the direct or immediate relationship of the artist to reality, the everyday reality of ordinary Russians. The era of Lermontov's individual protest was gone; no one believed any longer in the reality of the suffering of a variety of heroes who derived from Pechorin. Gogol' had directed Russian writers to the lives of ordinary people, and they were responding. The same, Grigor'ev grumbled, could not be said for the critics. They viewed every new literary phenomenon as personally threatening and went on demanding of literature exactly the same thing that they had asked of it ten years earlier. Literary criticism was in decay, growing ever more outmoded as it held up its narrow, artificial ideals to the ever-flowing stream of reality. Even worse was a resurgence of aesthetic criticism, which made the same demands on literature that a gourmet made on a meal.[43]

The profound influence of Gogol' was clearly evident in the series. During most of his years as a 'young editor,' Grigor'ev saw Christian humility as the salient characteristic of Russians. For that reason he relegated Lermontov and the literature of personal protest to a minor role. The egoist had to be reconciled to the spiritual demands of life. For the time being, the 'humble type' in Russian life and literature took pride of place in his thought; later he was to restore the 'predatory type' to an important role in Russia's spiritual development.

The theatre remained Grigor'ev's passion. As a young editor, he raised his praise for Ostrovskii's plays to a cult. In them he detected a 'new word' in Russian literature and nationality. His remarkable claims on Ostrovskii's behalf won him a great deal of ridicule. Botkin wrote to Turgenev in March 1852 that it was being said that 'Grigor'ev "had lost the last drop of sense remaining to him" in enthusing at a reading of [Ostrovskii's play *The Bride* (Nevesta)] in which he perceived a whole world.'[44] The novelist D.V. Grigorovich related bitterly how he called on Ostrovskii at his home to express his admiration for his plays *The Bankrupt* and *Don't Sit in Someone Else's Sleigh*. When he arrived at around eleven in the morning, Almazov, Edel'son, Grigor'ev, and Gorbunov were already there. His fulsome praise was received, he complained, like 'childish babble,' as if he were a man from the moon telling the world what it already knew. They treated him not as an interesting writer in his own right but merely as a St Petersburg dandy. 'Mutual praises, partiality and conceit in this circle surpassed the limits of the gates of Hercules. In that regard Apoll. Alek. Grigor'ev especially distinguished himself.' Grigor'ev's enthusiasm for Ostrovskii was unbounded. Once, Grigorovich sarcastically recounted, Grigor'ev pointed to a silent Ostrovskii and said, 'Look, look, what a Ciceronian silence!'[45] Almazov shared Grigor'ev's extremism with regard to Ostrovskii and was ridiculed for raising Ostrovskii above Shakespeare in one of his articles.[46]

Grigorovich was the victim of the war being waged by the young editors in Moscow against the natural-school critics of St Petersburg with whom Grigorovich was associated. Annenkov pointed out that one of the most effective fighters against the capital city's journalists was Grigor'ev.[47] More than one contemporary observer felt that Ostrovskii's association with *Moskvitianin* and the enthusiastic reviews of his plays by Almazov and Grigor'ev prevented him from being appreciated in St Petersburg for several years. A.F. Koni, for example, pointed out that Grigor'ev's exaggerated reviews had a negative impact on his popularity in St Petersburg, and it was only with the appearance of N.A. Dobroliubov's review of *Groza* (The Storm) that his earlier work was reevaluated.[48] Another example of such sentiments was an anonymous comment in *Otechestvennye zapiski*. The author noted that it was sad that a critic would praise a work in such a manner that he mocked the very thing that he was praising. How could *Moskvitianin* give space to verses that could only do harm to Ostrovskii's considerable talent?[49]

One of Grigor'ev's more extravagant celebrations of Ostrovskii did indeed come in a poem, 'Art and Truth. Elegy-Ode-Satire' (Isskustvo i pravda. Elegiia-oda-satira.) The elegy was to Mochalov, whose dominance of the Moscow stage in the 1830s, with his powerful portrayals of Hamlet and Richard III, Othello and King Lear, had made a lasting impression on Grigor'ev. Mochalov, he said, was a 'mighty, awesome magician.' He was Russia's greatest tragedian, but 'the volcano is extinguished, the lava turned to stone / He lived briefly but said much to us.' Russians had, however, paid a price for Mochalov's mastery: 'We loved *truth* in our tragedian / With him we buried the truth of tragedy.' The ode was to Ostrovskii, particularly to *Poverty's Not a Vice* (Bednost' ne porok). That play, Grigor'ev believed, spoke another, different, simpler, and more precious truth than had Mochalov. The dramatist had spoken a new word, though it served an old truth. That truth was found in Russia's own grandfathers and fathers, in Russia's customs and traditions. In Liubim Tortsov, the drunken but honest hero, Grigor'ev saw the embodiment of the 'pure Russian soul / unhappy, inebriated, wasted.' In Ostrovskii, comedy and tragedy mingled. 'There the soul of the national way of life now walked / There a Russian song rang out, free and resonant / There a man now weeps, now smiles / There a whole world, a world full and living.' Grigor'ev concluded that in Liubim Tortsov's humility 'Great Russian life reigned on the stage / The Great Russian principle / The treasury of Great Russian speech / Both in the dashing tale and the playful song / The Great Russian mind, the Great Russian outlook / All triumphed.'

The satire was a cruel assessment of the performances of the French tragic actress Rachel, who toured St Petersburg and Moscow in 1853–4. Grigor'ev found in her performances only a falseness of tone. 'The truth lies only in the heart: where there is no living feeling / There is no truth, no life / There is only falsehood – not eternal art!' He attributed the disingenuous nature of her acting and its enthusiastic reception on an earlier tour in the United States to the false spirit of 'old Europe' and the 'toothless immaturity' of the new, to which he contrasted the mature strength of Russia. The moral of the whole poetic tale was that only his own country possessed the truth.[50]

Pogodin himself had second thoughts about the wisdom of publishing Grigor'ev's poem and in the following number of the journal printed two satirical poems that ridiculed Grigor'ev. *Sovremennik* treated Grigor'ev's poem to two satirical reports in successive issues. In one the young editors were ridiculed as gnomes. Grigor'ev was the gnome 'with the wisp of bast' on his head.[51] In the other, the nihilist critic N.G. Chernyshevskii anonymously deplored the baneful influence that Grigor'ev exercised over Ostrovskii.[52]

Grigor'ev refused to be silenced by his critics. Instead, he was spurred to write another important programmatic article in the March 1855 issue of *Moskvitianin*, a detailed defence of his view of Ostrovskii as the purveyor of a 'new word.' The piece was an attack on authorities in literature and criticism who were interested only in their own theories rather than in the truth. Grigor'ev had at the time of Gogol's humiliation during the furore caused by publication of *Selected Passages* comforted the writer with the thought that the truth resides with the few or even only with the one. Now he reassured himself with the same thought. He stoutly declared that he who possessed truth had an obligation to proclaim it: 'Shame to him who, feeling in his heart a certain truth and understanding it historically, is afraid to declare it only because it seems ridiculous and improper; shame to him who having expressed a truth, although out of season and not whole but only in hints, recoils from it, on hearing himself ridiculed – because the first has too little faith in truth, and the second has too little faith in truth and too much self-regard.'[53]

The truth was, Grigor'ev continued, that with the four of the nine works written by Ostrovskii between 1847 and 1855 that were performed on the stage, the playwright had single-handedly created a national theatre. Ostrovskii was special for the way of life that his plays described, for his attitude to that way of life and the characters who expressed it, for the manner of its depiction, and for the coloration of the language in which it was depicted. Those attributes had awakened among all classes a common sympathy, altered people's view of their national being, and acquainted them with national types that they previously never even suspected to have existed. The plays were new in both form and content. By 'content,' Grigor'ev understood the world view of the poet, the types that he created, and the manner in which he depicted them. By 'form,' he meant the structure of the work and the uniqueness of its language. Ostrovskii's 'new word is the oldest word – nationality [*narodnost'*]: its new attitude is nothing more than a direct, pure, immediate relationship to life' – a claim that he had earlier made for Gogol'.[54]

He went on to define *narod* and *narodnost'*. Both had a wide and a narrow meaning. By *narod* in its broad meaning, Grigor'ev meant the whole national personality (*narodnaia lichnost'*), the collective person made up from the characteristics of all the strata of the nation. This collective person was constituted not mechanically but organically and had a general, typical, characteristic physiognomy which was distinguishable from all other collective persons. In the narrow meaning, *narod* referred to the part of the whole nation which, compared to the other parts, was in a spontaneous and undeveloped condition. Literature was national (*narodnyi*) in the wide sense when it reflected a view of life that belonged to the whole nation but was most completely and artistically expressed in the leading classes, at present the merchants. The types contained in national literature were both various and popular; the forms of the national literature were beautiful, in conformity to the national idea of beauty; the language was the language of the people, developed on the basis of fundamental etymological and syntactical laws.[55]

Grigor'ev then asked whether Russia possessed a national literature. Russians certainly had an enormous mass of writing in a language that they all understood. That language Grigor'ev attempted to demonstrate with examples from the chronicles and seventeenth-century *gramoty* (charters) of Tsar Mikhail, was rooted in a long literary tradition. In this mass of literature, he contended, lay the answers to all of Russia's religious, moral, and social questions. Since the beginning of the eighteenth century, an enormous body of writing had amassed, but the great bulk of it had by now lost all but historical interest. Only a small part of that huge body remained alive and fresh to contemporaries. He noted that the reading public of the day preferred to read Karamzin and Batiushkov rather than the more recent Polevoi or Kukol'nik; it had, he said, forgotten the novels of F. Bulgarin but loved to read Novikov and Sumarokov. The latter especially, he claimed, wrote in a language more refined, simple, and vital than the literary critics of Grigor'ev's own day. All Russian writers of influence, he insisted, had one thing in common: their language was near to that of the old Russian writings. The older Karamzin got, the closer he adhered to the ancient style of thought and language. The same was so of Gogol', Pushkin, and Zhukovskii. Not one of them, he noted, began that way; but all searched for *narodnost'* and all found a point of departure for it in the old memorials of Russian literature.

In the narrow sense, literature was national when it lowered itself to the ideas and tastes of the undeveloped masses with a view to educating them, or when it studied the masses and their concepts and mores as something exotic and unfamiliar. In its broad sense, literature expressed *nationalité* (*natsional'nost'*); in the narrow sense it expressed *popularité* (*narodnost'*). Grigor'ev argued that only *natsional'nost'* was of importance in Russia because 'there is no essential separation in the living, fresh and organic body of the *narod*,' and because in the narrow sense literature ceases to be art and falls into pedagogy or anthropology. In the merchant class, he concluded, Ostrovskii had found the fullest expression of contemporary Russian nationality (*natsional'nost'*) at its latest, but as yet unfinished, stage of development.[56]

Grigor'ev's attempt to explain himself did not impress his critics. *Otechestvennye zapiski* had long been amusing its readers at his expense by mocking his fondness for archaic words or ones not normally used in literary criticism. In an article of January 1853, one of its commentators asked whether Grigor'ev himself had said a 'new word,' and replied, 'The answer is not hard: he has said so many new words that all of the feuilletons taken together have not produced an equal quantity in a whole year.'[57]

Grigor'ev's article on Ostrovskii brought a further response from the journal. The anonymous writer agreed with Grigor'ev that all Russian writers were aspiring to *narodnost'* in their works. But Grigor'ev had failed to define *narodnost'*. He wished piously that Grigor'ev would get on with the task of further explication. Perhaps, he would explain what *Moskvitianin* wanted from literature, why it disliked the works of Turgenev, Evgeniia Tur, and others, why it found its sole joy in Ostrovskii's plays, why no modern writer could approach the majesty of the ancient chroniclers, and why no contemporary statecraft could compare with the politics of Pososhkov.[58]

Sovremennik, too, remained sceptical about Ostrovskii's new word. An anonymous critic, probably Chernyshevskii again, complained that while Grigor'ev had criticized the natural school critics for making idols out of young and inexperienced writers such as F.M. Dostoevskii, he had himself placed Ostrovskii on a pedestal. Other critics, he continued, had recognized Ostrovskii's importance. They had also, however, noted that the later plays were weaker both in form and in content than the earlier ones. Moreover, the merchant class depicted was not, as Grigor'ev claimed, representative of the whole of Russian life; Ostrovskii had by no means captured the great variety of Russian existence. Along with *Otechestvennye zapiski*, *Sovremennik* purported eagerly to be awaiting the second article in Grigor'ev's series.[59]

Grigor'ev did write a second article about the historical view in literature, but it was suppressed by the censors. It was, however, preserved and is revealing of Grigor'ev's attitudes toward literature and *narodnost'*.[60] He declined to define *narodnost'* as *Otechestvennye zapiski* demanded. He did so because he believed that any idea or 'word', new or old, had to be expressed gradually and clarified in a struggle with its own contradictions.

He went so far, however, as to say that the 'word' of the young editors was respect for tradition and for everything achieved by Russians. They therefore stood for re-establishment of links between the present and the past.

He then went on the offensive, criticizing *Sovremennik* for its slavish adherence to the ideas of Belinskii, whose false views in his last years had been so harmful to Russian literature. In Grigor'ev's view, Belinskii had been insufficiently literate to have been a good critic. He praised the ideas in 'Literary Musings' (Literaturnye mechtaniia), an early work in which Belinskii rejected authorities and looked on literature as the reflection of life. But even in his early period he had a false view of Russian *narodnost'* that derived from his reading of a handful of 'pseudo-historical novels.' Later he leapt onto the hobby horse of aestheticism (*khudozhestvennost'*), based on the abstractions of Hegelianism, which dragged him into his reconciliation with reality. Then he jumped off that horse and onto another – pathos.

More specifically, Belinskii's influence had been instrumental in persuading the natural school critics to attack Gogol''s positive side – his mysticism and aesthetic idealism. In his positive moments, as, for example, in his story 'Rome,' Gogol' contrasted tawdry, though glittering, civilization to the serene greatness of the world of art and simple memories of life's beauties. Gogol' preferred art to industry, simplicity to brilliance, serenity to ceaseless turmoil, beauty to artifice, Rome to Paris. Blinded by Belinskii's strictures, the natural school failed even to see Gogol''s positive side or to understand his negative side. Gogol' was unique, a true representative of Russian thought and language. Just as he was the best representative of his time, so too was Ostrovskii the best representative of his. Today's criticism was a poor reflection of Belinskii's. Nothing, Grigor'ev believed, better captured its impotence than the debate that followed publication of Annenkov's edition of Pushkin's works. The critics had nothing to say about Pushkin. Either they criticized the edition itself, its selection and production, or they merely paraphrased Annenkov's own introduction. Only Druzhinin, in *Biblioteka dlia chteniia*, had something to say about Pushkin beyond Annenkov's own remarks.[61]

This second article was another landmark in Grigor'ev's intellectual development. On the one hand, it marked the apotheosis of his regard for Gogol' and his dislike for Belinskii, who had done so much, in his view, to distort the meaning of Gogol''s work. On the other hand, it signalled his growing interest in Pushkin. Though he knew his works well, Pushkin had remained largely outside Grigor'ev's vision in his years as a young editor. After his rejection of the cosmopolitanism of his St Petersburg period,

Grigor'ev grew suspicious of Pushkin's own cosmopolitanism as well and focused instead on what he regarded to be the purely national (folk culture and the profoundly Russian plays of Ostrovskii) and on the Orthodox humility of Gogol' that Grigor'ev associated with the 'humble' Russian national type. But in his article on Ostrovskii, Grigor'ev had remarked that only premature death had prevented Pushkin from embodying in his works all the types of Russian life and history. And the more he studied Pushkin, the more he was to revise his views about Russian literature and literary criticism. Gogol' steadily declined in his esteem; Belinskii, who had recognized the significance of Pushkin, was increasingly to gain his admiration; and Pushkin was soon to dominate Grigor'ev's version of the Russian literary scene.

5

In the Light of the Ideal
1855–1857

[A]rt ... is impossible when the artist (no matter how
gifted artistically) has no contact with the people's life.

Alexei Khomiakov, 'On Humboldt'

Work on the editorial board of *Moskvitianin* (The Muscovite) was a continuing source of anguish, leading Grigor'ev to think by 1855 of taking
over the journal. Unwilling to pay even his nearest collaborators ade-
quately, Pogodin was even more reluctant to pay top price for the best
manuscripts. Grigor'ev blamed the eventual failure of the journal on its
editor's 'devilish miserliness.'[1] The business of the office was run badly,
and the typesetting and printing were of the poorest quality.[2] In addition,
Pogodin kept interfering in the sections of the journal that were supposed
to be under the control of the 'young editors.' In 1851, for example, he had
tried to impose a translation by Prince V. L'vov of a French work on them.
For his pains, he received an anonymous letter in which it was made clear
that the young editors would resign if he persisted.[3] In December of that
year, Edel'son, Grigor'ev, and Ostrovskii began negotiations for the outright transfer of *Moskvitianin* to the young editors. At first it appeared that
the details for a transfer had been worked out, but by January Pogodin
declined to give a definitive answer to the young editors about the change
of command.[4]

Relations among the young editors were frequently tense as well. In
October 1851, Grigor'ev had complained bitterly to Pogodin that Ostrovskii had altered several passages in an article that he had written on the
actress Vera Samoilova.[5] In 1852, Pisemskii had advised Pogodin not to
believe a word that his fellow young editor Grigor'ev said and had com-

plained that the latter's 'Russian Literature in 1851' (Russkaia literatura v 1851 godu) had far too much to say about its author's principles and far too little about the works being reviewed. Pogodin more kindly suggested to Grigor'ev that he had constructed a portico in the article but no building behind it. Grigor'ev hotly replied that a portico was precisely what he had intended.[6]

Relations between Pogodin and the 'young editors' had not improved during 1852. In November, T.I. Filippov acted as a mediator in the renewal of negotiations for the transfer of *Moskvitianin* to the 'young editors,' but the talks were as unfruitful as before. Further negotiations, in March 1853, were equally unavailing. From about that time, Ostrovskii began to withdraw from the editorial affairs of the journal, though he continued to publish in it. Grigor'ev's role became proportionately more important, but he did not enjoy Pogodin's confidence. In April 1853, he complained that Pogodin had altered the intent of an article that he had written in consultation with and on behalf of all the young editors. The article was to show the 'historical link between our activity ... and the activity of the Pushkin era.' In adding the name of the notorious reactionary journalist F.V. Bulgarin to the list of those who had the respect of *Moskvitianin* and eliminating the name of the progressive N.A. Polevoi, Pogodin, Grigor'ev concluded, was pandering to the authorities, because the former was and remained in the employ of the secret police while the latter was safely dead.[7]

To be fair, Pogodin had had little cause to trust Grigor'ev. The latter's article, 'Russian Belles-Lettres in 1852' (Russkaia iziashchnaia literatura v 1852 godu), had provoked a number of complaints. A St Petersburg acquaintance of Pogodin's reported that the editors of *Sankt-Peterburgskie vedomosti* (St Petersburg Gazette) had found that Grigor'ev had mixed up the titles of the novels that he had reviewed in the piece, had misconstrued their content, and had completely confused two quite different writers.[8] Evidently the combined strains of teaching, domestic turmoil, and writing were taking their toll on his concentration.

To make matters worse, Ostrovskii had already begun to distance himself from *Moskvitianin* and seek the wider audience and higher fees that the capital's journals could provide. In January 1855 Grigor'ev wrote to Pogodin, begging him to buy Ostrovskii's *Don't Live as You Want* (Ne tak zhivi, kak khochetsia) before someone else snatched it up. It was, he complained, bad enough that *Moskvitianin* had lost Pisemskii and that N.A. Potekhin had been enticed away.[9] The fact was that by this time the 'young editors' had ceased to exist as a group.

After trying in 1854 to replace the 'young editors' with a co-editor, P.P.

Sumarokov, with whom he immediately quarrelled, and failing in January 1855 to transfer the journal to E.F. Korsh, Pogodin had no one left to turn to except Grigor'ev. The latter agreed that for fifteen silver roubles per folio page he would write no fewer than four folio pages per issue, including a theatre chronicle. But he also demanded to be named co-editor, with full responsibility for the editorial stance of the journal and control of the literary and theatre sections. On hearing of the negotiations, Countess Rostopchina wrote to Pogodin deploring Grigor'ev's articles with their foolish adulation of Ostrovskii and suggested that B.N. Almazov be put in control of the criticism section because he was 'incomparably more intelligent, educated and pleasant.'[10] Pogodin was beholden to the countess and, perhaps due to her urging, postponed completing the arrangement with Grigor'ev.

Exploring all available options Pogodin opened negotiations with the Slavophiles about them taking over *Moskvitianin*. They, however, decided to launch their own organ, *Russkaia beseda* (Russian Conversation). That decision sealed the fate of *Moskvitianin*. Unable to attract an outsider to relieve him of the journal, Pogodin again reluctantly turned to Grigor'ev in January 1856. Grigor'ev replied that he had set out his terms a year before and had been rebuffed. But he declared himself to be passionately attached to the cause of *Moskvitianin* and wanted 'to return to the time when we all so believed in, so hoped for and so loved our cause.'[11]

Sometime late in 1855 or early in 1856, Grigor'ev had formulated a plan for *Moskvitianin* under his editorship. The document throws an interesting light on his views about the tasks of Russian literary criticism as well as on what Grigor'ev expected from a journal. In *Moskvitianin*, Grigor'ev wanted to separate serious literature, which was committed to analysing Russian attitudes, from 'frivolous and imitative' literature. The task of literary criticism was to explain to the ordinary reader the national significance of committed literature – to show how it was 'new by being old, that is, to show how the new literature had returned to a long-standing Russian point of view.' The duty of *Moskvitianin* was to point out the aesthetic weakness of the new writers such as Ostrovskii and Pisemskii in order to strengthen aesthetic criticism and force other journals to deal with Ostrovskii as an artist and not merely as a thinker. Readers had to be made aware that other publications were responding to Ostrovskii through the lens of their prejudices about his ideas and the nature of Russian nationality. Those prejudices arose from hatred for the humble, kind, reconciliatory nature of the Russian character.

The new literature had to be linked both spiritually and socially to pre-

Petrine literature, written and oral, as it was transmitted in songs and stories. It had to look not only to the language of the old literature, but also to Karamzin's work in his last years and to the mature ideas of Pushkin, who was the true father of an immediate and pure relationship of thought and feeling to the national essence. It was essential to distinguish the new literature from the literature of the natural school and from the false populist tendency that derived from Georges Sand's love for the French peasantry. It was best exemplified in Russia, in Grigor'ev's opinion, by the work of Grigorovich. The aim of the new literature was not proletarianism. Russia had no such phenomenon, though the natural school searched for it in the alleys and streets of St Petersburg. And readers must be made to understand that the new literature searched for the national way of life in the merchantry and common people not because it longed for democracy in the Western sense but because that was where the language, concepts, and types of Russian nationality were preserved.

Moskvitianin had to ridicule the narrowness of the vision of frivolous literature, reveal the moral and intellectual decay that it concealed, and satirize its preference for material well-being. Scientific literature, too, ought to be divided in the journal into major works that examined either Russian life or Western life from a Russian point of view and those 'exotic plants' of a specialist nature that examined the fates of Italy, Spain, and other countries without reference to Russia. In particular, the journal must warn young readers against what Grigor'ev called the 'microscopic monographs' of the Germans at a time when youth knew nothing of Russia.[12]

In a letter to Pogodin of 18 January 1856, Grigor'ev lamented the decline of *Moskvitianin*. Its tendency, he pointed out, was distinct from that of *Russkii vestnik* (The Russian Messenger) which had recently been founded by his acquaintance from university days, Mikhail Katkov, and of *Russkaia beseda*, the Slavophile journal 'which can hardly help but be the journal of the Troitskaia Lavra,' a nearby monastery with Slavophile connections. *Moskvitianin*, he cajoled Pogodin, stood for the tendency represented by Pogodin himself – 'democratic and progressive nationality.' *Russkii vestnik* was 'carrion' from its first number, characterized as it was by a 'lifeless eclecticism' or, even worse, disdain for 'nationality and the root principles of the national life.' *Russkaia beseda*, in its turn, would soon, he predicted, succumb to the reactionary tendency set out by *Maiak* (The Lighthouse), the ultra-conservative journal of the 1830s.[13]

A year earlier, Grigor'ev had complained to Pogodin that he (Grigor'ev) was 'muddled up morally and muddled up financially,'[14] and his circumstances had only deteriorated since then. His mother had died in 1854, and at the beginning of 1855 his beloved Leonida Vizard had married.[15] A constant theme of his letters of this time was that, suffering as he was from poverty and deprivations, he fell into apathy and dejection and was unable to work. In January 1856 he wrote, 'In order to serve the cause I have to be calm so that I can think about the cause and not about myself.' In February he joked that God had spared him from luxury, and he pointed out that from his literary work he needed 125 silver roubles a month, half of which would go directly to staving off his debtors. In April he lamented, 'I am heartily bored with thinking about myself and only about myself' and he longed to be locked up in a cell for three years with pens and paper.[16] He asked Pogodin to give him 250 roubles so that he could pay some of his debts, but Pogodin declined. Grigor'ev began to realize that he could not afford to participate in *Moskvitianin* on the terms to which he had agreed. His old mentor I.D. Beliaev approached Pogodin on his behalf in March to tell him that the six folio pages per issue that Grigor'ev had promised to deliver were beyond his strength and suggested that the millionaire tax-farmer V.A. Kokorev, who had strong Slavophile views, be involved financially in the journal in a last attempt to save it.[17] But none of these schemes was to be carried out. Pogodin agreed with Grigor'ev at the end of January 1856 on a plan to renovate *Moskvitianin*. In February they signed a document setting out the conditions for publication.[18] But Pogodin did not honour the agreement. Instead, after fulfilling his obligation to subscribers for 1856, he halted publication in 1857. In spite of frantic and chronic efforts on Grigor'ev's part to resuscitate it, it was never to be revived.

Grigor'ev was not without alternatives in the world of journalism. He so cherished his intellectual independence, however, that he always set terms that his potential employers could not accept. As early as October 1855, there had been rumours that Grigor'ev was about to become the official literary critic of the Slavophile journal *Russkaia beseda*.[19] In fact the editor, A.I. Koshelev, did offer him the position, but only in March 1856. The proposal provided Grigor'ev with an opportunity to reflect on his differences with the Slavophiles, which he set out in a long letter to Koshelev. Grigor'ev began by pointing out that Koshelev and he served the same cause but approached it from different points of view. The main point of difference between the 'old Slavophilism' and the stance of *Moskvitianin* concerned their attitudes to art. For the Slavophiles, said Grigor'ev, art had only a service role, whereas for the 'young editors' art was independent and of greater importance even than science. On all other points he claimed that they were in agreement, particularly on the questions of Russia's independent development and the immutability of Orthodoxy. He nevertheless went on to point out other differences. Though *Moskvitianin* was sympathetic to all Slavs, it, unlike the Slavophiles, believed in the special priority of the Great Russian principle. Believing, as did the Slavophiles, that the future of Russia was preserved only in those classes of the people who had preserved the faith, mores, and language of their fathers and were not spoiled by 'false' civilization, the 'young editors' maintained that not only the peasantry but the 'middle classes' as well, especially the 'industrial and merchant class,' had remained faithful to old, eternal Russia, with its good and evil, independence and imitativeness. Imitativeness had been a fault of the Slavs from the beginning. It accounted for much of the spoiling of the language of the middle class as well as its numerous comical features.

These differences between the two groups inevitably had certain consequences, Grigor'ev added. *Moskvitianin* leaned more toward Pushkin and less to Gogol' than did the Slavophiles. That was an interesting admission; Grigor'ev had only recently arrived at his preference for Pushkin over Gogol'. *Moskvitianin* attached greater importance to certain contemporary literary phenomena as expressions of the Russian present, especially the plays of Ostrovskii. Uncompromising as always, Grigor'ev demanded complete control over the literary criticism section of the journal. Koshelev refused to accept his conditions, and negotiations were broken off.[20]

Grigor'ev's options were not yet exhausted, however. In his letter of March 1856 to Pogodin on Grigor'ev's behalf, Beliaev had informed him that for all of his love for *Moskvitianin* Grigor'ev would be forced to transfer to *Sovremennik* (The Contemporary).[21] But there is no evidence that any offer had come from the editors of *Sovremennik* by the end of March. Around then, however, Grigor'ev himself must have planted in the mind of V.P. Botkin the idea that he should supplant N.G. Chernyshevskii as *Sovremennik*'s literary critic. Botkin was dissatisfied with the approach that Chernyshevskii was bringing to the journal and tried to enlist his fellow members of the editorial board, N.A. Nekrasov, I.I. Panaev, and I.S. Turgenev, to replace him with Grigor'ev. Complex negotiations followed, which, though they finally came to nothing, are interesting to relate, since they are both little known and involved some of the leading literary figures of the day.

On 19 April 1856 Botkin wrote to Nekrasov that Grigor'ev had visited him and expressed an interest in taking part in *Sovremennik*. He pointed out that Grigor'ev wanted access to the journal as a vehicle for his own opinions. In particular, he wanted full control of the literary criticism section, from which Chernyshevskii would be excluded. Chernyshevskii's exclusion was unlikely, Botkin thought, because although Grigor'ev was 'incomparably more talented' than the incumbent, the latter was 'incomparably more industrious' than Grigor'ev. He continued: 'Under your control Grigor'ev would be a treasure for the journal: he is the only man who has what the journal needs and for which, apart from him, there is no one. In addition he is incomparably nearer to us in everything than is Chernyshevskii. Talk it over with Turgenev, – it is really worth thinking about.'[22] Nekrasov must have spoken to Turgenev, who in a letter to Nekrasov at about the same time referred to a negotiation with Grigor'ev.[23]

On 26 April Grigor'ev wrote to Botkin that he had confidence in the editors of *Sovremennik*, among whom he listed Annenkov, Botkin, Druzhinin, Nekrasov, Ostrovskii, Panaev, Tolstoi, and Turgenev. In their hands, he felt, the general direction of the journal was secure. But he found it hard to believe in a journal that published unworthy articles. He particularly singled out Chernyshevskii's critical pieces, which 'offend all aesthetic and historical feeling,' and exposed their author's lack of subtlety and shallow thinking. Chernyshevskii saw art as a trade, like shoe-making, and Grigor'ev declined to have his own articles appear alongside such false views. He asked for the right to veto all articles for the critical section except those of Annenkov, Druzhinin, and Nekrasov. In addition, he demanded the right to publish works on religion, history, and contemporary life by certain Moscow colleagues. If his terms were accepted he would give his life to the journal; if not, he could do nothing. And he concluded: 'You are right in finding a similarity in my nature ... with the nature of the late Vissarion Grigor'evich [Belinskii]: I know this very well myself and therefore do not wish to be in the same position with regard to *Sovremennik* that he was in with regard to [*Otechestvennye*] *Zapiski* [Notes of the Fatherland].'[24]

In his preference for Grigor'ev over Chernyshevskii, Botkin was not as isolated from the other editors as is sometimes thought.[25] Turgenev had already expressed admiration for some of Grigor'ev's work. Early in May he was in Moscow, whence he wrote to Nekrasov that he would be seeing Grigor'ev the following evening and would report to him the results of the conversation.[26] If the report was written, it has not been preserved, but negotiations continued. Druzhinin had already met Grigor'ev in May 1855.[27] Exactly a year later he was in Moscow again and, along with Botkin, invited the critic to a dacha in Kuntsovo, outside Moscow. There Grigor'ev read some of the completed parts of his translation of *A Midsummer Night's Dream*, which he hoped to sell to Druzhinin. On that occasion, he also met L.N. Tolstoi for the first time. Druzhinin attended two literary evenings at Grigor'ev's home in the Zamoskvorech'e as well; there he met, as he put it, 'the whole of *Russkaia beseda*.'[28]

So well had these visits gone that Grigor'ev, as A.D. Galakhov wrote to A.A. Kraevskii, was heard to brag that not only had he been invited to collaborate in *Sovremennik* as resident critic but had also received an invitation from Druzhinin to work for *Biblioteka dlia chteniia* (Library for Reading) and would have an income of 3,000 silver roubles a year.[29] Though he had agreed to provide *Biblioteka dlia chteniia* with his translation of *A Midsummer Night's Dream* and some critical articles, he in fact, had no arrangement with *Sovremennik* to become its full-time literary critic. In July, Grigor'ev wrote to Druzhinin that he was once more penniless and had to make a firm arrangement with someone soon. And he asked for 500 roubles in advance for the translation of *A Midsummer Night's Dream.*'[30]

But the possibility of collaborating in *Sovremennik* remained open. In August, I.I. Panaev met Grigor'ev in Moscow and in a letter to Ostrovskii exclaimed, 'What an intelligent and most dear man!' In subsequent letters to Ostrovskii he always asked to be remembered to Grigor'ev.[31] Botkin continued to urge the case of Grigor'ev, and Turgenev, too, was strongly attracted to the unruly critic. In November he wrote to Ostrovskii from Paris that he was annoyed that circumstances had prevented him from seeing Grigor'ev in Moscow: 'I know that we would have quarreled until we dropped but feel that we would become intimates. I am attracted to him; he reminds me of the late Belinskii. He might not like that comparison; but that is how it is, – and for me everything that reminds me of Belinskii is precious.'[32]

There were a number of reasons why Grigor'ev in the end failed to secure a position on *Sovremennik*. Almost certainly Nekrasov did not share the others' enthusiasm for him. Under Nekrasov's direct editorship, *Sovremennik* had been the subject of a sustained critical barrage from *Moskvitianin*, led by Almazov and Grigor'ev. In an article written late in 1855, Nekrasov had pointedly referred to 'absurdities and comical self-glorification' in one of Grigor'ev's articles,[33] and he was unlikely to welcome him as the sole arbiter of his journal's literary criticism. Botkin was almost certainly wrong in including Nekrasov among those to whom Grigor'ev was 'incomparably closer' than Chernyshevskii, and the latter had no trouble maintaining his post with Nekrasov's support.

It is indicative of Grigor'ev's views that he was able to negotiate with both Slavophile and Westernizer journals for a position as literary critic. His failure to be taken on by either is even more indicative. Annenkov was almost certainly correct about Grigor'ev when he wrote: 'His artistic nature frequently could not abide the ascetic constraint of the [Slavophile] school, and they more than once regarded him as in the ranks of the adherents of western ideas and institutions. By the same token the diplomatic skill that was rather strongly developed in both camps was completely alien to this truthful man, and sometimes secondary considerations about the interests and needs of the parties did not obscure his convictions and influence his judgments.'[34]

And so Grigor'ev was destined not to publish his literary criticism in *Sovremennik*, but the failed negotiation with *Russkaia beseda* did not prevent Koshelev from publishing one of Grigor'ev's most important and, as the author himself later lamented, most ignored articles. It was addressed in the form of a letter to A.S. Khomiakov, the Slavophile 'theologian.' Entitled 'On Truth and Sincerity in Art: Concerning a Certain Aesthetic Question,' the piece marked Grigor'ev's coming of age as a literary critic and social thinker. In it, he consolidated a number of ideas from the 'young editor' period and began to build the walls of his later 'organic criticism,' behind the 'portico' that he had constructed as a 'young editor.' In particular, he here worked out his ideas on the relationship among art, morality, and social development.

Grigor'ev was responding in the letter to a question posed by Khomiakov: should an artist try to place himself into a spiritual condition, a world view, or a system of belief and feeling that is completely alien to him? Grigor'ev pointed out that the question had two dimensions – psychological and ideological. Could an artist, who had his own way of thinking and his own economy of feelings, place himself into a manner of thinking and economy of feelings alien to him? And could an artist as the product of a particular time and a member of a particular faith and people place himself into a different world view? The question, Grigor'ev said, concerned on the one hand the relationship between art and truth and the sincerity of the relationship of the artist to life, and on the other hand the relationship between artistic creativity and morality.[35]

In fact, a number of questions were embedded in Khomiakov's query, including those of the relationship between art and reality, art and morality, and art and truth. Grigor'ev's article was one of the early volleys in a debate about the role of art in social development that began about 1855 and continued almost unabated until 1870. The origins of the debate can be dated to the defence in May 1855 by N.G. Chernyshevskii of his MA thesis, 'The Aesthetic Relations of Art to Reality' (Esteticheskie otnosheniia iskusstva k deiatel'nosti). Chernyshevskii typified the second echelon of the new generation of the intelligentsia of which Grigor'ev represented the first. His cohort, roughly five to ten years younger than the first echelon, also reflected an urban, often provincial-city, experience. Like the first echelon, most of the second came from the bureaucratic gentry class, but a significant minority, especially among such leading lights as Chernyshevskii himself, came from the priestly estate and had been educated in seminaries.

This echelon, which Turgenev was soon to designate the 'children' whose 'fathers' had been the bright young men of Herzen's generation of the 1840s, particularly evinced the new tough-mindedness of Russian activists in the wake of the revolutions of 1848. Unlike the fathers, who believed in the primacy of art and philosophy, the children put their faith in science, especially in the new German materialist variant, of which L. Büchner and J. Moleschott were seen as the leading exponents. The fathers were more cosmopolitan, more cultured, more given to debate and strong friendships; the children were more seriously committed to testing ideas, more critical, more demanding, more desirous of action, and more inclined to choose their friends for their ideas than for their personal qualities.

Chernyshevskii's thesis set the tone for this generation of 'nihilists.' In it he rejected philosophical dualism in favour of a thoroughgoing monism, which was intended to eliminate any essential separation of real and ideal. The highest level of beauty was reality itself, and art was always inferior to reality. Art had its uses. It could serve as a substitute for reality, for example, to illustrate a seascape to a landlocked individual, or it could explain reality and teach the reader how to improve on reality. Here, idealism inevitably crept back into Chernyshevskii's aesthetics, since in order to judge reality one must have a point of view against which to compare it. But Chernyshevskii insisted that the ideal must always be sought in reality and not beyond it.

To the contention of Chernyshevskii and his followers that art should serve social goals, another group, which included P.V. Annenkov, Botkin, and Druzhinin, replied that art was an entirely independent phenomenon, free of all goals other than that of serving beauty itself. An important early moment in the extended debate was Annenkov's publication in 1855 of the collected poems of Pushkin. The utilitarian critics of Chernyshevskii's camp, culminating in 1865 in D.I. Pisarev's attack on Pushkin in his article 'Pushkin and Belinskii,' judged the poet to be a decadent and self-obssessed writer whose work was of little social value. The art-for-art school, on the contrary, glorified him for his aestheticism.

Throughout the fifteen-year debate, both sides engaged in extremes, and, on close examination, some at least of their declared differences are far from apparent. Grigor'ev quickly staked out an independent position in his article in *Russkaia beseda*. It was a position that he was to elaborate and firmly maintain for the rest of his life and one to which he was to convert in the early 1860s his most powerful ally in the struggle against the nihilists, Fedor Dostoevskii.[36]

In 'On Truth and Sincerity in Art,' Grigor'ev argued that art was truly art only when the artist was in a direct or unmediated relationship with the life around him. Such spontaneity had been Gogol's new word, as it was Ostrovskii's. Even when an artist was writing about another age, he was inevitably true to his own time and place. Otherwise, his work was false. An artist could not cut himself off from the life that he lived and, therefore, could not transform himself into an alien way of life and alien moral concepts. 'The life of a talented nature is truth'; an artist could not but be true to the reality of his own circumstances.[37] In that sense, all art was national.

Grigor'ev discerned three levels of artistic objectivity. At the simplest level, objectivity in art was the capacity of an artist to empathize with the object that he or she sought to represent or depict – an ability to cut himself off from his own personality and put himself into another personality or to enter another life and live it. Such objectivity was nothing more than a superior sensitivity to the totality of the national milieu of which the artist was himself a product. It required of the artist accuracy of expression but remained no more than a capacity to copy in a broad sense.

A higher level of objectivity was the ability to create types or general independent forms. These types were firmly rooted in the reality around the artist but were generated as artistic types unconsciously in the artist's soul. For all its individuality, the personality of the artist was a typical personality, and the types that it generated also existed in the reality of national life. These national types mingled in full harmony in the artist.

The highest level of objectivity brought Grigor'ev to the question both of art and morality and of art and truth. True objectivity lay in the capacity to expose the phenomena of life around one to the light of the ideal: '[True art] relates to life with an ideal, with a light that illuminates the accidental and assigns it a legitimate place; in this way art approaches phenomena with the highest, i.e. moral yardstick which is made up from the contemplation of the fundamental, most profound principles and rational laws of life.'[38] A great artist struggled not against that universal moral measure but only against conditional measures of morality. The artist waged war on false morality both in a positive and in a negative sense through two great weapons: tragedy, or lyricism, and comedy. Art therefore was the ideal expression of life. Truth was the light that lit life and separated the accidental from the essential, the temporal from the eternal. The artist, as the bearer of light and truth, was the highest representative of the moral concepts embedded in the life around him, that is, of his time and nation; otherwise he was not an artist. Art was in its essence moral. It was not subordinate to morality but was organically linked to morality through life. Indeed, by 'morality' Grigor'ev meant life. The particular truth of the artist was the general truth of life, universal but always expressed in a national guise. The highest objectivity was not, therefore, merely empathy for the life of the phenomena of reality but insight into their essence, informed by awareness of the ideal. Personality was essential to that process. The artist inevitably expressed his own internal life. For that reason, all the creations of even the most many-sided artist had a family resemblance, were linked by flesh and blood, and bore the stamp of a common origin.[39]

Since art was rooted in life and life was inseparable from morality, art served morality. But, Grigor'ev complained, the relationship between art and morality was seen by contemporaries in one of two ways, both of them mistaken: either art was annihilated in the name of morality and reduced to something explicitly morally and socially useful, or it was taken as a goal in itself, which could and ought to have no other purpose outside itself. Schiller and Gogol' were usually seen as examples of the first view, whereas Goethe and Pushkin were held up as models of the second. But, argued Grigor'ev, those who defended the two extremes fell into contradictions. Schiller, who was didactic, and Gogol', who was a jealous prosecutor of falsehood, were also both great artists who saw art as a force more potent than any other activity of the human soul. Goethe and Pushkin were both profoundly influenced by social movements and aspirations. All four recognized art as a powerful influence on humans, both on the individual and on the collectivity. All of them recognized forces in art that were both useful and necessary for life itself.

The rebellion that some critics had raised against art in the name of utility arose from a too-narrow understanding of the concept of usefulness. The rebels recognized only material usefulness, like street cleaning; they failed to apply the notion to the life of the spirit, of which art was but the manifestation. 'But without these expressions,' Grigor'ev warned, 'without these "tales," as the champions of utility see them, life would congeal and die, and humanity would fall into a condition in which the cleaning of streets would be superfluous.'[40] Dostoevskii later used this version of the utility of art as the centrepiece of *pochvennichestvo* (the native-soil movement).

In ages of more spontaneous literary creativity, such as the era of Dante or Shakespeare or Molière, Grigor'ev went on, the whole question of a separation between the creative side of art and service to society never arose. Even in Germany, the question came up only in theory but not in literary practice. Herder had managed to avoid it altogether. He smashed the conditional, classical understanding of beauty and revealed the highest ideals of art in places where previously no one expected to find them, not in artifice but in the spontaneous lives of individuals and the nation. But other German philosophers in their theorizing turned the artist and art into ideals, abstractions, and separated art from its organic roots in the soil. The issue entered Russia from Germany but had no meaning there. Russian writers experienced no feelings of separation between the artist and the person because literature there was firmly rooted in Russian life.

Grigor'ev illustrated his argument with a discussion of Lord Byron and Georges Sand, both of whom he saw as examples of artists who had fundamentally attacked Christian morality. Grigor'ev judged Byronism to have been a harmful phenomenon which was false and was also immoral to the extent that it was false. Byron stood accused of reducing human nature to irreverence, egoism, pride, malicious irony, and shamelessness toward women. But in Byron's defence, Grigor'ev noted that all those dark forces were in fact hidden in the morality of the eighteenth century and were merely being exposed by the poet. Thanks to his artistic nature, Byron proved incapable of enthroning egoism passively. He hated the mask of hypocrisy and dissimulation under which egoism concealed itself. His own egoism arose, therefore, from the capriciousness of a man who was profoundly dissatisfied with the falseness and hypocrisy of the life around him.

Byron's protest was a fiery, prophetic outcry by an individual against everything in the society that oppressed him. His strength was his melancholy and irony; his weakness, the absence of a moral point of view. Byron was not immoral, in Grigor'ev's opinion. He merely lacked a moral ideal. He protested against falsity without the consciousness of truth. He became the poet of despair and satanic laughter because he lacked the moral authority to be the poet of honourable laughter, the comic poet. Comedy was the appropriate attitude to what was false in life; comedy was the court in which life was judged when it strayed from the ideal. Byron provided a good example of the harm done when poetic meditation and moral contemplation were separated. Their separation deprived the poet's nature of wholeness and condemned him to remain a lyricist.

So Byron's truth lay in his blind protest and in the sincerity of his condemnation of the life around him. But Byron was harmful to art because of his one-sidedness, the absence of an ideal. Lermontov was often seen as the Russian Byron. But Lermontov's protest, Grigor'ev insisted, was not the same. Unlike in his earlier view, Grigor'ev had by now concluded that Lermontov was not without an ideal. His truth was exposure of the banality of life. His despair was that of loneliness, separation from life, and disgust with the pettiness around him that loneliness engendered. 'There is no serious possibility of speaking of Lermontov as a Russian Byron,' Grigor'ev concluded.

Grigor'ev saw Georges Sand, too, as a great artist. But he detected sharp differences between her early writing and her late work. In his opinion, Sand's artistic vision was increasingly diminished by the penetration of her writing by a conditional theory, a utopia. It was the narrow variant offered by the French socialists, one lacking in moral authority and constructed along the lines of the coercive forms of social life against which she was protesting. Sand aspired to a positive ideal but unfortunately upheld one derived solely from theory. But theory was impotent. Either it legitimized the decay of the social status quo or set up new but narrow concepts of good, honour, and love, which were merely contradictions of the status quo. Sand's truth lay not in her theory but in her passionate nature, which railed against the conditional morality of her day. The profound truth of her passion was fully expressed in a number of her works. And so Sand wrote both false works and true. The moral of her literary career was that wherever the constructed or theoretical replaced the born and living in art, falsehood resulted.

The lives of Byron and Sand demonstrated that the separation of art and morality harmed art's measure and harmony: 'The question about the link between art and morality, carried in this way to its natural boundaries, leads to the conclusion that artistic contemplation is inseparable in its nature from moral contemplation, that the separation of artistic from moral contemplation is reflected in art itself as a particular defect or weakness.'[41]

Grigor'ev had long believed that the universal was accessible only through the particular. The highest moral principles could be known only via the particular experiences of specific peoples. Christianity was never merely Christianity, but Italian or English or German Christianity. But the artist always expressed in his art his own internal being, which also shared in the eternal. And that was why all artists, though greatly different, also formed a single family, were related by flesh and blood, and displayed the stamp of a common origin. Only art could confront life directly. Since art was rooted in time and place, flesh and blood, it was an earthly matter, but of all worldly things it was 'the best, the truest, the most prophetic.'[42] The answer to Khomiakov's question, Grigor'ev concluded, was: 'Art, as the expression of the truth of life, could not even for a moment be false; *in truth* is its sincerity, *in truth* is its morality, *in truth* is its objectivity.'[43]

By the summer of 1856, Grigor'ev was both broke and ill. In July he told Druzhinin that his indebtedness had attained a new crescendo in which 'people came and took my piano, fur coats, clocks and the silver.'[44] Botkin wrote to Turgenev in September that during the summer Grigor'ev had asked him for 150 roubles so that he would not be put in prison: 'Under the circumstances there was nothing to do but to give him the 150. A short time afterwards I heard that Grigor'ev was appearing on all his walks in astonishing costumes. Then he visited me: a black foppish jacket, some kind of long waisted coat with blue plush lapels, a red silk shirt, white silk pants – in a word, a dandy of a special and unprecedented sort; add to this a beard. It set me off laughing. But he is no longer angry at me. A good, dear, gifted and somewhat half-witted man.'[45]

Grigor'ev's inability to put the generosity of his friends to good use was notorious. In his memoirs, A.D. Galakhov related a curious story about the critic's debts. One day, sometime in the 1850s, Galakhov visited Turgenev and found him in his study with an account book in his hand. The novelist was adding up the money he had lent to various people. Though it was a large sum, much of which he did not expect to get back, he said that he did not mind because each of the loans had been of benefit to the individuals, since it addressed what was only a temporary need. There was one exception. 'I'm afraid,' Turgenev sighed, 'that help will be of no use to him' – and he indicated the account of Apollon Grigor'ev.[46]

Grigor'ev was by now so poor that he was driven to extremes. His mother had left the house to him on condition that his father have the use of it until his death. For reasons that are not clear, his father had legally renounced the use of the house, and Grigor'ev proposed to mortgage it in order to clear up some of his debts.[47] A former chairman of the Moscow District Court, mistaking use for ownership, had issued a writ prohibiting transfer of the deed and had tied up the property against the debts of Grigor'ev's father. Apparently the writ could not be overturned in Moscow without an order of the Senate, but any court in a city other than Moscow could do so. One of Grigor'ev's creditors was Edel'son, who was himself in financial need and was pressing Grigor'ev for the money owed him. In July, Grigor'ev, who claimed the house to be worth 2800 silver roubles, offered it to Edel'son as guarantee of the loan and interest for the next year. At the same time, however, he requested Druzhinin to urge the owner of *Biblioteka dlia chteniia* also to take a mortgage on his house for 2,000 silver roubles.[48]

With the help from Botkin and the sale of his article to *Russkaia beseda*, Grigor'ev was able briefly to stave off financial ruin and, perhaps in gratitude, made a pilgrimage to the Berliukovskaia hermitage for some spiritual respite.[49] But the relief was short-lived. In August he fell ill with smallpox. He had promised an article for Druzhinin for the September issue of *Biblioteka dlia chteniia*, then postponed it to October. In December he wrote to Druzhinin that the article was still not finished, and finally he sent it in January 1857. Work on the translation of *A Midsummer Night's Dream*, which he had also promised to Druzhinin, was progressing no better. By February he had completed only four acts.[50]

The translation did, however, appear in August 1857. With it, Druzhinin published a letter from Grigor'ev about translating Shakespeare. He aimed, he wrote, to convey the odour and colour of the play rather than to reproduce it to the letter. A translator must convey the 'feeling' of the work. He had tried to capture the 'artistic and psychological transparency' of *A Midsummer Night's Dream*. All drama, he claimed, was democratic. Shakespeare and every great playwright expressed the most advanced point of view held by the masses. And although all great writers shared in the single truth of the human soul, all expressed it through local and national experience. A character has no credibility unless rooted in the real lives of real people.[51]

In the autumn of 1856, Botkin reported to Turgenev that Grigor'ev was drinking heavily again.[52] In fact, a number of the young editors were heavy imbibers. Almazov, Edel'son, Grigor'ev, Mei, Ostrovskii, and Pisemskii, with other of their associates, were notorious for their revels. Their 'club' was the Pechkin coffee-house, which was attached to the Gurin tavern. The Pechkin was a gathering place for Moscow's theatrical crowd. Mochalov had even married the tavern keeper's daughter, and Sadovskii visited it every morning until his death.[53] From there many adventures began. So dedicated a drinker was Grigor'ev that he even contrived to make piety serve his drinking habits. Galakhov remembered that when Grigor'ev turned from Europeanism to Slavism he began to imitate A.S. Khomiakov in his strict observance of holy days: 'Once on a Sunday during Lent I ran into him in the Pechkin tavern. We both ordered a cup of coffee. I, a sinner, began to drink it with cream, but he refused it and asked for something else. I saw that they brought him a carafe of cognac of considerable quantity. He's right, I thought, it's sinful to taste milk but cognac is not sinful, for [*zane*] in the church calendar for today it specified permission for wine and oil.'[54]

In the Russian people's fondness for drunkenness and carousals, Grigor'ev found not only vindication of his own habits but a certain wild beauty. Writing to Protopopova in 1858 from Florence at carnival time, Grigor'ev compared the pettiness of the carnival frolics of the Florentines with the poetry of Russian celebrations:

Our maslianitsa sketched itself before my eyes, our good, intelligent and capacious people with their sprees, hard drinking and colossal dissoluteness ... A winter snowstorm came to life in my memory, the Novinskoe, the wit of the conversation of the factory workers with the clowns, the *samokaty*, the songs of my fatherland, the cellars in which I and *** spent the night, he in drinking and depravity, I in songs and depravity, and I was right. In all of this dreadful deformity of a gifted, mighty and fresh tribe there is much more that is vital and compelling than in the final convulsions of a life that has outlived its time [i.e., Italy]. The summer, monastic holidays of my great, poetic, and along with it simple-hearted Moscow, its stations of the cross and other things came to my mind – everything which so few of us know how to cherish and which is as a matter of fact wholly true and fresh poetry, and to which, as you know, I always surrendered with all the passion of my peasant heart.

And he remembered a pub near the Kamennyi most (Stone Bridge), where he and two others, 'all three blind drunk but pure of heart, kissed and drank with the factory girls.'[55]

A couple of months earlier he had written to Edel'son: 'By the way ... they write me ... that the drunkenness and debauchery of Pisemskii and Ostrovskii has in recent times reached Herculean proportions and that Tolstoi is speaking about it with disapproval. Aha! I thought – there's a count's nature talking (ce n'est pas comme il faut!) ... Long may God help you not to drink but long may God preserve you and me from ever throwing stones at the drunkenness and excesses of Ostrovskii and Pisemskii.'[56] A few weeks later he picked up the theme again in another missive to Edel'son: 'With us these affairs of the tavern and the cellar are the Bacchanals of a new, emergent God, terrible and tragic Bacchanals for those who are spun round in them.'[57] The idea, of course, was borrowed from Schelling, who believed that the new in life often first appeared in the form of a Bacchanalian revel. It was a heady apologia for incipient alcoholism.

Grigor'ev must have gone on badgering Pogodin about re-establishing *Moskvitianin* and seems to have enlisted the help of his old mentor at the Moscow University, N.I. Krylov. In May 1857, E.E. Driianskii, an associate of the young editors, wrote to Ostrovskii that Krylov had bought shares in *Moskvitianin* with the object of combating the views of M.N. Katkov's new journal, *Russkii vestnik* (The Russian Messenger). The new *Moskvitianin* would announce its program in September, and Grigor'ev would be named head of the Slavic section.[58] Since this plan was not carried out, it is unlikely that Krylov actually did buy any shares.

But Pogodin did accede to Grigor'ev's pleas. On 7 June 1857, he petitioned to have *Moskvitianin* transferred to the editorial control of Grigor'ev from the beginning of 1858. A few days later, Driianskii wrote to Ostrovskii: 'Now [Grigor'ev] is mooing ardently – here's the reason: one fine day Pogodin summoned him and transferred *Moskvitianin* to him with the right of full and uncontrolled direction ... And from next year Grigor'ev will remain as the sole editor without the participation of Pogodin, who will have to provide only the capital for the publication and payment for the articles. An application has already been sent to the ministry on the 8th. The program has been shrewdly written.'[59]

After establishing through the director of schools in Moscow Province that Grigor'ev was a 'loyal' man, who had not been involved in any 'oppositional activities,' and that the Third Section saw no 'obstacle' to granting permission, the Ministry of Education, on 24 October 1857, granted the petition to put Grigor'ev in charge of *Moskvitianin*.[60]

6

Western Perspective
1857–1858

Is it not simpler to grasp that man lives
not for the *fulfilment of his destiny*,
not for the incarnation of an idea,
not for progress,
but solely because he was born ...

Alexander Herzen, *My Past and Thoughts*

In spite of the chaos around the running of *Moskvitianin* (The Muscovite) and the frustrating negotiations in the mid-1850s for work with other journals, Grigor'ev had by 1857 succeeded in formulating the outlines of an independent intellectual position in relation both to Westernism and Slavophilism and to utilitarian and aesthetic criticism. It was still far from a fully elaborated and philosophically anchored system, but it already contained nearly all the elements of the organic criticism of his mature years. In guiding him in fact to Italy, instead of to the helm of *Moskvitianin*, fate, with some help from Pogodin, provided him with the time to think more deeply and systematically about his views on art, morality, and society. It also gave him a chance to experience the West and test his preconceptions of it at first hand. By the time he returned to Russia, in the autumn of 1858, he had confirmed his commitment to Russian nationality and fully elaborated his views on art and life.

Grigor'ev was not destined to edit *Moskvitianin* as his own. In a letter of May 1857 to Ostrovskii, Driianskii reported that Grigor'ev had applied for a leave of absence from service; in June, he further informed Ostrovskii that though Grigor'ev was still in Moscow, the government had granted him leave. Grigor'ev had applied for a leave in order to assume in Florence the post of tutor to fifteen-year-old Prince Ivan Trubetskoi, scion of one of Russia's oldest and wealthiest aristocratic families. The prince's father had once been a student of Pogodin's and the latter had arranged the position – probably, Grigor'ev suspected, 'in order to drive a wedge between my past and future.'[1] His debts were still pressing. A regular salary and a period of separation from his familiar haunts and friends could not but mitigate his plight. Absence from the scenes of his pain and humiliation might conceivably begin even to effect a cure for his melancholy.

Grigor'ev longed to make a trip abroad. A consortium of his friends playfully informed Ostrovskii in July 1857: 'Grigor'ev has left for Italy, which attracts travellers with its monuments to the arts and salubrious air, about which he, Grigor'ev, has read in books. On the road at every hop he goes into raptures in advance about Venice.'[2] The 'hops' took him to several cities along the way. In Berlin, in a bookstore near the university, when he asked for a portrait of Schelling, the shopkeeper inquired, 'And who is Herr Schelling?'[3] In Prague, he stood on the Charles Bridge and wept at the sight of Hradčany Castle. And in Vienna, he 'spat on [the city] and the Austrians, abusing them with a variety of disgraceful curses at every step, running the risk out of some foolish daring of being heard by their spies.' At last he reached Venice, which met all his rapturous expectations. He was 'stupefied (literally stupefied) in Venice,' and the two days he spent there seemed to him to be a 'magical, fantastic dream,' he reported to Protopopova.[4] So enchanted was he by the sights around him that he stepped out of his hotel, across the pavement, and into the Grand Canal, from which he had to be rescued.

His destination was Florence. The Trubetskois occupied the Villa San Pancrazio, in the hills above the city, as well as a palazzo in town within sight of the Bargello and near the Palazzo Vecchio. Grigor'ev savoured the cultural delights of the great city. He attended the opera at the Pergola Theatre, where he saw Signor Albertini perform in Verdi's *Sicilian Vespers*, and the Pagliano Theatre, where Meyerbeer's *The Huguenots*, with its 'Jewish-satanic music,' 'set my heart beating wildly.'[5]

Once he was settled, however, life in Italy devolved into routine. Grigor'ev wrote to Edel'son: 'My life is defined in the following formula: I teach, I study, I write, I read Schelling, and drive more than 15 miles a day, and at the end of it all, when everyone around is sleeping, I write my strange poems consisting of sonnets. Through all of this I am melancholy and bored.'[6] Grigor'ev took his teaching duties seriously. They consisted of two sessions each day, in the mornings a half-hour each on Russian and

Slavonic grammar, Scripture, Russian history, and Latin, and after dinner a half-hour of reading to Prince Ivan and his sister from Russian literature. According to his own account, the prince was so attached to him that he could not be without him for two hours together.[7] For his part, the teacher soon grew to care very much for his pupil, in whom he saw considerable potential. But he found the young man to be stuffed with views that radically contradicted his own. Those attitudes came in part from the princess, his mother, and partly from Bell, his English companion, who saw the task of child rearing, Grigor'ev sneered, as consisting essentially of concealing from youth anything that might awake the passions. And so only children's books were prescribed, and any event in history that was the least bit disturbing was scrupulously extirpated. The result, said Grigor'ev, was that the prince's genuinely passionate nature was displaced onto petty passions: a horse with expensive tack and other vanities. The family's spiritual adviser, I.E. Betskii – who forced the young man to cram the catechism without a thought for its meaning and to every question of the pupil replied, 'That's the devil speaking in you' – only made matters worse. All that Grigor'ev could hope, he concluded, was to instill some understanding, in his pupil in the face of Bell, who feared nothing in the world more than understanding, and Betskii, who hated the world in general.

Grigor'ev perceived that young Trubetskoi had not only a passionate but also an artistic nature: he at once understood the *Odyssey* and grasped Schiller critically. But his artistic side was offset by the selfishness of the aristocrat, the 'coldness of the young Pechorin.'[8] 'No efforts on my part could stamp out in Prince Ivan the pernicious thought that [aristocrats] were created from different material than we sinners.' He admitted that in the struggle against Bell's 'heartless, cold system of discipline,' which encouraged his pupil's aristocratic condescension he perhaps carried too far his determination to stir things up. Grigor'ev despaired of a fifteen-year-old of great privilege who knew English but had read scarcely a word of Shakespeare, who was half Italian and had not read Dante, at an age when his own contemporaries, the children of the plebeians, had read everything that it was possible to read. 'Add to that again the routine of the day, which absorbs so much time fruitlessly. Oh, routine! It is not without reason that in the son, as in all Russian people, is concealed a deep-rooted, irreconcilable hatred for you.'[9] Almost certainly the teacher hated routine more than did the pupil.

Shortly before his death, Grigor'ev wrote a brief chronology of his life, called 'A Short Service Record in Memory of My Old and New Friends.'

Under the entry for 1857, he wrote: 'In 1857 the chance to go abroad turned up. There I wrote nothing but only thought. The articles in *Russkoe slovo* (The Russian Word) in 1859 were the result of my thinking.'[10] If writing is understood as publishing, then Grigor'ev's recollection is nearly exact. Except for an important article in *Biblioteka dlia chteniia* (Library for Reading), he published almost nothing during his time abroad. Much of the thinking was inspired by Schelling's recently published *Philosophy of Mythology*, which he had first read while lying ill with smallpox in 1856 and reread over and over again while abroad. But Grigor'ev's letters from Italy testify that, in addition to thinking, he wrote a great deal, though his writings, except for some poetry, have not survived. He had scarcely settled in Italy when he wrote to Protopopova that his book, *To Friends from Afar* (K druz'iam izdaleka), which he claimed to have half finished but which he never completed, encompassed 'the whole of me; there [is contained] the fruit of my entire internal life, the complete anatomy of my self and others.'[11] The title of the book evoked both Gogol''s *Selected Passages from Correspondence with Friends* (Vybrannye mesta iz perepiski s druz'iami) and Herzen's *From the Other Shore* (S togo berega). By January 1858, he reported to Fet that some of *To Friends from Afar* had been completed, as well as part of another work entitled *The Sea* (More) (which he elsewhere referred to as a portion of *To Friends from Afar*). In them, he said, he had addressed all of the philosophical, historical, and literary questions that he had set for himself. Before publishing them, however, he wanted to refine and sharpen them.[12]

Grigor'ev's recent reading of Schelling's *Philosophy of Mythology* had consolidated his membership once and for all in the camp of the opponents of what has been called the 'scientific universalism' of the Enlightenment. Such critics have a long history that stretches from Hamman and Herder in the eighteenth century to Schelling and Carlyle, Schopenhauer and Nietzsche in the nineteenth, and on to Bergson and Heidegger in the twentieth. The idea of progress and its product, material well-being, lay at its centre. Reason, embodied in science and technology, was for Enlightenment thinkers the instrument of progress. Through application of rational and utilitarian principles to the human condition, they anticipated the steady improvement of the material, social, and even spiritual life of humankind. A more uniform 'humanity' would emerge, with progressive reduction of differences among individuals and nations. At the heart of the ideal of 'humanity' stood the 'autonomous personality,' governed by reason and utility and free of the prejudices and traditions of the past. Most important, the autonomous personality was endowed with abstract, 'inalienable human rights.' The spirit of scientific universalism was evident in the nineteenth century in Hegelian transformism, left-Hegelianism and its offspring Marxism, the utilitarian and positivist movements, and even liberalism.

The critics of this philosophy were motivated by an aesthetic revulsion for 'progress.' They saw the universalizing thrust contained in the idea of progress as a threat to the variety of human life, to the uniqueness of nations and regions, to the originality of national cultures, to social differences, and to true individuality and personality – all in the name of universal human rights. For the natural, progress substituted the artificial; for the concrete, the abstract; for the parochial, the universal, and for the organic, the rational. The ideal of a more uniform humanity and an individualism that rested on the possession by all of identical rights cut people off from their own time and place and set their moral sense adrift in a sea of rationalist abstractions. The critique was associated most often with political and social conservatism, but elements of it appeared, at least in Russia, in some varieties of radical thought, most notably in Herzen and later in the populist N.K. Mikhailovskii.

Grigor'ev fully shared the concerns of the critics and for the most part drew conservative conclusions from them. His reading of Schelling focused his thoughts on the differences between Russia and the West and the relationship between art and nationality. It helped him to refine his ideas about the various cultural groupings in Russia and reinforced his earlier views about the centrality of art in the uncovering of truth.

Though the manuscript of To Friends from Afar has not survived, it is possible to reconstruct much of its content from Grigor'ev's letters to friends and acquaintances in Russia. At the centre of his reflections while abroad was the question of Russia and the West. While campaigning to broaden Prince Ivan's young mind, Grigor'ev, at least at first, resolutely closed his own to new perspectives on western Europe. Like so many patriotically inclined Russians before and after him who travelled abroad, he expected to find the West decadent and moribund. The belief that the West had already made its contribution to universal development and now was exhausted was an article of faith of Slavophilism. Grigor'ev shared it not only with the Slavophiles but with Pogodin and, from another perspective, Herzen, whose Letters from the Avenue Marigny (Pis'ma iz Avenue Marigny) and From the Other Shore, written in the wake of the failed revolutions of 1848, condemned the West for its inability to inaugurate the age of socialism.

Grigor'ev, too, went on at length about the pettiness of western Europeans and their concerns. He found Italy a 'bloody land' that he wanted to leave.[13] He judged the Italians to be a passionate but not a vital people: 'they love the noble rags, the tinsel of life.'[14] They were concerned only about money and material interests. Nothing could be more 'prosaic' than women there, with their coarse features, the masculine throatiness of their voices, their narrow interests, and what he called their 'male giftedness' in music and the plastic arts. He complained about the street songs that he heard under his window, which seemed to him to be all sentimental rubbish. Italian drama was obsessed with a 'stupid comicalness' without any serious meaning, and opera was dominated by 'talk of hangmen, masks, the sound of guitars ... dark glances and the most passionate vibratos on certain words such as "Vendetttttt'a," "Curi patrrria," etc.'

Most striking, in his view, was the enormous contrast between the 'greatness of the past and the pettiness of the present (for they are all ants and not people).' All the strengths of the Italian past were now gone, he believed, because they had served their purpose.[15] To Apollon Maikov, he wrote that contemporary Italy, out of old habits, occasionally created 'this opera of Verdi, or that powerful soprano or this talented painter. Here only the past is good but it is good to the point of intoxication. In the present I do not know what of a poetical nature you could find. Paltriness, pettiness, old phrases and gestures without their old meaning: in life triteness, the absence of scope and poetry – bovine ignorance.'[16]

Grigor'ev found comfort only in the great monuments of art. He had been urged by Pogodin to study painting and sculpture in Italy. Now he fervently thanked his old mentor for the advice. As he wrote to him, 'Salvation lies only in the Uffizi and the Pitti.'[17] Earlier, he had written to Edel'son that 'to live ... is possible only in Russia, even, speaking officially, in Moscow.'[18] He explained why that was so:

[In the galleries] only the old is good. Life ahead is ours, ours, ours! ... Even our carnival (maslianitsa), which is gross, drunken without surcease and accompanied by the excesses of the tempter, contains more of the seeds of life, amplitude, brotherhood than their [Florence's] present carnival (karnaval). To poeticize Italy and its life at the expense of ours as did Gogol' one would need to have an egotistical, not to mention, Ukrainian (khokhlattskaia) soul. Insolence, you say, and then repent and say, 'he's right, only one cannot tell him so.'[19]

What was true of Italy was true of the rest of the West. Grigor'ev complained to Edel'son that all Europeans, because they were all specialists, appeared to him insignificant, 'small ants, occupying themselves with petty work amid the magnificent and enormous monuments of a past life.'[20] The West was dominated by theory. It had reached the conclusion that humanity existed only for itself, for its own happiness. The most conscientious representatives of Western thought – the socialists and left Hegelians – had placed the rights of the flesh ahead of the needs of the spirit. In the slogan of the French Revolution, 'Liberté, Égalité, Fraternité ou la mort,' the strivings of western Europe in the nineteenth century were fully contained. Only the last part of the slogan had been realized, but the goals of liberty, equality, and fraternity were not at fault for their fatal consequences. To blame were the means through which the goals had been pursued. The ideals of the socialists were outmoded and reduced to gestures, phrases, and effects.[21] The West had arrived at an abstract person – humanity – to which, in the name of utility, it sacrificed everything that was individual and unique. All of the West's philosophical strivings were the result of a futile effort to reassert through theory the principle of natural or organic unity, which it had lost to atomization.[22]

For all his hostility to Herzen, Grigor'ev greatly valued what he called his 'negative truth,' and Herzen's influence was apparent in Grigor'ev's ruminations in Italy. In *From the Other Shore*, Herzen had mounted a far-ranging critique of western European thought since the Enlightenment. While throwing off the old classical and religious authorities, he argued, Western man still lacked the courage to do without ideals and so adopted new authorities in order to give meaning to human existence. The most tyrannical of the new absolutes were humanity and the theory of inevitable progress. They were ideals located in the future, but Herzen believed that meaning in life should be sought only in the present. There was no single, unifying ideal to harmonize life. Instead, human values and meaning were the products of self-creation against a background of the bewildering but aesthetically satisfying and desirable variety of human experience. Herzen believed that progress was by no means inevitable and that no single social ideal was final. He stressed the one-sidedness of theory and insisted that to be valuable a theory had to take on flesh.[23]

These thoughts were to be prominent in Grigor'ev's 'organic criticism.' But as much as he agreed with Herzen, he believed that the delusions arising from Herzen's 'vanity' and his 'cynical atheism' prevented him from understanding Russia's future.[24] Whereas Herzen was content to look for freedom in contingency, Grigor'ev sought it in Orthodoxy. But he, unlike Dostoevskii who also saw the nation's future in Orthodoxy, never confused that faith with dreams of utopia.

The contrast between Italian and Russian religiosity particularly impressed Grigor'ev. On one of the many drives that he took while living in the Villa San Pancrazio he came across a Madonna in a nearby church that reminded him of the Suzdal' Madonna in the Russian village of Spasskoe. But the Italian villagers, in worshipping the Madonna's image as if she were God, betrayed their paganism, whereas the Russians were true Christians, who understood in their hearts that they were praying not to the icon but rather to God.[25] He complained to Edel'son that whereas in Russia, on Christmas Eve, a reverential silence fell on the cities, in Italy hawkers continued to shout, children sang, and a night market went on in the streets. He attended a service at the Church of the Annunciation and found the choir singing like an opera chorus and the organist playing excerpts from Verdi.[26] All of this confirmed for him the decline of Catholicism.

In the East, in contrast, another principle reigned. The East bore the seeds of the new life, which were nurtured in the humility of Orthodoxy. Belief in the miracle of God's creation, in 'the light and shadows of his canvasses,' remained. In the East, humanity was seen as testament to the living variety of human existence. Easterners believed in the human soul, not in the abstract notion of humanity. The East recognized that the human soul was eternal and did not develop. Only in Russia did the living life live and grow, in everything from popular faith to folk songs.[27] 'Believe only in the *narod*,' he wrote to the poet A.N. Maikov, 'old and new together – it is great and to it belongs the whole future world, for apart from it there is nothing living.'[28] The new was growing out of the starting point of Orthodoxy, which bore within it the force of a new world.

Though Grigor'ev believed that his country's future was inseparable from Orthodoxy, he had little use for the Orthodox church or its defenders. In the first place, Orthodoxy, unfortunately, travelled in bad company. F. Bulgarin and N. Grech, the reactionary editors of the journal *Maiak* (The Lighthouse) of the 1830s and 1840s, were the symbols for him of official Orthodoxy. *Maiak* represented for him a narrow, formal, 'dilettante' Orthodoxy that stood against true morality.[29] He was appalled by the defection of the former young editor T. Filippov to official Orthodoxy.[30] Nearer to home, he found the embodiment of the worst in the native religion in the Trubetskois' family counsellor, Betskii.

Indeed, Grigor'ev experienced a profound religious crisis while in Italy. He noted that his Orthodoxy was expressed in conventional observance of the religious festivals but detected inside himself another person who was attracted to all kinds of doctrines. After a while, he confessed, he had come to believe 'all $747\frac{1}{2}$ of the heresies' of Orthodoxy. He discussed his doubts with the resident Orthodox priest in Florence, Father P.P. Travlinskii, and with a 'serious, noble woman,' probably V.A. Ol'khina. He resolved the crisis by dismissing questions of dogma and accepting Orthodoxy as a broad cultural-historical force of universal significance: 'I, myself, understood by Orthodoxy simply a certain elemental historical principle, which was fated to live and to give new forms of life and art in opposition to that other principle, Catholicism, which has already outlived and delivered its word, its bloom. That this principle in the soil of Slavdom and primarily of Great Russian Slavdom, with the breadth of its moral embrace, should renew the world – that is what became for me not a troubling but a simple faith ...'[31]

All of this great future was as yet contained in Russia, only in 'antediluvian forms.' Russians were not yet ready as individuals for the task before them. 'The entire living future,' he wrote, 'belongs to us, but to our type and not to individuals – our individuals are nowhere, nowhere ready – the best are not those who act but those who become drunkards and wanderers.'[32] Almost no one in Russia understood his nation's destiny. Even among the young editors, Grigor'ev believed, only Ostrovskii instinctively, Edel'son in flashes of consciousness, and Grigor'ev himself grasped the significance of Russian nationality. Of the older generation, only Pogodin, with his views on the continuity of Russia before and after Peter the Great and the necessity of incorporating both new and old into developing nationality, was sound. Everyone else was in error.[33]

Grigor'ev was appalled by a feuilleton that appeared in the St Petersburg journal *Nord* (The North) which celebrated as proof that Russia was a European nation with a European destiny the fact that the capital had a demi-monde, expensive femmes de nuit, and juicy scandals. It symbolized for him the emptiness of the liberal Westernizer view of his country's future 'progress' as an annex of a dying Western culture. Russian youth, with its socialist leanings, was highly critical of the past and of many of the things that made the hearts of his own generation beat with wild enthusiasm. In much of their criticism they were correct, but the price of correctness was the clipping of their wings and a preoccupation with trifles.[34]

The Slavophiles, too, were mistaken. Though Grigor'ev retained his affection for them, he saw the Slavophiles in relation to the young editors 'as Judaism to Christianity, or the Raskol (the Schismatics) to the true Church.' The Slavophiles did not believe in life. Instead of the unhindered development of the *narod*, they advocated its development according to a prescribed theory. In particular, they, like all theoreticians, had no sense of the importance of the individual. 'The annihilation of the indivdual in the communality of the Russian soul is precisely the weak side of Slavophilism,' he wrote to Maikov.[35]

Grigor'ev could not decide what he most hated, 'Petersburg progress,' the 'dilettante Orthodoxy of *Maiak*, the 'cynical atheism' of Herzen, or the 'dry, theoretical, extreme Puritanism' of the Slavophiles.[36] He believed, however, that all of them were the product of the same source: lack of faith in life, in ideals, and in art. He remained, he declared, convinced that 'everything living enters the world only through Art.'[37] Without art, the world was dominated by theory, either by a utilitarian utopia aimed at material gratification and spiritual slavery or by stagnation under the external authority of a church without the internal unity of 'Christ, the Ideal, Measure and Beauty.' Only through art did truth enter human consciousness. 'Everything great enters life through its embodiment in art, science was always a draft, an elaboration of art. Art – it is the second world of the second creator.' Like the human soul, art was eternal. There was no such thing as a new art, and dreams about a new art were but the spasms of a dying Germano-Romantic world in the persons of its best representatives, Georges Sand and Franz Liszt.[38]

Though Grigor'ev was not to express the thought publicly until his series of articles in *Russkoe slovo* in 1859, he had already formulated his view of Pushkin as the embodiment of Russian art while still in Italy. He planned to write an article in a revived *Moskvitianin*, showing how everything in Russia began and returned to Pushkin. Pushkin's centrality to Russian nationality was apparently prominent in Grigor'ev's lost *To Friends from Afar*. In the fragment called 'The Sea,' he claimed, he had compared the sea, with its eternal yet ever-changing physiognomy, to the manifestations of the human soul in various nations. Pushkin was Russia, a sea, who through the tide of his creativity defined the 'boundaries of our being.' The principle of art was, for Grigor'ev, inseparable from that of nationality. In the linkage of art and nationality, he found the guarantee of spontaneity in national life and the defence against theory. In his view, Pushkin was Russia's first, whole, and synthetic expression. In his works were the sketches of Russia's future. 'Pushkin,' he wrote to Maikov, 'is the first, but full, outline of our typical physiognomy.' Pushkin created both the 'humble Belkin and the critical Aleko,' the two basic Russian types. Everything that followed after Pushkin, if it was true to his original vision, only filled in his sketches with colours.[39] Pushkin and the Polish poet Adam Mickiewicz were the 'water and fire, the sea and the mountains of the new world' that was coming into being in succession to old Europe.[40]

It was also in Italy that Grigor'ev recognized the need to become 'reconciled with Vissarion [Belinskii] and his extravagances.' Though he had always had some sympathy for Belinskii's earlier views, which were formed under the influence of Schelling, he had seen his later ideas, which reflected attachment to the Hegelian notion of universal progress, as essentially damaging to Russia's autonomous cultural development. But Belinskii had been the first to recognize the genius and cultural significance of Pushkin, and his importance in Russian cultural history was undeniable. Grigor'ev therefore began to look on him as a necessary contributor to the nation's cultural growth, though he by no means agreed with all, or even many, of his views.

Grigor'ev had not entirely despaired of propagating, in a revived *Moskvitianin* or in a successor journal, the thoughts on Russian culture that were taking shape in his mind while he pursued the education of his teenaged charge in Italy. Indeed, he professed to Pogodin that since his private life had been stripped away from him, all that remained was his cause. The closing of *Moskvitianin* pained him most of all, but he still hoped to buy it from Pogodin. Later he was plotting to get control of it and rename it *Moskovskii Telegraf* (Moscow Telegraph). The new publication would exclude all literature except translations; it would make its stand on the basis of opposition to the 'journalistic coterie of literary people.' It would appear in four small numbers a month, like the old *Moskovskii Telegraf*, and be devoted to politics, criticism, and 'merciless' review of competitor journals.[41]

But even Grigor'ev's faith in his cause was tentative. After a lengthy discussion with Pogodin, on the 'life' of the East and the 'theory' of the West, in which he expressed his hope for the triumph of the Orthodox idea, he betrayed his despair and feelings of unnecessariness:

The new is coming into life, but we are its victims. Victims, who do not even have the consolation of recognition. Victims of Herzen – even I, an Orthodox believer, appreciate him, but no one recognizes our sacrifices.

Nothing will come from me or from our movement in general, and nothing can come of it because the time is not right. We are the people of some distant future which still has to be redeemed by a long, long process. We will die without honour, without victories, but nevertheless we alone see the dim, real goal.[42]

Grigor'ev's reflections on art in this period did not remain unpublished. They found their fullest expression in his 'Critical View of the Basis, Meaning, and Method of Contemporary Art,' which appeared in *Bib-*

lioteka dlia chteniia in January 1858. The article was a further response to the debate that was blossoming in Russian literary criticism between the adherents of art-for-the-sake-of-art and the utilitarian critics. It represented a major attempt to get beyond contemporary polemics and to place the debate in a wider historical context. In a letter to Druzhinin, Grigor'ev called the article 'my complete and completely heartfelt literary testament.'[43] To Pogodin he recommended it as a 'sermon thought out at length and ... clear.'[44]

Grigor'ev began from the position that the roots of the separation of life and thought, which he believed to be the essence of the Western European cultural crisis, lay in the Enlightenment. Eighteenth-century European thought, particularly its French variant, had created the notion of universal humanity, a universal human education, and a universal human aesthetics. Thanks to the great genius of Voltaire, a whole century had been led to believe in a narrow, rational formula based on pure analysis. Symptomatic of the new rationalism had been the rationalist literary critics' contempt for Shakespeare. The French Revolution and its principal actors embodied the new anti-historical rationalism. But inevitably the utopia of Condorcet perished under that of the Mountain, which was in turn threatened by that of Marat.

Eighteenth-century rationalism, with its theoretical formulations, provoked a reaction that Grigor'ev named 'historical feeling' and defined as *'a feeling for the organic connectedness of the phenomena of life, a feeling for the wholeness and unity of life.'*[45] J.W. von Herder was one of the first to respond to the rationalism of his age. Herder affirmed a new belief in the past, in history, and in the wholeness of humanity. He was obsessed with the artistic monuments of the early lives of peoples. He took his contemporaries into the peasants' huts in order to reveal to them the beauty of the popular arts. He turned their attention to the past, where they could savour the splendours of folk epic poetry.

The new 'historical feeling' evident in Herder gave birth to romanticism, but it, like the Enlightenment, proved to be separated from the living life and crumbled into dust. The intense examination of the past undertaken by Herder, Schiller, Goethe, and the romantics, however, fostered the sense among at least some nineteenth-century thinkers that the past was organically linked with the present, and the dead with the living, and so nurtured the tender new shoot. The real enemy was Hegel. With his formula 'what is real is rational,' he transformed 'historical feeling' into the 'historical view.' That view, Grigor'ev maintained, was a revival of the eighteenth-century idea of universal human progress. It was based on the notion of unlimited development. It was devoid of morality because it located its ideal in the future, to which end it was prepared to sacrifice everything in the present.

Grigor'ev regarded Hegelianism as the most cheerless of all world views; in it every separate moment of the life of the world was reduced to being only a transitional form to yet another transitional form. History became a bottomless pit into which all human activity rushed headlong without hope of gaining a moral foothold. But the idea of progress toward some future ideal was alien to human nature; humans demanded an ideal in the here and now. Consequently, they arbitrarily declared a halt to the march of unlimited progress and with Hegel declared, 'This is the spot' where the ideal has been reached. Paradoxically, therefore, Hegelianism proclaimed eternal development while it halted all development at the present level of the German nation, as if some final boundary of human capacity had been reached.[46]

The new theoretical despotism declared that the part of humanity that had not lived according to the ideal existed in a bestial state or at best was in transition to the German form. In Hegel the soul of man, which always aspired to truth, beauty, and love, was devoured by the abstract spirit of humanity, with its siren song of gradually widening consciousness of the World Spirit. Longing for the eternal, Hegelian despotism ended in dead materialism; wishing to explain the nature of nations, it subordinated them to humanity: 'And all this arises from the fact that instead of a real point of departure – the human soul – an imaginary point of departure is seized upon, the abstract spirit of humanity is taken to be something real. To it, this spirit, idolatrous religious rites are performed, unprecedented sacrifices, illicit sacrifices are made, because it is always an idol, arbitrarily decreed, always only theory.'[47] The essence of the 'historical view,' Grigor'ev concluded, was the most complete moral indifferentism and fatalism, in which neither nations nor individuals were accorded any independent being but were only tools of an abstract idea. On this point Grigor'ev and Herzen agreed.

In spite of Hegel's vast influence, Grigor'ev went on, historical feeling was never entirely subsumed in the historical view. Carlyle and Coleridge in England, Thierry and Savigny in France, and Emerson in the United States remained true to the essence of Herder's earlier legacy. But the man who smashed the Hegelian formulae was Schelling. Grigor'ev called him the Plato of the new world: 'The greatest significance of Schelling's formula as it has emerged in his recently published works consists in the fact that everyone, both peoples and individuals, are restored to their full, autonomous significance, that the abstract spirit of humanity and its development is smashed.'[48] Leaning on Schelling, Grigor'ev stressed the primary unity of humankind. That original unity, was not abstract but represented a historical moment. Firmly rooted in its initial unity the human soul adhered to a single truth and did not develop. The soul could be enriched through experience and knowledge of the world, but its knowledge of truth, beauty, and love was independent of experience.

The human soul did not develop; but national organisms did, while retaining traces of their distant membership in the primary unity of the human race. Grigor'ev brought an almost Jungian sensitivity to the underlying cultural unity of humanity, which, however, was expressed in a great diversity of forms and national myths. Grigor'ev pointed out that every national organism gradually modified the primary tradition into its own traditions and beliefs. Each gave birth to its own organic principle and introduced it into the collective life of the world. Each was justified in itself, was entitled to live according to the laws appropriate to it, and was not obligated to serve as a transitional form for another organism.[49]

What united these national organisms, in all their variety, was the single and unchanging truth of the human soul, or what he earlier had called 'the truth of life.' The ideal of the human soul was eternal truth, which was the only criterion of good and evil. Centuries and peoples did not judge that truth; they were judged by it and measured according to the extent to which they approximated the truth of the human soul in their lives. The ideal, the truth of the human soul, was eternally present but was accessible only through the real, the particular, the concrete. 'Every ideal,' Grigor'ev wrote, 'is nothing but the aroma and colour of the real.'[50] In the realm of knowledge, only that was living and precious to humans which took on flesh and blood; only that was dear to the human soul which appeared to it in an artistic form: 'The great significance of art is that it alone ... brings into the world the new, organic, and necessary in life. In order for a thought to be believed it is necessary that the thought take on a body; and on the other hand, a thought cannot take on a body unless it is born and not made artificially.'[51]

Art was the product of a particular time and place; the artist was the child of a particular epoch, country, and locality. The artist was merely a more gifted member of his group, more sensitive and responsive to ancestry, locality, and history. He belonged to a certain national type and was one of its fullest expressions. An artistic nature of true genius was organically joined to all around it and to the past, present, and future; it severed no links with its environment, mastered all, and embraced all in love. But despite its special sensitivity to time and place, it never lost its own particularity. Genius was always self-conscious in the highest degree. A genius had an undivided world view, carried the future within him, and understood the ties that joined past, present, and future.

The creative act began when the artist's reserve of observations about life reached a critical mass in his soul. At that point some flash of lightning illuminated the artist's spiritual world and attitude to life. The artist employed every means available – his region, time, and personal experiences – to create. Creativity was neither completely personal nor impersonal: it was a living national or local product yet informed by the eternal truth of the artist's own soul. The artist made conscious what he had divined in life and in so doing augmented the common treasury of the human soul.[52]

Art was in its essence ideal, but it could not illuminate a sphere broader than the sphere of phenomena in which it was created. Art was a human or earthly activity and reflected in an ideal light only what life set before it. It could perceive the ideal not directly, but only through the medium of time and place. But art, Grigor'ev repeated, was the best of all human activities. It embodied in its creations that which was invisibly present in the air and sensed the approaching future in advance. Art reflected in its lens everything that was in the air of an epoch, permanent or transient, and reflected it in such a way that each person felt the truth of the reflection. A great work of art had a despotic attraction and could dominate a whole epoch, through imitation or variations on its theme. Herzen had also stressd the prohetic nature of art. 'Poets really are,' he wrote, 'as the Romans called them, prophets; only they utter not what is not and what will be by chance, but what is unrecognized, what exists in the dim consciousness of the masses, what is already slumbering in them.'[53]

Grigor'ev turned next to literary criticism. If art was the reflection through real living phenomena of the ideal, then criticism was the elucidation of that reflection. Grigor'ev argued that there had never been a truly art-for-art's-sake form of criticism. Only among the ancients had there been a tendency to focus solely on the beauty of art because in the ancient world there was no separation of the world view of intellectuals from that of the people. Since art was always embedded in the particular national and social milieu in which it was created, it could not be viewed only formally as it was by the art-for-art's-sake critics. 'It is clear that criticism has ceased to be purely artistic, that for it social, psychological, and historical interests are connected with the products of art, in a word, the interests of life itself.'[54] In England, Coleridge and Carlyle had founded a new criticism, based on a moral point of view, and other national critics were also working from a moral or national point of view.

Criticism bore the same relationship to art that art had to life. It elucidated, interpreted, and disseminated the 'light and warmth' that were contained in a beautiful creation. The critic linked the particular work of art to the soil in which it was born and examined the attitudes of the artist to life. He did not discuss the technical blunders of the artist. Every artist knew his own mistakes. Technical errors in art arose from a moral deficiency; they indicated either an incomplete view of life or a confused and stubborn sympathy for an uncommon solution to a psychological or social question. Artists resisted ordinary solutions and dry, logical conclusions. In their quest for living solutions to life's questions, they inevitably committed errors. In such a case the critic should note the error and probe its causes. In particular, he had to try to understand why art had resisted an ordinary solution to a particular problem. Though the critic had a duty to ask why a living, artistic question was posed or resolved incorrectly, it was not the task of criticism to direct life; only art could do so.[55]

Grigor'ev noted that during the 1840s and early 1850s the leading body of literary criticism in Russia had been the so-called historical school. In his opinion, that school had reached a dead end. Its critics had forgotten the greatness of Pushkin and Gogol' and failed to assess Ostrovskii accurately; but the public had not: 'The fact is that the public, the mass, no longer believes in criticism precisely because criticism does not believe in itself.'[56] The weaknesses of historical criticism were the same as those of the historical view; both had no moral criterion. The first error of historical criticism was its conviction that in everything false there lay a bit of the truth or that every falsity was a relative truth. And so its adherents concluded that there was no absolute truth or unconditional beauty or good. But the reality did not correspond to the theory. Relative truth was only a phrase. The human soul demanded an ideal and invariably seized on the last relative truth as the ideal. 'The absence of a firm, unconditional ideal, the absence of conviction – there lies the disease of historical criticism, the reason for its decline and the reaction against it.'[57]

Believing only in an arbitrarily adopted theory, the practitioners of historical criticism could not separate truth from their own narrow, personal ideals. Beginning from the idea of eternal development, they ended in oriental-style stagnation. Theory had to be replaced with a new, living principle, for only that which was born, which was incarnated in flesh and blood, lived and acted. Such a principle was a 'new word' of life and art, always born and never artificially made. A practitioner of 'true historical criticism'

(Grigor'ev had not yet begun to use the term 'organic criticism') viewed literature or any other spiritual activity as the organic fruit of the age and nation and linked to the development of current social concepts.

Though Grigor'ev did not mount a direct attack in this article on the utilitarian criticism being espoused by Chernyshevskii, preferring instead to focus on the 'historical school' of which he believed Chernyshevskii was the direct heir, the main outline of his critique of the utilitarians was clear. He would develop it fully in *Russkoe slovo* and later in *Vremia* (Time) in conjunction with the further elaboration of his own 'organic criticism.' His contempt for the art-for-art's sake critics was equally apparent, a contempt that he never abandoned.

In spite of the freedom that Italy provided him to think, Grigor'ev felt out of sympathy with it. One summer evening, as the scent of the lemon blossoms drifted to him on the gentle evening breeze, he heard a Chopin waltz being played by someone with great feeling but no measure. As he concluded gloomily to Protopopova, 'it follows that both Chopin's music and my dissolute soul get along very badly with Italy.' Fate had condemned him, a 'northern bear' to live in Florence for a whole year.[58] Even the rapture that Venice had first aroused in him could not for long suppress the spleen that arose in his soul. In the midst of Venice's magic, he now recalled, as he floated on the Grand Canal in the evening in a gondola, 'I tasted the well-known dish called melancholy (*khandra*).'[59] Guilt at the abandonment of his family also tortured him. He even had fond thoughts of his father, to whom, he wrote to Fet, he had become passionately attached in recent times. He claimed to be sending most of his tutor's salary to his family, keeping only five or ten rubles a month for himself.[60] His personal failures had, he declared, ended for ever his hopes for a personal life. To Protopopova he wrote, 'My life is over, completely over, I feel that. Nevertheless, I am healthy: the sea at Livorno, the riding every day at the Villa San Pancrazio ... have strengthened my physical powers.'[61]

On 8 and 9 March 1858 (n.s.), Turgenev, who was often abroad, dropped in on him in Florence. They talked all night, and Grigor'ev read to Turgenev what he had written while abroad away from Russia. During the discussion, according to Grigor'ev, Turgenev put his finger on the sore point of his personality – the disorderliness of his thought. Turgenev nevertheless, or so Grigor'ev claimed, went on to say that

(1) only in me [Grigor'ev], at the present moment, is energy, that only in me is the wholeness of some specific doctrine that is wholly inexclusive, like Slavophilism ...

(2) that to succeed I have to reiterate like the late Vissarion, to limit myself, to repeat without the least remorse: in a word to reiterate, reiterate, reiterate, (3) that for me there is nowhere to reiterate at the present time, because I cannot join any of the existing tendencies, that is, that not one of them will take me and I cannot in all honour and conscience make concessions for I have worked out my own strong and whole position.

Turgenev apparently declared his readiness to write under Grigor'ev's principles, but Grigor'ev doubted it, 'for he is fully a Westernizer by development, a Hegelian by principle, and a society man by education and manners.'[62] Though Turgenev mentioned his meeting with Grigor'ev in his correspondence, he did not record their conversation. On Turgenev's recommendation (he particularly emphasized the attractions of Grigor'ev's friend Mme Ol'khina, 'a pretty woman'), Botkin also visited the critic in Florence and found him 'fresh and healthy and passionately in love with art.'[63]

In spite of these visits, Grigor'ev felt alone. He captured his sense of having no allies among Russian critics in a poem that he wrote in Italy. He lamented that he was destined to leave a sad legacy of 'suffering, passion and doubt' and went on:

> My tongue is my enemy, a long-standing enemy ...
> But, unfortunately, I am prepared
> As an Orthodox Christian
> Always to forgive my enemy.
>
> Whether I fall in stormy battle,
> Or end my days in 'hard drinking,'
> I pray to be remembered in a virgin's
> Prayer that here went a man
> Who frankly and selflessly
> Gave his soul over to transports,
> Fought honourably, long and in vain,
> And was killed or fell worn out.[64]

Apart from the prose works to which Grigor'ev treated Turgenev, he was also busy writing his 'strange poems.' Most of them appeared in the cycle *Venezia la Bella* (Venice the Beautiful), which was published in *Sovremennik* (The Contemporary) in 1858. Inspired by his love for

Leonida Vizard, the cycle was the first part of a continuing novel, *Odyssey of the Last Romantic* (Odisseia poslednego romantika), to which he was to add parts over the next years. It also marked the purging of his love for Vizard and even of the ideal kind of love that it represented. In a later instalment of *Odyssey of the Last Romantic* – a poem written in 1862, in which he described the course of a passionate 'carnal' love with a woman – he recalled a time when he 'loved a different love,' 'pure as heaven.' But its image was, he wrote, 'entombed in my "Venezia la Bella."'[65]

The Venice cycle consisted of 48 sonnets (some, though, with fifteen lines), which, Grigor'ev noted, sustained a 'feverishness of tone' throughout.[66] The theme was familiar. The poet wandered through Venice, but wherever he went she shadowed him. Again he struggled to submit to his fate and accept the suffering that life inflicted on him through love. A new theme crept into the work, however, that anticipated the conceit later employed in his autobiography. The poet began to examine his fate in light of his own history and the history of his time. He stressed in particular the romanticism of the time of his youth:

> Forgive me! A romantic from minority
> To majority years – alas! I have preserved
> The legacy of Mochalov's times
> And, like Tortsov, 'love tragedy.'
> From childhood I experienced a proclivity
> For the heroic, stored it in my soul
> Like a kind of hoard, tried every means
> To live a fast life and drank outrageously;
> But there was in this wild Quixotism
> Not just petty self-regard:
> He who weeps is capable of greatness,
> The heart that thirsts is full of truth,
> The fanatic is capable of humility,
> On him lies the stamp of election and service.

The cycle ended on a familiar note, with his determination to 'get used to wandering on the sea *senza amare*.'[67]

But Grigor'ev could not live *senza amare* and once again found himself in love. In Italy he had been living a completely chaste life, which, as he pointed out to Pogodin, was 'bad for a man of his temperament.' Indeed, he continued, things had reached such a pass by the spring of 1858 that he could not even look at his cleaning woman with indifference, though she was quite ugly.[68] His new love provided little physical respite, however; it was as platonic as was the one with Vizard.

For all his frequent complaints about having no personal life, Grigor'ev was not without society in Florence. In the fall of 1857, he was introduced to the Mel'nikov family, which was living in Florence, partly for the health of one daughter, Olga Alexandrovna, who was convalescing from consumption. Grigor'ev fell for her: 'In this subject,' he wrote to Protopopova, 'was everything I love in a woman: the quiet responsiveness of the guitar and the litheness of the cat ...' Once again, he wrote, he lived the whole gamut of passion; every day from three o'clock he spent by the couch where she lay, the 'ailing kitten,' as he called her, until eleven, when her sisters would come and say 'Isn't it time you were going home A.A.?' He understood the 'hopelessness of this new passion, suffering her coughing shyly like a slave, anticipating her every movement and, like a despot, steering her thoughts and impressions to their moral essence ... There was no past or present for me ... There was only the moment and I seized it passionately.'[69]

As usual, love inspired him to poetry. He wrote a number of poems in Olga Alexandrovna's album. Some were published; the rest survived in the album in the St Petersburg archives. These poems were lighthearted and teasing. One was written in St Petersburg; evidently, Grigor'ev renewed his acquaintance with Olga Alexandrovna after his return to Russia.

He was also inspired by Olga Alexandrovna to write more serious poems. In Florence, he had been for the first time in his life deeply moved by the plastic arts. He spent three days in Siena in order to see its monuments and discover the Siena school of painting. Beautiful though he found its legacy, it did not move him.[70] In Rome, in contrast, 'there was a place for him,' as he exclaimed to Protopopova. His pulse quickened at the very name. There he found something old that was eternally young.[71] But to Protopopova he also wrote that 'Italy is poison to a nature such as mine: there is something narcotic in it that strongly irritates the nerves.' Its great art kept the soul in a 'state of dizziness.'[72]

He fell under the spell particularly of Murillo's *Madonna*, the 'highest ideal of womanhood,' an ideal that he had not even seen in his dreams. When he first saw her, he recalled, he wanted to cry; he visited the painting three times for every visit he paid to other works of art.[73] He felt that the painting contained a mystery in its creation that was partly technical and partly spiritual:

The darkness, which surrounds this transparent, eternally tender, virginally severe and meditative face, plays as important a role in the painting as the Madonna, herself, and the child who stands on her knee. And this is not a *tour de force* of art. For me there is not the slightest doubt that this darkness is the darkness of the soul of the artist himself from which rushes out, escapes and volatilizes the holy vision, the image, which is created not out of the rays of daylight but from the rosy-straw-coloured glimmering of the dawn ... everything has been created boldly, simply, expansively ...

He saw in the masterpiece a parallel with Beethoven's creativity, which also arose out of the depths and darkness and 'with its simplicity overcomes everything that is discordant, everything that is Jewish (though the Jewish, that is, Meyerbeer and Mendelssohn, I passionately love, as you know).'[74] He also told Protopopova that in the features of the Madonna he saw his own tormentor, Vizard.[75]

The profound impression made on him by Murillo's great painting was recorded in a number of poems. A short five-poem cycle, *Improvisations of a Wandering Romantic* (Improvizatsii stranstvuiushchego romantika), brought together his new feelings of love for Olga Alexandrovna, whose young life he expected would be cut short by illness; his own renewed despair at a fate that prevented him from attaining love; and the dark mystery of the Madonna.

In the first poem he lamented that the beloved was fated to die young while the poet lived and studied to live 'fully, broadly, freely and passionately.' In the second he spoke of her as a cat with hidden claws; but he is prepared to suffer all the torments of her claws to be near her. He took up in the third poem the theme, which he had developed in his letter to Protopopova, of the profound darkness out of which shone the virgin face of the Madonna. Here it was the close proximity of good and evil, creativity and destructiveness, that fascinated him:

> In you, yourself, is the seed of destruction –
> I tremble for you, o my phantom,
> Limpid and youthful apparition;
>
> And your companion, the silent gloom, is terrible to me,
> O, how can you, bright one, become intimate
> With the sinister darkness that embraces you?
>
> In it, ruinous chaos lies concealed.

In the fourth poem Grigor'ev looked into the darkness itself, into 'the bottomless chaos of both good and evil / Everything that the soul madly endures / In pursuit of a hidden riddle.' And he concluded: 'O, I believe that into that gloomy hell / You would shine a ray of love and reconciliation ... / That you would overflow with a virgin and pure / Entreaty, as with a healing blessing.' In the cycle's fifth and final poem, he dreamed that the Madonna had left the frame of the picture to comfort him. But he knew that these were foolish and harmful dreams. 'The gloom is inseparably part of you / You are unmoving, stern, implacable ... You only gave me fresh suffering.' And so once again he ends with the need to submit to the 'irony of life.'[76]

Grigor'ev was less prepared to submit to his employer's tyranny. At first, he had bowed to the domestic order of the Trubetskois.[77] But the regimen had soon driven him from the palazzo and into his own apartment. Apparently the princess rebuked him for not returning home before ten. He initially laughed it off, but when she did it a second time he left.[78] Though Pogodin was furious at him and after an angry letter to him broke off relations, Grigor'ev continued to tutor Prince Ivan. And he felt that the youth was making progress. When the Trubetskois returned to Moscow, as was planned for the next year, Ivan was to attend Moscow University, for which Grigor'ev was preparing him; he hoped to continue to tutor him for the first year. 'Moscow University and the society of orderly people will finally make a man out of this intelligent, highly gifted, but childish Florentine.'[79]

In late spring 1858, Grigor'ev travelled with the family to Paris. They went by sea from Livorno to Genoa, where, he noted, the portraits of Mazzini and Garibaldi on tavern walls provided an air of freedom, on to Marseilles, and by train to Paris. He arrived there with only a ten-rouble note but, determined not to fall again under the regimen of his employer's household, settled in the Hôtel Maroc, rue de Seine, for 25 francs a month. He claimed to be contented there, travelling around Paris and making a favourable impression on Trubetskoi's older brother, Nikolai, and his wife. Nikolai had converted to Roman Catholicism and was the centre of a religious circle in Paris. Grigor'ev delivered a paper to some of its members.

Unfortunately, he ran by chance into a certain Maksim Afanas'ev, whose exact identity remains unknown. He had apparently been an associate during the young editors period and worked in a wine-importing business in Moscow. According to Grigor'ev, who mentioned him a couple of times, he was an admirer of the Cossack rebel leaders Stenka Razin and Emelian Pugachev and an advocate of extreme violence. Grigor'ev had ceased writing to him previously because of his 'awful theories.' But Afanas'ev had not lost his fascination for him. Grigor'ev saw in him an exemplar of the Russian common people, more cunning than his compatriots and more disreputable than the most disreputable among the educated. Afanas'ev informed Grigor'ev that Ostrovskii was cursing him for trying to persuade him to sell one of his stories to *Russkoe slovo*. He also told him that Grigor'ev's own wife was drinking and carousing.

Whatever equilibrium Grigor'ev had achieved while abroad was smashed at once. He began to drink, in the morning alone, but was unable to get drunk. At night he dragged himself back to his lonely room after the 'orgies and all sorts of nasty things,' convinced that God had cursed him. As if on purpose, his room was decorated with a print of a Paul Delaroche painting in which Christ 'is depicted forgiving the prostitute.' After a night of drinking and debauchery, he would go to the Louvre and pray to the *Venus de Milo*, 'with surprising sincerity,' to send him a woman who would be a 'priestess' and not a 'commercial voluptuary.'[80]

In his despair, he 'stretched out his hands' to Murillo's Madonna in distant Florence. In a desperate poem he explained to her that his sins were the 'fruit of profound torment / Of a hopeless and venomous boredom / Of despair, of melancholy without end!' From the heights of her inaccessible sanctuary, she could not know 'our sinful world with its groans ... nor the torment of struggle.' He longed to join her in her eternal realm but was lost in the same darkness that surrounded his soul as well as her bright image:

> But I wander alone in the boundless darkness,
> In the darkness of melancholy, and grumbling, and anger,
> In the darkness of harsh and mutinous enmity ...
> Forgive me, my holy Maiden,
> My sins are the fruit of a hopeless sorrow.[81]

Grigor'ev's behaviour in Paris became notorious. In 1863 N.A. Potekhin, who specialized in scandal and whose brother's works had been dismissed by Grigor'ev, wrote a play, *Russians in Paris* (Nashi v Parizhe), which was published in a book entitled *Nashi bezobrazniki* (Russian Rascals). Grigor'ev appeared in the play as the character Vagabundov (the vagabond), a pun on the title of Grigor'ev's memoirs, *My Literary and Moral Wanderings* (Moi literaturnye i nravstvennye skital'chestva), which had recently begun to appear. Vagabundov was described as a wandering

Slavophile with uncombed hair cut in the Russian manner, a wedge beard, passionate speech, and a hoarse voice. Wherever he went in the streets of Paris, he attracted large crowds with his bizarre array of Russian folk costumes. Only in Italy, he complained, did people not make fun of his clothes. He was forever speechifying about the rotten West and insisted that the 'Slavic current' (*veianie*) was being felt in the whole of Europe. Whenever he spoke a foreign word, he afterward spat and searched for a Russian equivalent. He compared Paris unfavourably to Moscow, denounced all French literature as false; but then went on to label all his Russian friends traitors. After complaining about the false beauty of Western women, he went off with a prostitute.

At another party, where two of the guests, Dozhdin and Shepelev, were obvious caricatures of Pogodin and Shevyrev, Vagabundov performed a prodigious feat of drinking absinthe and then, after declaring that he would never betray his convictions, settled down to drink glass after glass of wine. Dead drunk, he accompanied himself on the piano in a 'folk song' at full volume and was eventually dragged off to his bed. At the end of the play he appeared with a sheaf of papers on which the Masonic doctrine was portrayed allegorically. Though he said that he recognized the truth of Catholicism and saw escape from his moral torment only in Catholicism (a reference to his association with Nikolai Trubetskoi's circle), he nevertheless talked about joining the Masons because he needed money and 'they do put one's affairs in order.' He expressed the view that 'to drink is to die and not to drink is to die, so that it is better to drink and die.' When the subject of debtors' prisons came up, Vagabundov knew them well and compared the *dolgovoe* of St Petersburg with the *iama* of Moscow. By the end of the play, he was so drunk that he searched wildly about the stage for his head. He was last seen asleep on the floor.[82]

Exaggerated and vicious as Potekhin's account was, it was not inconsistent with Grigor'ev's own recollections of his time in Paris. Through it all he continued to teach the young prince. He had already begun to suspect that the family's plan to return to Moscow would be abandoned, and his suspicions were confirmed in Paris. The princess herself had been intriguing against a return to Russia. Now she argued that the 'university corrupts young people.'[83] Grigor'ev's pupil himself was showing signs of rebellion against a university education.

It is perhaps a measure of the place that Grigor'ev had won for himself in the household that when the Trubetskois decided in August 1858 to return to Florence and not to Moscow, he was asked to go with them. Even the princess, who had monitored his hours in Florence, had come to cherish him. Observing teacher and pupil together in Paris's Jardin de Mabille or the Château des Fleurs, gathering places for prostitutes, she jokingly remarked that teacher, as well as pupil, needed a governor. It was even more surprising that Grigor'ev agreed to return to Italy. While visiting Rome before setting out for Paris, he had met Count G.A. Kushelev-Bezborodko, who was in the process of setting up a new journal, *Russkoe slovo* (The Russian Word). Kushelev had offered Grigor'ev the position of chief literary critic and given him 1,100 piastres (1,500 roubles) to confirm the appointment. Grigor'ev was delighted. He took half of the money and sent it to his family in Moscow. The rest he used to pay off his debts and purchase some books and prints. He also wrote to Turgenev asking him not to make the inquiries about state service on his behalf that Turgenev had promised because he now had an outlet for his writings.[84]

For all his posing about his boredom and alienation in Italy, he had grown fond of his life there. He had, by his own admission, become attached to his pupil and in Paris, in anticipation of the return, persuaded Princess Trubetskoi to buy a supply of books on history, political economy, and classical literature in the hope that he could still instill some knowledge into his pupil in the 'interstices of the prince's licentiousness and worldly distractions.' He had come to love '*cara Italia, solo beato*' as his fatherland. Russia had offered and still offered nothing to him. He once more expected to live in his own apartment in Florence and 'naively intended to read lectures,' encouraged as he was by his success in the Trubetskoi circle in Paris.

But it was not to be. At a dinner at the Palais Royal, in aristocratic company, he drank 'like a tradesman.' He knew that the princess would not forget it, though she said nothing at the time and the others made a joke of it. But he sensed that he had fallen, certainly in his own eyes. On what was supposed to be one of his last nights in Paris, 29 August, he went on a spree with some of Russia's young 'demagogues.' When he woke up the next morning, with a prostitute in the bed,[85] he remembered that it was Alexander Ostrovskii's name-day. All his love for Russia and his hopes for its people flooded over him. The Trubetskois had already left for Turin where Grigor'ev was to meet them. In an instant he had written to them that he intended to return to Russia.

The present difficulty was how to scrape together enough funds to get back to St Petersburg. Hoping to scrounge some money from someone, he lingered in Paris for two more weeks. Continued dissipation ate further into his reserves, so at last he departed for Berlin, hoping to sell there some books and prints that he carried with him. The evening of his arrival was cold; he had only his light Parisian jacket and, by that time, possessed not even a penny. He remembered, however, the Roter Adler, an inn where on his way to Italy he had stayed and met P.A. Bekhmetev, who later served as a model for Chernyshevskii's Rakhmetov in his novel *What Is to Be Done?* There the owners recognized him at once and provided him with a warm room, unlimited tea from the *Thee-maschine*, and strong Russian cigarettes. 'The enemy of all comforts, I understand comfort only as tea and tobacco.'

From this haven he petitioned Kushelev-Bezborodko in St Petersburg to send him more money. It took three weeks to come, ample time during which to be disgusted, in good Russian patriotic fashion, by Berlin. He returned to St Petersburg in October 1858.

PART THREE

Organic Criticism

7

True Realism
1858–1860

Cosmopolitanism is nonsense;
the cosmopolitan is a cipher; ...
Outside nationality there is neither
art, nor truth, nor life.

Ivan Turgenev, *Rudin*

In his 'Short Service Record,' which he wrote in debtors' prison in September 1864, shortly before his death, Grigor'ev described his return in October 1858 to hated St Petersburg as 'brilliant': 'At last they were prepared to grant me patent to the title of super-critic (*ober-kritik*).'[1] In the same month, he wrote optimistically to Protopopova that he was back and hoped to 'act, act, and act.'[2] For all his bravado, he was already wallowing in self-doubt and anticipation of failure. A. Druzhinin had reported to Ostrovskii at the end of September: 'I have received a letter from Ap. Grigor'ev which is full of all sorts of nonsense – it seems that he is utterly washed up and nothing of use will come from him.'[3]

But at first all went well. In December, Druzhinin informed Ostrovskii that he saw Grigor'ev often and added, with reference to Grigor'ev's recent involuntary exile from and then return to the world of journalism, that since 'the whale had disgorged him from its belly, he is conducting himself meekly.'[4] The fruits of his ruminations and writings while abroad began to pour out in a series of critical articles in *Russkoe slovo* (The Russian Word), which Grigor'ev himself designated his 'course' in organic criticism. The response was gratifying. According to Grigor'ev, the censor (and novelist) I.A. Goncharov expressed his admiration for the articles. He also noted that the Dostoevskii brothers, Fedor and Mikhail, N.N. Strakhov, Dm. Averkiev, and others had surprised him with their high opinion of his work. One admirer even learned whole passages by heart. Grigor'ev was euphoric, convinced that the day of his ideas had at last dawned.[5] He was all the more sure that his fortunes had changed when Nekrasov purchased his cycle of sonnets *Venezia la Bella* (Venice the Beautiful) for *Sovremennik* (The Contemporary) as well as his translation of Byron's 'Parisina.'

Success was to be short-lived; Grigor'ev's meekness was not destined to last for long. The editor-in-chief of *Russkoe slovo* was his old friend from student days Ia.P. Polonskii. He had recommended Grigor'ev as chief literary critic to Count Kushelev-Bezborodko primarily at the urging of A.N. Maikov, who, in a letter to Polonskii on 2 March 1858, had said 'I am writing to you about Apollon Grigor'ev not because I see in him a second Belinskii and not because he is well disposed towards me but because he is the best of the contemporary critics and the only one who loves art with a pure heart.'[6] With his fanatical faith in the correctness of his own views, Grigor'ev had long ago proven that he was difficult to work with. In particular, he refused to submit his articles to editing, and Polonskii, as editor-in-chief, was determined to see to it that at the very least the copy that appeared in the journal should be comprehensible. By the New Year, the two men were at daggers drawn. Turgenev wrote to Fet on 16 January 1859, 'Grigor'ev is drinking without stopping and Polonskii looks like a field turned under by a plough a week ago.'

The problem, according to Turgenev, was a phrase in an article that Grigor'ev had written about the historian S.M. Solov'ev: 'Every person in our time experiences two formulae at the same time' (Kazhdyi chelovek v nashe vremia razom perezhivaet dve formuly). Polonskii wanted to know what it meant; Grigor'ev, who believed that the meaning was evident, regarded such questions as tantamount to censorship. The two men were canvassing their acquaintances for their opinion about the clarity of the phrase; Turgenev jokingly told Fet that he was convinced that Tolstoi would affirm that it was perfectly clear to him.[7]

Among the radicals, a plot to take over *Russkoe slovo* was forming. In April 1859, G.E. Blagosvetlov, who was to become the editor of the journal in 1860 and turn it into an instrument for the nihilist views of Dm. Pisarev, wrote to V.P. Popov from France: 'Of course nothing could be stupider than to hire on a toady in criticism like Ap. Grigor. But what is Polonskii thinking of? Why don't others protest? ... I am afraid of omissions, corrections and changes in my articles were they to pass through the editing of Ap. Grigor'ev.'[8] To Polonskii himself, Blagosvetlov wrote on 1 May 1859 that he was interested in participating in *Russkoe slovo* but 'suddenly I find out that Apollon Grigor'ev, who has been called a literary lackey [by Kavelin in *Russkii vestnik* (The Russian Messenger)] is a sworn Slavophile and a man positively harmful to the journal because of his Moscow-Viazemskii convictions, predominates in *Russkoe slovo*.' He refused to publish a line in the journal while Grigor'ev 'reigns' there. 'After all, our tendencies are somewhat different.'[9]

Both Grigor'ev and Polonskii threatened to resign over the stalemate, but it was Polonskii's offer that Kushelev-Bezborodko accepted. The last issue of *Russkoe slovo* in which all three names – Grigor'ev, Kushelev-Bezborodko, and Polonskii – appeared on the masthead as co-editors was June 1859. Many years later, Polonskii expressed a lifetime of frustration at Grigor'ev's contradictory nature: 'I remember Grigor'ev preaching submission to the Russian knout and singing the student song which he set to music: "Long the landlords have oppressed us, beaten our backs"! I remember him believing in neither God nor the devil – and in church on his knees praying himself into a bloody sweat. I remember him as a sceptic and a mystic, I remember him as my friend and my enemy – as the most honest of people and flattering Count Kushelev for his puerile articles!'[10]

On Grigor'ev's recommendation, A. Khmel'nitskii was named to be co-editor with Grigor'ov. But Khmel'nitskii soon proved to be even more intractable than Polonskii. In July a quarrel about the use of the names of certain Slavophile writers flared up between the two men. Grigor'ev wrote to Kushelev-Bezborodko in Paris demanding an explanation. By that time the radicals were increasingly influencing Kushelev, who did not reply. Later Grigor'ev learned that Khmelnitskii had been put in charge of all editorial matters. Grigor'ev resigned.

As the tensions around *Russkoe slovo* mounted, Grigor'ev again resorted increasingly to alcohol for solace. In spite of his claim in January 1860 to Protopopova that he was drinking moderately despite being surrounded by 'drunks who believe in life,' it is apparent that he had been drinking heavily since his return from the West.[11] In February 1860, for example, Turgenev reported to Tolstoi that Grigor'ev was imbibing steadily.[12] So were many of his friends. In his memoirs, P.D. Boborykin recalled disapprovingly that there were never so many alcoholics and drinkers among writers as during the period of the emancipation of the serfs and social reform of the late 1850s and the 1860s. He claimed that Kushelev-Bezborodko had, under the auspices of *Russkoe slovo*, gathered together a number of known drinkers, including Grigor'ev and the poet L. Mei. The count more or less kept an open house at his palace in St Petersburg, and the regulars permitted themselves all kinds of drunken disorders in his drawing-room. Boborykin saw it as exploitation and compared the count to an old *barin* (gentry landlord) who fed and gave alcohol to the literary brotherhood as if its members were serfs, in order to command their labour.[13]

Throughout much of this period, Grigor'ev was ill, both 'physically and spiritually.' To Protopopova he complained that the chaos of his life was incompatible with work.[14] Though he had been briefly reunited with his wife after he returned from Italy, she had not accompanied him to St Petersburg. Early in 1859, on one of his prowls through the brothels of the capital, he met Mar'ia Fedorovna Dubrovskaia. In a further instalment of his continuing novel *Odyssey of the Last Romantic* (Odisseia poslednego romantika), a lengthy poem called 'Along the Volga: A Diary without Beginning and End' (Vverkh po Volge. Dnevnik bez nachala i bez kontsa), written in 1862 in Orenburg, Grigor'ev analysed his relationship with Mar'ia Fedorovna.[15] She was the daughter of a schoolteacher from the northern town of Ustiug, who, filled by her mother with romantic notions and ambition but deprived by her drunken father of the opportunity to acquire any useful knowledge, had fled to St Petersburg in search of her fortune. There she fell first into destitution and then into prostitution. Grigor'ev removed her from the brothel and established her in separate quarters in his boarding-house, from which apparently she continued to ply her trade during the day.

At first he did not seek a sexual relationship with Mar'ia Fedorovna, though he was physically attracted to her. He claimed that he paid no personal attention to her relationships but tried to counsel her as a friend that she could not carouse for ever, youth would not last, and she ought to seek marriage. At that time Grigor'ev had money, which he spent freely. He was also consorting with students at the university. Ostrovskii and Fet, he reported to Protopopova, frequently reproached him for his student connections. But he excused his behaviour on the grounds that he refused to allow himself to get old.[16] Polonskii, it will also be recalled, remembered Grigor'ev in this period for his participation in the radical song-making of the students.

At that stage, Grigor'ev later recorded, he loved only dissipation and lived solely for the moment. Love was for him the memory of Olga Alexandrovna Mel'nikova; he wanted freedom from all binding relationships. But Mar'ia Fedorovna was apparently drawn to him and his circle of young friends; in spite of himself, he in turn increasingly found himself wishing to attract her while avoiding exploiting whatever gratitude she felt toward him. He noticed that when he returned home late there was usually a light in her room; once he went to her door, she received him, and they kissed.

After that, he often returned late, drunk, and flung himself on her sofa. Finally they confessed their love for each other and began a stormy relationship. Unlike his previous love affairs, which he idealized, this one was built squarely on passion. Pogodin denounced it as purely carnal and without moral foundation. Grigor'ev replied that his old mentor knew passion 'only by rumour' and pointed out that his distinction between carnal and moral love was 'absurd.'

In December 1859 Mar'ia Fedorovna bore a child. By this time Grigor'ev was again impoverished, and it was winter. In 1862 he recollected the scene in a letter to Strakhov: 'There was a time during the winter of 1859 in December – a poor woman, not yet recovered from labour, lay on a bed in my cold, unheated apartment in the house of Longinov, and in another room moaned an ill and dying child without a wet nurse, and the good, generous Evgenii Edel'son appeared to me as the spokesman for family responsibilities. He … had come to advise me to give all this up, was surprised that I had not taken from the mother the first fruit of her first ever human attachment and tossed it into a foundling home.'[17] In the same letter he recalled another scene in which, in order to provide Mar'ia Fedorovna with some money, he sold his own household goods. She went berserk, smashed the windows of the apartment, called the police, and accused him of violent behaviour toward her and of stealing her from her parents. She claimed that Grigor'ev had left her without a kopek. The authorities were bewildered, since she had the proceeds of Grigor'ev's sale in hand.[18]

Grigor'ev wanted to divorce his wife but was frustrated by the strict laws of the church, which made that procedure both difficult and fraught with future consequences for anyone who might wish to remarry. In a letter to Pogodin in September 1861 he complained that 'in any other country, the Church and the state would long ago have freed me from this noble lady [*barynia*], and even in our Fatherland if only she would on her side bring a complaint against me we will still see a *result. We have nothing to lose.* For many reasons I am so truly and simply disillusioned with the delights of this world, that be it the penance of a monastery or exile to a colony I will take it with great indifference; but will she?'[19]

Grigor'ev's flirtation with solvency during his editorship of *Russkoe slovo* was short-lived, and he was soon in serious financial difficulties once again. The actor I.F. Gorbunov, a friend of Grigor'ev's, reported to Ostrovskii that when Grigor'ev had left the journal in late summer 1859 'Khmel'nitskii had alerted all his creditors and now God knows what will happen. He appears to be happy but I do not think that all will come out well for him.'[20] There was even some suggestion that Grigor'ev had stolen some money intended for P.L. Lavrov, who had contributed an article to *Russkoe slovo*. By the time the sum was to be paid, Grigor'ev and Khmel'nitskii had already parted, and each man accused the other of not paying the writer. Lavrov, for his part, declared that he did not trust Grigor'ev.[21]

In an attempt to get work after being dropped from *Russkoe slovo*, Grigor'ev approached P.A. Pletnev, a former editor of *Sovremennik*, asking for a meeting with him for a 'literary conversation.'[22] Nothing appears to have come of the request. In the fall of 1859, he met the young poet K.K. Sluchevskii, the editor of *Syn otechestva* (Son of the Fatherland). Early in the new year, Grigor'ev began to write a polemical feuilleton in *Syn otechestva*: 'Conversations with Ivan Ivanovich about our Contemporary Literature and about Many Other Provocative Subjects for Reflection' (Besedy s Ivanom Ivanovichem o sovremennoi nashei slovesnosti i o mnogikh drugikh vyzyvaiushchikh na razmyshlenie predmetakh), which was intended to be a continuing feature.

Ivan Ivanovich had appeared earlier in a feuilleton in *Russkoe slovo* entitled 'The Great Tragedian' (Velikii tragik). He was Grigor'ev's double, expressing the more romantic side of the writer's character. His creator called him the 'last of the romantics': 'I still love Ivan Ivanovich because he is in no way a theoretician but a man of life, because while under forty he has still retained faith in life and a thirst for life, because by the word "life" he means not the blind current of the moment but the great, inextinguishable and forever whole mystery ... Transcendentalism of a certain kind links Ivan Ivanovich and me although I can never go so boldly and completely along the path of transcendentalism as my friend ... either in life or thought.'[23] Ivan Ivanovich was the 'unnecessary man' who did not change to suit the times. Unlike his friend Ivan Ivanovich, Grigor'ev claimed that he himself was developing, influenced by the sterling examples of the changes in public opinion led by the progressive people of the day.

The feuilleton was dropped after two numbers. It failed in part because it was unpopular. But there was another reason. In 'Conversations,' Grigor'ev had praised Sluchevskii's poetry with embarrassing extravagance, and the radical press had satirized the claims mercilessly. Sluchevskii was so humiliated by the reaction that he ceased publishing poetry for several years.

Grigor'ev did manage to sell one of his most important articles in this period, 'After Ostrovskii's "Storm"' (Posle 'Grozy' Ostrovskogo), to *Russkii mir* (The Russian World) in 1860, and in March of that year he became editor of *Dramaticheskii sbornik* (Drama Miscellany). He soon abandoned his post there to pursue larger game in Moscow. Thanks to an article that he had written in *Russkoe slovo* in defence of Pushkin, M. Katkov invited him to Moscow to work for *Russkii vestnik* (The Russian Messenger), a journal from which, he had written while in Italy, he expected little because it lacked 'vital fluids.' Desperate as he was for work, he went to Moscow in April to sign a contract with *Russkii vestnik* anyway, then returned to St Petersburg at the end of the month in order to put his affairs there in order. On 1 May he sent a letter to the Society for Grants to Needy Writers and Scholars; he asked the society to lend him 800 roubles, which he would repay at the rate of 250 roubles (allowing interest of 50 roubles a year) over four years. The loan, he said, would enable him to put his tangled affairs in order and make it possible for him to work again. The society dealt with his case the following day. Though it regretted that it could not meet his request because it did not give loans, it did grant him 300 silver roubles in recognition of his 'gifts, knowledge, and the honourable tendency' of his literary work.[24] The gift enabled him to take a dacha in Poliustrov near St Petersburg for May and June.

Grigor'ev returned to Moscow to take up his duties with *Russkii vestnik* at the end of June 1860. His experience there was unproductive and unhappy. He was put to work on what he regarded as minor matters such as reports on Sunday schools and various translations. Asked to read manuscripts, he found that those which he recommended for publication were not accepted. Later he declared that only God knew why he had been invited. Perhaps it was to accuse him, he conjectured, of stealing a tenkopek piece from a table in the office, which the journal did.[25] E.M. Feoktistov reported to Turgenev that '*Russkii vestnik* has a fresh misfortune: its collaborator, A.A. Grigor'ev, has taken money in advance and then disappeared! So much for a poetic nature. ...' Turgenev replied that Grigor'ev's flight did not surprise him, but he could not understand why Katkov would have trusted him.[26]

Grigor'ev's fortunes had reached a new low. Late in September 1860 he wrote to Pogodin, his relentless conscience, in anguish: 'Oh, you stern judges of human dissipations. You are stern because you have a defined future, you do not know the awful inner life of the Russian proletariat, i.e. the Russian developed man, this life forever on the eve of poverty, on the eve of the Debtors' Prison or the Third Section, this life of the fear of Cain, the grief of Cain, the regrets of Cain!' His past, he admitted, was full of failings, and knowledge of them was a heavy burden. But the past continued to bind him hand and foot. He needed to destroy the past and get rid of his chains. He needed first freedom and then strict moral responsibility. He confessed that his circumstances could not excuse his dissipation, which he deplored with 'bitter tears' and paid for with 'hellish torments.' His actions were, however, the 'cry of a man who wants to live honourably, according to God and Orthodoxy, and sees no chance of doing so.'[27] He was convinced that he and his cause were out of step with the times. Now he more or less became Ivan Ivanovich and began to sign his articles One of the Unnecessary People; N.N. Strakhov, who had met him in the autumn of 1859, affirmed that he intended no sarcasm by it.[28]

Throughout his trials, Grigor'ev had kept alive the possibility of re-establishing *Moskvitianin* (The Muscovite). He had gone to Italy rather than take its editorship because his affairs had been in such disorder that he had neither the material nor the spiritual resources to carry out the burden of editing a major journal. He did not abandon the idea, however, and while in Italy had pestered Pogodin about selling *Moskvitianin* to him. When he decided to take up the editorship of *Russkoe slovo*, he later confessed to Pogodin, he had lost faith in *Moskvitianin* and had hoped to make a fresh start.[29] In the spring of 1860, with *Russkoe slovo* snatched from him and his failure to establish for himself a permanent place on other journals, he had made one last effort to convince Pogodin to revive *Moskvitianin*.

Late in March or early in April 1860, Grigor'ev wrote to Pogodin that *Moskvitianin* could stand successfully on a platform of *narodnost'* because nationality was an attractive idea to the young. He claimed that since meeting Strakhov in the autumn of 1859 he had attracted a circle of young friends who believed in his cause. He tried to convince Pogodin of his capacity for work and went on to list the participants whom he hoped to attract. They included some of his old collaborators, such as Edel'son and L.N. Mei, but also some new names, 'fresh, young, noble, and committed forces,' several of whom were soon to be active in *Vremia* (Time), run by the Dostoevskii brothers. The new recruits included V. Krestovskii, I. Shill, and Strakhov himself.[30]

In early August 1860, Grigor'ev informed Pogodin that he was working on a grand project that would make or break their enterprise. He reproached Pogodin for scolding him and pointed out that though he had twice been in Moscow since returning from Italy, he had not dared to approach his mentor. And he asked Pogodin whether he was willing to 'take a vital and active part with your articles, advice, and Slavic connections in the new enterprise' that he was organizing.[31] On 21 August he reported that the fate of the new enterprise would be decided by mid-September. His confidence, however, was waning. In the same letter he told Pogodin that he had offered to teach in the Smol'nyi Institute (a girls' school in St Petersburg founded by Catherine the Great) and expected to be hired. He went on to complain about having to live in a country that was too immature to provide a legitimate niche for any honourable conviction and to declare his unhappiness in the capital, where a year's residence had reconciled him neither to the city nor to its literary men. But, he wrote, 'I nevertheless believe that God will in the end give me a task that is to my liking or send the tranquility of death.'[32]

The attempt to revive *Moskvitianin* was interrupted by Grigor'ev's brief employment at *Russkii vestnik*. With that experiment going badly by October 1860, Grigor'ev was ready to try again with his old project, especially since Pogodin had been sympathetic to his earlier approach. Along with B.N. Almazov, Grigor'ev met Pogodin several times in September and October. The fruit of those meetings was a petition to the Main Censorship Administration on 15 October to revive *Moskvitianin* under Grigor'ev's editorship. Anticipating problems, Grigor'ev, on 24 October, wrote to A.N. Maikov and to P.A. Pletnev asking them to do whatever they could to persuade the Censorship Administration to approve the transfer. But it was not to be convinced. It refused the request on the formal grounds that Grigor'ev was already editor of *Dramaticheskii sbornik*. P.A. Viazemskii wrote privately to Pogodin that the problem was not *Moskvitianin* but its proposed editor and suggested that Pogodin reapply under a different editor.[33] Pogodin followed his advice and approached B.I. Ordynskii, someone Grigor'ev had already rejected as a collaborator. Ordynskii replied that though it was important to attract the young to their movement, the path of Almazov and Grigor'ev was not the right one. He argued that the 'young editors' had done a lot of harm to *Moskvitianin*. And he added that Grigor'ev inspired in him a superstitious fear because every journal that he was associated with had failed.[34]

Grigor'ev took his shattered hopes hard. Again in despair, he spent much of November wandering from friend to friend in Moscow in search of drink and a bed.[35] In late November or early December he returned to St Petersburg. There his luck improved, and he began to write for the journal *Svetoch* (The Beacon), which was edited by A.P. Miliukov.

Grigor'ev's accustomed pessimism was not typical of the mood of the literate Russian public in the late 1850s. The death of Nicholas I a few months before the end of the Crimean War in autumn 1855 and the unfavourable outcome of the war itself had transformed the relationship between government and society. Under the new tsar, Alexander II, the government was pledged to undertake major reforms. At the head of the list was emancipation of the serfs, but the magnitude of the effect of bringing for the first time several million people into the civic life of the nation presaged a whole host of related reforms. The government was particularly anxious to promote a relatively free public debate about the issues at stake during the proposed transformation. With that in mind, it liberalized the censorship laws. The result was the burgeoning of journals and newspapers in Russia as pragmatic interest groups and reforming ideologists alike began to vie to influence public opinion. The journalists and the public were enjoying themselves, and confidence in the progressive intentions of the autocracy still ran high among the progressively minded.

Liberalization of the censorship laws did not mean the end of censorship. The government invited the public to discuss such matters as terms of the proposed emancipation of the serfs, reform of the judicial system, and local self-government, but the political dispensation of a reformed Russia remained out of bounds. Publicists of all stripes did manage to discuss politics, however, in 'Aesopian language' which employed coded words and veiled analogies to other times and places.

Though his critique of the Enlightenment notion of the rights of man made him a conservative, Grigor'ev was little interested in political questions. He had long ago declared Pogodin's conservative nationalism, with its blend of autocracy, Orthodoxy, and nationality, in the context of the Westernizing direction set by Peter the Great, to be his own. His primary concern, as it had been in *Moskvitianin*, was with the development of an independent Russian literature and culture, and that was the cause he once more took up in the pages of *Russkoe slovo*.

Politics was not so easily avoided, however. Grigor'ev's powerful sense of the organicism of Russian historical and cultural development, his belief in the traditional merchant class as the principal bearer of an autonomous Russian culture, and his hostility to 'theory' inevitably implicated him with the 'conservatives.' The 'progressive' forces placed him in the 'reactionary' camp and treated him accordingly. For his part, Grigor'ev had strong views about his opponents from right to left and was prepared to engage them vigorously at the philosophical level. His formulation of organic criticism at the end of the 1850s also laid down many of the principles behind the *pochvennichestvo* (native soil movement) of *Vremia*, the journal of the Dostoevskii brothers in the early 1860s. *Vremia* soon proved itself a leading protaganist in the ideological battles of the journals in the emancipation period.

The first fruit of Grigor'ev's new labours in *Russkoe slovo*, which advanced one of the most important ideas of *pochvennichestvo* – the attack on centralization in the writing of Russian history and literary criticism – was a major review in May 1859 of the early volumes of S.M. Solov'ev's monumental *History of Russia*. Grigor'ev argued that since N.M. Karamzin's *A History of the Russian State*, historians had been preoccupied with the vast task of destroying the forms into which Karamzin had cast his nation's history. Educated in the French manner, Karamzin had not been disposed to accept Herder's concept of nationality and had produced a highly centralized, Moscow-dominated version of the Russian past. Solov'ev, in Grigor'ev's opinion, had not overcome the problems of Karamzin's history. Instead, he, too, subjected Russian history to the formula of centralization: 'The artificial, contrived, theoretical sympathy which our historian substitutes for faith in the living, national principle of life comes down to a common denominator that we from the beginning have labelled centralization.' Solov'ev's history was, to Grigor'ev, too obviously written from a Moscow office in the absence of knowledge about the regions and their fundamental differences. He objected to Solov'ev's contention that geography was the chief determinent of national development. Climate and geography, he admitted, had an influence, but the human soul was free to rise above such material limitations. He objected particularly to Solov'ev's view that northern peoples tended not to develop sociability, especially between the sexes, or to be suited to the arts.

Grigor'ev was equally troubled by Solov'ev's treatment of the early Slavic tribes, which, he complained, the historian regarded as no more than future material for a state. The truly national moment in Russia was, for Grigor'ev, the moment of local diversity that preceded the triumph of the central state over regional differences. Since national principles were alien to Solov'ev, that diversity appeared to him to be only a transitional moment to the unity imposed by Moscow. Finally, Grigor'ev objected to Solov'ev's view that Russian paganism was weak and easily swept away by Christianity. On the contrary, it was deeply embedded in the Russian psyche and was incorporated into Orthodoxy from the beginning.[36]

The main vehicle in which Grigor'ev advanced his philosophical position was not history, however, but 'organic criticism.' He had previously attributed 'organic criticism' to Coleridge and Carlyle and subscribed to its tenets but had not yet used the term to describe his own approach. Now he embraced the term wholeheartedly and began his 'course' on organic criticism in *Russkoe slovo* in order to explain its intricacies to the reading public. He offered what was essentially a recapitulation and elaboration of the ideas first expressed in the earlier articles 'On Truth and Sincerity in Art' (O pravde i iskrennosti v iskusstve), of 1856, and 'Critical View of the

Basis, Meaning, and Methods of the Contemporary Criticism of Art' (Krit-icheskii vzgliad na osnovy, znachenie i priemy sovremennoi russkoi kritiki iskusstva), of 1858. Grigor'ev's opponents, indeed, accused him of repeating himself or of plagiarizing whole sections from his own previous articles. The accusations were often true, but the copied passages were the continuous theoretical background to Grigor'ev's thought and usually appeared in quite different contexts than had the originals. The articles in *Russkoe slovo*, for example, focused the earlier ideas and transformed them into a theory and method of literary criticism.

Organic criticism rested on Schelling's belief in the primacy of art in bringing truth into the world, a belief that Grigor'ev had passionately embraced:

Works of art … are linked organically with the lives of their creators and that means with the life of the epoch; as living offspring, they express in themselves what is living in the epoch, often, as it were, they foretell far into the future, explain or define difficult questions without, however, in any way setting themselves the task of such explanation. Everything *new* is brought into life only by art: it alone incarnates in its creations what is invisibly present in the air of the epoch. More than that: art often senses the approaching future in advance, as a bird beforehand senses fair or foul weather.[37]

Art conditioned life, which moved eternally forward; moulded its multifarious moments into forms; and linked it to the universal ideal of the human soul. The world view of the artist was not something completely personal to the poet but was conditioned by temporal and local historical conditions. An artistic genius was a focus for the true limits of contemporary thinking, the highest development of social concepts and convictions. The genius reflected the strivings of the age but never slavishly; rather, he or she made them his or hers and reconciled their contradictions through love. The critical attitude of a genius to reality appeared hostile, but closer examination revealed that behind the indignation lay love and an eternal ideal. The world view of an artist, invisibly present in the work, reconciled the reader to the life process and explained to him the meaning of life. True art therefore was always moral. By 'moral,' Grigor'ev meant not the conditional or conventional morality but the morality inherent in the flow of life itself. 'In the heart of a man,' he quoted himself from an earlier work, 'lie simple eternal truths and they are especially clear to a nature of true genius.'[38] Since all humans shared these truths, all true works of all literary epochs had the same world view; only the colours, which expressed the time and place of the work, were different. The same note sounded, for example, in Shakespeare, Gogol', Pushkin, and Goethe. The differences among them were only in the colouring of the portrayals.

Truth therefore revealed itself first not in the reflections of the scholar but in artistic forms or 'types.' 'Love for types and the aspiration towards them are the aspiration towards life and to the living and rejection of the moribund, stale, decayed – living or logical.'[39] Types were the product of specific times, nations, and regions. The rationalists, Grigor'ev said, were wrong in supposing that a collective person called humanity existed. Only nationalities, races, families, and individuals were real. Whether the multifarious hues of nations and individuals would some day amalgamate into a single colour, he professed not to know, but such a circumstance had not yet happened. Organic criticism therefore, he concluded, correctly recognized types and their development and not the mingling of types into an undifferentiated mass. 'Every type, as something organic,' he wrote, 'is a necessary link in creation and in degenerating, regenerating or transforming itself, nevertheless lives an eternal, organic life.'[40]

The eccentricities of Grigor'ev's language here opened him up to a good deal of ridicule in rival journals, especially in *Svistok* (The Whistler), a satirical supplement to *Sovremennik*. In 'A Few Words about the Laws and Terms of Organic Criticism,' he defended the language that he had adopted as the tools of his criticism. One term that had attracted attention was 'antediluvian,' which, Grigor'ev explained, referred to works or creative talents that had expressed an early formulation, as yet incomplete, of an organic idea. He refused, he said, to call such artists 'incomplete talents.' Another was vegetale. By 'vegetale [*rastitel'nyi*] poetry,' Grigor'ev meant popular, anonymous, artless creativity, which he contrasted to personal creativity. 'Locality' [*mestnost'*] referred to the territory occupied by a particular tribe or race. By '*veianie*' (current), he was expressing his belief in certain forces at work in any age that invisibly shaped life's manifestations and expressions and which the artist sensed in the air around him.[41]

As well as noting the peculiarities of his language, Grigor'ev's critics pointed to the rambling, seemingly disjointed character of his articles of literary criticism. But the theory of organic criticism inevitably dictated the form that his articles of positive criticism took. Neither detailed plot analysis nor formal criticism was of much interest to him. Instead, since the measure of artistic genius was the sensitivity of the artist to the social and moral processes going on around him or her, Grigor'ev concentrated on the place of the artist's work in the general socio-moral development of the nation and on the artist's personal moral attitude, reflected in his or her world view, to that general development, as expressed through the psychology and attitudes of his or her characters.

That method of literary criticism made Grigor'ev's articles highly discursive. Whereas criticism based on what Grigor'ev called the 'historical view,' which considered works as steps in a development toward an ideal, pursued sequential, linear relationships among works of art, criticism arising from 'historical feeling,' which valued each work for itself and not as a step toward an external goal, precluded linear discussion of artistic phenomena. Grigor'ev therefore deliberately eschewed traditional, linear argumentation. Much of the material in an article ostensibly about Turgenev, for example, dealt with what preceded that writer, but as an organic whole and not a sequence leading to the work being discussed, with the *veianiia* that whispered to the artist's soul, and with the types in Russian life and literature with which the artist had to grapple. Grigor'ev once remarked that when he began an article, he did not know the direction it would take or how it would end.[42] There was a good deal of truth in the remark, but it should not be construed too readily as criticism or self-criticism. Instead, it reflected the non-linear, almost kaleidoscopic writing that organic criticism demanded. The organic method therefore shaped Grigor'ev's articles of functional criticism, and only the inattentive or hostile reader, as many of his contemporaries were, could, on finishing them, pronounce them incoherent.

In his 'Critical View' published in *Biblioteka dlia chteniia* (Library for Reading) in 1858, Grigor'ev had set out his thoughts on the development of historical feeling in Europe and Russia since the eighteenth century, the role of art, and the tasks of literary criticism. In his 'Look at Russian Literature since the Death of Pushkin,' in *Russkoe slovo* in 1859, he set out to apply the principles of organic criticism to Russian literature since the time of Pushkin. The determining element of Grigor'ev's applied criticism from 1859 on was the primacy that he accorded Pushkin as progenitor of the whole of contemporary Russian literature. He had recognized the centrality of Pushkin in Russian culture while in Italy; now in *Russkoe slovo* he set out to promote a cult of Pushkin. He had also announced in Italy the need he felt to be reconciled with the legacy of Belinskii; now he raised Belinskii to an eminence approaching that of Pushkin. For Grigor'ev, the two men were inseparable and were the measure of Russia's cultural future: 'The analysis of Belinskii's nature is the analysis of our critical consciousness, at least in a particular epoch, just as the analysis of Pushkin's nature is the analysis of all of the creative powers of our national personality, at least for a very long time, and readers must excuse me for my endless recurrences to Pushkin and Belinskii, to elemental force and to consciousness.'[43]

Grigor'ev's article on literature since Pushkin marked as well the continuation of his battle against both the utilitarian critics and the school of art-for-the-sake-of-art, which had begun in 1855, around the time when Pushkin's collected works appeared. The utilitarians had done their best to coopt Belinskii's heritage as their own. Now Grigor'ev offered the early Belinskii – the enthusiast of Pushkin and author of the 'Literary Musings' (Literaturnye mechtaniia), written under the influence of Schelling – in support of his own position. Belinskii, he averred, was the leading representative of his age and bore in his soul all the doubts and the hopes of the era. Though he was attracted by theory, Belinskii's love of the truth had always intervened to raise him above theory. In 'Literary Musings,' Belinskii himself had contrasted the dead hand of intellect (rassudok) with the living force of reason (razum).

According to Grigor'ev, only Belinskii had understood the enormous significance of Pushkin. In 'Literary Musings' he had pointed out that Pushkin was the voice of his age and the only true voice of Russia. Grigor'ev agreed with Belinskii that Pushkin was everything to Russia:

Pushkin is the representative of everything *spiritual* and *particular* to us, everything that remains spiritual and particular to us after clashes with alien, other worlds. Pushkin is, for the time being, the only complete sketch of our national personality, a naturally gifted person who incorporates, after all possible conflicts with other particularities and organisms, everything that ought to be incorporated, rejects everything that ought to be rejected, a full and whole image of our national essence, but not yet coloured in but only sketched with contours – an image that we will for a long time shade in with colours. The scope of Pushkin's sympathies excluded nothing from his past and nothing that was or will be after him which is appropriate and organically our own.[44]

Grigor'ev contrasted Belinskii's insight into Pushkin with the dumb incomprehension or indifference that Annenkov's edition of the poet's works had elicited. Russian critics either saw no value in Pushkin, he complained, or saw only his literary-artistic significance. They missed completely his vast moral-social importance for Russia. All of the types in Russian literature since Pushkin, Grigor'ev claimed, flowed from his characters. It will be recalled that Grigor'ev first mentioned his theory of types in Russian culture in *Finskii vestnik* (The Finnish Messenger) in 1846. The early native Slavs represented the 'humble' (smirennyi) type or element in

the Russian physiognomy, and their Western Varangian rulers, the 'predatory' (*khishchnyi*) type or element. In Italy, Grigor'ev had associated these
types with characters in Pushkin. Now he placed the idea at the centre of
Russia's cultural travails in the nineteenth century. Pushkin re-created
these basic Russian types in his works. For example, Ivan Petrovich Belkin,
hero of *Tales of Belkin* (Povesti Belkina), represented the indigenous, humble side of Russian life. Belkin had reappeared in the works of Turgenev,
Pisemskii, Tolstoi, and even Ostrovskii. Belkin's type stood for simple
common sense and correct feeling. His was a meek and humble type, who
embodied the capacity of Russians to feel and understand the culture and
sympathies of other peoples. The predatory type, with its Western-oriented
frame of mind, was, in Grigor'ev's view, best exemplified in Aleko. In
Pushkin's 'The Gypsies' (Tsygany), Aleko went to wander with the gypsies, loved the gypsy woman Zemfira, and finally killed her and her gypsy
lover. The 'predatory' type had often reappeared in Russian literature since
Pushkin, notably in Lermontov and Turgenev and in Grigor'ev's own fictional works.

Grigor'ev went on in the article to place Pushkin more fully in the context of Russian historical development. Before the time of Peter the Great,
Russians had lived a spontaneous existence, not yet provoked to consciousness by conflict with other living organisms. Peter's reforms, however,
placed the old Russian type, with its elemental richness and critical common sense, into conflict with other, alien lives and a host of complex ideals.
The first response of Russian literature to the challenge of the other was
critical, as in the satirical works of Fonvizin in the reign of Catherine the
Great. Soon, however, the old elemental type was caught up in a terrible
storm and rapidly evolved.

Here Grigor'ev introduced another of his major contributions to *pochvennichestvo*. It was the idea of the universality of Russians. For it turned
out, Grigor'ev enthused, that his compatriots were sympathetic to all the
ideals reaching them from foreign climes and inimical only to those that
contradicted the basic Russian spiritual type.[45] Grigor'ev's was not a new
idea in Russia. In 1802 Karamzin remarked that, after Peter, his countrymen 'looked at Europe, so to speak, and at one glance we assimilated the
fruits of her long labours.'[46] In 1846 Belinskii had referred to the many-
sided nature of Russian nationality, which would permit it 'to adapt and
assimilate all foreign elements.'[47] Herzen, too, spoke of the 'receptive character of the Slavs' and of their 'great capacity for assimilation and adapta-
tion.' He concluded that no people but the Russian was absorbing the
thought of others while remaining true to itself.[48]

According to Grigor'ev, Pushkin embodied the whole of Russia's spiritual capacity and the complete struggle of national life was reflected in his work. Out of the struggle of Pushkin grew the outlines of the national essence. By that essence, Grigor'ev meant the essence not of Russia before or after Peter, but an organic whole, Russia as it had become after confronting other national organisms and after incorporating various elements from them. In Pushkin was the Russian physiognomy, the Russian type, which measured itself against other European types, which were also captured in his works. Nothing was excluded from Pushkin's expansive nature, neither romanticism nor rationalism, passion nor cold reflection. He justified and reconciled all of Russia's divided feelings. Pushkin never slavishly served any ideal but always emerged as himself, a completely new and special type. His Onegin, for example, was not, Grigor'ev contended, a Russian version of Byron's Childe Harold but a unique creation.[49] Gogol' had expressed a parallel view of the poet's significance as early as 1832. 'Pushkin,' Gogol' wrote, 'is an extraordinary and perhaps unique manifestation of the Russian spirit: this is Russian man in his developed stage, what he perhaps will be in two hundred years.'[50]

In Grigor'ev's opinion, Belinskii had not only understood Pushkin but had also been the only one to realize that Gogol''s role in Russian literature had been purely negative. Grigor'ev's disenchantment with Gogol' as the representative of Russian humility, which had been growing for some time, was now complete. Whereas once he had seen Gogol' as the true expression of Russian Orthodox humility, he now saw him as no more than the measure of Russian aversions – that is, as a negative force. Gogol' was incapable, he now concluded, of embodying a positive Russian ideal because he was a Ukrainian as well as a troubled and isolated artist. Gogol' himself understood his own task, which was to expose the banality of contemporary life. 'Gogol',' he now understood, 'was called to unmask the falsehood of everything that in our life was borrowed from alien lives or that, under the influence of external formalism, developed as a non-organic excrescence.'[51] Gogol' accomplished his mission through humour. Grigor'ev's understanding of the function of comedy in Gogol''s work was unchanged from his earlier view. Humour arose from love and was the appropriate response of the artist to deformities and contradictions in the reality around him.

Having established the centrality of Pushkin in the evolution of the nation's culture, Grigor'ev turned in a four-part article, 'Turgenev and His Activity: On "A Nest of Gentlefolk,"' which ran from April through

August 1859, to the Russian writers of his own day. True to his belief that every great artist was the representative of the age and place in which he created, Grigor'ev conducted his discussion of Turgenev on the premise that 'the analysis of Turgenev's activity is ... the analysis of our whole epoch with the majority of its processes.' Grigor'ev believed that Turgenev, with his highly sensitive, artistic nature, engaged in his writings most of the types sketched out by Pushkin and elaborated by others since him. Turgenev, unlike Pushkin, was not, according to Grigor'ev, a genius. He was unable to prophesy the future and define its limits; but his artistic nature responded to all the trends of his time. So in Turgenev was reflected the literary map of Russia, which included, in Grigor'ev's terminology, Lermontovian romanticism, sentimental romanticism, sentimental naturalism, and idyllic populism.[52]

Turgenev began with the Lermontovian type, embodied originally in Pushkin's Aleko, the proud, hot-headed individualist represented in Turgenev's early work by Vasilii Luchinov, the hero of the poem 'The Landlord' (Pomeshchik). The type repelled Turgenev. Having elaborated it in 'The Landlord,' he mercilessly satirized it in 'Hamlet of Shchigrovo District' (Gamlet Shchigrovogo uezda). In *The Diary of a Superfluous Man* (Dnevnik lishnego cheloveka), he further exposed the 'moral weakness' and 'spiritual impotence' of the type.

Having temporarily disposed of the egoist, Turgenev turned to the portrayal of the simple and artless type in *A Hunter's Sketches* (Zapiski okhotnika). But the egoist re-emerged in *Rudin*. But *Rudin*, said Grigor'ev, turned out to be more than an attack on a type. Rudin, for all his futility, proved attractive to readers; in his portrait, Turgenev legitimized the type of the superfluous man, again first exemplified in Pushkin's Evgenii Onegin. And so the moral process in Pushkin that pitted the brilliant egoism of an Onegin against the simplicity, common sense, and spontaneity of a Belkin was recapitulated in Turgenev's artistic development.

Turgenev's latest creation was *A Nest of Gentlefolk* (Dvorianskoe gnezdo), which Grigor'ev judged to be incomparably better than anything else that had appeared in literature in the last two years, with the exception of Ostrovskii's play *A Protégé of the Mistress*. But he also judged it to be unfinished or sketchy. The novel was conceived as a huge canvas; to succeed, it had to bind the characters and story to the larger, unique world of the gentry and the region. But Turgenev, Grigor'ev declared, did not believe in the possibility of achieving his original conception. Ostrovskii, too, lacked faith in the realization of his great conceptions. The reason for their inability to attain their ideal was that the age in which they wrote was one of great potential but also one lacking in scope for action. It aroused artists to grand ideals but condemned them to the disillusionment of hopes unfulfilled. The failure of Turgenev and Ostrovskii demonstrated that the social question and the artistic psyche were intimately intertwined.

The hero of *A Nest of Gentlefolk*, Lavretskii, Grigor'ev continued, was the last word in Turgenev's struggle with the Lermontovian type of passions and extremes that had so disturbed and provoked him. Lavretskii was the fullest expression of his protest on behalf of the good, the simple, the humble against the predatory, the overly passionate and intense. Grigor'ev located the source of that protest, too, in Russian social reality. In a passage reminiscent of Herzen, he pointed out that in Russia a thought once uttered was immediately given a practical application. Every trend became a religion, and ideal and reality, thought and life were united. Books were not merely objects of study or amusement but were converted into flesh and blood. Such intensity led to a reaction against thought.

Turgenev's Rudin had protested against reality, but his was a futile struggle. Lavretskii, on the contrary, achieved real humility because he had a greater internal psychological affinity for the soil that produced him and the environment that shaped his first impressions. In other words, Grigor'ev concluded, the moral process achieved by Pushkin in Belkin, in which the predatory type was overcome by the humble, was again achieved by Turgenev in Lavretskii: 'Humility before the soil, before reality, rose up in his soul as the soul of a poet, not because of a purely Rudin-like or Mikhailovich-like requirement, but as an outgrowth of the soil itself, of the environment itself, of Pushkin's Belkin.'[53]

In his discussion of *A Nest of Gentlefolk*, Grigor'ev betrayed his profound distaste for liberalism. The character Panshin, he wrote, was a man of theory, who contrasted with Lavretskii, the man of life. Panshin was a reformer who believed in the abstract law and abstract justice, which, Grigor'ev avowed, were so offensive to the Russian soul. Grigor'ev believed, however, that Panshin did not clearly emerge as a type in the novel because Lavretskii, his contrast and foil, was also not clearly conceived. In Turgenev's mind, Grigor'ev believed, Lavretskii was a contrast to and protest against the brilliant, predatory type. The novelist had intended him to be a simpleton, slob, and laggard, but he turned out to be a man uniquely alive. In Lavretskii, Turgenev created not merely a protest to a type but a real type in its own right. His uncertain attitude to the type, however, caused him to confer some of Panshin's qualities as a type on Lavretskii, and some of Lavretskii's on Panshin.[54]

Lavretskii, Grigor'ev went on, was an Oblomov, the eponymous hero of

Goncharov's novel. He was real, he was Russian, he was what Peter the Great's reforms had made of Russians. He was not yet action oriented, but he was Russia's defence against the Panshin reformers or the aimless activists such as Stolz in *Oblomov*. Lavretskii displayed love for the soil, for traditions, for the native way of life. He was Russia's shield against dry practicality and dreary methodicalness. A child of the soil, Lavretskii humbled himself before it.

Grigor'ev turned next in the series on Turgenev to an analysis of Goncharov's novels *An Ordinary Story* (Obyknovennaia istoriia) and *Oblomov*. He saw Goncharov as an artistic talent who had permitted rational analysis to destroy his creativity. He denounced *An Ordinary Story* as a contrived development of a theory prescribed in advance, not a living product of life. Its hero, Petr Ivanovich Aduev, was merely the embodiment of a particular point of view, the glorification of dry, lifeless practicality. *Oblomov* espoused the same point of view, though Grigor'ev judged it to be psychologically more profound and artistically superior to *An Ordinary Story*. *Oblomov* catered to a small group of people who thought that Russia's salvation lay in reconstructing the country according to some narrow theory. The hero of his time, Grigor'ev maintained, was not Stolz, nor Petr Ivanovich, and the heroine not Olga, who, if she lived to an old age, would become a repulsive woman with a 'perpetual and unfounded neurotic anxiety.' The real heroine of Goncharov's creations was Agafia Fedoseevna, an ordinary woman with whom Oblomov at the end of the novel cohabits; she was more of a woman than Olga. Goncharov's heart inclined to Oblomov and Agafia, said Grigor'ev, but his head to Stolz and Olga.[55] And the persecutors of Oblomovism attacked Oblomov, and his predecessors in Russian literature – Onegin (Pushkin), Pechorin (Lermontov), Beltov (Herzen), and Rudin (Turgenev) – in the name of Stolz.

Turgenev did not follow the path of theory as had Goncharov. He loved, trusted, doubted, execrated, and aspired on behalf of the entire age. He gave himself over to every enthusiasm: 'What was revealed in *A Nest of Gentlefolk*? All the intellectual life of the post-Pushkin age, from its hazy origins in the Stankevich circle to the shrill questions asked by Belinskii, and from Belinskii's shrillness to the concessions (quite important concessions) that contemporary thinking has made to life and the soil. The struggle of Slavophiles and Westernizers, and the struggle of life with theory – Slavophile or western, it's all one – ends with the victory of life over theory in the poetic formulations of the Turgenev type.'[56] That passage was a précis of the program of *Vremia* (Time) nearly two years later.

Though Turgenev had assumed a central place in Grigor'ev's pantheon of contemporary writers, he had not displaced Grigor'ev's old hero Ostrovskii. In 'After Ostrovskii's "Storm,"' which appeared in *Russkii mir* (The Russian World) in 1860, Grigor'ev reasserted his faith in Ostrovskii as the bearer of a 'new word' in Russian literature. The article was a response to N.A. Dobroliubov's assessment of Ostrovskii's play *The Storm* in a famous piece called 'The Dark Kingdom.' Dobroliubov had interpreted Ostrovskii's work to be primarily a protest against the patriarchalism, obscurantism, and petty tyranny (*samodurstvo*) of the merchants of Moscow and, by extension, of the old Russian way of life.[57] In replying, Grigor'ev attacked not only the realist approach to literary criticism of Dobroliubov, which he condemned as driven by theory, but also the aesthetic approach, which, he maintained, betrayed a dilettante's indifference to life and its fundamental questions. Art, Grigor'ev repeated, was organically joined to life and embraced life more wholly than could any theory. He agreed with Dobroliubov that Ostrovskii's work had an accusatory side in which he attacked the idiocies of life. But Ostrovskii did not write or create literary types for the benefit of Dobroliubov or Grigor'ev or anyone else except the masses; for them Ostrovskii was both poet and teacher. 'A poet is the teacher of the people only when he judges and scolds life in the name of the ideals inherent in life itself, and not manufactured by him, the poet.'[58] By 'the masses,' Grigor'ev went on, he meant not only the 'poor folk' but the whole of society.

Dobroliubov, Grigor'ev continued, traced Ostrovskii's plays back to Gogol' and tried to understand them as primarily an attack on stupidity. They were, however, the portrait of a whole world. Liubim Tortsov aroused sympathy not because he protested against injustice but because he was a mighty personality. Ostrovskii was not a satirist, he was a poet who played on all the strings of national life. His subject was not stupidity but nationality: 'Petty tyranny [*samodurstvo*] is only the integument, the froth, the comic side; it is, of course, depicted comically by the poet – and how else could it be depicted? – but it is not that that is the key to his creations.'[59] Dobroliubov, Grigor'ev reported, believed that Gogol' had not accurately depicted reality but rather had exaggerated it. Grigor'ev argued, on the contrary, that many of Gogol''s stories had no hint of exaggeration and that his talent lay precisely in the accuracy of his depiction of reality. But, said Grigor'ev, the relationship of Gogol' to life and his manner of depicting it were in any case completely different from Ostrovskii's. Ostrovskii, like Gogol', had been accused of falsifying reality; his language had been called inappropriate; and some critics denied that characters such as those in *Poverty Is Not a Vice* existed in life. '[This] dissatisfaction with the jargon of the dramas of Ostrovskii was closely related to dissatisfaction with the very way of life depicted by him.'[60]

Between 1847 and 1855, Grigor'ev continued, Ostrovskii had created a national theatre. He did not initiate the search for nationality but defined it more clearly, precisely, and simply. His understanding of it was not, however, final. In defining nationality in this article, Grigor'ev resorted to the broad and narrow definitions of *narodnost'* that he had developed in earlier pieces. Literature was national in the broad sense when it reflected in its point of view the outlook on life peculiar to the whole nation as precisely defined with and artistically expressed in the leading classes; national types varied but they all shared an essence that all understood. The form of literature corresponded to the national understanding of beauty, and its language was the language of the people and not of a caste or local dialect. Ostrovskii was national, Grigor'ev maintained, in that broad sense.

In the narrow sense, literature was national when it attempted to educate the masses or to teach them morals, concepts, and language. It was merely pedagogy or anthropology. A good example, Grigor'ev suggested, was the work of D.V. Grigorovich, who sought to be a Russian Georges Sand in his attitude to the peasants but who had no real knowledge of the national way of life or an ear for the people's language. Dobroliubov, he concluded, wished to make Ostrovskii's plays serve that narrow definition of nationality.[61] For Grigor'ev, in contrast, the 'dark kingdom' was not merely patriarchy, though it was that in part, but a profound place, the darkness from which the national creativity erupted in the same way as the creativity of Murillo or Beethoven 'volatilized' from the dark depths of their souls.

Grigor'ev next turned in his article on Ostrovskii to an attack on the aesthetic critics. The time in which a work of art could be considered a luxury had long passed. There was no such thing as art-for-art's-sake. Such a phenomenon could appear only when the consciousness of the few was separated from that of the nation. Life, he pointed out, demanded solutions to the questions that it posed. Those solutions were shouted out in a variety of voices, voices of the soil, of regions, of nationalities. True art therefore was always national and democratic. The poet was the voice of the masses, of nationality, of the locality in which he wrote, the spokesman for the great truths and great secrets of life, the bearer of words that served as keys to the riddles of 'epochs – organisms in time, and nations, organisms in space.'[62] Theory was never greater than the sum of understanding achieved in the past and so was always true only in relation to the past. But the past was a corpse, rapidly left behind by the forward-moving current of life. Theory derived laws from particular data and wanted to force life into those laws. But such laws were viable only in a world without creativity. It was necessary to love life; without humility before life, the individual would always be in a false position relative to it. The primary theme of Grigor'ev's poetry – struggle to submit to the irony of life – had now become explicit as well in his literary criticism.

Writing in *Svetoch* (The Beacon) in 1860, Grigor'ev returned to the theme of morality and art that he had first raised in 1856 in *Russkaia beseda* (Russian Conversation). The earlier article, he said, had been in embryo and in order to live needed life support. He pointed out that art and morality had been separated in contemporary life and needed again to be reconciled. He hastened to add that he did not mean, as had the reactionary editors of *Maiak* (The Lighthouse) in the 1830s, the subordination of art to a narrow moralism. Instead, he maintained, as in his earlier piece, that art provided the highest earthly revelations of the eternal. Neither the advocates of art-for-art's-sake nor those who saw in art a slavish reflection of life grasped the meaning of artistic creativity. Art was free: 'Art is an organically conscious response to organic life, as a creative force, and as an activity of creative force is not and cannot be subordinated to something conditional, including morality, and should not be judged or altered by anything conditional even be it morality.'[63]

Art did not learn from morality, but morality from art. That was not, Grigor'ev asserted, as 'immoral' a position as the theoreticians of all schools thought. By 'morality,' most people meant a conventional expression of the concepts of their own society. Social, conventional morality functioned as a kind of Inquisition that pushed aside true morality and victimized and slandered people. It forced the noble fighters for ideals, the defenders of unconditional morality, into an apologia for the fallen and a protest on behalf of the slandered. Unconditional morality was either negative, as in 'Thou shalt not kill,' or positive, as in 'Love thy neighbour.' An art that recommended immorality, that encouraged humanity to kill or to steal, could not, in Grigor'ev's opinion, exist. Art therefore was a corrective to conventional morality, not its agent. Art had answered puritanism with Shakespeare and petty-bourgeois philistinism with Byron and Sand.

In Russia, Turgenev had recently offended the defenders of conventional morality with *On the Eve* (Nakanune). Grigor'ev judged that work to be weak. It had set for itself two problems. The first was the psychological and poetic problem of depicting the meeting of two passionate beings; the other was the social question of whether Russia could have heroes, and, if so, whether its heroes were capable of love. Though Turgenev achieved both tasks well separately, in Grigor'ev's view he had failed to unite them into a whole. The Bulgarian hero, Insarov, was an isolated figure and not credible because the novelist had failed to surround him with his own countrymen, who in their devotion to him would have given him depth. Elena, who fell in love with him, was too limited a portrayal of Russian woman. She represented a privileged and advanced part of society. Turgenev had failed to ask himself about Russian women outside that narrow circle. In Russian literature, Grigor'ev noted, there were very few full female characters. Pushkin's Tat'iana, Mar'ia Andreevna of Ostrovskii's *The Bride* (Nevesta) and Liubov' Alexandrovna of Herzen's *Who Is to Blame?* (Kto vinovat?), along with Turgenev's Liza in *A Nest of Gentlefolk*, were the sum total. The last-named was really a replica of Pushkin's Tat'iana. And of these characters, only Tat'iana was, in Grigor'ev's opinion, the full expression of Russian women. Dostoevskii was to echo that view exactly many years later in his famous Pushkin speech of 1880.

It was, said Grigor'ev, Turgenev's portrayal of family life in *On the Eve* that offended the public. Pursuing one of his favourite themes, Grigor'ev pointed out that in the 1840s Russian literature had been highly critical of the Russian family and most of the reading public had sympathized with that criticism. Then, in the 1850s, a reaction had set in. Literature began to portray reality more objectively and even began to sympathize with the Russian family principle. In his early plays, Ostrovskii had poeticized familial and folk principles, in opposition to the protest of the 1840s. The favourable portrayal of the family had not, however, occurred because it was suddenly found to be good or had miraculously improved. Approval of the family was merely part of a larger struggle to discover the nation's ideals. Life now had to move, however, from the realization of the ideal in art to the victory of the ideal in life:

Only those who, aspiring to reach new shores, boldly burn their boats behind them are capable of bearing witness to the truth of any moral fact and of going beyond it, of going forward, – and the unsophisticated, thousand-headed child called the masses instinctively goes steadfastly and inexorably forward. The priests want always to turn thought back for the simple reason that there is a warm and honourable corner for them. Timid moral philistinism, in the name of self-preservation, hides behind the skirts of priestly costumes, just as in the name of faith in life the masses aspire ahead instinctively.[64]

And so the slavery and mire of the old family life continued to be exposed as well during the 1850s, most notably in S.T. Aksakov's *A Family Chronicle* (Semeinaia khronika). Ostrovskii, too, returned to that tack in his later plays. And in *The Storm*, he fully expressed his protest against the family's disorders. *The Storm* and Turgenev's *On the Eve* offended the defenders of the status quo, who had been temporarily appeased by the earlier poeticization of family life.

In a second article in *Svetoch*, published in early 1861, Grigor'ev returned to a related theme – realism and idealism in art. Realism was, in his view, the literary expression of the historical view. The realist depicted reality either in the absence of any ideal or from the point of view of an arbitrary ideal derived not from life but from theory. Since the deaths of Byron, Pushkin, Lermontov, and Mickiewicz, he said, idealism had passed out of art and everyone demanded realism in the depiction of life. Not, he pointed out, that the previously listed artists had failed truthfully to depict reality in their art as well. Grigor'ev detected three kinds of contemporary realists: those who depicted the world from the vantage point of the bureaucrat or the reformer, like Goncharov's Stolz; those who viewed everything sceptically and fell into moral apathy, and those who looked at reality from the viewpoint of the provincial administrator.

Among the realists were many talented writers, but all their works were accusatory and all were written as a foil on behalf of certain civic or social objectives. Such realism, in spite of public demand, did not finally satisfy the reader. And so true poets such as Turgenev, who possessed an ideal, continued to attract readers. Grigor'ev agreed that realism in form was essential in the present age and that its prevalence represented one of the victories of modern literature. But the real issue, he insisted, was realism not of form but of content and of the artist's attitude to life.

In order to define contemporary realism, Grigor'ev compared Turgenev and Pisemskii. Turgenev was, he granted, a realist of form, but in content his work was the sole surviving representative of the poetic element of an age now past. Pisemskii was a realist of content and of attitude to life. Though not devoid of poetic elements, his work was obsessed with realism. His realism was rooted in Gogol''s attack on the banality of the banal man, which in Gogol' was raised to a higher, though still negative, level, by humour. In the young Dostoevskii, Grigor'ev noted in passing, the same realism had turned into the 'moan' of sentimental naturalism. Pisemskii, perpetuated Gogol''s protest against the false and contrived, but without the humour. His weakness was that his ideal was that of the petty gentry and provincial bureaucrat. He identified with the life that he depicted and analysed so conscientiously, but his protest against it was limited by the narrowly conditional social ideal that flowed from his very attachment to it. Ostrovskii, whose ideal was national, had carried Pisemskii's types further and analysed them more deeply. Pisemskii believed not in the possibility of national development but only in the victory of his narrow ideal.

Pisemskii was therefore a follower of Gogol' to the extent that he ruthlessly exposed every lie and falsehood, a trait that he shared more or less with all writers of the period, but especially, in Grigor'ev's view, with Ostrovskii and Tolstoi. All lies, Grigor'ev maintained, were exposed in the name of some ideal. Gogol' exposed falsehood in the name of the European ideal of the beautiful soul. He was destined never to grasp Russia's national ideal. Ostrovskii carried Gogol''s comedy forward because he truly expressed the Russian national ideal. Not so Pisemskii and Tolstoi, who perpetuated the purely negative realism of Gogol'; neither had a defined ideal with which to judge reality apart from reality itself.

Turgenev, said Grigor'ev, was the opposite of Pisemskii. He was the last representative of the 'gentleman's brand' of literature, educated, secure, and highly developed. Like Lermontov, Turgenev was hostile to reality, but whereas Lermontov's hostility was angry, Turgenev's was melancholic. What distinguished him from Pisemskii was that he criticized reality in the name of an ideal and not a program. In his writings, two principal types emerged. The first was proud, bold, and predatory; the second, cowed by the environment or by fate, shy, and hesitant. The first was Lermontovian, and the second derived from Pushkin's Belkin. These two views of life clashed in Turgenev. One expressed the experience of an upbringing on foreign ideals; the other that of being nurtured on the soil of reality. Turgenev had moved gradually toward the poeticization of the cowed and humble man. The clash of the two types exposed the inadequacies of both. From the resolution of those inadequacies a new type emerged, planted firmly in the soil in which he was born and raised – Lavretskii.

Turgenev placed his characters in a general milieu where they were free to develop. The realists, on the contrary, placed their characters in a narrow, practical milieu that imposed certain 'unavoidable requirements' on them. In the latter milieu, Turgenev's analysis of the relationships of his characters could never have been so precise, deep, and true, and their feelings would have rung less true. Depicted as they were by Turgenev, however, his characters carried the reader away and nurtured his or her soul. Grigor'ev was to return again to the issue of realism in Russian literature. Later he was to designate Turgenev's work as 'true realism'; realism as typified in this article by Pisemskii's work he renamed 'stark or naked (*golyi*) realism.'[65]

These thoughts in *Svetoch* on realism marked the end of the phase of his life that had begun with such promise with his 'brilliant' return to St Petersburg in October 1858. Though Grigor'ev had succeeded since getting back from Italy in setting out his organic criticism for the literary public, he had so far failed to establish a secure spot for himself on a major journal. Since leaving *Russkoe slovo* in late summer of 1859 he had contributed to a number of journals, but none of them offered him regular employment. *Svetoch*, a newly established journal, had provided another chance, but the fees received by Grigor'ev for the two articles he published in it were inadequate to meet his pressing need. A.P. Miliukov, the editor of *Svetoch*, whom Grigor'ev had met early in 1860, recalled that on New Year's Eve 1860 he received a note from Grigor'ev offering him two translations from Byron in return for cash. On them, Grigor'ev desperately hinted, depended whether he would spend the New Year of 1861 in jail or not. In the event, he arrived with only one poem in hand, the proceeds from which saved him from debtors' prison only until 11 January 1861.[66]

8

Native Soil and Self-Exile
1860–1862

But like a wine the sorrow of days past
Grows stronger in my soul the longer that it lasts.

Alexander Pushkin, 'Elegy'

Grigor'ev's views on art and nationality were fully formed by the time he met Fedor Dostoevskii in 1860. Even his preoccupation with the role of the 'predatory' type in Russia's spiritual odyssey, which characterized his thought from the late 1850s on, had been clearly anticipated in his articles in *Russkoe slovo* (The Russian Word) in 1859. Not only had he staked out a distinctive position with his organic criticism, but he also had developed his own critical vocabulary and imagery. In *pochvennichestvo* (the native soil movement), Dostoevskii shared most of Grigor'ev's views on art and society, Slavophilism and Westernism, Russian history and nationality. He also adopted much of Grigor'ev's vocabulary and form of expression. At a deeper level, the two men had in common a religious outlook on the nature of human suffering and on the dangers inherent in the quest of modern man to usurp God.

Their collaboration was both fruitful and tense. One point of contention was Dostoevskii's early flirtation with the nihilists, an attempt on his part to 'reconcile' all differences in a new nationality. A more profound disagreement arose over Dostoevskii's emerging messianism, a belief that Russia was destined to reconcile all the differences of East and West and renovate a dying Europe. Such messianic universalism had become as objectionable to Grigor'ev as liberal cosmopolitanism, with its notion of universal human rights. For Grigor'ev, the task of nations was to be themselves; no nation had a universal role to play. On his side, Dostoevskii found Grigor'ev to be irascible and impractical, but he greatly admired him. He made many of Grigor'ev's ideas and judgments his own, and the critic's influence was often apparent in his mature work.

Grigor'ev was still in debtors' prison in mid-February 1861 and bitterly resentful about his fate. Better, he wrote to Pogodin, that he join the camp of the radicals. They at least were all of one mind and did not betray their own kind. His own so-called allies had shown him nothing but duplicity and weakness: his father refused to relieve him financially; Edel'son preached morality at him; and Pogodin himself addressed him in a 'preceptorial tone.' He concluded on a martyr's note that the cause was more important than any single individual who served it.

In the same letter he declared that when he was bought out of debtors' prison – and, he boasted, there were still some good people who would buy him out – he was going to take up a military service post teaching in the Orenburg Cadet Corps on the southeastern frontier.[1] The 'good people' were probably the Dostoevskii brothers, Fedor and Mikhail, and their associates, for whose journal, *Vremia* (Time) Grigor'ev was already writing. It is not clear how Grigor'ev was recruited to *Vremia*. Friendship with N.N. Strakhov from the fall of 1859 and with A.P. Miliukov from early in 1860 had brought him into the orbit in which F.M. Dostoevskii began to turn on his return from exile in the last days of 1859. Vl.F. Odoevskii recorded in his diary that after Grigor'ev returned to St Petersburg following his failures in Moscow, he appeared at his apartment in a pitiable state of impoverishment late in 1860 to offer him one of his articles. Impressed by the item and sorry at its author's plight, Odoevskii recommended the down-and-out man to M.M. Dostoevskii, who hired him as *Vremia*'s chief literary critic.[2] Strakhov, who later maintained that he had written to Katkov urging him to hire Grigor'ev as the critic for *Russkii vestnik* (The Russian Messenger), also laid claim to the credit for recommending Grigor'ev to F.M. Dostoevskii when the latter attempted to recruit Strakhov to *Vremia* as literary critic.[3]

Fedor Dostoevskii had been well prepared to welcome Grigor'ev into his new enterprise. Even before he was permitted by the authorities to return to European Russia, he had been told by his old friend A.N. Pleshcheev that Grigor'ev was speaking of him 'with great sympathy.'[4] Then in March 1860, Pleshcheev wrote to Dostoevskii: '[Grigor'ev's] criticism has a lot of nonsense in it; but I know his heart to be perfect – the very best. I have always loved him as a person very much.'[5] To Strakhov's recommendation that he hire Grigor'ev, Dostoevskii replied that he too loved Grigor'ev very much and greatly desired his participation.[6] Though the invitation to join

Vremia came too late to squeeze one of Grigor'ev's articles into the first number, which appeared in January 1861, his pieces were featured regularly from March.

Grigor'ev's incarceration was not without advantages for his journalistic collaborators. Grigor'ev wrote well while in debtors' prison, whereas when at large he lazed about whole weeks, not completing promised items and refusing to 'write to order.' Once M.M. Dostoevskii told him, only half-jokingly, 'Apollon Alexandrovich, do you know what I'm thinking? You need money; I'll give you a short-term loan and put you for debt into debtors' prison and there you will write for me a worthy article. Isn't that a good idea?'[7] As A.P. Miliukov, who knew Grigor'ev well in the early 1860s, recalled, Grigor'ev occupied a privileged position in St Petersburg's debtors' prison, rather in the manner of Dickens's Mr Dorrit. The warder was a warm-hearted soul who took considerable personal interest in the city's literary fraternity, of which he saw a good deal. Grigor'ev was often permitted to leave the prison during the day, on his word that he would return in the evening. When he had a visitor he was allowed to receive him or her in his own room rather than in the common hall. All the warder asked in return was the privilege of himself being present so that he could enjoy some intelligent conversation.[8]

Perhaps on the strength of his new employment with *Vremia*, Grigor'ev was released from the debtors' prison sometime after mid-February. It is not clear why he was let out, since he still owed 400 roubles to a certain D.K. Lazdovskii, who was the person who had had him imprisoned in the first place. Now suddenly unable to locate Grigor'ev, the local police issued a notice to all home owners and apartment managers to report Grigor'ev's residence to the police at once and took measures to prevent him from leaving the city.[9] The debt must have been redeemed, however, because Grigor'ev remained free until his departure for Orenburg in May.

Grigor'ev played an important role in *Vremia* not only through his own writings, but also because he attracted to the journal a group of capable young writers who deeply admired his work. P.V. Bykov, who described himself as a 'passionate fan' of Grigor'ev's at the time, recalled the 'gallery of writers' that surrounded the offices of *Vremia*.[10] Strakhov noted two distinct groups of contributors – one coterie of young writers gathered around Grigor'ev, and another centred around F.M. Dostoevskii and Strakhov himself. The offices of *Vremia* were in M.M. Dostoevskii's house in the Malaia Meshchanskaia, and the other editors lived nearby in that somewhat undesirable section of the capital – Strakhov in the Bolshaia Meshchanskaia, F.M. Dostoevskii in the Sredniaia Meshchanskaia, and Grigor'ev in a furnished room in the Vosnesenskii Prospekt. The editors usually met at the offices at three in the afternoon to discuss policy and the latest antics of competition papers and journals. In the evenings, Grigor'ev often met his young friends in his room, while at seven F.M. went for tea to Strakhov's quarters, where he talked with the group that usually gathered there.[11]

As will be seen, differences between F.M. Dostoevskii and Grigor'ev emerged, but the centrality of organic criticism in *Vremia* was apparent to all. Dostoevskii, whose own life's journey had pointed him toward similar ideas, found in organic criticism a form and language in which to express the thoughts that had taken root in his mind during his years of prison and exile. In *Vremia*, he turned his formidable journalistic and artistic talents to making them accessible to a broad public. *Pochvennichestvo* was therefore the product of the meeting of the two men's minds and hearts, at least on a number of essentials.

Vremia was the journal of a movement that soon came to be known as *pochvennichestvo*. The native soil movement was a development of many of the ideas that had begun among the 'young editors' of *Moskvitianin* (The Muscovite) and continued in Grigor'ev's organic criticism.[12] Intelligentsia conservatism, of which *pochvennichestvo* was one manifestation, was at least in part a reaction to intelligentsia radicalism, which in the 1860s was expressed in the so-called nihilism of Chernyshevskii, Dobroliubov, and Pisarev in the journals *Sovremennik* (The Contemporary) and *Russkoe slovo*. The nihilists, particularly in the person of Pisarev but in their other leaders as well, fully represented 'scientific universalism' in its mid–nineteenth-century form. The nihilists rejected all authority, including that of science, unless it was empirically based. They looked on history as a story of oppression and traditions and institutions as the instruments of the oppressors that distorted the human personality and its relationships. They wished to subject everything to the stern test of utility and live lives of strict social service. Art, too, should serve the utilitarian aims of society, and philosophy was a mere diversion from action. Grigor'ev accepted none of the premises or the aims of nihilism.

The principal task of *Vremia*, Dostoevskii announced, was to analyse the 'nature of our time ... and, particularly, the nature of the present moment of our social life.'[13] The tools for the analysis were essentially the same as those employed by Grigor'ev in his organic criticism. Dostoevskii shared Grigor'ev's anti-rationalism and like him believed in the primacy of life over theory and abstraction. 'Idealism stupefies, captivates and kills,' he wrote, echoing earlier statements of Grigor'ev's, especially his review of

Stankevich's story 'The Idealist.'[14] Elsewhere Dostoevskii wrote, 'The mistaking of incomplete thought for complete reality – here is the root of all the errors of mankind.'[15] Abstract thought always strove to level, to set aside differences, and to reduce life to a monochrome. The *pochvenniki* aimed their criticism of the centralization inherent in abstract theorizing at the idea of universal humanity. Dostoevskii believed that humankind would attain its fullest expression only when all peoples had made their contribution to the human treasury: 'Only universal mankind can attain a full life. But mankind will attain it in no other way than by *emphasis on the unique nationality (natsional'nost')* of every people. The idea of the soil, of nationalities, is the fulcrum, *Antaeus*.'[16]

Since all peoples contributed to the totality of human life, each nation must have some ideal or principle immanent in its history. At first that ideal lived only unconsciously in the national life, but gradually it attained consciousness. Consequently, the cultural, political, and social forms and institutions of a people expressed the national ideal at its present level of development. 'Under the term soil are meant those basic and distinctive capacities of the people which are the seeds of all of its organic manifestations. Whatever the phenomenon is ... be it a song, story, custom, or a private or civil form, all these are recognized as legitimate, as having real meaning, in so far as they are organically linked to the national essence.'[17] Nations were therefore organic wholes; no manifestation of the national life was superfluous or wasted. Every stage of development was essential to the life of the whole, and no stage was merely preparatory to another. Humans and nations were in essence their past. As Strakhov wrote: 'To some degree human life has already become firmly established, has worked itself through and taken shape; it is no longer simply life; it is historical life. Mankind forms for itself a soil, a firm foothold, history. At the present time, man can no longer reject history, cannot be separate as was the first man, cannot sever his ties with the common world of humankind.'[18]

Like the Slavophiles, the *pochvenniki* stressed the peaceful relations of the social classes in Russia. Drawing on the work of the French historian Augustin Thierry, whom Grigor'ev had singled out as one of the bearers of 'historical feeling' in the West, the Slavophiles argued that the ruling classes in western Europe were originally conquerors of the people over whom they ruled and different from them in ethnic origin. That had not been the case in Russia, where social antagonisms were few. In the West, conflicts in society had to be overcome through the external compulsion of the law, whereas in Russia the native sense of fraternity guaranteed internal social unity and harmony. The *pochvenniki* shared these Slavophile views. 'The

Russian nation,' Dostoevskii wrote, 'is an extraordinary phenomenon in the history of all humankind. The character of the Russian people does not resemble the characters of all the contemporary European peoples.'[19]

On the question of the role of Peter the Great in Russian history, the *pochvenniki* departed radically from the Slavophiles, however, and followed, as had the 'young editors,' in the footsteps of Pogodin. Though the Slavophiles, with the exception of Konstantin Aksakov, did not deny the benefits of the Western education that Peter had introduced into Russia, they maintained that the tsar, by imposing rigid Western forms on learning, had excluded the possibility of a native art or science. His reforms had affected only the upper classes and left the lower classes with their native way of life and the principles of old Muscovy intact. As a result, a total state of disunity had arisen between the educated and the uneducated. The Slavophiles concluded that Peter's reforms had separated intellect and body, knowledge and life.

The *pochvenniki* believed, in contrast, that the reforms were a necessary aspect of their country's cultural development. Dostoevskii agreed with Grigor'ev about Russian universality. His compatriots, he said, 'spoke all languages, understood all civilizations, and sympathized with the interests of every European nation.'[20] Peter's reforms were merely a response to that innate Russian longing for universality. The *pochvenniki* acknowledged the great gulf that separated the educated and the uneducated in Russia and agreed that the educated had forfeited the trust of the masses, at times even incurring their hatred. But they denied that there was any fundamental rift between the two sides. Dostoevskii accepted Grigor'ev's broad definition of nationality as an organic whole, made up of elements drawn from all classes of society:

Why should nationality belong only to the common people? Does nationality disappear when the people develops? Are we, the educated, not really the Russian people? To us the opposite appears to be the case; with the development of the people, all of its natural gifts, all of its wealth develops and strengthens and the spirit of the people shines through more brightly ... We only know that we were divided by purely external circumstances. These external circumstances did not permit the residual mass of the people to follow us, thus including *all* the forces of the national spirit. We only know that we are a too separate and small part of the people and that if the people do not follow us, we will never be able to express ourselves completely ... not as we would have expressed ourselves had the whole Russian people been with us. But it does not follow from this that we have lost our national spirit, that we have degenerated.[21]

Their exposure to European civilization had broadened the outlook of the educated, but they 'did not become Europeans.' Now, they realized that they could not become Europeans but had to create a 'new form, our own native form, drawn from our soil, drawn from our national spirit and national principles.'[22] But the universality of Russians, Dostoevskii concluded, perhaps destined them as well 'to bring about the universal-human solidarity of the world.'[23]

The 'new form' would be neither the old Muscovite ideal of the Slavophiles nor the liberal or socialist ideals of the Westernizers. Dostoevskii wrote: 'We do not go to ancient Moscow for our ideals; we do not say that first everything has to be transformed in the German manner and only then can we consider our nationality to be suitable material for a future, eternal edifice. We have worked directly from what is and only wish to permit the greatest freedom of development to what is. Given such freedom of development we believe in the Russian future; we believe in its independent potential.'[24] The present era, Dostoevskii wrote, was indifferent to the quarrels of Slavophiles and Westernizers. 'We are talking about the reconciliation of civilization with the national principle.'[25] The journey into civilization that had been begun by Peter the Great had now reached its culmination in the concrete reality of the Russian soil.

Like Grigor'ev, Dostoevskii believed that Pushkin had sketched out the contours of Russia's future cultural development in his works. In 1861 he wrote, 'We see in Pushkin the confirmation of all our thoughts ... For all Russians, he is the living exposition in full artistic completeness of the Russian spirit.' Pushkin was proof that the Russian ideal was 'wholeness, universal reconciliation and universal humanity.'[26] Again like Grigor'ev, Dostoevskii rejected both the utilitarian definition of art and that of the school of art-for-art's-sake. It was wrong, he argued, to 'demand' that a work of art serve a social purpose, though it was correct to 'urge, wish, and ask' that it do so. To prescribe a utilitarian goal for art was to deprive it of its true utility. Unconstrained art was useful not just to a single society but to the whole of mankind.[27] Moreover, an inartistic work could not effectively serve a useful purpose. The greater the artistry of a work the greater was its utility: 'The fact is that art is the best means for presenting to the masses precisely that cause about which you [Dobroliubov] are so concerned, the most business-like way if you will, you who are a business-like man.'[28] And finally, Dostoevskii agreed with Grigor'ev that true art was always about the life that it was born from, the spontaneous reflection of reality: 'The important thing is that art is always faithful to reality in the highest degree, its deviations are fleeting and temporary; art is not only always faithful to reality but cannot be anything else but true to contemporary reality. Otherwise it would not be real art. The mark of real art is that it is always contemporary, urgent and useful ... Art that is not contemporary and does not answer contemporary needs cannot exist. If it does exist it is not art, it becomes shallow, degenerates, loses its force and all artistic value.'[29] Pushkin, Turgenev, and Ostrovskii, Dostoevskii concluded in 1861, could do more for Russia's development than could the political section of any of its journals.[30]

In its early months, Grigor'ev's articles occupied a prominent place in *Vremia*, functioning more or less as editorials. Though most of the ideas expressed were familiar from earlier works, the new series not only broadened and deepened his views about Russian cultural development, but also introduced an important new idea. From the time of his infatuation with Gogol''s *Selected Passages from Correspondence with Friends* (Vybrannye mesta iz perepiski s druz'iami), through the period of *Moskvitianin*, and even in the months in which he gave his course in organic criticism in *Russkoe slovo*, Grigor'ev had believed in the primacy and eventual victory of the 'humble' over the 'predatory' type in Russian development. The humble type represented for Grigor'ev the primary trait of Russian personality and nationality. Now, however, he recognized that alone the humble type could produce only stagnation and that the predatory type was an essential aspect of the full development of personality and society. In *Vremia*, he accepted for the first time the continuing necessity in Russian social development of the 'predatory' type and the preservation of at least some of its characteristics in the new nationality.

Grigor'ev had several times begun to write an intellectual and spiritual biography of Russia since the eighteenth century, but circumstances had so far enabled him to produce only a fragmentary and incomplete account. Now he seized the opportunity afforded him to develop his views on Russia's cultural growth at length. He opened his new series of articles with one called 'Nationality and Literature' (Narodnost' i literatura) and followed it with 'Westernism in Russian Literature' (Zapadnichestvo v russkoi literature), 'Belinskii and the Negative View in Literature' (Belinskii i otrizatel'nyi vzgliad v literature), and 'The Opposition of Stagnation: Features of the History of Obscurantism' (Oppozitsiia zastoia. Cherty iz istorii mrakobesiia). Two concluding articles, 'Lermontov and His Tendency' (Lermontov i ego napravlenie) and 'Our Literary Trends since 1848' (Nashi literaturnye napravleniia s 1848), were published after his return from Orenburg in spring 1862. Other articles on Khomiakov, Nekrasov, and Tolstoi reinforced and supplemented the themes developed in the series. The whole represented an insightful and, in its day, highly original account of Russia's intellectual growth from the eighteenth century to the period of the emancipation reforms. A number of Grigor'ev's insights remain the conventional wisdom of today.

The series focused on the origins, course, and consequences of the split in Russian consciousness between Slavophilism and Westernism. The rift, he pointed out in 'Nationality and Literature,' was not as many supposed readily apparent in the eighteenth century, when, thanks to the reforms of Peter the Great, Russians entered the universal life of humankind for the first time. Russians looked, on the one hand, to M.V. Lomonosov, Russia's first great scientist and educator, for the new knowledge and, on the other hand, to Prince M. Shcherbatov, a caustic, aristocratic defender of the old Russian way of life, for an old foundation on which to base the new education. The reforms therefore by no means destroyed the ties with the old Muscovite world. 'The separation of our consciousness from the pre-Petrine way of life was accomplished gradually.'[31] Russian literature bore neither a national nor a European stamp, because Russian life in the eighteenth century still contained neither one nor the other. While the rest of Europe was ruled slavishly by French thought and enraptured by Voltaire, D.I. Fonvizin, the satirist, was establishing the foundations of a Russian drama; Tred'iakovskii was studying the roots of the Russian language; N.I. Novikov, the Freemason, was publishing a collection of folk songs and stories; and even Catherine the Great was collecting Russian proverbs. Russia experienced neither the imitation of French culture nor the struggle against it that the Germans had passed through: 'With us there was still none of this – neither the negation by us of our nationality, nor a struggle for it, and the vows of the youthful companions of Klopstock before the Irininsaüle were fated to be repeated by us only after 1836.'[32]

According to Grigor'ev, the historian N.M. Karamzin, whom he described as the first real talent in Russian literature save for Fonvizin, initiated the division in life and in literature that separated the old and new. With his 'Letters of a Russian Traveller' and his sentimental novels, Karamzin introduced Russians to everything great and beautiful in the European ideal. Thanks to his great artistry, Russian moral and social life fell under the spell of that ideal. He gave Russian society its first education in morality and in so doing also bestowed on the nation's literature its didactic function.

The European ideal, which Karamzin at first held in common with his contemporary A.N. Radishchev, the radical author of *A Journey from St*

Petersburg to Moscow (Puteshestvie iz Peterburga v Moskvu), proved inef-
fective, however, in the face of harsh reality. In Russia, said Grigor'ev, an
idealist at the end of the eighteenth century could either perish like Radishchev or submit to reality like Novikov. But a third path emerged, the one
that Karamzin followed. Rather than challenging reality and being
destroyed by or accepting it, Karamzin tried to deceive it, to pretend that it
was something that it was not. He became the historian of the Russian state
and applied the western European ideal to the raw data of his country's history. He wrote that history from an entirely Western point of view and
promoted the idea that Russia had a common path with western Europe.
Karamzin imposed European forms on Russian nationality and so
destroyed its integrity. He wrote of events and historical actors not in a
manner proper to them but in a way appropriate to their putative Western
analogues. Karamzin's history became the cornerstone of national self-con-
sciousness and drew Russians into the circle of European life. Karamzin –
not Lomonosov, as Belinskii had believed – was the Peter the Great of Russian cultural awareness.

Karamzin's *History of the Russian State*, as a great poetic creation, exercised a profound influence on Russians. It was, however, a false portrait of
the past and became the source of cultural mistakes and of false literary attitudes toward nationality. Sceptics such as N.A. Polevoi tried to correct
Karamzin's view by writing a history of the Russian people. The sceptics,
however, contributed nothing positive to the understanding of Russian
nationality and succeeded only in generating the view that the nation had
no worthwhile history at all. It was only with the publication of the sources
of Russian history, which got under way in the 1840s, that the process of
destroying the false forms of Karamzin's history properly began.

On the heels of Karamzin came the great romantic poet V.A. Zhukovskii, who imposed a Western mould on Russia's poetry, just as Karamzin
had imposed one on its history. But Zhukovskii was soon followed by
Pushkin. Pushkin incorporated the whole of the nation's divided subcon-
scious – both its longing for the West and its rootedness in its own past.
'Pushkin was everything – the fundament of our spiritual life, the reflection
of our moral process, its expression, as mysterious as our life itself.'[33] It was
therefore not surprising that on his death a division into two camps took
place.

In his 'Philosophical Letters' (Filosofskie pis'ma), written in 1829, P.Ia.
Chaadaev set out the central dilemma of Russian culture. He was by conviction a Catholic who believed fanatically in beauty and in the necessity of
the humanizing concepts of Western morality – honour, truth, and good-

ness for universal human development. He applied those ideals to Russia's past and at once discovered their absence, said Grigor'ev in 'Westernism in Russian Lieterature' (the second article in the series for *Vremia*), and so divined the falseness of Karamzin's representations. Since Russian life did not fit the forms of Western life, which Chaadaev took to be universally human, he concluded that Russia did not contain good, truth, honour, or morality. To his question 'What is Russia's role in universal development?' two answers could be given: Either Russians were not human and to become so had to reject their past and Westernize as quickly as possible; or their life was different from Western life but no less human. The two camps, Westernizer and Slavophile, were born of the two answers.[34]

Chaadaev's Westernism, Grigor'ev believed, arose not only as a protest against Karamzin's history but also against those forms in Russian romantic literature that his history had inspired. A host of historical dramas appeared in the 1830s and 1840s that struck the false notes of Karamzin's influence. Even Pushkin sounded such notes in *Boris Godunov*, but he, for the most part, detected the falseness of Karamzin's view and resisted it. Others, however, fell completely under his spell, and in the period that Belinskii called 'romantic-national' artists rejoiced in their 'discovery' of Russian nationality. Grigor'ev particularly blamed Walter Scott's novels, with their profoundly bourgeois morality, for giving a boost to the romantic-national falsification of Russian nationality that Karamzin had initiated.

The most destructive of the historical novelists, Grigor'ev believed, was N. Zagoskin, whose works were full of false language and characters. Zagoskin, he complained, presented Russian people either as moral eunuchs or as court jesters. He portrayed Russian nationality as a love for stagnation, exclusiveness, and submissiveness. To him, all protest was crime, and he justified the most revolting phenomena of the old life with a good-natured but stupid equanimity in their depiction. Zagoskin saw the sole quality of the *narod* as humility. His was not, in Grigor'ev's opinion, the humility of the Slavophiles, which was based on the community and legitimate order, but the humility of sheeplike submissiveness. In drama, Polevoi and N.V. Kukol'nik perpetuated the false view of Russian nationality found in Zagoskin.[35] Later, in a review of Alexei Tolstoi's historical tale 'Prince Serebrianyi' Grigor'ev portrayed Tolstoi as Zagoskin's contemporary successor. Tolstoi's story fell into the Zagoskin mould, being both false in content – the boyar aristocrats were not, in Grigor'ev's view, defending the *narod* against tyranny when they opposed the *oprichnina* of Ivan the Terrible – and artless in execution.[36]

Grigor'ev did not disapprove of all the historical novelists of the romantic-national period. The false nationality in the works of Zagoskin, Polevoi, and Kukol'nik was, in the distinctive vocabulary of this second article in the series, an 'antediluvian' form that was developed and corrected by I.I. Lazhechnikov. Lazhechnikov's opposition to the false Karamzinian forms, Grigor'ev believed, was only semi-conscious and incomplete, but in some ways he anticipated the nationality of Ostrovskii and Ostrovskii's protest on behalf of Russian cultural independence.[37]

A more conscious reaction against the false nationality of the romantic-national period came in the form of Gogol''s satire, on the one hand, and Westernism, on the other. Grigor'ev emphasized that Westernism arose as a reaction not against Russian nationality but against the false forms into which it had been forced. The fault of Westernism was not that it struggled against false forms but that at first it mistook, like Chaadaev, the false forms for the idea of Russian nationality itself. In time, however, Westernism too rejected the false forms of nationality. 'As soon as the real forms instead of the false ones were revealed [Westernism] had to decline and has truly declined.'[38]

In his piece on Belinskii – the third in his *Vremia* series – Grigor'ev developed a theme that he had previously broached while writing for *Russkoe slovo* but which became central to his thinking in the last years of his life. He believed that at the heart of what he called the negative view of Russian history, by which he meant Westernism, lay the idea of 'centralization.' Grigor'ev had come to admire Belinskii, whom he portrayed as Russia's teacher and a passionate seeker after truth who was able to contradict himself when he sensed his errors. Great as he was, however, Belinskii had harmed Russia's development. As Grigor'ev wrote to Pogodin, 'Surely, I undermined [in the article on Belinskii] the "centralization" in the doctrine of one of its most gifted proponents.'[39] Grigor'ev astutely pointed out that the historians S.M. Solov'ev, K.D. Kavelin, and even B.N. Chicherin were merely Belinskii's students.[40]

Grigor'ev remarked that Karamzin had introduced the idea of centralization, which lay at the heart of the Westernizer view of Russian life. It was at bottom a false idea. Though in pre-Petrine Russia, Moscow had sought to impose itself on the rest of the nation and had succeeded in enforcing a formal unity, the vitality of the regions had not disappeared. The land did not resist Moscow's political centralization with force but stubbornly withdrew into itself and preserved the vital sap of localism. Those local forces led to the Church Schism and the revolts of pretenders such as the two false Dmitriis of the Time of Troubles in the seventeenth century. Grigor'ev was deeply interested in the Russian schismatics and successfully lobbied to have A.N. Shchapov's work on the Schism published in *Vremia*.

In the revolt and schism, the Westerners saw only chaotic and inhuman expressions of poverty and immorality. But they also, said Grigor'ev, detected a countervailing force, beginning with the Tatars, a force that smashed through all that immorality and disorder. It was the force of centralization, and its apotheosis was Peter the Great. Kavelin first wrote specifically of Russian history in this way, but Belinskii, Grigor'ev maintained, had said it all before him. Obsessed as they were with Western ideals, Belinskii and the Westernizers could understand nothing that did not fit the prescribed model. For them, only Ivan the Terrible and Peter the Great stood out. Under the influence of Balzac's *Histoire de Louis treize*, Belinskii cast Ivan psychologically and artistically in the same mould as Louis, as a reformer. Later he moved on to portray Ivan as Peter's predecessor. Solov'ev's later idea of Ivan's 'mission' derived from Belinskii's notion of Ivan's 'calling to a great deed.'

In Grigor'ev's assessment, Belinskii clung to his centralist conception of Russian history throughout his life. From it derived his dislike for pan-Slavism and Ukrainians. He understood Russians, Grigor'ev believed, solely in terms of the yardstick of abstract humanity. Grigor'ev deplored above all else that yardstick: 'Humanity! this abstract humanity of a badly understood Hegelianism, a humanity which does not exist, for there are only organisms that grow, age, are transformed but are eternal: nations. In order for this abstract humanity to exist, it is necessary without fail to recognize some conditional ideal of it. And to this ideal everything national, local, organic is sacrificed.'[41]

Yet for all his faults, Belinskii was not entirely blind to Russian cultural developments. He understood that Russia had absorbed everything useful from the West, yet had remained itself. He recognized the living, organic nature of Russian society but believed that love for one's society meant wishing to see the ideals of humanity realized in it. That view derived from his Hegelianism, which ultimately was a cosmopolitan and not a national doctrine. 'The sole ideal thinkable for such an outlook in its extreme consequences,' Grigor'ev insisted, 'is a single level – centralization, whether Catholic or socialist, it is in essence all the same – centralization.'[42] Thus, Belinskii was always a cosmopolitan and centralizer, who eliminated the spontaneous in favour of the abstract, and the local in favour of the universal. His cosmopolitanism led him to prefer composed to folk poetry and, in his last days, to the view that a nail is preferable to a flower.

Grigor'ev cited an article that had recently appeared in *Svetoch* which suggested that in his final years Belinskii was neither a Westernizer nor a Slavophile but was evolving an independent Russian way. Grigor'ev did not entirely agree. He granted that it was possible that had Belinskii lived on into the 1850s he might have broken with his past, but in reality he had been a centralizer and the enemy of *narodnost'* to the moment of his death. To him, civilized development was precluded by the principles of Russian nationality, which, consequently, had to be overcome. The *narod* and *narodnost'* were, for him, merely transitional forms to a Westernized humanity. The fault lay, Grigor'ev once again pointed out, with his left-Hegelianism, which separated spirit from nature and led to the sacrifice of the national to the universal and the spontaneous to the artificial.[43]

Grigor'ev returned frequently in *Vremia*, in pieces outside his history of Russian consciousness, to these themes of centralization and localism in the life and culture of the empire. In an obituary for Taras Shevchenko, he compared the beauty of expression of the great Ukrainian poet to that of the Russian Pushkin and the Polish Mickiewicz. Shevchenko, said Grigor'ev, possessed the charm of the former and the passion of the latter. So far, only he had written anything that came straight from the soil of Ukraine. Grigor'ev went on to lament that centralizers such as Belinskii were hostile to Ukrainian poetry. Gogol' had been a victim of that theoretical attitude, which compelled him to write in Russian. His significance in Russian literature, Grigor'ev erroneously believed, was already in the past, whereas his influence in Ukrainian literature would have been eternal.[44]

At the beginning of 1863, the appearance of N.I. Kostomarov's historical work on Ukraine prompted Grigor'ev to return to the theme of localism and to promote the writing of regional history. For Grigor'ev, Kostomarov was a brilliant representative of a new school of historians that opposed centralizers such as Solov'ev and Kavelin. It saw the political society of any people as related to its internal essence. The ability to comprehend the political structure of a people rested on understanding the people in question. 'It is not necessary to prove to us that the external phenomena of political life cannot constitute for us the history of a people because it is too obvious in itself.' Great Russia's nationality had received the most attention because it held political power, but Russia was diverse. The centralizers placed everything national, local, and individual in the realm of the animal or anti-social. It is interesting that Grigor'ev named in this article the man who had prepared him for his university entrance examinations – I.D. Beliaev – as one of Kostomarov's predecessors.[45]

Returning to his history of Russian cultural consciousness, Grigor'ev, in the fourth article of the series in *Vremia*, pointed out that pure Slavophilism was largely unknown to the public in the 1840s. But even then, he noted, 'as now the old boyar tendency of Slavophilism was marked by its fanatical hatred of contemporary life and its literary expressions.'[46] Grigor'ev's attitude to Slavophilism was ambivalent. He deeply admired Khomiakov and to a lesser degree Ivan Kireevskii. He had responded ecstatically in the 1850s to Konstantin Aksakov's patriotic play *The Liberation of Moscow* (Osvobozhdenie Moskvy). But he also believed that the Slavophiles had failed because they did not understand Russian national development. 'The exclusively folk outlook of Slavophilism,' he had complained in 'Nationality and Literature,' 'did not meet sympathy among the masses, and overtaken by fate, [it] lost its most brilliant representatives.'[47] Reacting to the extremes of the Westernizers who denied the value of Russian history before Peter the Great and the possibility of an autonomous Russian cultural path, the Slavophiles, too, fell into extremes. Grigor'ev emphasized that Khomiakov and Kireevskii were deeply appreciative of the beauties and high ideals of Western life. They grew up on them and even fought German rationalism with the tools of German rationalism. They, and even more their heirs, accepted that Western ideals were the lastest word of humanity. They convinced themselves that the West was now exhausted and that Russia was awakening to further the development of that very same humanity.

Though familiar with pre-Petrine history from documents, they knew little of contemporary national life. On the basis of their historical researches, they came to believe that Russia was unique. And so they began to deny any significance to Peter's reforms, apart from the harm that they inflicted on Russia's special nature: '[Slavophilism] forgot that even if we slept over the course of 150 years, we nevertheless slept a watchful sleep, measuring ourselves against the ideals we dreamed about, developing our spiritual powers or our potential for struggle, even though with phantoms, and, however we are or will be awakened it will not be by those with whom we went to bed but for better or worse by a certain storehouse of accumulated data which inevitably must form the basis of our new life.'[48] In defence of life before Peter, the Slavophiles ran to extremes. For example, though marriage was, of course, a spiritual and holy union, the Slavophiles turned it from a union based on love or mutual attraction into mortification of the flesh.

Elsewhere in *Vremia*, in 1861, Grigor'ev noted that the Slavophile view of the people, its way of life, its history, its customs, and its poetry had been closer to the truth than was the negative view of the westernizers but, like the latter, was only theory:

Slavophilism is already now precisely as much an historical phenomenon as is Westernism; it does not take the *narod* as it is in life but searched always in it for its own ideal of the *narod* and trimmed the shoots of this enormous vegetale life according to a conditional pattern. In its theoretical blindness Slavophilism shook hands with Shishkovism which led straight to *Maiak* and *Domashnaia beseda*; Slavophilism in essence did not love Pushkin exactly in the same way as g. –bov [Dobroliubov, a leading radical], on the one hand, and g. Askochenskii [a leading reactionary], on the other, did not and perhaps until now is still alienated from contemporary national literature at the head of which stands Ostrovskii.[49]

Peter's reforms happened, Grigor'ev asserted, and to deny them as false was tilting at windmills. But Slavophilism looked for its ideal people only in Russia before Peter and in the steppe. Russia could not return to its pre-Petrine past as the Slavophiles hoped. If it could go back anywhere, it would in any case be to the twelfth century, not to the centralizing Muscovite state of the seventeenth century.[50]

Grigor'ev did not reduce the protagonists in the 'romantic-national' period to Slavophiles and Westernizers. He was deeply interested as well in the reactionaries of the time, who were epitomized for him in the journal *Maiak*. In order to expose the nature of their views, he quoted a letter written by the historical novelist Zagoskin to P.A. Korsakov, editor of *Maiak*, in 1840. The epistle expressed Zagoskin's support for *Maiak* and especially his appreciation for its contention that there could be no literature without religion. He claimed that the Russian romantics, by whom he meant the historical novelists, were fundamentally religious. Grigor'ev rejected that opinion. Compared, he said, to the religious light cast by Khomiakov and Kireevskii, the romantics were obscurantists. And obscurantism, he averred, had nothing in common with religious feeling. Zagoskin concluded that religiosity in a novel was intended to remind the reader that life on earth was merely a means to salvation and deplored the falsity of Western philosophy, with its rampant materialism. That, Grigor'ev pointed out, was a typical obscurantist ploy in which lofty thought was mingled with petty dislike of philosophy. For Zagoskin and his kind, philosophy was mere words; for the true Christian, religion had already answered all of philosophy's questions. If, for example, one sought for proof of the immortality of the human soul in Plato, one was not a true Christian. And so the obscurantists demonstrated their hostility to all inquiry.

Maiak espoused a mixture of mysticism and St Petersburg nationalism. Its mysticism was, in Grigor'ev's opinion, its best side. Its editors had correctly identified the falsehood of the Westernizers' cosmopolitanism but combated it with their own false view of Russian nationality. *Maiak* was distinguished by a negative attitude to everything contemporary and a desire to affirm the old. It was not conservative but reactionary and shamefully promoted a bigoted Orthodoxy, with the support of the official church. Only Pogodin's *Moskvitianin*, Grigor'ev maintained, espoused at the time a correct, if limited, view of *narodnost'*.[51]

Grigor'ev observed that *Maiak* was particularly hostile to Lermontov, especially to his *Hero of Our Time* (Geroi nashego vremeni). The novel epitomized for the obscurantists the tyranny of the 'ego' in the nineteenth century. *Maiak* found Lermontov empty, but only because it looked for its own theories in him. His poems were only words, of which, Grigor'ev commented ironically, he used far more, in the opinion of *Maiak*, than he needed to express his thoughts. The truth was that the obscurantists feared Lermontov because he powerfully expressed what they most opposed.[52]

Grigor'ev had himself recently come to value Lermontov's contribution to Russia's spiritual growth more highly than he had earlier. In his new assessment (in article no. 5 of his *Vremia* series), Lermontov possessed that instinctive, prophetic foresight of great poets, which was the product of their spontaneity and receptiveness. He was not the master of the forces of his age, but their blind representative. He was the representative, in particular, of true Russian romanticism. Grigor'ev believed that though romanticism was a broad and varied phenomenon, it had certain constant characteristics: 'Romanticism in art and life arises on the one hand out of an enslaved, subordinated, unconscious relationship of the soul to life, but, on the other hand, something that dwells in the heart is disturbed and eternally dissatisfied with this subordinated relationship, and the whole world is unsatisfactory to it.'[53] Romanticism therefore was the principle of disquiet in art and life.

Lermontov's Pechorin, the hero of our time, was the best artistic representative of romantic disquiet. He was the predatory type in all its fullness. As a type, Grigor'ev insisted, Pechorin was as legitimate as the humble type. The type contained many of Russia's most positive qualities. But since its appearance, the predatory type had been resisted in Russian literature. 'Morally affrighted at the extreme consequences of logical thought, separated from reality and finding no answer in the soil', Grigor'ev explained, we fell into despondency and even profound despair.'[54]

But the predatory could not be eliminated or transformed into another type. Maksim Maksimych, another character in *A Hero of Our Time*, was a simple and good type who deserved more sympathy than Pechorin. But by nature Maksim Maksimych was stupid and merely incapable of falling into Pechorin's extremes: 'The voice on behalf of the simple and good that arises in our souls against the false and predatory is, of course, a fine voice, but its value is only negative. Its positive side is stagnation, rust, moral philistinism.'[55] Consequently Lermontov and his type were essential. Without the predatory, protesting Lermontovian type, Russia would fall into the sheep-like humility of the type of Maksim Maksimych: 'And that is why all of our attempts, both healthy and pathological, to laugh at our discontent, to defeat once and for all the charming type which is set out before us, the type which in the person of Pechorin recognizes in itself "unlimited powers," while dissipating them on trifles, the type of the strongly passionate man, turned out to be in vain. We annihilate only the false, conditional aspects with comedy.'[56]

Since his conversion to Gogol''s 'Christian humility,' Grigor'ev had believed that the humble man was the quintessential Russian type. But increasingly he realized that such a personality was incapable of effecting social improvement. In order to change society, the critical, analytical personality was essential. There was no concession here to the primacy of the 'social' that had characterized the Fourierist section of his little book of poems in 1846. The 'ethical' remained paramount, but the Russian personality had acquired for Grigor'ev a new complexity. Both the Slavophile and Westernizer, Russian and Western, humble and predatory were essential elements of the Russian personality and nationality. They were held in equilibrium in art, or in the personality of the artist, where the universally true or the moral met the social. Art either affirmed the social through love or condemned it through the sharp scourge of comedy. There was no end to the process, no utopia, no overcoming of one by the other, but only the ceaseless unfolding of life itself and its unending confirmation in art.

Grigor'ev placed the significance of the predatory type for Russia's future at the centre of his assessment of his contemporaries. On a number of occasions, he had made passing reference to the strength of L.N. Tolstoi as a writer, but he had also often remarked on his inability to discover meaningful content in his work. In *Vremia*, in 1862, he wrote a long, two-part assessment of Tolstoi, whose *War and Peace* (Voina i mir) was yet to be published.[57] The task of literary criticism, Grigor'ev declared, was not merely to welcome and declare sympathy for a new talent but to capture what was specific or individual in it. The mission was most difficult with talents who were distinguished not by the breadth, clarity, or importance of their social concepts but by their internal powers and virtuosity. Tolstoi was, in Grigor'ev's view, a writer of bold originality and psychological power. Tolstoi, he noted, had been met so far with indifference by the critics, but Grigor'ev found it hard to account for the lack of response to him. He was not, in Grigor'ev's opinion, a strong lyricist, or story-teller, or historian. Instead, Tolstoi was most remarkable for his trenchant analysis of the individual soul and for his uncompromising enmity toward the false.

Tolstoi's strength was thus his power of analysis, and all artistic analysis, said Grigor'ev, was expressed in poetic images. The broader the artistic nature of the writer, the wider his ideal and the more national his work. Tolstoi analysed spiritual developments so far unexamined in Russia. He was not interested in the 'evil of evil men,' as was Gogol'; did not sneer at the advanced man, as did Turgenev; did not contrast the healthy way of life to one based on mere tinsel and artificiality of feeling, as did Pisemskii; and he did not limit his idealism to narrow practicality, as did Goncharov. But Tolstoi had something in common with each of them because, like them, he rejected everything superficial and affected. He, like the others, dug in the Russian soil in order to unearth the foundations of nationality. But Tolstoi was special, in Grigor'ev's assessment, because he went deeper than any of them. Turgenev was like Moses and never reached the promised land of Russian nationality, Pisemskii was shallow, and Gogol' was too reconciliatory.

As with all national tasks in Russia, it was Pushkin who had set out Tolstoi's subject for him when he created Belkin, the meek and humble type. Again Grigor'ev asserted that on its own that was inadequate. With it there could be no forward movement, because it lacked a passionate principle. The passionate type was equally necessary to Russia. Pushkin and Turgenev had both looked for that type in foreign ideals; Ostrovskii and Dostoevskii searched for broad types in Russian national life. But Tolstoi distrusted all elevated and extraordinary feelings and attached himself – and here Grigor'ev displayed remarkable insight – to the type of the simple and humble man. He believed that Tolstoi had stumbled on the type primarily because of his dislike for the brilliant and predatory rather than directly through the soil. 'Tolstoi's analysis is inadequate,' he judged, 'because it is not based on the soil and because it does not accord significance to the truly brilliant, truly passionate, truly predatory type which in nature and history has justification.'[58] Russia would be a poor nation were it to take its ideal only from the humble type. But Russians had a sympathy for all ideals, a fact that had caused a colossal struggle in the Russian psyche, especially within artistic natures. They were also resistant to regulation. They rejected external order and contrived unity. They were incapable of any utopia, be it that of the bureaucrats or that of the Fourierists, the barracks or the phalanstery. Tolstoi had fallen into one-sidedness. Unlike Pushkin, who mastered all the types and remained himself, Tolstoi, with his analytical talent, attacked all types except the humble and could not see other types in the people: 'Only by directly experiencing the national life, bearing it in one's soul like Ostrovskii, Kol'tsov and in part Nekrasov, or going down into the subterranean depths of *The House of the Dead* [Zapiski iz mertvogo doma], like F. Dostoevskii, is it possible to legitimate both types equally, both the passionate type and the humble.'[59]

In an 1862 review of Nekrasov's collected poetry, Grigor'ev took up the role of the editor of *Sovremennik* and the favoured poet of the nihilists in revealing the passionate type in Russian culture. For Grigor'ev, Nekrasov stood among the best of Russia's writers. But everyone, complained Grigor'ev, interpreted his poetry to suit their own purposes. The critics at *Russkoe slovo*, for example, praised his poetry for depicting Russian life accurately, without idealizing it. But, replied Grigor'ev, Nekrasov did not merely expose the horrors of peasant life; he also described the development of the national spirit. Russians loved Nekrasov not only for his merciless criticism of social reality but for his profound understanding of Russian nationality.

The real task of the critic, he once again asserted, was to discover the poet's particular nature and its relationship to nationality. In the 1840s Nekrasov wrote, along with everyone else, in a negative or critical manner. But even in that decade, it was apparent that he was a poet with a national heart, that he experienced the national essence. Grigor'ev compared Nekrasov's sympathy for the common people in the 1840s to Dostoevskii's compassion in *Poor Folk* (Bednye liudi). But Nekrasov was and remained too bitter. His poetry misled the young aesthetically, intellectually, and morally. His alluring clarity spared his young supporters thought, and his passion spared them many-sided feeling. To the theoreticians (Grigor'ev's name for the nihilists of *Sovremennik* and *Russkoe slovo*), Nekrasov was a hero because he upset and annoyed authority and the public, but not because he was a poet. With his focus on petty annoyances, he had no ideal and so failed to reveal the full truth. But Renan had correctly observed, said

Grigor'ev, that it is narrow ideas that rule the world: 'Narrow, i.e. theoretical, thought can always be stated, with a bit of talent in the stater, with "alluring clarity." Its development is very uncomplicated. The fullest negation on the one side ... and, on the other side, a distant little ideal, though one shrouded at the time in the most mysterious cloud, but nevertheless very accessible. That's all you need!'[60]

Nekrasov then was narrow in his analysis of Russian life, but, on the whole, critics had not attacked his narrowness or his subservience to theory. That was because, Grigor'ev asserted, during the 1840s literary criticism began to reject everything subjective in favour of the objective. Criticism became one-sided, and Nekrasov fitted the desired mould. Such poets as L. Mei and A. Maikov did not, and consequently they were largely ignored. Nekrasov's adherents clung to him and ignored whatever did not fit their narrow vision.

Nekrasov's opponents were as confused as his supporters. A good example, in Grigor'ev's opinion, was the review of his poetry in *Otechestvennye zapiski* (Notes of the Fatherland). Its strategy was to single out Nekrasov's weaknesses and engage him in a polemic. The journal's critic saw the main element of his poetry as 'bile.' He wanted not to understand the poet but merely to use him, in order to flog his supporters. But, said Grigor'ev, bile had its necessary uses. Wherever there was poetry, there was not only life but also protest. 'Poetry is the highest, best, and most effective legitimation of this most sacred of rights of the human soul' – the right of protest.[61] Poetry was changeless in its function, according to Grigor'ev. Though the poetry of the past lost its propelling social force, it retained the power to perfect the individual. But in its role in shaping the future, poetry was protest and forward social movement.

Nekrasov loved the soil as much as others, but his Russian nature was disturbed by exposure to the theories of civilization. Dostoevskii, Grigor'ev believed, brought a purer understanding to the Russian people. Grigor'ev portrayed Dostoevskii's *Notes from the House of the Dead* in his article about Nekrasov as one of the great works of the era; though much admired in the rest of Europe, it had made little impact in Russia: 'We either ignored it because it was not English, as *Russkii vestnik* ignored it, for whom its phenomena are of a magnitude infinitely small, or we see nothing in it except lies, as Slavophilism sees it, or we simply cancel out its importance, along with the importance of literature in general, as something completely superfluous in that perfected world where the moon unites with the earth and where Bazarov will be perfectly right to enthuse over "frogs," as did the theoreticians.'[62] Grigor'ev believed that in *Notes from the House of the Dead* Dostoevskii, the educated man, had united fully with the people. The search for roots in the soil that began with Pushkin had ended with Dostoevskii.

Grigor'ev was disturbed that the abuse of literature by forcing it to serve a narrow ideal was by no means confined to the nihilists. He contended in his 1862 article on Tolstoi in *Vremia* that the Slavophiles, like the nihilists, saw art as a subordinate phenomenon. They condescendingly accepted Pushkin, but only with extensive reservations; they recognized in Lermontov a stray comet, failed to understand Ostrovskii, and managed to see in Gogol' what no one else could see. They placed all contemporary literature on a level beneath the *The Family Chronicle* (Semeinaia khronika), Sergei Aksakov's great portrait of Russian patriarchalism, or any work by Gogol'. In other words, Grigor'ev concluded, Slavophilism viewed literature only as a means to serve its purposes. Like the theoreticians, the Slavophiles placed life on a Procrustean bed. The two groups were similar in the consistency of their views, in their unquestionably honourable thoughts and feelings, in their strict civic seriousness, and in their understanding of social obligation. The only difference between Khomiakov and Chernyshevskii, or Ivan Aksakov and Dobroliubov, was that Chernyshevskii and Dobroliubov were more Russian by nature. They were more capable of burning their boats and bolder and more ruthless in their application of the communal principle in Russian life: 'The Slavophiles built a cathedral to this communal principle in the old Byzantine style but [Chernyshevskii and Dobroliubov] built in the simplest barracks style. In the future Slavophilism will perhaps be stronger than they because it has ready-made moulds for its ideal ... But at the moment the theoreticians are rather more the masters of the situation.'[63] Everyone kowtowed to them. And they were, in Grigor'ev's opinion, a fully Russian phenomenon. Their view did not embrace the entire essence of the nation's life but represented its negative side in its latest manifestation. The present negation could go no further, however, and the theoreticians, Grigor'ev suggested, would reign for only a while longer.

Mikhail Katkov's *Russkii vestnik*, he pointed out in the same article, with its Anglomania, also despised Russian literature and life. Only European, especially English, life was legitimate, according to *Russkii vestnik*, and Russian life and literature had to rise to that level. *Atenei*, a St Petersburg liberal-minded journal, represented ultra-Westernism for Grigor'ev, by which he meant both extreme centralization, in the name of an abstract humanity that swallowed up the national, and belief in endless progress.

Atenei took the ideas of centralization and abstract humanity more seriously than the idea of progress. For it, the human ideal was the Germano-Romance nationality to which Slavs were supposedly inferior. At the heart of the Germano-Romance nationality, Grigor'ev pointed out, lurked two ideas: either (1) the subordination of the individual to the community of the Papacy, the Puritans, the Convention, or Fourier, or (2) extreme individualism and nationalism.'[64]

But of all Russian trends, only the theoreticians pushed their aesthetic views to their logical extremes. Only they held that artistic beauty was inferior to living beauty; that philosophy, history, poetry, and art were nonsense; that all life was about social structure and material prosperity. Their great advantage was the simplicity and clarity of their ideas. They chewed and rechewed the same food and then put it in their sympathizers' mouths for them. Nihilism eliminated the effort required to think; indeed it ridiculed thought. It deeply despised life, with its organic laws, history, and literature. But it also had a practical gumption that kept it close to life and literature. The Slavophiles merely noted all in life and literature that they disliked and labelled it decay and deformity. The theoreticians were more energetic and not only saw but also forced others to see only what was useful to them in life and literature and ignored the rest. In Ostrovskii, they lionized the painter of the 'dark kingdom' and ignored everything else in his work. In fact, Ostrovskii pulled the various strings of the Russian soul and revealed a whole new series of new natures. But the theoreticians would continue to lead until life itself displaced them by revealing new phenomena. The majority of the public would, until that time, continue to see them as correct, and only a minority would notice those phenomena unremarked on by the theoreticians.

Even A.S. Khomiakov's collected poems, Grigor'ev lamented, were used by the nihilists for their purposes. In an 1861 review of a recent edition of Khomiakov's poetry, Grigor'ev pointed out that *Sovremennik*, in its assessment of the work, had adopted Belinskii's view of the writer's verse. His poems, according to Belinskii, had no structure and were as artificial as was his idea of Russian nationality. Poetry, the critic had maintained, was not about peoples, as Khomiakov believed, but about individuals. A great poet did not choose his subjects, but Khomiakov, Belinskii complained, consciously chose to sing a hymn to old Russia. As a result, his poems rang false and lacked true feeling or a sense of conflict.

Grigor'ev maintained that Belinskii, as a centralizer, failed to see the meaning of the lines of Khomiakov's poetry or the innovation of some of his historical poems. Belinskii was partly motivated by his hostility to Slavophilism and so was blind to many of Khomiakov's virtues. But Belinskii was a true critic and was right in seeing Khomiakov as a poet of the head and not the heart. What Belinskii did not grant was that a poet of the head could be a true poet by virtue of drawing the reader into the magic of the world of his creation. Khomiakov was even better than that, Grigor'ev concluded. He was a poet of beautiful forms, of objectivity, who carried the reader into the past in speech and outlook. His poems bore no trace of the deep and original spirit that marked his other works, but they were the product of profound and independent convictions and the reflection of a full moral and intellectual life.[65]

Tolstoi suffered in the same way as Nekrasov, Ostrovskii, or Khomiakov from literary factionalism. In working through a number of psychological problems in his work, he achieved moral results that contradicted the views of the theoreticians. And so they were silent about him. Instead, they droned on about Oblomov and the baselessness of Russian life. But an analysis of Tolstoi's psychological approach, Grigor'ev insisted in his article about Tolstoi, would reveal more about Russian lives than all the Oblomovs put together. Few believed, however, that literature was an expression of life. Instead, the theoreticians boldly faced their own truth and drew all the conclusions from their narrow analysis. Though Grigor'ev frequently acknowledged that nihilism was a necessary part of the national process, he was less sympathetic to the defenders of art-for-art's-sake; they also failed to see that literature was an expression of life. But they, unlike the nihilists, had no purpose whatsoever. For them, art was pure dilettantism.

Russkii vestnik and the Westernizers therefore saw no significance in Russian literature, the Slavophiles saw no utility in it, and the theoreticians denied nationality in favour of humanity. All forgot that literature was necessary. 'Everything real,' Grigor'ev repeated, 'is nothing but the aroma and colour of the ideal and, as such, is inevitably expressed in literature. If the scent is alien to you and the colour hateful, you are in essence at war with the soil and the air.'[66] Germano-Romance art, Grigor'ev insisted, could not be recapitulated in Russia. Again with that Jungian sense of the underlying unity of cultures, particularly mythic similarities, he remarked that all art came in a national cocoon but that it was also universally human: 'The foundation of the universally human lies even in the vegetale, apparently unique phenomena of art, i.e., for example, in the poetic world of folk sayings and the mythical notions expressed in all Indo-Caucasian races most obviously and in the race in general, although it is a hidden but necessary linkage. The more broadly a nationality develops, the more it amalgamates with other nationalities, though at the same time it does not lose its own particularity in life and art to the very summit of its development.'[67] The great national writers were all worthy of universal attention, yet all were national. Russian art was joined to the art of the whole of Europe but was marked with a Byzantine-Tatar stamp that was new and unique to Russia.

In the sixth and concluding article in his *Vremia* series on Russian cultural evolution since the eighteenth century, Grigor'ev traced the development of Russian literature from Belinskii's death in 1848.[68] The period immediately following the critic's demise was one of protest against civil, religious, moral, and social deformities. It was a time when Russian history, traditions, folk songs, and oral literature were perceived by many as obstacles to civilized development. The counterattack on this kind of Westernizing negation was led by the obscurantism of *Maiak*. Slavophilism was a 'comic' movement at the time, and Pogodin's views were relatively unknown. Even the latter had confused his democratic outlook by wedding it in the early *Moskvitianin* to an extreme attachment to Russian traditions and historical continuity.

The great strength of the negative view held by the Westernizers had been its laughter at the monstrously absurd phenomena of Russian life, its protest on behalf of the individual, and its intensification of the individual's expectations of life. Gogol''s humour was full of love and sympathy for life. Returning to an old theme, Grigor'ev pointed out that not everyone had seen the love but only the form of Gogol''s work. To them, Gogol' had opened up a new mine for exploitation – analysis of ordinary reality. That led to the numerous satirical sketches and stories of the 1840s. Most of those stories were false in their criticism of Russian reality and led those unfamiliar with reality into error. But one-sided hostility to reality could not go on indefinitely, and reconciliation with reality became necessary. People began to doubt that reality was as black as it was painted in the literature. Russians were prepared to acknowledge their faults but not to exaggerate them and to fall into despair.

The result was a protest against the demands made on reality by the romantic. At first the protest was taken up on behalf of Russia's most obvious reality – the bureaucratic state. Goncharov led that protest. His work boasted neither profound content nor any aspiration to the ideal. It was dogmatic and analytical. Goncharov's *An Ordinary Story* (Obyknovennaia istoriia) was the height of this official, bureaucratic view, the disparaging of individual protest and the triumph of lifeless practicality. *An Ordinary*

Story catered to the needs of the moral philistines. His *Oblomov* added nothing: the Russian devil was still Russian nature, and salvation lay in Russians' making themselves over according to some narrow theory. The whole message of *Oblomov* was 'love work, eschew idleness or fall into Oblomovism.'[69] Honourable but short-sighted people such as Dobroliubov, who had praised Goncharov for exposing the superfluousness of the superfluous man, and incidentally of the gentry, in his famous article in *Sovremennik*, 'What Is Oblomovism?' (Chto takoe oblomovshchina?), rejoiced at that theme, but it was a theme with limited applicability.

The short-sighted were, however, temporarily in the ascendancy. In *Vremia*, Grigor'ev resumed his pessimistic identity as the 'unnecessary man.' In an article about the 'gradual but precipitous and universal spread of ignorance and illiteracy in Russian literature,' he pointed out that Russians were now living in a practical age in which Dobroliubov, at the beginning of every article, demanded humility from his readers, and Chernyshevskii explained all knowledge in terms of the great ideal of material well-being. It was also an era in which Pushkin was deprived of all national significance. In such a time, a man such as Grigor'ev was unnecessary. Voices such as his could have only a negative impact. Theirs were the few voices of scepticism:

Above all, in us the 'unnecessary people,' in the face of a profound sympathy for progress, the most dismal faith in an infinity of progress that is rooted to the point of incurability, and the consequence of that faith, rests the sad conviction that the human soul with its multi-various strings remains and will always remain the same, that the moon will never unite with the earth as Fourier hoped; neither will the variegated colours of nationality and individuals coalesce into a universal, continuous, salubrious, and monotonous mass of humanity; nor will the human passions be reduced to mathematically determined and voluntarily acceded to needs – nor will art, that eternal hymn and eternal howl of the human soul, wither and disappear.[70]

That thought made it impossible for the unnecessary people to believe in Chernyshevskii's comforting theory and to prefer with him a real apple to a painted one. The progressives always forgot today what happened yesterday and hoped that what was achieved today would be cancelled out tomorrow. They were a people of the moment.

Grigor'ev went on in the article to compare the fathers and the children. The period of Karamzin and Pushkin was many-sided and encyclopaedic. Russians then were raised on the classics and were profoundly humanistic in outlook. They also had a firm understanding of the rest of Europe. Over time, that encyclopaedic and humanistic knowledge had bred pedantry and hindered the Russians from coming to know themselves. It was even considered chic to know nothing of Russia. Now that the new era had eschewed encyclopaedic knowledge, it might be expected that the 'young generation' would know at least its own land. But it did not. To the 'young generation,' knowledge of Russia meant knowledge of today, whereas yesterday was ignored. Gogol' was yesterday, and Pushkin the day before. Anything before Pushkin was confined to examinations; anything before Peter the Great was unknown. 'It is possible to say without the slightest exaggeration that the greatest number of our writers, i.e. our scholarly class, are as separated from the national life as was the previous generation.'[71] And, along with the persistence of scholarly alienation, the general level of education in Russia, Grigor'ev was convinced, had declined.

Though Grigor'ev wrote frequently in *Vremia* about Russian drama and the theatre, he had little new to say on the subject. In particular, he repeated his contention that Ostrovskii had been the founder of a Russian national theatre with his 'new word' of the 1850s.[72] In a letter to Strakhov written in Orenburg, Grigor'ev made it clear that Ostrovskii's new word on nationality was not, however, Russia's final word. Ostrovskii, too, was one-sided, and his portrait of Russian nationality would also give way to other 'essential elements of the national spirit.'[73]

Grigor'ev's only original piece on Russian drama in *Vremia* was a comment on Griboedov's *Woe from Wit* (Gore ot uma). Grigor'ev portrayed it as a comedy that represented Russia's secular life at the time. The depiction of the upper classes, he contended, was not Russian. It came from France via Balzac. Griboedov attacked the ignorance and philistinism of high society in the name of Christianity and humanity. Grigor'ev judged Griboedov's hero, Chatskii, to be the only heroic individual in Russian literature. He was the heir of Novikov and Radishchev, who were prepared to die in protest against their environment. An honourable, passionate, and active character, he alone in Russian literature fought positively for morality in the milieu into which fate had placed him.[74]

Grigor'ev's tenure at *Vremia* was punctuated by his departure at the end of May 1861 for Orenburg, where he remained until May of the following year. Within a couple of months of joining Dostoevskii's journal in January 1861, Grigor'ev's customary restlessness at having to work under the constraints imposed by others reasserted itself, and he announced his intention to carry out his plan, formed while in debtors' prison, to teach in the military school in Orenburg. In a number of letters from Orenburg to Strakhov in St Petersburg, Grigor'ev blamed the editors of *Vremia* for his flight. In a comment that accompanied the published version of the letters that appeared in 1864, Strakhov went to some lengths to explain that Grigor'ev did not leave *Vremia* for reasons of philosophical disagreement with the other editors. The interference in his work of which Grigor'ev accused the editors in his letters, Strakhov maintained, was a minor matter, often the product of misunderstanding, and insignificant compared to their broad agreement on questions of editorial direction. Strakhov emphasized the leading role that Grigor'ev had played· in the formation of *pochvennichestvo* and the importance attached to his views by the editors.[75]

The 'minor matters' were reminiscent of Grigor'ev's problems at *Russkoe slovo*. The editors of *Vremia*, like Polonskii at *Russkoe slovo*, had questioned the respect with which Grigor'ev referred to the Slavophiles I. Kireevskii and A. Khomiakov, as well as to M. Pogodin and S. Shevyrev. M.M. Dostoevskii, whose own views were much more liberal than Grigor'ev's or even his brother's, apparently objected to Grigor'ev's generous references to those thinkers and dared to delete from one of his articles the word 'profound,' which the author had used to describe Kireevskii's thought. Strakhov explained that the piece had been published with the word 'profound' reinstated. In questioning Kireevskii's profundity, said Strakhov, M.M. was only reflecting a widely held view. Besides, he went on, while everyone read German 'rubbish,' no one read the Slavophiles, so that it was useless to cite them and expect to be understood.[76] As a compromise, the Dostoevskii brothers suggested that Grigor'ev's articles in *Vremia* be published anonymously. Then, when their brilliance was widely recognized, their author's name could be triumphantly revealed. Grigor'ev asked whether he was such a reactionary that his name would compromise the journal and threatened to withhold the article he was writing about Tolstoi.[77]

Grigor'ev admitted that a feeling of being unnecessary had led to his voluntary exile in Orenburg and even confessed to feelings of hurt pride. But he also made it clear that he did have problems with both the editorial policy and the management of *Vremia*. The journal, he wrote, could become an 'honourable, independent and for that very reason a leading organ in the end,' but only if it took as its slogan 'absolute *truth*' (Orthodoxy), broke off its 'shameful' regard for *Sovremennik*, embraced 'Slavism (not Slavophilism, but Slavism),' dropped some of its contributors who aspired to 'Liberalism *quand même*,' and ceased to drive the enormously talented Fedor Dostoevskii like a 'post horse' and protect him from feuilleton work, which would destroy him both 'physically' and 'in a literary sense.'[78]

Grigor'ev left little doubt that he felt uncomfortable contributing to a journal that often sided with *Sovremennik* in the journalistic battles of the day: 'I very much love [Fedor Dostoevskii] and in general both brothers – though I do not go along with them in all and in much I depart with them completely. In my opinion – and they at one time agreed with me – it is impossible to "serve God and Mammon": it is impossible *to recognize* philosophy, history, and poetry and be friendly with *Sovremennik*.'[79]

In the early months of its existence, Fedor Dostoevskii regarded *Vremia* as among the progressive journals. It advocated abolition of corporal punishment, called for sweeping hospital and prison reform, recommended that Jews be granted full civil rights, pressed for female emancipation from the worst excesses of patriarchalism, and defended the nihilists against semi-official charges that they were responsible for the fires that swept Russian cities in the summer of 1862. When in October 1862 Nekrasov, editor of *Sovremennik*, refused to contribute any more of his poems to *Vremia* because he did not wish to compromise himself in the eyes of his radical friends, Dostoevskii was shocked. 'Is our journal really retrograde ...?' he asked Nekrasov. 'But I am convinced that the public does not regard us as retrograde.'[80]

Grigor'ev did not especially oppose any of the causes embraced by *Vremia* but did not see them as essential: 'There is a question both deeper and wider in its implications than all of our questions, both the question (what cynicism?) about the serf condition, and the question (O, horrors!) about political liberty. This is the question about our intellectual and moral *independence*.'[81] Here again, Grigor'ev raised the ethical above the social. In order to be independent, he said, *Vremia* had either to get rid of him and Strakhov and 'woo' Chernyshevskii or 'be consistent in its faith in poetry and life, in the idea of nationality in general (as opposed to abstract humanity), take advantage of the mistakes of Slavophilism ... and take [Slavophilism's] place.'[82] He was constitutionally incapable, he informed Strakhov, of writing anything that was opposed to his beliefs. The literature of 'Progress' was hateful to him. It was better to teach the Kirgiz grammar than to participate in a literary debate without the capacity to praise and criticize other trends and personalities freely.

To Pogodin he wrote from Orenburg that he had left *Vremia* because it had an 'obvious leaning toward Chernyshevskii and company.' He had left St Petersburg because 'there I was for the most part an unnecessary man. Here, in Orenburg, teaching Russian, trying honourably and earnestly to awaken love for nationality, tradition, the Church, and the cultured, I am at least not a useless worker.'[83] It was no one's fault that he was unnecessary, he assured Strakhov. It was the times. But he did not despair: 'Do not tell me that I expect the impossible, what the times do not and will not yield. In everything life is a profound irony. In a time of the triumphs of rationalism it suddenly shows the opposite side of the coin, sends a Cagliostro and others; in the century of the steam-engine life turns the tables and raises the curtain on some hidden, ironical world of strange, capricious, mocking, even obscene spirits.'[84]

Strakhov also pointed out that Grigor'ev left for Orenburg for financial and personal reasons as much as for his dissatisfaction with the direction of *Vremia*. He had made the decision to take up the military teaching post while he was in debtors' prison. Since Orenburg was a frontier 'hardship' post, the terms of employment were very favourable. Teachers who stayed for three years were entitled to double the regular teachers' salary. As a youth, Grigor'ev had dreamed of going to the uncomplicated Siberian wilds to teach, and in his struggle not to get old the realization of that youthful fantasy probably attracted him. From his room in the debtors' prison, with his failed family relations and collapsed literary hopes, the central Asian city, with its modest reputation for culture, must have appeared to him as a haven. His relationship with Mar'ia Fedorovna was complicated by her social aspirations and limited social skills. A fresh start in Orenburg perhaps appealed to them both.

Grigor'ev was named teacher of Russian language in the military cadet school in Orenburg on 29 March 1861.[85] He did not, however, arrive there until 9 June. The reason may well have been that he did not have enough money to make the journey and had to petition for an advance on his salary. By the day he left St Petersburg, 20 May, he had received 364 roubles, been provided with an orderly and a standing order for a pair of post horses, and had procured an additional personal loan of 63 roubles. Typically, when he left the capital, he failed to report his departure to the headquarters of military educational institutions. That body sent an inquiry to Orenburg on 23 August about whether he had arrived. Asked for an explanation, Grigor'ev said that on the very day of setting out he had put a report about his departure in a city post box, 'not considering it *obligatory* to deliver it in person.' This defence was accepted.

He had taken his time on the way to his new posting, visiting Tver', which he found to be dead, and Iaroslavl', which overwhelmed him with its beauty, history, and 'gifted and intelligent' people and 'communal life.' Between Tver' and Iaroslavl', he stopped in Korcheva in order to visit Father Fedor (A.M. Bukharev), who had been banished to the provinces for advocating the closing of the monastic orders and the monasteries.

Grigor'ev had met Bukharev in the early 1850s but failed to see him on this occasion.[86] He disliked Kazan', with its 'Tatar filth and pretensions to the Nevskii Prospekt,' and the 'government haunts,' such as Samara and Orenburg, that were without history or interest. During the trip down the Volga, Mar'ia Fedorovna suffered a miscarriage.

The advance and loan that he got before leaving St Petersburg should have been a great deal more than enough to get to Orenburg, but he arrived there penniless and had to petition for a further advance of 200 roubles to set up a household. The pattern of destitution continued throughout his stay. Though he earned 1,000 roubles between May and October, he never had any money. He was not, at least in the early months, sending it to his wife in Moscow, because she wrote several times to Governor-General Bezak as well as to the director of the corps to have part of his salary garnisheed. Instead, he was giving his money away to various newly found friends in Orenburg.

He and Mar'ia Fedorovna took two rooms in a merchant's home (where he led a most 'irregular' life) only a few paces from the school. As a man of learning, he was received by the whole of Orenburg society. To Pogodin he wrote grandly, 'Service here is a less nasty thing than elsewhere. Here they value people who know their work, and the officials (director and inspector) are honourable people, though, of course, little experienced.'[87] One of his new acquaintances was V.V. Grigor'ev (no relation), one of the country's greatest geographers and ethnographers, who was working out of Orenburg at the time.

At first, A.A. Grigor'ev was popular in society. A quarter-century after he left Orenburg, he was still remembered by many of the inhabitants, often for his witty verses. Once, for example, the teachers of the school received an order to appear on church parade along with the cadets on the fourth Sunday of Lent. Required to sign the order, Grigor'ev improvised: 'Though I have many sins, / Of which I repent and am ashamed, / I do not confess on command; / I do not pray at the beating of the drum.'[88]

The school was divided into two squadrons, the first for the Russian children of Orenburg's gentry and merchants, and the second for the offspring of Kazak (then called Kirgiz) officers and other non-Russians. Grigor'ev taught the second squadron, which the locals regarded as much more open and talented than the first. It did not take him long to alter the prescribed curriculum. He objected in particular to a text by a certain Alexei Razin, *God's World* (Bozhskii mir), which served as an introduction to natural science. It was, he complained to Strakhov, full of materialism and utterly meaningless; no child could understand it, and even if it could be understood it would not interest a dog. The book was, in his view, an extreme consequence of the realism of the past fifteen years that had killed humanist and classical education even in the gymnasia.[89] Strakhov, himself a teacher, later commented that Razin's book was an excellent introduction to natural science and criticized Grigor'ev for his ignorance of the subject.[90] Grigor'ev refused to use the book and substituted historical readings for it. He also would not teach rote lessons to the upper class and read it proper lectures instead. He taught Slavonic grammar to the middle class, in addition to Russian. To Strakhov he boasted that the officials came to his classes every day and were beginning to pay attention to his fight for humanism, by which he meant his efforts to have the Russian and Kazak schools amalgamated.[91]

Grigor'ev was popular with his students. P. Iudin, who later gathered stories about him at the time of his tenure in Orenburg, wrote of him: 'Apollon Alexandrovich, loving his "literature" not only as a teacher but as a writer, with all the ardour of youth and passionate expansiveness, tried to instill in the hearts of these listeners his insights and to develop in them an aesthetic feeling for everything good and beautiful. And all of the students loved him and always listened to his keenly felt lectures with visible enjoyment.'[92] At first, he was popular in society as well. Even after events had taken a turn for the worse and Grigor'ev was ostracized by others, the students came to him in his rooms to hear him read 'Minin' – a reference to K. Akasakov's patriotic play, *The Liberation of Moscow*. These were for him emotional moments. He wept, he said, and they wept, and by nightfall he was convinced that there was something to life apart from personal suffering.[93]

Things began to go badly when, encouraged by his success in the classroom, Grigor'ev decided to reach out culturally to the larger community. According to Iudin, he set out to give a series of lectures 'On Contemporary Education and the Improvement of Learning for Youth.' In Iudin's version, the first and only lecture was not well received. The local intelligentsia, especially the teachers, whom Iudin labelled hidebound and backward, ridiculed him, and he felt rejected and humiliated. From then on he shunned the company of his co-workers and distanced himself from society. Soon he began to drink, to miss classes, and to be generally unpleasant. His friends began to avoid him, and the officials to supervise his work more closely.[94]

Grigor'ev did not mention such a lecture in his letters to Strakhov. Instead, he wrote in January 1862 that he had given four public lectures on Pushkin during the holidays in order to raise money for the Literary Fund, with admission at a rouble a lecture or three roubles for the four. He raised

320 silver roubles, but the people of Orenburg did not understand about the Literary Fund. The governor-general asked him to donate the money instead to the poor of the city. The first lecture, he said, was directed against the theoreticians (Chernyshevskii and Dobroliubov) and created no small perplexity in his audience. The second apparently elicited stormy applause. In the third he defended Pushkin as a Russian citizen and national poet, embittering all who understood him. In the fourth, he chided a generation that knew only the poetry of Nekrasov and made fun of Fourier's utopian imaginings, earning again enthusiastic applause. It was a good audience, he said, but it would have been twice as large had he brought an elephant. The governor-general, he bragged, gave a reception following the lectures.[95] Though Iudin made no mention of these lectures, the posters announcing them have been preserved.

Grigor'ev was bored in Orenburg. He hated cities without a history or architectural monuments and called it the 'muddiest slum in the whole of the Russian Empire.' But he also admitted that no matter where he was, spleen and apathy soon overtook him.[96] He even expressed his feelings in a poem that became well known in the region: 'Boring city of a boring steppe, / Vile camp of despotism, / At the gates a gaol and chains, / And within either boor (*kham*) or khan.'[97]

Mar'ia Fedorovna was also bored. Her position in Orenburg society was far from comfortable. The petition of Lidiia Korsh, Grigor'ev's legal wife, to the authorities concerning her husband's failure to support her and the children and her legal action to claim part of his salary alerted society to the fact that Mar'ia Fedorovna was not married to Grigor'ev. In a letter of May to Strakhov, Grigor'ev claimed that the 'authorities' had not raised difficulties about his 'illicit cohabitation' and that his wife's complaint against him was reaching a judicial solution. He went on to describe his life with his companion. Unfortunately, Mar'ia Fedorovna left no record of her own feelings. It appeared that she was trapped in her social ambition and in her vanity and the disadvantages of her vulgar birthright. She aspired to respectability – longed, Grigor'ev said, for the life of the 'lady.'

She suffered for her past, he went on, but he could detect not a scrap of moral feeling in her suffering. She chided him for his poverty. She would never, she informed him, marry a man for whom she had to do the cooking herself. He arranged piano lessons for her, and he taught her French. But, he complained, she did not try to learn. He tried, he claimed, to harness her vanity by making an actress of her. That failed because of shyness, the 'shyness not of talent but of petty vanity.' Her début ended in a tantrum in the wings and a public quarrel with Grigor'ev. She attended his lectures but was, he suggested, jealous of every society lady who touched his hand. She abused all servants, was always angry toward society, and had an 'immoderate maternal attachment to a little dog.' She reproached him for her plight noon and night.[98]

That Mar'ia Fedorovna loved Grigor'ev and felt concern for him was not in doubt. She wrote secretly to Strakhov from Orenburg in May 1861 to beg him to persuade Apollon to stop drinking because 'wine kills his talent and can harm him in the service.'[99] Grigor'ev himself recognized that she acted as she did from love for him. 'Yes, she loves me, loves me with all her heart, in the way an egotistical being, deprived of any light, can love, loves me only, to be exact, because "those who were before me" did not even arouse any feeling.' He considered sending her away but feared to lose someone who loved him – a forty-year-old who had 'lost his looks.' He was powerfully attracted to her sexually. He considered suicide but checked himself, excusing his weakness on the grounds that since she was suffering he should be patient and himself suffer for her. Such resolutions were hard to keep, however; he began to fear that living as he did in sin and under social censure meant for him both moral and creative death. 'That thought ripened and ripened, my melancholy deepened and deepened and, of course, debauchery was the result.'[100]

It is clear from Mar'ia Fedorovna's scant testimony that Grigor'ev was drinking from the time he arrived in Orenburg. Wherever he lived, he later told Strakhov, he went on 'ten-day benders.'[101] After the failure of his lecture on education and the ridicule that he suffered for it, he became less sociable and more susceptible to the temptation of wine. Now he visited only a few people. His best friend was an unsavoury character, a junior officer named Stepan Nikolaevich Fedorov, who became his drinking companion. He began to miss classes and incur the distrust of the school officials. Only one inspector of classes, P.V. Miturich, stayed true to him and defended him from the attacks of officials and teachers, but he too was known in society for his drinking.

In January 1862 Mar'ia Fedorovna, not surprisingly, could stand no more and fled the city for St Petersburg, leaving Grigor'ev alone. He ceased to take care of himself, appearing in a dirty and torn old suit, with his hair long and unkempt. He began to wander from house to house demanding vodka.[102] Sometime in the second half of June, Grigor'ev, too, could bear it no more and took a leave of absence until 1 August, ostensibly to go to Moscow in order to arrange to move his legal family to Orenburg. Instead, he went to St Petersburg and did not return or even report his intention not to return.

On 4 December, the remarkably patient director of the school reported that Grigor'ev had deserted his post. Ten days later, Grigor'ev petitioned to leave the service, explaining that he had fallen sick with hepatitis in St Petersburg but, hoping to be cured, had not notified his commanding officers. 'Now my illness has become worse and I am no longer able to continue in service.' Attached was a medical report, written by a St Petersburg doctor and dated 19 August 1862, testifying that Grigor'ev had been ill since at least 27 July with hepatitis, complicated by catarrh in the duodenal intestine (colitis). The army demanded a second medical report, which was submitted on 31 December. It diagnosed chronic pulmonary catarrh and peritonitis with dyspepsia and recommended constant care. His resignation from service was granted in May 1863. Since he had not stayed on for the requisite three years and had taken part of his doubled salary in advance, he ended by owing the Cadet Corps 810 roubles.[103]

Grigor'ev had long since ceased to theorize in his writings about the woman question. In his own mind, he had settled the matter in his letters to Gogol'. There he had argued that men and woman were different and in some ways unequal but were complementary. Their relations, however, had been distorted by social attitudes and conventional morality. The present education of girls merely encourged their dependence on men. Marriage was debased. Instead of being complemented by their wives, men tyrannized over the girl/woman that society insisted on preparing. Consequently, the essential complementarity of men and women was destroyed. It could be restored, in Grigor'ev's view, only through a change in social attitudes and major improvements in the education of women. Years later, in his notes for the 'Diary of a Writer,' Dostoevskii, in commenting on Strakhov's hostility to J.S. Mill's feminist views and especially his thoughts on women's education, suggested that Grigor'ev had agreed with Mill.[104] Grigor'ev's preference for experience over theory caused him to give up writing about the woman question but not to stop thinking about his personal experience of relations with women. It remained the subject of much of his poetry.

He examined his relationship with Mar'ia Fedorovna in the last instalment of his continuing novel *Odyssey of the Last Romantic* (Odisseia poslednego romantika) – the poem 'Along the Volga' (Vverkh po Volge). The poem was published in *Russkii mir* in 1862. Unlike the egoistic lovers in his earlier works, for whom love was a battle of self-assertion, the characters in 'Along the Volga' were real and living persons with a much more complex relationship. Trapped in the web of their social origins, from which they could not escape, the lovers, for all their passion, were doomed to separate. In Grigor'ev's earlier poems, women were essentially moral beings, in whose presence he felt spiritually purified. The relationship in 'Along the Volga' was primarily physical, not only in the sexual but in the existential sense.

In the poem, he wondered whether the kind of elevated moral love that he felt for Leonida Vizard would fail if tested by the ordinariness of real life. Now he had learned that a purely physical love could endure the rigours of daily routine no better. The poem was another version of 'The Struggle' (Bor'ba), played out this time not against the romantic background of the gypsy taverns of Moscow but against the realistic greyness of provincial towns, the boarding-houses of St Petersburg, and a cold, bare room in which a child perished. Like Turgenev's *A Nest of Gentlefolk*, in which Grigor'ev's failed marriage was alluded to, Grigor'ev's 'Along the Volga' was about the impossibility of happiness. It was a rejection of theorizing about the relationship of the sexes in the face of life's pressing realities, a desperate recognition of the irresolvable complexity of life and the ironic principle that gave those fated to live it such joy and such pain.[105]

When Grigor'ev returned from Orenburg to St Petersburg, he resumed his relationship with Mar'ia Fedorovna. In one of his letters, he mentioned that he had bought furniture in order to meet her minimum demands for a household.[106] Strakhov reported that for a time after his return, Grigor'ev's circumstances improved considerably. The apartment that he had set up with Mar'ia Fedorovna was orderly, and he began to affect a certain dandyism in his dress.[107] He was again contributing to *Vremia*, but still chafing at having to publish only in someone else's journal. And once again the temptation to take over as an editor-in-chief was put in his way.

9

Beauty, Suffering, and Art
1862–1864

O friends, I do not wish to die,
I want to live to think and suffer.

Alexander Pushkin, 'Elegy'

The publisher of *Iakor'* (The Anchor), of which Grigor'ev became editor in 1863, was F.T. Stellovskii, a music-store owner, with whom Grigor'ev had already collaborated as editor of the short-lived *Dramaticheskii sbornik* (Drama Miscellany) in 1860. In March 1863, Grigor'ev set out from St Petersburg for Moscow to arrange for contributors for the journal. He took on the task, he wrote, as 'the last serious gambit of my life.'[1] Mar'ia Fedorovna, with whom he was still living, shared his sense of urgency. On 9 March she wrote to Strakhov to tell him that Apollon had gone to Moscow and urged Grigor'ev's friend to contribute to *Iakor'*, as he had promised.[2] But the emotional stress of the visit to Moscow, where his father was near death and his estranged family lived, and where he had spent happier years, proved to be too much for Grigor'ev. He drank up the funds given to him by Stellovskii to set up the journal and returned to St Petersburg without achieving anything.

In spite of Grigor'ev's failure in Moscow, the first number of *Iakor'* appeared at the end of April 1863. The full title of the journal was *Iakor'. Vestnik obshchestvennoi zhizni i literatury, teatra, muzyki i khudozhestv* (The Anchor. Messenger of Social Life and Literature, Theatre, Music, and the Arts). It was published in St Petersburg weekly, on Saturdays. In addition to Grigor'ev, *Iakor'*'s most important contributors were the composer A.N. Serov, who wrote occasional music reviews and a number of lengthy articles on Wagner; the writer K. Babikov, the Moscow correspondent; the youthful collaborator of *Vremia* (Time) Dm. Averkiev, who wrote about art and music; and N.N. Strakhov, who published a translation of Schelling's *Philosophy of Mythology* in *Iakor'*. A regular feature was a political section, which published articles on Poland, the Schleswig-Holstein question, other European events, and the U.S. Civil War. It also ran a regular column about life in the provinces and followed theatre and music, especially opera, in St Petersburg closely. Grigor'ev contributed a combative column on contemporary Russian journalism. With the ninth issue, a satirical supplement called *Osa* (The Wasp) was added in which Russian manners and mores were entertainingly examined and the foibles of rival journals excoriated.

Iakor' enjoyed considerable popularity in theatre circles. It did not succeed, however, among the general public. Grigor'ev at first threw himself into the new task with much of the enthusiasm he had shown for *Moskvitianin* (The Muscovite) and later for *Russkoe slovo* (The Russian Word). But soon the old pattern reasserted itself, as public indifference and his personal struggle against melancholy and apathy combined to destroy his confidence. His pessimism was apparent from the first number of *Iakor'*, in which he revived the 'unnecessary man.'

Disappointment at the lack of success of *Iakor'* was only one of Grigor'ev's problems. His relationship with Pogodin had deteriorated steadily since he had abandoned the Trubetskois. On his failed trip to Moscow to garner contributors for *Iakor'*, he saw his stern mentor Pogodin, who lived until 1875, for what turned out to be the last time, and no letters between them survive after September 1861. It is likely that Grigor'ev visited his father in Moscow on the same trip. If so, it was also for the last time: the old man died in April or May 1863. The simultaneous loss of the father whom he had despised and the surrogate father whom he loved and who had rejected him because of the chaos of his personal life must have disoriented and demoralized Grigor'ev.

His last love had also gone. No evidence exists after March 1863 that Mar'ia Fedorovna and Grigor'ev continued to live together. Konstantin Leont'ev, who met Grigor'ev for the first time in March 1863, called on his new friend at his apartment during Easter week (1–6 April). He described the place as poor and empty. Grigor'ev, he noted, appeared to be living alone. When Leont'ev inquired about his marriage, Grigor'ev replied bitterly, 'Ask what kind of marriage I have.' Though Leont'ev went on to hint at the rumours he had heard about Grigor'ev's family life, he declined to say more. Shortly after that visit he returned to find Grigor'ev gone. After a long search, he found him living in a poor room in a poor district.

Grigor'ev was not in when he called; Leont'ev never again saw him.[3] His friends recalled that no amount of money could assist Grigor'ev since he continued to give away whatever he had. P.V. Bykov observed, that Grigor'ev handed out money 'right and left, both to friends, often passing, and to every Tom, Dick, and Harry, forgetting his own expenses.' He also neglected to eat. 'Only the greatest hunger would wake Grigor'ev up, recalling him to himself. He did not eat but more or less bolted titbits prepared by his landlady or in some filthy tavern.'[4]

At the end of May, *Vremia*, for which he had continued to write, was closed by order of the censors for an article written by Strakhov on the Polish question, depriving Grigor'ev of an additional source of income. By the end of June he was again in debtors' prison, and once more his friends managed to get him out. Though he nominally remained editor of *Iakor'*, he had effectively ceased to play any role in it by January 1864. By the beginning of 1864 the Dostoevskii brothers had reconstituted *Vremia* under the new name *Epokha* (The Epoch). Grigor'ev resumed his relations with the enterprise, publishing in the March and May issues of *Epokha* the continuation of his autobiography, *My Literary and Moral Wanderings* (Moi literaturnye i nravstvennye skital'chestva), which he had begun in *Vremia*; further articles on the theatre in Russia; and several other major pieces, including his final effort to explain organic criticism in 'Paradoxes of Organic Criticism' (Paradoksy organicheskoi kritiki).

In a series of editorials in *Iakor'*, Grigor'ev set out the aims of the new journal. Its first task was, he declared, negative, or critical. He noted the proliferation of programs in Russia for solving the nation's problems. Many of those schemes, he maintained, were false, and *Iakor'* would explore and expose such flaws wherever they appeared.[5] Consequently, *Iakor'* devoted a good deal of space to examining the ideas of rival journals.

Grigor'ev declared *Iakor'*'s solidarity on many issues with *Den'* (The Day), the Slavophile journal edited by I.S. Aksakov, but insisted that *Iakor'* was pursuing a more practical path. In particular, it rejected the Slavophile ideal of the Russian past, especially its Muscovite centralism, which he accused *Den'* of wishing to prescribe for the present by force. He pointed out that, much as he respected Moscow Slavophilism, he differed with it on a number of issues. Unlike the Slavophiles, he understood Russian nationality to be an organic phenomenon that combined both pre- and post-Petrine elements; he saw the people not just in the old boyars and the steppe peasantry but in the whole of the nation; he believed in particular that the national type in both its good and its bad manifestations had developed in the merchant class. Much in contemporary social life was unimportant to *Den'* but precious to *Iakor'*. The best example was contemporary art and literature, which *Den'* dismissed as filth and lies.[6]

Grigor'ev also tried to set out some of his more profound differences with the Dostoevskii brothers. His journal, he declared, shared with *Vremia* its passionate belief in the narod but felt that *Vremia* did not understand the national essence. It did not comprehend that the spiritual life of the people was founded on Orthodoxy: 'Apart from our profound faith in the highest dogmatic essence of Orthodoxy, we believe in its enormous historical significance ... In spite of all its numberless schisms, which indicate among other things the full vitality of its living juices, Orthodoxy is a vigorously alive phenomenon, and like everything alive is strongly joined to its essence. The life of the land may have deviated from the norm on many points, but, all the same, it stubbornly clung to its spiritual independence, to its collective and national mores.'[7]

Grigor'ev disavowed Dostoevskii's claim that Russians were perhaps 'destined by fate to bring about the universal-human solidarity of the world.' The Slavophiles had made the same error of supposing that Russia was the heir to the Hegelian mantle and would continue or complete the quest of World Spirit – a quest that did not exist. Grigor'ev dismissed both Dostoevskii and Aksakov when he wrote, 'But we definitely do not intend either to reconcile West and East or to force Peter the Great to hop to Muscovite church councils.'[8] Grigor'ev did not assign to the nation itself any European or universal mission. Reconciliation of East and West meant to him simply the uniting of the two halves of Russian national consciousness. In Italy he had spoken of Orthodoxy as revitalizing the West, but the reference was to Western Christianity, not directly to the cultures of the other European nations. In spite of the great importance that he attached to Orthodoxy as a potent religious principle, he nevertheless consistently opposed the obscurantism of the official church.

In an editorial called 'Theory and Life,' Grigor'ev pointed out the essentially conservative nature of all doctrines that were based on theory. In order to defend their theory and preserve its purity, theorists were forced to deny reality and resist the phenomena that life cast up. For example, the radical journal *Sovremennik* (The Contemporary) was compelled to attack Turgenev's Bazarov – the nihilist of his novel *Fathers and Children* (Ottsy i deti). But, Grigor'ev contended, Bazarov merely gave a name to what was already present in the air. Or the satirical supplement of *Sovremennik*, *Iskra* (The Spark), opposed the music of Wagner simply because it was a new trend that required something more than thought to understand.

Grigor'ev went on, however, to allow that theory that arose out of the careful analysis of real social life had a place. And he took the opportunity to flog once again the hated 'literary gastronomes' of the art-for-art's-sake school. At least the analysis of the theoreticians was not dilettantish indifference to life and its problems. One could argue with a theoretician, but not with a dilettante. But neither could answer the burning questions to which life demanded solutions.[9]

Grigor'ev pursued *Iakor''s* critical task in a series of articles on the world of Russian journalism. In it, he reviewed the history of journalism in the country and went on to evaluate journals in contemporary Russia. Between Belinskii's death and the advent of Chernyshevskii and Dobroliubov as its ideological leaders, *Sovremennik* had lacked convictions. Belinskii's successors had turned it into a 'socialist stable.' The chief characteristic of the new *Sovremennik*, he went on, was its attempt to harness life to logical thought. *Russkoe slovo*, the journal of Dm. Pisarev, had no raison d'être. It merely said what *Sovremennik* said, but to less effect.[10] Elsewhere he said that in *Sovremennik* were congregated 'the aristocrats of negation.' They were sure that art, history, and philosophy were the record of savagery. But at least one knew where one stood with them. *Russkoe slovo*, in contrast, seemed unable to decide about anything.[11] Ivan Aksakov's *Den'* was a journal of strong beliefs but had no sympathy for the voices of life. *Russkii vestnik* (Russian Messenger) sported something that resembled convictions, but its anglomania was out of step with Russian reality. *Vremia* had been a confused but essentially correct expression of nationality.[12]

In his declared war on obscurantism, Grigor'ev devoted as much time to attacking the reactionary journals, such as *Domashniaia beseda* (Domestic Conversation), *Vestnik iugozapadnoi Rossii* (Messenger of Southwestern Russia), and *Kievskii telegraf* (Kievan Telegraph), as he did the radical and liberal ones. He traced their origins to *Maiak* (The Lighthouse) and to what he, somewhat arbitrarily, labelled Admiral Shishkov's 'St Petersburg Slavophilism,' about which he had written extensively in *Vremia*. Once again he characterized them by their hostility to all inquiry into life. *Maiak's* negation, he repeated, had, however, been necessary and had helped to give birth to a positive view of nationality. But the new obscurantist journals were merely spitting into the wind. *Domashniaia beseda* was, for example, the heir to *Maiak*, but was utterly lacking in the latter's talent.[13]

Osa was *Iakor''s* own satirical supplement, which Grigor'ev also edited. Consistent with his views on the function of comedy, he saw satire as the most valuable weapon available in the struggle against falsehood. But, again in conformity with his earlier views, he pronounced that satire had to be employed with care so as not to undermine the faith of the masses in literature and journalism. Satire was effective as a form of negation only when it negated in the name of a positive ideal and shared a living faith in truth, beauty, and order.[14]

Grigor'ev admitted that *Iakor'*'s positive task was as yet unclear: 'We know only one thing: that we have a positive haven, nationality [*narodnost'*] with its typical-historical features, profound faith in its strength, and a foothold in the unbroken chain of its traditions. In this haven we put down our anchor.'[15] He pointed out that *Iakor'* was not alone in seeking refuge in the harbour of nationality and pointed to Aksakov's *Den'* and Dostoevskii's *Vremia*. Hard as it was to define a positive task, Grigor'ev maintained that it would be unfair to demand of *Iakor'* more than of the other journals of *pochvennik* leanings. For all of them, their positive task was more one of feeling than a defined, theoretically formulated thought. Not theory but art held the key to the future. *Iakor'*, he declared, believed in democracy in art and boldly affirmed its faith in art despite the sneers of the theoreticians and others. The realization of *Iakor'*'s positive program, he conceded, was a long way in the future, but it was gaining sympathizers.[16]

Grigor'ev also staked out a spare political position in *Iakor'*. From the point of view of popularity, he granted, the journal was not wise to be 'backward' in the political sense. And by the standards of the nihilists and liberals, he allowed, *Iakor'* was backward politically. So be it, he declared; were the editors of *Iakor'* 'as we ought to be we would die.'[17] Grigor'ev's whole outlook on life was profoundly conservative, but it was based on what he called 'conservatism in the best possible sense.' Such an approach was rooted in the national traditions, was sympathetic to all reasonable phenomena of the past, and examined and criticized every new need in social life in light of the spirit of the people and its best interests. Grigor'ev's conservatism allowed for change and recognized the need for advocates of change. Indeed, his conservatism was strongly reminiscent of Ralph Waldo Emerson's in his brilliant essay of 1841, 'The Conservative.'[18] Grigor'ev mentioned Emerson favourably more than once, but it cannot be shown that he knew that particular essay.

Grigor'ev had long since accepted Pogodin's argument for autocracy in Russia and had at one time declared himself to be a Slavophile at least in politics, sharing the belief in the autocrat and the *zemskii sobor* – a kind of consultative body of sixteenth- and seventeenth-century Muscovy. He had also been an enemy of liberalism for many years, expressing his hostility in attacks on characters such as Panshin in Turgenev's *A Nest of Gentlefolk* (Dvorianskoe gnezdo). Now he reaffirmed his opposition to liberal principles. 'The formula of despotism of 1792 (liberté, egalité, fraternité, ou la mort) is as hateful to us as the formula of any other despotism,' he wrote in *Iakor'*.[19] Rejecting the idea that the self was an abstraction, Grigor'ev also rejected the notion that the self could be defined in terms of abstract rights. Indeed, the greatest threat to the autonomous personality lay in the abstract theory of individual human rights. Bourgeois individualism, which eliminated human differences in favour of a commonality of rights, was, in his view, fundamentally hostile to individuality.

Grigor'ev interpreted the emancipation reforms more as a social than as a political change. He stressed the importance of the emancipation in bringing the peasantry back into the full life of the nation. He also wrote vaguely about the necessity of providing land to the peasants. He pressed for an end to secret court activities and their replacement with public juridical procedures. Grigor'ev believed that the overriding principle of social change in Russia had been the vast growth in consciousness in the last few years which required action to correspond to its development. 'Life demands action, order, reason.' Highly important, therefore, was *glasnost'*, with its freedoms of speech and conscience, through which the nation could express its wishes to its sovereign. That was some measure of his political education, since earlier he had declared the meaninglessness of such words.[20]

Grigor'ev also returned to a question dear to his heart in *Iakor'* – the cultural rights of nationalities. It was not a popular issue in Russia at the time. The rebellion in Poland, which got under way in January 1863, was producing among his countrymen a wave of chauvinism that was to lead to massive Russification of the non-Russian nationalities. Undeterred, Grigor'ev argued in the spirit of Herder that every nationality had the right to an independent existence, to its own colour within the general painting of the world structure. Contrary to government policy, which did not recognize Ukrainian as a separate language, Grigor'ev argued that Ukraine had a right to its own language and literature.

There were two kinds of arguments made against national autonomy, he pointed out. The adherents of the first kind argued merely from political expediency as reason enough to suppress national differences; proponents of the second wished to extirpate nationality in the name of an abstract humanity. Both denied life and relied only on thought. 'In their eyes, any little political idea or any beastly social utopia is incomparably dearer and higher.' Ultimately, he agreed, nationalities would in some measure amalgamate and mingle, but only at their own behest and not under compulsion.

Grigor'ev, however, defined nationality in terms of language, race, and beliefs and warned that an attempt to define it beyond those limits was to invite strife and suffering.[21] It was by no means a thorough denunciation of Russian imperialism, but his rejection of Russian cultural domination in the Empire stood out not only among conservative voices but also among liberals and even many radicals who saw Russian cultural pre-eminence as a necessary concomitant of the advance of European civilization. Elsewhere, *Iakor'* with equal temerity supported the admission of Jews to the Odessa Club.[22]

In *Iakor'* Grigor'ev again catered to his pessimism, reviving the side of his character that he had named the 'unnecessary man.' The reason that he was unnecessary, he explained, was that he was not an artist. He was the sort of person who understood everything and achieved nothing. To be an artist, one had to live a life within oneself; an artist required calm and concentration. But Grigor'ev declared that he preferred to experience life in reality rather than to contemplate it. Not only was he not an artist, he went on, but, strictly speaking, he was not a thinker either. 'My thinking is rather kaleidoscopic. That's the truth! I can never see a subject from one side only and therefore cannot form a clear theory about it.' Others could build theories and even believe in them. But he could not. In order to make a hole in a wall, he philosophized, one needed to keep butting it in the same place. 'That is what a theory does, butts with all its might on one spot because that is the only spot it can see.' Nor, he went on, was he a scholar, because he understood no subject through and through. The time of people of his kind had passed. Perhaps people of encyclopaedic knowledge and philosophical ideas were once needed in order to awaken life from the sleep of dullness, but life had now awakened and required action, and 'we are abolished.'

He warned the nihilists, however, that their time too would pass, because life moved on quite independently of those who tried to shape it. 'Life, then, is a strangely mysterious matter: it contains a principle of irony and is in some ways a two-faced Janus; smash Obolomovitis with a hammer and you will get Stolzitis, and you will feel that Stolzitis is rather worse than Oblomovitis.'[23] In another article, the 'unnecessary man' warned the nihilists not to try to serve the public (the educated). The Slavophiles were right to have contempt for it. 'Only a literary louse serves, has served, and will serve the public.' The people loved and understood Ostrovskii, 'its great poet,' and K. Aksakov's play *The Liberation of Moscow* (Osvobozhdenie Moskvy), whereas the public did not.[24]

Iakor' was primarily a journal of drama and music. Grigor'ev set about enthusiastically promoting them and advocating establishment of truly indigenous theatre and opera companies. He had since youth been a student of Russian folk music and was deeply interested in the collection of folk songs and their performance. Over the years he had written a good deal on the subject. In 1854 he had written a review of M.A. Stakhovich's *Collection of Russian Folk Songs* (Sobranie russkikh narodnykh pesen') in *Moskvitianin*, and in 1860 he had returned to the subject in an article in *Otechestvennye zapiski* (Notes of the Fatherland). The two pieces exhibited his remarkable familiarity not only with the songs themselves but with the method of their collection and preservation.

Grigor'ev maintained that the Russian folk song and the songs of Slavs in general were still alive and developing at a time when in other European nations folk songs had become an archaeological curiosity: 'Our singing is not stored in an archive: it lives in the people, is created according to the old laws of its independent creativity; a new feeling, a new content is sometimes brought into the prepared, customary old forms, the old does not die, it lives and continues in the new, sometimes remains whole and untouched, sometimes grows, is sometimes, if you will, perverted, but in any case lives.'[25]

Since the Russian folk song was still evolving, it could not be recorded once and for all. Grigor'ev advocated instead that collectors concentrate on preserving types of songs rather than trying to produce a definitive version of one song from many variants. He believed that the song was inseparable from its performance. 'The metre of the verses of a Russian song is incomprehensible without singing.'[26] Too many academic collectors looked on folk songs as only a written form and apparently had never heard them sung. But all of the life was taken out of a folk song unless it was repeated in the form in which it was actually sung.

The folk song was a 'poetic-musical or musical-poetic whole.' In order to be effective, a collector had to possess both poetic and musical feeling and understanding, as well as deep familiarity with the forms of poetry and music, taste, and a good ear.[27] But even those qualities were insufficient. Since the folk song was a product of a long, organic process of development from the popular consciousness, the collector must be empathetic to the mind and heart of the people. If a collector permitted education to become a barrier between himself and the people, he could not penetrate the folk song. 'In the truly educated person the links with life, with the soil, are not severed by education.'[28] Few collectors were sufficiently acquainted, in Grigor'ev's opinion, with the real sources of the songs – the singers themselves. But that deficiency was not easy to overcome. Russian folk singers would not simply perform on request; one had almost to catch them at it. 'One can only happen upon Great Russian singing: one has to have a method of approach – successfully approached, then you catch it!'[29]

At first glance, Grigor'ev pointed out, every talented folk singer in Russia was a product of patriarchy. Each was a natural talent beyond the external world of learning, art, and civilized life. But no matter how dark their sphere of life, they were all linked directly to other, less dark spheres, and expressed the ideas, concepts, feelings, tastes, and sympathies of the whole of the life around them. Grigor'ev dismissed many of the performers of Russian folk songs who made a living by performing them. Most of them were distinguished by the way they used the songs to express some aspect of their own talent and not by their love of the works themselves.[30]

Grigor'ev went on to talk about the place of gypsy music. He believed that the gypsies had played over the centuries an important part in the development of the Russian folk song. For Grigor'ev, their music was characterized by its innate sense of musical harmony, but not by melodiousness. They harmonized any motif in a distinctive way and had a gift for instrumentation and for blending the voices of a chorus in original ways. Their principal contribution to Slavic music had been instrumentation of Slavic melodies. They had given them their passionate coloration and preserved many traditional lyrics and motifs. The gypsies were, Grigor'ev noted, a race that sang by nature but had little of their own to sing. Grigor'ev claimed to be aware of only three purely gypsy songs. The gypsies were not original, therefore, but merely preserved what they had received from the Slavs. Grigor'ev was, however, sensitive to the way in which gypsies could alter songs through variations.[31]

Grigor'ev's enthusiasm for Russian folk music was undiminished in *Iakor'*, but he was increasingly preoccupied with the development of Russian classical music. He had known Nikolai Rubenshtein since his days as a young editor and was acquainted as well with his brother Anton. The latter had pressed for establishment of a conservatory of music in Russia for several years, and in September 1862 the St Petersburg Conservatory opened its doors, with Anton as its director. Nikolai later became director of the Moscow branch of the conservatory. Though the opening of the conservatory was welcomed by Grigor'ev, he soon realized that its mere existence was no guarantee that Russian music would be its focus. In fact, the conservatory was almost indistinguishable from its counterparts in Germany or France. Few Russian compositions were performed there, and classes in theory and composition were based on western European models.[32]

Grigor'ev's friendship with E.S. Protopopova also brought him into contact with Alexander Borodin, a future member of the Russian five who are regarded as the founders of Russian classical music, whose wife she became. But it was no more than an acquaintanceship. More important for Grigor'ev's ambitions for Russian music was his close friendship with the composer A.N. Serov – not one of the celebrated five – whom he had met sometime shortly after his return from Italy. Serov was very attached to Grigor'ev. Once, during a period of ill health, Serov refused to see anyone except Grigor'ev, who had a standing invitation to call at any time.[33] Serov's wife, who wrote lovingly of Grigor'ev in her memoirs, first encountered the critic lying on a couch in her apartment, where he had arrived to congratulate the couple on their marriage. Finding no one home on his arrival, Grigor'ev had settled down on the couch to wait and soon fell asleep. Returning, Serova discovered the rumpled sleeper with head buried in a pillow, emitting a din of snores and whistles.

For his part, Grigor'ev worshipped Serov. He once said that when he heard certain passages from the composer's opera *Judith*, he wanted to kiss Serov's boots. Once he said to his friend: 'We are old, Sasha, but I tell you, I would not exchange my age for their [the radicals'] youth – they understand nothing of art, they do not value genius and talent or know that genius and talent are not mortal creatures but demigods, inhabitants of paradise ... ; when they descend to us kneel to them, honoured people! – they let you sip that invigorating nectar that feeds them; they give you that fire which they keep alight on their eternal credences in front of their holy altars; these altars are sacred art!'[34] Grigor'ev encouraged the writing of *Judith*. After the opera opened successfully in St Petesburg in May 1863, Serov wrote to K.I Zvantsov, a music critic: 'It was a total triumph just as Apollon Grigor'ev promised me when he had just become acquainted (a year ago) with my *Judith* ... through the sound of an out-of-tune organ by which he convinced me through hints only of what the true effect would be.'[35] So deeply involved was Grigor'ev in the opera that at a performance in the capital city he became so enraptured that he anticipated some of the dialogue at the top of his voice and was unceremoniously ushered out of the theatre.

Serov was in turn greatly influenced by Grigor'ev to search for a native theme for an opera. Zvantsov recalled that in the winter and spring of 1864, Serov organized a number of literary Thursdays. At the centre of them was Grigor'ev, 'a man of genius and chaos, but sincere and good as far as I could judge.' A frequent visitor at those evenings was Hans von Bülow.[36]

Serova reported that under Grigor'ev's influence she and her husband read more Russian works and their love and understanding for the national deepened.[37]

Grigor'ev's intellectual influence was felt more formally in the circles in which Serov moved as well. A group formed around the dramatist A.A. Potekhin, about whose work Grigor'ev had not been kind in the past. Serov was a member, and Grigor'ev's ideas about the moral independence of art and his dislike of the aesthetes occupied a prominent place in the discussions. Serova wrote: '*Expressiveness, life, a preference for Russianism* [*russitsizm*], *absence of the routine* became the motto of our circle, and beauty, as an obligatory element, did not enter our artistic catechism, or at least did not play an essential role.'[38] Near the end of his life, Grigor'ev urged Serov: 'Write a national opera, Sasha, you have enough talent; something national, "ours," is more vital than something foreign. Surely, even the Greeks wrote about what was theirs, national, and the more their art was theirs, Greek, the more invaluable it became. It is nonsense to say that our people possess no beauty. That is up to the artist.'[39] Serov did not write a national opera, but after Grigor'ev's death he did attempt to collaborate with Ostrovskii on one. The plan did not bear fruit.

Grigor'ev had high hopes for the development of opera in Russia, in terms of both composition and performance. Apart from Glinka and Serov, he granted, Russian composers had so far produced little opera. But he saw Serov's *Judith* and its initial success as a promise of the great future of the form in Russia. He believed development of domestic opera to be a matter of the greatest urgency and predicted that it would some day outshine all its competitors.[40]

Though Grigor'ev took pains to make it clear that he loved other music, he insisted that the music of Wagner, or the musical drama, was the wave of the future. *Iakor'* even printed a portrait of Wagner in its pages. For Grigor'ev, Wagnerism was 'true realism' in music – consistent with his views about literature – a realism of form on the stage through which an ideal was clearly visible. True realism, he said, arose in parallel in Wagner and Serov, Hugo and Ostrovskii. Like drama in general, musical drama was profoundly democratic. No matter what the critics thought of it, Wagnerism, he maintained, was understood by the people as a true expression of the time. In Serov's *Judith*, Grigor'ev saw the triumph of Wagnerism in Russia. Though he felt that in some ways *Judith* was closer to Meyerbeer than to Wagner, it was nevertheless Wagnerist because of its true realism. He expected Russians to improve on Wagner. The latter, he said, was strong on harmonies but suffered from the general poverty of melodies in German music. Serov and his fellow Russians, in contrast, had a wealth of melodies in the Russian folk tradition on which to draw.[41]

In *Epokha*, Grigor'ev developed his views on the democratic nature of drama and the new opera: 'Art in general and dramatic art in particular would play a most pitiful role in the history of nations were it solely the object of enjoyment by the dilettantes. It flows out of the masses and has the power to illuminate the masses. It is the lens in which is concentrated the light of consciousness, but this light comes not from outside but so to speak also "rises" from the depths of the life of the masses. It is its own light, but concentrated, defined, and in that sense possessing a leading role.'[42] For that reason, the theatre had to subordinate itself to literature so that what appeared on the stage would be recognized by literature as literary. Critics in Russia as well as impresarios should pay greater attention to Russian and less to German and French theatre. Russian national theatre was an aid to social development and betterment. The time for both a Russian theatre and a Russian opera had come. Opera was as democratic as any other art: 'As a democrat, I am of necessity a Wagnerite, because the principle that opera is drama, the principle of which Wagner is the highest and at the same time purest representative in our time – is a fully democratic principle which eliminates dilettante enjoyment and gives pleasure to the masses.'[43]

Grigor'ev was also encouraged by the development of opera performance in Russia. Unlike performance in the theatre, which had in his view declined in quality, opera companies had steadily improved. Though there were as yet, he lamented, no good baritones and too few contraltos, there was nevertheless the real possibility of creating a true performing opera. As in the theatre, Grigor'ev approved of naturalism on the opera stage. He disapproved of virtuosity alone and demanded that singers have strong acting talents. He urged the imperial theatre administration, during the period of internal reform that it was passing through, to begin to pay attention to the needs of opera.[44]

The passion of Grigor'ev's life since youth – theatre – still excited him. He was still himself acting in amateur performances. P.D. Boborykin met him for the first time in 1859 in Kronstadt at a performance of Griboedov's *Woe from Wit* (Gore ot uma), in which Grigor'ev was playing the role of Repetilov. Boborykin had heard a great deal about Grigor'ev from Edel'son and others and was delighted to meet him. They sat in the billiards room of the local hotel before the rehearsal and chatted about Florence. Boborykin noted Grigor'ev's attractive demeanour, 'in the old Russian manner,' and the 'characteristic jargon' of Muscovite literary men of the 1840s that larded his speech. Grigor'ev appeared to be sober but had a bottle with him when Boborykin, who was playing Chatskii, went off to rehearse. When the fourth act, in which Repetilov first appears, came, the critic had not arrived in the theatre; he was found, dead drunk, on the floor of the billiards room.[45]

Grigor'ev was convinced that only *Iakor'* was seriously interested in the theatre: 'The theoreticians do not want to follow the theatre and treat it as a thing utterly useless and contributing little to the creation of the phalanstery; the daredevils [imitators of *Sovremennik*] in imitation of their masters spit on [the theatre].'[46]

But he was pessimistic about the prospects for drama and the theatre, especially in Moscow and St Petersburg, Russia's old and new capitals, respectively.[47] There were, he opined, too few dramatists of quality. Ostrovskii was the sole exception. The stage in the capitals was dominated by foreign plays in translation or various kinds of vaudevillean rubbish. Moreover, since the great days of the 1830s and 1840s, Russian acting had declined. Only a handful of actors of quality remained, among them Grigor'ev's favourite, P. Vasil'ev. Since the retirement of Vera Samoilova, he declared, there were no good actresses in the capitals at all, though he granted that there were some young actresses of promise. In Moscow and St Petersburg, he concluded, no native or foreign play could be performed at the level of acting competence at which it ought to be. In hopes of strengthening the theatre through competition, Grigor'ev strongly advocated that private theatres be permitted to compete with government-sponsored theatres, at least in St Petersburg.

He was somewhat more optimistic about provincial theatre. While in Orenburg, he claimed to have seen productions of Ostrovskii's plays that served the author's intentions much better than peformances he had seen in the capitals. In the theatres of Moscow and St Petersburg, actors spoke in unnatural, mannered tones. 'Not a word do they speak with simplicity – everything is done with a grimace.'[48] Theatre schools taught declamation in speech and mannerism in gesture. The provincial actors had been spared such training and, from their love and care for the material, spoke and moved naturally. The epitome of the false and petty in acting was, in his opinion, an actor called Burdin; Grigor'ev coined the word 'burdinism' to describe everything that he disliked about the stage in Russia. After Grigor'ev's death, Burdin himself wrote a furious letter to Dostoevskii, after the term appeared in *Epokha*, demanding an apology. Dostoevskii coolly informed him that Grigor'ev's opinion was also the journal's.[49]

Grigor'ev also attempted to explain in *Epokha* why only Ostrovskii had so far succeeded in writing Russian national drama. If Ostrovskii was a truly national playwright, Grigor'ev asked, why had he never written about peasant life or about advanced people of the upper social classes? The answer was that it was impossible to write dramas about either. The peasantry represented either serfdom – that is, a historical anomaly that no longer existed – or was as it had always been – remote and untouched by Western influence: 'I know very well that such a peasantry, the ideal of the Slavophile doctrine which I deeply respect, is morally higher and purer than the urban population as the result, of course, of the exclusiveness of certain local factors.'[50] But art could immortalize only fundamental types, and these emerged only among the free classes that had tested their strength in the clash with civilization or the forces of the West. Drama was the cult of nationality, the re-creation in art of the nation's whole, full types, both good and evil ones; one-sided types, no matter how clear, could not be made into drama. One could include the peasant way of life in a play, but it could not stand on its own. The upper sphere of Russian society was a mirage, neither Russian nor Western, and not part of the national drama. Only the merchant class, which contained both the essence of Russia and that of the West, had sufficiently developed a conscious Russian nationality. Consequently, Russian types had developed only among the merchants, and only they were the subject of drama.[51]

In his last years, Grigor'ev was preoccupied with what he called 'true realism' not only in opera and drama but in the rest of the arts as well. In *Iakor'*, for example, he reprinted verbatim his article on realism that had been first published in *Svetoch* (The Beacon) in 1861. He also wrote a lengthy review of Pisemskii's novel *The Turbulent Sea* (Vzbalamuchennoe more). In Pisemskii, he said, realism had found a real artist. But Pisemskii's realism was the realism of the gentry and sometimes of the bureaucracy. Though the idea of nationality and the soil lay behind his work, Pisemskii believed only in the Russia of the nobility and despaired of its transforming itself into the new. Pisemskii continued Gogol''s work in pointing up all the moral falsehoods in Russia. But he had no ideal, merely the sad reality of gentry life. Pisemskii, then, was a negative realist, and not a true realist because he lacked an ideal.[52]

In one of his last articles in *Epokha*, Grigor'ev returned to one of his favourite targets – Dmitrii Grigorovich. There were, he wrote, writers such as S. Aksakov, Dostoevskii, Ostrovskii, Pisemskii, Pushkin, L. Tolstoi, and Turgenev who had great empathy for the people in general and the peasants in particular and had an understanding of nationality in both its broad and its narrow senses. They captured a variety of national types without a one-sided focus on a single aspect of the life of the nation. There were other writers, such as G. Uspenskii, who turned to the *narod* in the narrow sense because they knew nothing else. But those people, too, performed an organic task in their own narrow way. Finally there was a type such as Grigorovich, who craved simplicity, rejected social questions, and merely yearned for a pastoral life. The love of landscapes and commune of such artists did not penetrate to the depths of the national way of life but viewed it in a distant mirror, in imitation of foreign writers such as Georges Sand.[53]

The first instalments of Grigor'ev's autobiographical *My Literary and Moral Wanderings* had appeared in *Vremia*, which was closed by police order in 1863. With the establishment of *Epokha* in 1864, the instalments resumed. Grigor'ev first conceived of preparing a memoir while he was in Orenburg. Originally he thought of it as a portrait of the provincial 'backwoods' (*glush'*). At the urging of Mikhail Dostoevskii, however, he was persuaded to write a memoir that included his childhood. Grigor'ev was well aware of Herzen's autobiographical reflections in *My Past and Thoughts* (Byloe i dumy) and of the comparison between Herzen's experience and his own. There were several points of contact between the two works. They had in common a childhood and youth in Moscow, and both were powerfully evocative of time and place. Both authors aimed to disclose through the example of their personal lives the greater historical forces that were shaping the days of their youth. Both emphasized their affinity for the culture of the Russian people as well as the profound influence on them of the literature of the West. But Grigor'ev's memoir should not be seen as a comment on or polemic against Herzen's. It was an autonomous entity that recounted a parallel but unique experience.

In spite of their many similarities, the two works differed in fundamental ways. Herzen's was the autobiography of a cause, of an attitude to life, and of a political and social stance. His personal story was told in the larger context of great events – Napoleon's invasion, with which the memoir opened; the Decembrist rebellion; his father's influential friends, as well as the little people of the household; and sightings of Tsar Alexander I in Moscow and later of Nicholas I. It was a tale of obstacles overcome, oaths sworn, sacrifices made, and regrets disavowed, a story of heroic dimensions.

Grigor'ev's *Wanderings* was the autobiography of an individual or, perhaps, of a type. The story unfolded in the little world of the Zamoskvorech'e district of Moscow and behind the walls and closed gates of the family home. The great events were faintly echoed or completely unheard, and there were only the little people. Grigor'ev's was a tale of weakness, flawed character, failure, compromise, and sensuality – decidedly unheroic. If there were heroes, they were the currents (*veianiia*) of the time that made him what he and those around him were.

Whereas Herzen's memoir celebrated the education of the personality through social struggle, Grigor'ev's stressed the inner contradictions of the personality that rendered it immune to the lessons of the social environment. True to his notion that the ideal was accessible only through the real, Grigor'ev's memoir was a tour of the Zamoskvorech'e, a specific time and place, the real through which the ideal currents of the age made themselves known, and a guide to his inner self, the self-conscious product of those currents.

Grigor'ev's most important contribution to *Epokha* was his article 'Paradoxes of Organic Criticism.' The piece took the form of a letter addressed to F.M. Dostoevskii and represented the author's final effort to clarify his views. He complained that when he used the words 'life,' 'living process,' and 'living forces' no one understood their meaning. To him, he explained, life was something mysterious, inexhaustible, beyond total comprehension.[54] Between the totality of life, on the one hand, and reason, on the other, lay a wide gap. But humans were not blind and incapable of understanding something of life. In the vast history of the living life, humans could discern the organic laws of the living process. They could also understand that those organic laws of the past would repeat themselves in the future, but in different forms and under different guises. Each age gave names to the laws and categories of the living process, and those names became living forces that gave birth to and directed the life of the age.

Since the organic links that joined those living forces were discernible, humans, of necessity, gradually formed an organic outlook. Belinskii's historical view was, for example, one-sided, and had he lived his historical view would have evolved into the organic. That was clearly a revision of Grigor'ev's earlier position that Belinskii would probably have remained a centralizer. On the difference between the historical and organic views, Grigor'ev wrote: 'The most essential difference of that view that I call organic from the one-sided historical view consists in the fact that the first, i.e., the organic view, recognizes as its point of departure creative, spontaneous, natural, vital forces, in other words: not mind with its logical requirements and those demands of theory to which it inevitably gives rise, but mind and its logical requirements – *plus* life and its organic manifestations.'[55]

Naked reason could lead only to theories, and theories were always out of date from the moment of their conception. 'Consciousness can explain only the past: creativity casts its, in a manner of speaking, clairvoyant views into the future, often very far, flinging up such features that only subsequent development fills in with colours.' And Grigor'ev quoted approvingly Tiutchev's line in the poem 'Silentium,' 'A thought spoken is a lie.'[56] The theorists dismissed art as rubbish except as a means to mobilize human energy for something they regarded as more important. They saw nationality as nonsense, destined to disappear in an all-human amalgam. They regarded history as nonsense, a skein of absurd errors, ignorant blindness, and confused enthusiasms, and they saw science, except in its mathematical and natural forms, as the greatest nonsense of all, a distraction that numbed the mind and prevented action. Finally, they dismissed all thinking as useless and unnecessary. All that was required was an upbringing on five or six intelligent books, in which all the necessary wisdom was contained.

Grigor'ev recognized the legitimacy and necessity of nihilism in Russia. The moment of consciousness represented by Bazarov and nihilism was understandable, he said, and had every right to be a part of the general process of human consciousness. That was why he had refused to make fun of the *veianiia* of the age, even if he ridiculed individual nihilists. Historically, he pointed out, this period of materialism was necessary to the evolution of the organic view: 'Thought, science, art, nationalities, history are definitely not steps in some kind of progress, not a husk shed by the human spirit immediately on the attainment of some positive results – but the eternal, organic work of eternal forces, inherent in it as an organism.'[57] If the nihilist idea of progress were true, it would follow that it would not be worth reading Homer after Shakespeare wrote, or Shakespeare after Hugo. That would be true of all fields of knowledge. Like the Westernizers before them, the nihilists had fallen slave to the Germano-Romance tribes and the philosophy of centralization. In that sense, the nihilists were merely continuing the Westernizer movement. But nihilism was organically necessary and flowed out of Russia's past history. At fault was Hegelianism, especially the left variant, with its 'all-devouring progress' and the triumph of the 'extreme limits of logical thinking,' which fostered a 'mechanically comforting structure of life and the world.' Only Schelling, with his deep faith in art pulled life back from the abyss of 'final reason.'[58]

But if nihilism was necessary, it was also doomed. Life's calculations rested not on reason but on beauty (variety, balance, proportion). The capacity of the human mind was not coterminous with the potential of the universe.[59] What appeared to the mind to point in one direction was subject in life to sudden changes of direction. Those changes constituted the irony of life, and that irony was governed by the principle of love:

The task of this passionate and, at the same time, complete love of the secret power ... is, so to speak, artistic in its broadest and deepest meaning: to lead us up a blind alley, to strike us dumb, to turn our intellectual calculations inside out, to demonstrate to us every hour, every minute the fact that though the logic that is in our skull is the same as that that is poured into the immeasureable whole, the calculations in life's logic are made *en grand*, in immeasurably wide spaces. Yes, life would not only be murderously boring but also meagre if everything in it were fulfilled according to cerebral calculations.[60]

Life was a tale of beauty told over and over again in a variety of forms that continuously surprised, shocked, renewed, and enriched the human soul.

Grigor'ev's article had been inspired by a number of failings that Dostoevskii had found in organic criticism. What his concerns were can only be inferred from Grigor'ev's reply, but they apparently included vagueness of definitions, lack of a clear program, and, most devastating for Grigor'ev, the accusation that organic criticism, too, was only theory. Grigor'ev was deeply hurt to have Dostoevskii call him a theoretician:

It was particularly bitter for me to hear [this accusation] from you for many reasons, and first because in the moral process, under the influence of which our view of life and literature formed, the doctrine on behalf of which you were once one of the activists played a very important role.

You, however, without willing it, are yourself in part also responsible for the many literary misunderstandings arising between us. You were in a certain measure, an *obstacle* to me in the clarification and development of my views on the course of our literary and moral and social development.[61]

In *Vremia*, Grigor'ev explained, he had begun a series of articles intended to explain the relationship of literature to life from Pushkin to the present. Those pieces had reached the point where the early stages of independent Slav thought had been attained. But they went no further. They stalled, said Grigor'ev, because Dostoevskii had refused to accept certain Slavophile beliefs.[62] Grigor'ev was referring here to the disagreements that had played some part at least in his flight to Orenburg in 1861, particularly, Dostoevskii's unwillingness to place Orthodoxy in the forefront of the program of *pochvennichestvo*.

The affinity between Dostoevskii and Grigor'ev was great. They shared an aesthetic appreciation of life, identified Christ with Beauty, and believed that 'Beauty would redeem the world.' Both had delved deeply into the human psyche and discovered there the complexity of being, the ambiguity of happiness, and the 'joy of suffering.' Grigor'ev, together with Strakhov, exerted on Dostoevskii a powerful influence in the early 1860s, drawing him increasingly away from the 'flirtation' with the nihilists and toward a more openly religious understanding of Russian nationality. Dostoevskii's fascination with Grigor'ev survived the latter's death by many years.

That death came as a severe blow to Dostoevskii, following hard on the heels of his brother Mikhail's sudden death in July 1864. It was also a blow to *Epokha*, which survived Grigor'ev's funeral by only a few months. Of Grigor'ev's role in *Epokha* Strakhov wrote, 'It is true that the public almost never read [his articles], just as they do not read them to this day; but in our eyes and for serious literary people he gave weight and colour to our journal.'[63]

Grigor'ev's condition had deteriorated rapidly from the middle of 1863. Strakhov recalled that in his last year of life Grigor'ev often needed to be cared for like a child. Periods of recovery, optimism, and activity were followed by further lapses. Eventually even help did no good. Grigor'ev immediately spent or gave away any money given to him and then simply asked for more. Strakhov wrote of him at this time, 'A less practical man neither I nor many others who knew him had never met. He knew how to do nothing for himself; he had no idea how to look out for his own interests.' He was drinking heavily. P.D. Boborykin reported on Grigor'ev's drinking exploits with L. Mei and later with Dm. Averkiev and V.V. Krestovskii. 'Wits recounted at that time that they [Averkiev and Krestovskii] along with Grigor'ev were capable in the absence of vodka of drinking pure alcohol, eau de cologne, and even kerosene.'[64]

Even his writing was becoming controversial again, not only because of its content but because he was transferring whole passages from earlier articles into new ones. Accused by his friends as well as his enemies of plagiarizing himself, he pointed out in his own defence that Belinskii, too, had moved whole articles from *Nabliudatel'* (The Observer) to *Otechestvennye zapiski*.[65] He also had to hear again and again the old story about how he had stolen ten kopeks from a desk at *Russkii vestnik*.

By July 1864 he was again in debtors' prison. To N.V. Mikhno, editor of *Russkaia stsena* (The Russian Stage), he wrote that his detention did not

bother him because he was working hard. He offered Mikhno his translation of *Romeo and Juliet* and an article to accompany it; they were published in *Russkaia stsena* in August. He also reported that he was writing
something for *Epokha*. In another letter, he asked Evgenii Edel'son to
bring him a book by Kavelin and an article by Pavlov. V.S. Serova remembered him in the prison in these last days of his life: 'I remember his miserable room, his intelligent, talented face which ennobled those grey, dirty
walls; his ardent, sincere conversation which under these conditions penetrated all the more deeply, made an even greater impression on my young
mind.'[66]

Others visited his shabby room. Fedor Dostoevskii called on him and
encouraged him to list his debts. Grigor'ev complied with a note to Dostoevskii: he owed 200 roubles to a certain Lazdovskii, 35 to the Beliaev shop,
100 to the tailor Stepanov, and 19 to the debtors' prison – 10 to the overseer
and 9 to the latter's assistant. He begged Dostoevskii to make the sacrifice
and buy him out because he was going mad with boredom. As well, he
complained, his haemorrhoids were developing with 'awesome force.' He
promised to settle down near Dostoevskii and place himself in his hands.[67]
Dostoevskii sent him some money, which Grigor'ev, following his friend's
advice, used to pay off the tailor.[68]

Strakhov, too, called on him around 15 September. They discussed
Slavophilism under whose influence *Epokha* was steadily falling. Grigor'ev
saw dangers in a full surrender to the Slavophiles and told Strakhov that he
had spent the previous night pacing the corridors of the prison, drinking
tea, and arguing with the ghosts of Strakhov and the editor of the
Slavophile journal *Den'*, Ivan Aksakov.[69]

It is not clear when Grigor'ev left the prison. His freedom was probably
purchased by the wife of a general, A.I. Bibikova, a woman previously
unknown to Grigor'ev, who hoped to ensnare him to correct her own compositions. Grigor'ev was, in one version of the story, released on 21 or 22
September.[70] Meeting his benefactress on the street outside the prison, he is
reported to have fallen on his knees before her in a dramatic display of gratitude.[71]

Other evidence suggests that he left the prison earlier. In a letter to Strakhov that is dated only 'Saturday,' Mar'ia Fedorovna, who though apparently no longer living with Grigor'ev was still seeing him, wrote that she
had gone to visit him at the prison on Friday and was told that he had left.
She begged Strakhov to tell her where they had 'concealed' Apollon Alexandrovich. She went on to say that on leaving the prison she had met an
acquaintance, who had told her some unpleasant and painful news (pre-

sumably that another woman had rescued him in order to exploit him). She asked Strakhov to help her to be reconciled to Grigor'ev and to tell him at least that he should treat her as other acquaintances, without anger and jokes and the nervous outbursts that he so often had when angry. 'I feel terribly sorry for him,' she wrote.[72] Saturday was 19 September, so he must have been released at the latest on the 18th, before Mar'ia Fedorovna called.

Grigor'ev died on 25 September 1864, apparently of a stroke, alone in his apartment after a heated quarrel with a publisher. He was buried in the Mitrofan'evskii Cemetery in St Petersburg; in 1930 his body was reinterred in the Volkovo Cemetery in Leningrad. The funeral took place on 28 September. Boborykin reported that it was the poorest possible burial on the greyest possible day. Among the mourners were Fedor Dostoevskii, Dm. Averkiev, N.N. Strakhov, V.V. Krestovskii, A. Serov, and several of his friends from the debtors' prison, among them the comic actor Lev Kambek. The artist Bernadskii also attended, as did the actor P. Vasil'ev and the actress Vladimirova.[73]

Boborykin later included an accurate description of Grigor'ev's funeral in a short story written in 1875. In the procession were about fifteen people. Behind walked a woman dressed in mourning, followed by her two-seater carriage. The church at the cemetery was nearly empty. In a corner apart stood a young woman, wearing a scarf and silently weeping. The woman who had come in the carriage stood on the family side of the grave. Boborykin speculated that she was Grigor'ev's landlady. After the service, the mourners gathered in a shop for tea and traded stories about the deceased. Grigor'ev's saviour, Mme Bibikova, appeared toward the end of the tea to tell her reluctant listeners about how she had purchased Grigor'ev's freedom in return for the theatre royalties of his translation of *Romeo and Juliet*.[74]

None of the unidentified women at the funeral was Mar'ia Fedorovna. She learned of Grigor'ev's death only after the burial. On 4 October she wrote to Strakhov that 'they did not want to let me know about Apollon's end.' She continued, 'How sad and painful it is to me to know that I lived so near and knew nothing.' And she begged Strakhov to send her 'his portrait.' She was also angry at Mme Bibikova, whom she accused of shedding tears in public only because she had lost a hundred roubles. 'But those tears that no one ever sees or hears, they are tears from the depths of the soul and heart.' She asked to be shown his grave or for Strakhov at least to write to her where he was buried.[75] Nothing more was heard of her until May 1866, when she wrote to Strakhov that she was in an 'insupportable position' and begged for his help. After that she disappeared.[76] Grigor'ev's wife, Lidiia, was also apparently not among the mourners. She was reported to have died some years later, in a fire started when she fell asleep while smoking in bed.

Epilogue

Only a few regretted Grigor'ev's passing. Ostrovskii learned of the death of his greatest advocate from Dm. Averkiev, who wrote: 'I must begin my acquaintance with you, Alexander Nikolaevich, with sorrowful news. Our Apollon is no more. He died of a stroke at three o'clock yesterday. I consider it my duty to inform you, whom Grigor'ev so passionately loved, about this first. I know that you will weep with us. In times of great sorrow it is comforting to know that you do not grieve alone.'[1] Serov took the loss hardest. K.I. Zvantsov returned from abroad a month to the day after Grigor'ev's stroke and found Serov in a lamentable state:

Alexander Ivanovich was in inconsolable mourning, having buried his beloved Grigor'ev; he spoke of him frequently and with ardour and gave me [Grigor'ev's] superb translation of Shakespeare's "Romeo and Juliet" in the form of reprints from some journal which he had got to give to his friends and wrote on the cover: 'From A. Serov in memory of the death of the translator, 27 [sic] September 1864.' To read such a translation was a great pleasure because, being familiar with the original, one could see in it not a sterile struggle of some stupid romancer against the text but the deeply felt re-creation of a great poet.[2]

Serov's wife recorded how much she regretted Grigor'ev's death because only his enthusiasm could have supported Serov through the moments of bitter doubts about his talent that at times assailed him.[3]

In the light of Grigor'ev's dissipated existence, it was not surprising that rumours soon were rife that he had died in a back alley in a drunken stupor. None of his close friends reported such a death. The only hint that the passing was other than as it was reported came from Dostoevskii some years later. In the notes to a *Diary of a Writer* (Dnevnik pisatel'ia), he asked after mentioning Grigor'ev's name, 'Is it known how he died?'[4] The comment is enigmatic and by no means conclusive. Grigor'ev's pattern had been to pull himself together after release from incarceration and pass through a period of optimism before melancholy and then drink once more overtook him. A bout of drinking on a scale sufficient to kill him so soon after his release was inconsistent with that pattern and supported the version of his death recounted by his friends.

D.I. Pisarev set the general tone of the press's response to Grigor'ev's early death in an obituary in *Russkoe slovo* (The Russian Word). Labelling the deceased a 'pure and honourable fanatic of an outmoded romantic world view,' Pisarev concluded that the 'whole development of our intellectual life has gone contrary to the sympathies and hopes of Grigor'ev.'[5] *Otechestvennye zapiski* (Notes of the Fatherland) praised Grigor'ev for his critical ability but condemned him for his exaggerations and 'obscure Slavophile doctrine.'[6] Writing in *Den'* (The Day), the Slavophile I.S. Aksakov was kinder than was the radical press. Aksakov noted Grigor'ev's exaggerations and the oddities of his views and expressions but saw him as a man who was sincerely and ardently devoted to Russian art. 'We were not close to him personally,' Aksakov concluded, 'but we regret his passing, regret the disappearance of committed people, of gifted originals, of ardent idealists.'[7]

An anonymous obituary in *Sovremennik* (The Contemporary) used the occasion of Grigor'ev's death to berate Dostoevskii and Strakhov for distancing themselves from their colleague in the notes that they had written to accompany his letters to Strakhov from Orenburg, which were posthumously published in *Epokha* (The Epoch).[8] The whole episode was embarrassing for Dostoevskii and appeared to rankle with him for years. He was surely correct when he asserted in those notes that Grigor'ev knew nothing about the practical side of running a journal; he went on to agree with Annenkov's earlier assessment: 'In [Grigor'ev] there was definitely none of that tact, that flexibility, which a publicist and any proponent of ideas needs.'[9] But Dostoevskii also understood the man's great gifts and the problems inherent in possessing them. In a note to the obituary that Dmitrii Averkiev published in *Epokha*, Dostoevskii compared the deceased and Dobroliubov: Grigor'ev was broader than Dobroliubov, broader and deeper and incomparably more richly gifted by nature than Dobroliubov. Dobroliubov was very talented but his mind was slighter than Grigor'ev's, his outlook incomparably more limited. That narrowness and limitedness were even partly Dobroliubov's strength. His horizon was narrower, he saw and understood less, consequently he had to convey and explain less and everything was all one; thus he himself spoke more intelligibly and clearly than Grigor'ev.[10]

In *Epokha*, Dostoevskii did move further away from the radicals and closer to the Slavophiles, as Grigor'ev had urged. An article in *Epokha* written by Strakhov went so far as to declare that 'Slavophilism has conquered.'[11] Though Grigor'ev had approved of the Slavophiles, he nevertheless had felt moved to plead with Strakhov to defend the 'independent life of the regions' against their Moscow centralism. No wonder Dostoevskii called Grigor'ev a Hamlet:

Grigor'ev was doubtless a passionate poet, but he was capricious and impulsive like a passionate poet ... Grigor'ev was, if you will, a real Hamlet, but beginning with Shakespeare's Hamlet and ending with our contemporary Russian Hamlets and female Hamlets, he was one of those Hamlets who were less divided than the rest, who reflected less than the others. He was spontaneously and in many matters even unbeknownst to himself a man of the soil, of the hills. Perhaps of all his contemporaries, he was the most Russian, by character (I do not say as an ideal; that goes without saying).[12]

Dostoevskii agreed with Grigor'ev that *Vremia* (Time) had experienced a number of problems. But he maintained that they were not of belief but of strategy and tactics. Had he still been alive, Grigor'ev would not have concurred. As noted in the previous chapter, he had already rejected in *Iakor'* (The Anchor) Dostoevskii's mission in *Vremia* to reconcile the West and the East, and Dostoevskii's new understanding of the mission of Orthodoxy would have appeared to him equally objectionable. One of the first and arguably clearest statements of Dostoevskii's Orthodox messianism appeared in his notebook for 1864:

After the appearance of Christ *as the ideal of man in the flesh*, it became as clear as day that the highest, final development of the personality must reach the point at which ... man discovers, knows and believes with all the strength of his nature that the highest use that man can make of his personality, of the fullness of the development of his *ego*, is to eliminate this *ego*, to surrender it wholeheartedly and selflessly. And this is the greatest happiness. In that way, the law of the ego joins with the law of humanism, and in their mingling, both the *ego* and the *all* ... mutually annihilate one another, and at the same time, each one also attains separately the pinnacle of its individual development.

Here is Christ's paradise. The whole history of mankind ... is only the development of, struggle for, aspiration toward and attainment of this goal.

But if this is the final goal of mankind, then it follows that man on attaining it completes his earthly existence. So man on earth is being, only developing being, consequently, not finished, but transitional.[13]

Such teleological thinking was utterly alien to Grigor'ev. The human soul was eternal and not transitional or developing, it would never be annihilated and had no goal beyond its own truth, which was ever present in it. For all his hostility to Herzen's atheism and his approval of Dostoevskii's religiosity, with the rejection of teleology Grigor'ev stood closer to the former thinker than to the latter.[14]

From 1864, Dostoevskii increasingly viewed history as a vast theodicy in which Russian Orthodoxy was destined to play the decisive role in completing man's earthly existence. As much as Dostoevskii in his famous Pushkin speech of 1880 drew on Grigor'ev's thought for his understanding of the significance of Pushkin in national development, the conclusions that he drew about the meaning of that process were very far from Grigor'ev's. For Dostoevskii, Pushkin's universality signified that 'to become a genuine Russian means to seek finally to reconcile all European controversies, to show the solution of European anguish in our all-humanitarian and all-unifying Russian soul, to embrace in it with brotherly love all our brethren, and finally, perhaps, to utter the ultimate word of great universal harmony, of the brotherly accord of all nations abiding by the law of Christ's Gospel!'[15] For Grigor'ev, Russia had no such mission. The task for Russian culture was to be itself and to permit other cultures to be themselves. Pushkin's universality signified the unity of West and East but also the reuniting of the divided Russian self.

Grigor'ev remained on Dostoevskii's mind long after the critic's death. In the early 1870s Dostoevskii encouraged Strakhov to write an article about Grigor'ev's literary significance. At the same time, however, he discouraged him from writing a memoir of Grigor'ev and the years of *Vremia* and *Epokha*. 'I think it is both too early and will not be interesting to others,' he wrote.[16] It is more likely that Dostoevskii remained sensitive about the criticisms that Grigor'ev had levelled at *Vremia* and did not want the controversy resurrected. In his notes for the *Diary of a Writer*, he hinted that he intended to write an article about Grigor'ev and mentioned his death several times.[17] The article was never written. Some commentators have seen in Dmitrii Karamazov many of Grigor'ev's characteristics – for example, his love of gypsies, carousing, and women. There were some similarities, and Dostoevskii was also aware of Grigor'ev's deep dislike of his father, which in Dmitrii Karamazov turned to patricide. But if Dostoevskii drew on Grigor'ev at all in creating Karamazov, he did not reproduce him whole.[18]

Others who had known Grigor'ev were less ambivalent about him than was Dostoevskii, and the critic was never entirely without a voice to speak out for him over the decades. Strakhov often referred to his ideals in the journal *Zaria* (The Dawn), which he published in the early 1870s; in 1876 he published the first of what was intended to be several volumes of Grigor'ev's collected works. The response was so poor, however, that nothing more ever appeared.[19] The most adulatory portrait of Grigor'ev in the decade following his death came from the pen of Konstantin Leont'ev, who shared many of his ideas about aesthetics.[20] Leont'ev fondly conjured up a portrait of Grigor'ev as he had been ten years before, in 1860 – his 'intensity,' his 'beautiful aquiline nose,' his 'serene, ponderous movements that concealed ardour,' his 'peaked cap' and 'long frock coat,' and his movement, 'stout and slow,' as he walked on the Nevskii Prospekt or drank tea, nodding his head as he listened. 'He resembled a good, intelligent merchant, naturally a Russian one.' So that this truly Russian personality not be lost, Leont'ev urged Grigor'ev's friends to write down for posterity everything they knew about the critic.[21]

Such views were rare, however, and Grigor'ev was systematically consigned as near to oblivion as publicists and critics could contrive. When, for example, the first volume of Strakhov's edition of Grigor'ev's works appeared in 1876, a reviewer in *Russkii vestnik* (The Russian Messenger), which by that time was increasingly conservative in outlook, took the opportunity to point out that Grigor'ev's obscurity among the public was well-deserved. Though a few of his ideas were interesting, he was out of touch with the times and seemed to be perversely interested only in those things that educated Russian society was not interested in. He also complained that Grigor'ev often took pages to prove what was 'obvious' and that little thought was evident in his writings – an extraordinary charge for anyone who has read Grigor'ev with any attention, but nevertheless typical.[22] The 'unnecessary man' would not have been surprised at that outburst. Harsher yet, and more viciously obtuse, was the judgment of the radical polemicist N.V. Shelgunov, who maintained that though Grigor'ev's radical opponents might have made mistakes and fallen into contradictions, their efforts contained life, 'whereas Grigor'ev preached death.'[23]

Only in the late 1880s did a more balanced assessment of Grigor'ev's life's work begin to creep into the literature. In 1886 S. Vengerov published a lengthy study of the 'young editors' of *Moskvitianin* (The Muscovite), in which he attributed to Grigor'ev the leading role.[24] The literary historian A. Skabichevskii, in an assessment in 1888 of Russian literature after the deaths of Belinskii and Gogol', wrote of the 'living democratic spirit' that pervaded Grigor'ev's writings and described him as a man of 'honourable, humane and national instincts'.[25]

The twenty-fifth anniversary of Grigor'ev's death marked the modest revival of his reputation. Strakhov pointed out in a memorial that Grigor'ev's reputation, like Pushkin's, would grow with the development of Russian literary consciousness. Though he was still out of favour with the public and his ideas passed over the heads of most readers, professors of literature such as A.D. Galakhov, O.F. Miller, and A.I. Nezelenov were teaching his ideas to their students. Strakhov pointed out, as proof of his growing popularity, that most of the 2,000 original copies of the 1876 edition of Grigor'ev's works were sold.[26] To mark the anniversary, a memorial service was held beside his grave in the Mitrofan'evskii cemetery.[27] K.K. Sluchevskii, who had been so embarrassed by the extravagant praise that Grigor'ev had heaped on him at his poetic début, read a poem over the grave. Two garlands of white roses decorated the new cross which the family had erected, thanks to a public subscription organized by the actor M.I. Pisarev.[28] The service was followed by a dinner and panygeric, which included a chorus of singers. There were no speeches, but a lively exchange of anecdotes and memories about the deceased took place. The event was attended by an interesting cross-section of the official, journalistic, academic, and artistic worlds. Guests included T.I. Filippov, the former young editor and now a very conservative government official; the actors I.F. Gorbunov and M.I. Pisarev; the journalists and writers D.V. Averkiev, S.V. Maksimov, and N.N. Strakhov; and professors G.P. Danilevskii, Gr. Gradovskii, A.I. Nezelenov, I.N. Shchelgov, and M.A. Zagulaev. Perhaps the most curious presence was that of N.A. Potekhin, author of the scurrilous play about Grigor'ev's exploits in Paris in 1858.

During the 1890s interest in Grigor'ev grew, perhaps stimulated by Vengerov's entry on him in the ninth volume of the *Entsiklopedicheskii Slovar'* (Encyclopaedic Dictionary) published in 1893.[29] The end-of-the-century revival of aesthetics among the so-called decadents also favourably affected Grigor'ev's fortunes. In 1892 Vasilii Rozanov named Grigor'ev as the founder of 'scientific criticism' in Russia, and two years later the critic Iu. Govorukh-Otrok judged him to be the true founder of an independent Russian literary criticism, as well as a critic of general European significance.[30] In 1896 A. Volynskii treated his organic criticism at length in his study of the

Russian critics. He concluded that his method had no scientific value and found his essays to be as malformed and disorderly as their author's life.[31]

Volynskii's dismissal of Grigor'ev's achievement was an early sign that Grigor'ev's ghost was to be dragged into the arena of literary politics. In 1899, the thirty-fifth anniversary of the critic's death, a writer in the conservative *Moskovskiia vedomosti* (Moscow News) complained the the 'liberal' press had completely ignored the anniversary on the dubious grounds that because Grigor'ev was unknown he was no good as a critic. The truth was, the author confided, that the liberals were interested only in simplistic messages rather than in serious literature. 'In the person of Apollon Grigor'ev our liberal press fears a serious intellectual force who by the whole tendency of his thought is a living reproach to liberal routine.'[32] In fact, liberal literary historians did not ignore Grigor'ev but merely continued to assess him coolly. P. Morozov, for example, called him a 'stepson' of Russian literature of the 1850s and 1860s; Iv. Ivanov pronounced him a confused enthusiast, who was in large part to blame for his own superfluousness. 'Grigor'ev,' he wrote, 'reaped what he sowed.'[33]

After the turn of the century, the Symbolist poets, especially Alexander Blok, discovered Grigor'ev's poetry, and Blok used Grigor'ev's 'Kometa' (The Comet) as the epigraph to one of his own collections. The link between Grigor'ev, who liked at times to call himself the 'last romantic,' and Symbolism was aestheticism. But the romantics understood aesthetics in terms of nature and the natural, whereas the Symbolists understood it in terms of cultural creativity. Grigor'ev, with his indifference to the natural and the stress that he placed on culture, occupied a central place in the reorientation of aesthetics from romanticism to Symbolism.

In spite of Blok's enthusiasm, Grigor'ev's reputation was again on the wane in the years before the First World War. In September 1914, marking the fiftieth anniversary of Grigor'ev's death, Rozanov, who had hailed Grigor'ev's organic criticism at the beginning of the 1890s, now speculated in *Novoe vremia* (The New Times) that the war might help to revive Grigor'ev's reputation among the Russian public. He pointed out that Grigor'ev was the first and only Russian literary critic to construct his criticism on foundations wider than a literary party or personal taste. 'For Chernyshevskii there was no Russia "beyond Chernyshevskii" and for Dobroliubov "human reason" ceased where *Sovremennik* was not read.' Grigor'ev was not like that and had paid a high price for his independence, in ridicule and isolation when alive and ignominious obscurity when dead. Rozanov likened his fate to that of Prince Vladimir Odoevskii, a talented writer who had shared Grigor'ev's enthusiasm for Schelling.[34] Earlier, Rozanov had praised Grigor'ev for being the first to recognize that beginning with Pushkin Russian writers had begun to create original native types of unquestionable moral beauty, who were in harmony with spiritual types living among the common people and to whom even Western writers were prepared to bow.[35]

Rozanov's prediction that the war would foster a renaissance of Grigor'ev's writings proved accurate. By November 1914, Leonid Grossman's lengthy and enthusiastic appraisal of Grigor'ev's organic criticism had appeared in *Russkaia mysl'* (Russian Thought).[36] In Grossman's opinion, Grigor'ev's primacy in Russian literary criticism was beyond dispute. He was, wrote Grossman, superior to Belinskii, Pisarev, and Dobroliubov in literary, linguistic, and philosophical erudition, in the completeness of his aesthetic doctrine, and in the gifts of analogy and the exact art of critical formulations. More than a Russian critic, Grigor'ev was, according to Grossman, 'one of the greatest European critics of the new school,' a predecessor of Henri Bergson and the bridge in European thought between Schelling and Bergson. Grigor'ev anticipated Bergson's notion of 'élan vital.' Like Bergson, he understood that whereas inanimate matter was the proper study of reason, eternally moving life was the proper subject of intuition, which itself was built on sympathy or love. Even more impressive to Grossman was the contemporaneity of Grigor'ev's concerns with the preoccupations of Grossman's own pre-war generation of artists and writers and the applicability of organic criticism to current literary analysis and commentary.[37]

The war also saw revival of the project of publishing Grigor'ev's collected works begun and abandoned by Strakhov in 1876. In 1915–16 V.F. Savodnik edited and published fourteen of Grigor'ev's major essays, including his 'Autobiography.'[38] Rozanov greeted the collection enthusiatically. 'Russian criticism was founded by Apollon Grigor'ev,' he reiterated, and he urged Russian youth to abandon the 'juvenile, glittering, but not very sophisticated' school of criticism founded by Belinskii and perpetuated by Pisarev in favour of the profundity of Grigor'ev.[39] Savodnik's efforts were seconded by V.S. Spiridonov. In 1918 he undertook to produce Grigor'ev's collected works and letters in a projected twelve volumes. Only one volume was ever published.[40]

While others busied themselves with making Grigor'ev's critical legacy available to the reading public, Alexander Blok in 1916 published the critic's collected poems.[41] He introduced the volume with a long biographical essay in which he sketched Grigor'ev's 'fate.'[42] Like Rozanov, Blok was outraged by the ridicule and neglect that Grigor'ev had suffered. In his view, the central question of Grigor'ev's thinking, the 'question about our independence,' was largely alien to the nineteenth-century intelligentsia which was obsessed with social and political questions. Only at the end of the nineteenth and the beginning of the twentieth centuries was there a Russian cultural renaissance and a new appreciation of Russian architecture, painting, philosophy, music, and poetry. For Blok, Grigor'ev was the 'only bridge thrown across to us from Griboedov and Pushkin: rickety, suspended over the awesome abyss of intelligentsia immaturity [*bezvremen'e*], but the only bridge.'[43]

In Blok's judgment, Grigor'ev was not pre-eminently a critic but was rather an artist. But the 'poet' in Grigor'ev was never able completely to subdue the '*intelligent*' who constantly made of him a thinker. In 'The Struggle' (Bor'ba), Blok saw Grigor'ev's best cycle of poems. 'In this struggle,' Blok wrote, 'one must look for the key to all of Grigor'ev's judgments and constructions.' Grigor'ev did not 'excoriate' the 'dark forces' of life, he struggled with them; and the contest was for him as for any artist a struggle with himself.[44] Grigor'ev passionately loved life, and life rewarded him with both deep melancholy and great joy. This 'derelict' and 'drunk' never aspired to be a 'serene being' or to seem 'pure'; he did not set ideals for himself 'to which it is proper to aspire.' He was without such hubris and because of that, and despite his 'outrageous behaviour,' he dwelt 'in the hands of the gods.'[45] Grigor'ev's soul, Blok believed, was connected with the 'depths,' though 'not as firmly and obviously as the soul of Dostoevskii and the soul of Vladimir Solov'ev.'[46]

Not everyone during the war had a taste for Grigor'ev, however. The critic Iurii Aikhenval'd complained that Grigor'ev placed limits on his own great talent by valuing writing not because it was free but because it was natural. But Aikhenval'd praised the critic for his 'literary courage.'[47] In contrast to Blok's claim that Grigor'ev had all the qualities required of a lyrical poet – a direct and deliberate challenge to Belinskii's judgment of 1846 – Aikhenval'd supported Belinskii and denied Grigor'ev's poetic gifts. 'He did not know,' Aikhenval'd wrote, 'how to transform the rich content of his internal world into true artistry, into vivid and living form, into uncomplicated melody.' Only occasionally did he triumph over 'creative impotence' and begin to resonate 'mightily and energetically.'[48]

Another reviewer of Blok's edition of Grigor'ev's poetry was angered by Blok's introduction. He saw it as intended to 'provoke a storm' with its unwarranted attack on the intelligentsia, which deserved better than Blok's abuse. As for Grigor'ev, he was by no means the only bridge between

Blok's generation and that of Pushkin and Lermontov.[49] Yet another hostile critic confidently dismissed Grigor'ev as 'not a progressive' but merely a 'negative' force against social evil.[50] The cruellest summation of Grigor'ev's brief life was penned by Zinaida Gippius. Unable to choose between right and left, she noted, he died 'like a dog' between the lines of battle.[51]

Interest in Grigor'ev's work sparked interest in his life. A few biographical or semi-biographical studies appeared before the war. The best of them was published just as the war began by S. Ashevskii in *Golos minuvshego* (Voice of the Past).[52] Until the war, however, the materials for Grigor'ev's biography remained scarce. Some of his letters had been published in *Epokha* in 1865, the year after his death. Others of his letters or fragments of letters found their way into N. Barsukov's vast literary monument to M.P. Pogodin, Grigor'ev's mentor and conscience, which appeared between 1888 and 1910. There were memoirs as well, the most important of which were by the poet A.A. Fet.[53] Then, in 1917 Vladimir Kniazhnin published a volume of materials for Grigor'ev's biography, including his non-fictional autobiographical writings, a large collection of his letters (prudishly edited) to a number of correspondents; archival materials relating to Grigor'ev's birth, education, and state service; and a comprehensive bibliography of works in which the critic was mentioned.[54]

Interest in Grigor'ev did not entirely dissipate in the wake of the revolution. In 1922 an exhibition of Grigor'ev's life and work was mounted in the Pushkinskii Dom, and M.D. Beliaev and V.S. Spiridonov prepared for the occasion a pamphlet biography of Grigor'ev and exhibition guide.[55] In 1924 P. Sakulin returned to a debate that had begun before the revolution about whether Grigor'ev had in the 1840s held socialist, especially Fourierist, views. He concluded that Grigor'ev had never been a socialist,[56] but the urge to classify him within the Marxist framework grew during the 1920s. In 1929 V. Friche distinguished Grigor'ev's organic criticism from Slavophilism, which he categorized as the ideology of the gentry class, from 'pure Westernism,' which was the ideology of the industrial bourgeoisie, and from socialism, which was the ideology of the advanced levels of the petty bourgeoisie. Organic criticism was, according to Friche, the ideology of the Russian commercial bourgeoisie, which was as yet uncorrupted by Western civilization.[57] N.L. Rubinshstein, writing in the same year, labelled Grigor'ev a petty bourgeois nationalist, who saw in the great bourgeoisie – that is, the merchant class – the only independent expression of the national way of life.[58]

After the 1922 exhibition, the most notable expression of continuing

interest in Grigor'ev was publication in 1930 of a volume of autobiographical writings, along with an extensive collection of memoirs about the critic,
edited by the former Socialist-Revolutionary ideologist R.V. Ivanov-
Razumnik. He provided a biographical sketch of Grigor'ev that eschewed
ideological classifications. He did, however, maintain, against the accepted
view that Grigor'ev was never a socialist, that for a time in the 1840s
Grigor'ev was a committed Fourierist.[59]

Though Grigor'ev did not disappear from the histories of Russian criticism and surveys of Russian literature, references to him in Soviet scholarship declined sharply in the 1930s, 1940s, and on into the late 1950s. In 1940
he did receive a surprisingly sympathetic assessment in the journal *Teatr*
(Theatre). The author agreed that Grigor'ev was a bourgeois nationalist but
pointed out that to be a bourgeois ideologue was not necessarily to be an
indiscriminate admirer of everything bourgeois. Grigor'ev's tragedy, he
concluded, was that he stood between two generations, between the
'fathers' and the 'children': 'He even knew, perhaps, on what side the truth
lay but that truth was alien to him.'[60]

A new history of Russian criticism published in 1958 re-examined
Grigor'ev's ideological leanings and rekindled interest in him. Though earlier commentators had not denied Grigor'ev's links with Slavophilism, they
had not dwelled on them either. The authors of the new history of Russian
criticism, in contrast, discovered the foundations of Grigor'ev's world view
in the doctrine of the Slavophiles and located him on the 'democratic left-
wing of old Slavophilism.' They argued that since Grigor'ev, unlike the
early Slavophiles, was acting in an environment in which the feudal serf
structure of society was collapsing and being replaced by industrial capital-
ism, he had taken on certain 'bourgeois tendencies' that prevented him
from accepting fully the Slavophile version of patriarchalism.[61] Like the
Slavophiles and unlike the left-wing *raznochintsy*, who oriented themselves
to the future of the people, Grigor'ev, they said, oriented himself to the
people's past, idealizing the patriarchal and preferring it to the new future
that was being born. They concluded that both his social and aesthetic theories were moribund and anti-historical and that their holder followed an
'objectively reactionary' path.[62] The view that Grigor'ev was, if not exactly
a Slavophile, then at least a Slavophile fellow-traveller, was reasserted in
1969 in a special section of *Voprosy literatury* (Problems of Literature)
devoted to Slavophilism. In it, A. Ianov characterized Grigor'ev's organic
criticism as the 'furthest development of Slavophile ideas,' its highest stage,
at least in the realm of literary criticism.[63]

Since the end of the 1950s, Grigor'ev scholarship in Russia has modestly blossomed. In 1959 a scholarly edition of his collected poems was published. It was followed in 1966 by a second scholarly edition, which was, in turn, reissued in a condensed and more popular format in 1978.[64] A short selection of his poems was recorded in a Melodiia series on Russian poetry from the eighteenth to the twentieth centuries.[65] A selection of Grigor'ev's critical works appeared in 1967, and a number of collections that brought together his articles on such topics as the theatre or literature and morality followed, revealing the great range of his artistic and critical interests.[66] In 1980 a new edition of his autobiographical writings, including most of the fictional ones, was published in Leningrad. In 1988 his *Odyssey of the Last Romantic* (Odisseia poslednego romantika) was gathered together and published as a single work.[67] In the past thirty years, the remaining relevant materials about Grigor'ev in Soviet archives have been published. In the early 1960s, B.F. Egorov had made available a large number of Grigor'ev's previously unpublished letters; since then other letters have been discovered and published.[68] Most recently, a selection of Grigor'ev's articles, poems, autobiographical fiction, and letters came out in two volumes.[69]

By no means all recent Russian commentators on Grigor'ev have accepted the view that he was a spiritual Slavophile. As early as 1959 P.P. Gromov pointed out that in the social-political struggle Grigor'ev tried to occupy a middle position among the contending camps in an effort to unite the extremes. The result was frequent crises and reversals in his thinking and contradictions in his creative work.[70] In 1980 V. Rakov observed that Grigor'ev possessed such a copious creative nature that commentators on his work were able to discover there anything that they wanted to find. In his view, Grigor'ev's ideas were stimulated by the philosophical searchings of the Slavophiles but developed far beyond their Slavophile origins.[71]

From the 1960s a new direction in Grigor'ev studies was the detailed exploration of the critic's relationship with F.M. Dostoevskii, in particular the nature of *pochvennichestvo*. Most scholars grant that Grigor'ev played the decisive role in the formulation of the native soil movement and agree that, while not carrying Dostoevskii completely with him, the critic did exercise an important influence on the novelist.[72] The consequence of associating Grigor'ev with Dostoevskii has been a tendency to distinguish more sharply between Slavophilism and *pochvennichestvo* and so to distance Grigor'ev from his Slavophile roots. Contrary to earlier assertions by Soviet writers that Grigor'ev's thought was, like Slavophilism, an idealization of the patriarchal past, A.L. Ospovat declared in 1980 that the secret of *pochvennichestvo*, of which Grigor'ev was the principal author, lay in its 'orientation toward the future.'[73] The latest and best major Russian work on Grigor'ev is the short life and times by S.N. Nosov published in the Soviet Writer series in 1990.[74]

Scant attention was paid to Grigor'ev by Western scholars before the 1950s. Alexandre Koyré in France and Tomaš Masaryk in Czechoslovakia, the latter writing in much greater detail than the former, were two exceptions. D.I. Chizhevskii's *Hegel in Russia* (Gegel' v Rossii), published in Paris in Russian in 1939, also included sections on Grigor'ev. After the Second World War, Italian scholars took the lead in exploring the work of Grigor'ev. Ettore Lo Gatto translated some of his critical studies into Italian in 1947.[75] W. Giusti provided a perceptive analysis of Grigor'ev and his work in 1958.[76] On the basis of their work, Laura Satta Boschian wrote a fine biography in Italian in 1969.[77] Few others have attempted to capture their subject whole. An exception was Jurgen Lehman, who prepared a major assessment of Grigor'ev's work in terms of its German idealist roots.[78]

The publication in English of Masaryk's *Spirit of Russia* in 1955, together with a translation two years earlier of V.V. Zenkovskii's *A History of Russian Philosophy* (Istoriia russkoi filosofii), in which Grigor'ev's philosophical idealism was discussed, probably helped to stimulate interest in Grigor'ev among Western scholars.[79] Their examinations established the critic in Western scholarship as an important Russian romantic nationalist. René Wellek, in his monumental *History of Modern Criticism, 1750–1950*, which appeared in 1965, revealed Grigor'ev, much in the spirit of Leonid Grossman, as a significant European literary critical theorist.[80] Those two approaches have guided Western scholarship about Grigor'ev; since the 1960s, scholars have most often studied him either primarily as a romantic nationalist or primarily as a literary critic.[81]

Grigor'ev's legacy cannot easily be so divided, and the present work has tried to bring its two sides together again. Without an understanding of his basic philosophical position and of his place in the intellectual debates of the day, Grigor'ev's role in the literary/critical battles of his time cannot be fully appreciated. Grigor'ev was widely acknowledged to be among the best-read men in the Russia of his day. He read extensively and deeply in Russian and European history, literature, and philosophy. In addition to Russian and several other Slavic languages, he was familiar with the classical languages as well as English, French, German, Italian, and almost certainly one or two others.

Not only was he thoroughly versed in European romanticism and idealism, but he also kept abreast of the new materialism, positivism, and utilitarianism in philosophy, historicism in history, and realism in literature. Of all the many influences on him, the most formative was that of Schelling, from his early works on idealism to the later philosophy of mythology. Partly through Schelling, and also directly, Grigor'ev was deeply influenced by Herder as well. He was familiar with the works of other idealists of the time, especially those of Carlyle, Coleridge, and Emerson.[82] Like them, one of Grigor'ev's important roles was to interpret Schelling and adapt his work to his national culture. In performing that task, he was neither more nor less derivative or eclectic than they. Within the broader context of European idealist thought, therefore, Grigor'ev was an innovative and important Russian exponent of a pan-European intellectual movement.

Belinskii's powerful presence was important in Grigor'ev's intellectual development, as it was for most thinking Russians of his generation. But his borrowings from Belinskii were few. Grigor'ev was much better educated than Belinskii and infinitely better read. He once commented, as noted earlier, that Belinskii was too poorly educated to be a good critic. In that sense he had little to learn from him. Even more important, Grigor'ev far more often disagreed than agreed with Belinskii and completely rejected his impoverished Hegelianism and the anguished liberalism of his last years. Grigor'ev, it is true, admired and approved of the Belinskii of 'Literary Musings,' which was written under Schelling's influence. But organic criticism was not merely a form of what Grigor'ev called Belinskii's historical criticism, which was loosely based on Hegelianism. On the contrary, it was a rejection of the philosophical foundations of historical criticism. That both were in some sense related to German idealist philosophy is undeniable, but to account them similar on those grounds is not to appreciate the vast differences between Schelling and Hegel.

Belinskii was the eclectic's electic who, through his passion and the purity and strength of his conviction and character and far less through the quality of his ideas, challenged Russians to think and talk about the abjectness of Nicholas I's Russia and helped to inspire a generation of protest. Grigor'ev grew to appreciate better than most how necessary Belinskii had been to the nation's struggle for cultural independence and how important it was to deal with his mighty legacy. He shared Belinskii's passion for the Russian theatre and for Pushkin, and if it is possible to speak of a direct influence it is in those two instances. For the most part, however, he struggled with Belinskii, rejecting many of his philosophical premises and often

criticizing his literary judgments, all the while honouring without reserva-
tion his role, his moral force, and his passionate commitment.[83]

Grigor'ev's contributions to Russian intellectual history were many. At
the heart of all his thought was the philosophical rejection of what became
known as scientific universalism or the philosophy of 'mastery' – the belief
in material and moral progress, and even human perfectibility, through
application of science and technology.[84] Along with Herzen, he deplored
all teleological modes of thinking in which some defined future goal shaped
present thought and action and reduced everything in the present to its
instrument. He subjected Hegelian historicism in particular to a searching
critique and found its universalism and instrumentalism wanting.
Grigor'ev, however, clearly understood the movement and dialectic of
thought. Consequently, though he deplored nihilism, with its materialism
and scientism and its own determinist outlook, he gave the devil his due
and recognized the vitality and necessity of the nihilists in the nation's cultural development.

In Grigor'ev's view, all national phenomena were organically necessary,
though always partial. For him, life was infinite and mysterious, and no
theory could contain, let alone direct it. Such was life's irony. In the assault
on scientific universalism, Grigor'ev occupies a leading place among Russians and an honourable one among Europeans. At the end of the twentieth
century, the inadequacies of the philosophy of mastery are nowhere more
apparent than in the former Soviet Union. Both Grigor'ev's critique of left-
Hegelianism and nihilism and his own thoughts on life and morality, art
and the nation are of interest today to a nation in search of autochthonous
cultural and philosophical sources. It is in that sense that Grigor'ev's time
has come again.

Organic criticism flowed directly from Grigor'ev's philosophical position.
There was nothing fragmentary or eclectic about organic criticism. It was
deeply rooted in a carefully considered philosophical stance, was fully elaborated in theory, and was applied in a number of articles of practical criticism. Building on Schelling's notion of art and genius as the mediators
between the ideal and the real, Grigor'ev endeavoured to show the relationship between art, on the one hand, and moral, social, and national development, on the other. Art, especially literature, expressed the universal ideal
through the particular experiences of real people living in specific times and
places, by which he meant nations (not states). Art brought the universal
moral truths that resided in every human heart into consciousness through
the creation of types. Beauty and morality were one, and the task of literary

criticism was to assess the degree to which the artist had measured the particulars of his own time and place against the universal standard of beauty and morality. Art and nationality were inseparable, and criticism raised the nature of their relationship to a wider consciousness. In an age that insists on a strict relativism in morality and artistic expression, the attempt to validate not only the uniqueness of all works of art as well as the particularity of their moral expression, but also their common membership in the moral universality of an ineluctable human condition, is refreshing and even, perhaps, necessary.

Grigor'ev applied organic criticism to the works of the best writers of his day. Most of them knew him personally, and many of them loved the man and admired his work. Along with Belinskii, Grigor'ev did more than any other writer to create the Pushkin cult that culminated in the Pushkin Day celebration of 1880, and a number of his thoughts about the great writer were repeated there without acknowledgment.[85] He perceived the significance of Gogol's writings more clearly than most of his contemporaries, though he underestimated his lasting importance in Russian literature. He did much to draw the attention of the public to the talent of Ostrovskii and in promoting him also contributed significantly to the development of a national theatre. For several years, he almost singlehandedly espoused the cause of Russian theatre and acting. Though he died before either Dostoevskii or Tolstoi had written their major works, he perceived both the potential and the direction of their talents. Turgenev believed that Grigor'ev's was the only Russian critic's opinion worth having.

Along with organic criticism came the critique of utilitarian criticism. Grigor'ev's was one of the most effective voices in the theoretical struggle with the nihilsts. And the multi-dimensionality of his judgments about writers and their works is welcome after the narrow views of the social critics. Indeed, Grigor'ev's criticism has stood the test of time better than has theirs. Narrow ideas have ruled in Russia, and elsewhere. Dostoevskii was surely right when he said that Grigor'ev understood more than Dobroliubov but was handicapped in the contest for public understanding by the very breadth and subtlety of his vision.

Apart from his contribution to the Russian philosophical and critical heritage, Grigor'ev also left his mark on Russian historiography. His analysis of Russian intellectual development from the eighteenth century through Karamzin and Chaadaev and on to the Slavophile-Westernizer split has become so much a part of the historiography that no one remembers that it was Grigor'ev who first set that development out fully. As in other intellectual arenas, Grigor'ev fought against the mainstream of Russian historians of the time. Along with a handful of regionalists such as Shchapov and Kostomarov, he led the attack on the 'centralizers' in Russian historical writing. Better than many, he grasped the lasting importance of regionalism within the Empire. The theme was important then, as it is now.

Grigor'ev disliked politics and devoted much of his life to defending the independence of art from politics of all kinds. He understood, however, that intellectual politics could not be completely avoided in Russia and acknowledged his own conservatism. Among the contending groups in Russia, he was closer to the Slavophiles than to others. But he was not a Slavophile in anything but the broadest definition of the term. Their conservative utopianism was fundamentally alien to him. Though part of the present and future, the past, for Grigor'ev, could in no sense be retrieved. The Slavophile dream of rediscovering Russia's guiding principles in the past and recreating them in the present was to him mere theory. He was deeply engaged with life as it was and believed that life would impose its own principles on Russia.

Zinaida Gippius missed the point entirely when she charged that Grigor'ev's failure was his inability to choose between right and left. Choosing extremes was the failure of much of the Russian intelligentsia, but not his. He understood that the choices at the extremes, which were the only ones offered, were ultimately destructive of the independence of Russian spiritual and cultural life. In Russian conditions, he granted the need for extremes, but not for their triumph. His was a struggle for middle ground, for creation of a cultural and social milieu that was capable of tolerating life's full variety and complexity. The centre, in his view, was not merely a compromise between the extremes but an independent force that could embrace and contain them both. Such a position was rare among Russians, and rarer still among Russian conservatives. Much of his originality therefore lies in his preference for middle ground, and his most important contribution to Russia's future may yet lie there.

Grigor'ev does not rank among the top poets of Russia. A few of his poems are remembered almost as folk poetry, and those who recite them often do not know the name of their author. But even his lesser poems are of interest to more than literary historians. They are memorials not just to the end of the Russian romantic era but to the personal struggles of a talented individual in an intellectual and social environment become alien and hostile to him.

In spite of their highly personal nature and period references, they often convey a universally familiar condition in striking language and imagery.

Though at times a childish even foolish, man, Grigor'ev's great strength was the emphasis he placed on the complexity of life and the varieties of personalities and human experiences, his tolerance and encouragement of cultural differences, and his understanding of the dehumanizing potential of science and technology. He clearly grasped the despotic power of modern ideologies, their centralizing urges, and the moral indifferentism by which they sacrifice the few for the sake of the many. His fundamentally religious view of the world – that is, his appreciation of human limits – was at odds with the dominant materialist and positivist ethos of Europe. He was the 'unnecessary man' and an easy target for the radical intelligentsia in Russia, which had few doubts that it was capable of engineering a better future.

His weaknesses were multiple. His personal failings – petulance, impracticality, selfishness, and deadly taste for alcohol, among others – marked him as a social misfit. He called himself the last of the romantics and identified that as the source of his unnecessariness. But his alienation was as rooted in his social disfunction as in his intellectual preferences. In his failure to fit into society he was like many members of the first generation of the intelligentsia, who frequently expressed their alienation either in dissipation or in revolutionary dreaming. The core of Grigor'ev's thought remained remarkably consistent from his earliest poetry to his last article on organic criticism: the belief that truth enters life only through the concrete and particular; but it also led him to the extremes that so bemused his friend and rival Polonskii.

Complex as was his thought, Grigor'ev chose to express it in an uncompromisingly difficult language and style, which limited the number of his readers and made the task of defending him arduous, as Dostoevskii well knew. He stubbornly insisted on every nuance and obscurity and, in doing so, greatly harmed his own cause.

At the level of ideas, Grigor'ev failed to perceive, or perhaps only to acknowledge, the extent and depths of change arising from the industrial and scientific revolutions. The lure of cosmopolitanism, which he so deplored, was far more powerful than he allowed. For all the trenchancy and relevance of his critique of materialism and scientism, he could not advance a viable alternative. Grigor'ev's view of art as the sole purveyor and arbiter of truth was too exclusive and ignored other essential ways of knowing. The Orthodox heart of his idea of Russian nationality was too narrow theoretically and practically to encompass and direct the flood of the new and too weak to mitigate the effective secularization of society and social attitudes that was already under way.

Grigor'ev placed his hope for social harmony and unity in a romantic national consensus based on a common religious faith. Like other conservatives who criticized liberal notions of individual rights, he could offer no defence against political, social, cultural, or spiritual tyranny when the national consensus broke down. While lionizing individuality, he offered no means of preserving it against the very despotic forces of which he warned. The rights of man were to Grigor'ev the death knell of the uniqueness of individuals. But pluralism based on social or cultural consensus and not on rights has proved to be an elusive goal in Russia and elsewhere. Russian nationality did survive the communist experiment, most strikingly through the agency of art, as Grigor'ev would have expected. With the experiment ended, Russia is again in search of a basis for consensus. Grigor'ev's inability to reconcile Russian cultural independence with a firm foundation for individual liberty, tolerance, and pluralism was in his time, and today remains, the main dilemma of Russian conservatives.

Notes

INTRODUCTION

1 See my 'Echoes of *Pochvennichestvo* in Solzhenitsyn's *August 1914*,' *Slavic Review*, 34, no. 1 (March 1975), 109–22.

2 [Apollon Grigor'ev], 'Bezvykhodnoe polozhenie (Iz zapisok nenuzhnogo cheloveka),' *Iakor'*, no. 1 (1863), 2.

3 Aleksandr Blok, 'Chto nado zapomnit' ob Apollone Grigor'eve,' in V.N. Orlov et al., eds, *Sobranie sochinenii*, VI, *Proza, 1918–1921* (Moscow and Leningrad 1962), 28.

4 Ibid, 27–8.

5 Anon., 'A.A. Grigor'ev,' *Otechestvennyia zapiski* (September 1864), sect. I, 511–12.

6 M.D. Prygunov, Iu.A. Bakhrushin, and N.A. Brodskii, eds, *Neizdannye pis'ma k A.N. Ostrovskomu* (Moscow and Leningrad 1932), 456.

7 Vlad. Kniazhnin, 'Materialy po istorii russkoi literatury i kultury. Neizvestnaia stat'ia K.N. Leont'eva: Neskol'ko vospominanii i mysli o pokoinom Ap. Grigor'eve,' *Russkaia mysl'* (Sept 1915), 124.

CHAPTER ONE: A Feverish Imagination (1822–1842)

1 G.A. Fedorov, 'Novye materialy o rannikh godakh zhizni Ap. Grigor'eva,' in Apollon Grigor'ev, *Vospominaniia* (Leningrad 1980), 370.

2 Vl. Kniazhnin, ed, *Materialy dlia biografii A. Grigor'eva* (henceforth *Materialy*) (Petrograd 1917), 317–18.

3 A.A. Grigor'ev, *Moi literaturnye i nravstvennye skital'chestva* (henceforth *Skital'chestva*), in Grigor'ev, *Vospominaniia*, 13. Aksakov's autobiographical novel was published fully in 1856 and was immediately recognized as a classic of

Russian literature. For an English version, see S.T. Aksakov, *A Family Chronicle*, Ralph E. Matlaw trans (New York 1961).

4 The Table of Ranks was established by Peter the Great at the beginning of the eighteenth century. Its fourteen ranks correlated social standing with rank in state service. In the early nineteenth century, ranks 14 to 9 conferred personal nobility and ranks 8 to 1 brought with them hereditary nobility.

5 Fedorov, 'Novye materialy,' 370.

6 Grigor'ev, *Skital'chestva*, 14.

7 Ibid, 17.

8 Letter to M.P. Pogodin, 16 Sept. 1861, *Materialy*, 276.

9 Grigor'ev, *Skital'chestva*, 63–4.

10 A.A. Fet, *Rannie gody moei zhizni* (Moscow 1893), 149.

11 Fedorov, 'Novye materialy,' 370.

12 Fet, *Rannie gody*, 149.

13 Grigor'ev, *Skital'chestva*, 16.

14 Fet, *Rannie gody*, 148.

15 Grigor'ev, *Skital'chestva*, 14.

16 Ibid, 31.

17 Apollon Grigor'ev, 'Olimpii Radin. Rasskaz,' *Sochineniia v dvukh tomakh*, 1 (Moscow 1990), 139–40.

18 Grigor'ev, *Skital'chestva*, 7. In a brilliant piece, Robert Whittaker shows that Grigor'ev employed the social geography of the Zamoskvorech'e district in *My Literary and Moral Wanderings* as a map of the cultural forces that shaped the Russia of his day. Robert Whittaker, '"My Literary and Moral Wanderings": Apollon Grigor'ev and the Changing Cultural Topography of Moscow,' *Slavic Review*, 42, no. 3 (fall 1983), 390–407.

19 N.N. Strakhov, 'Vospominaniia ob A.A. Grigor'eve,' *Epokha*, no. 9 (1864), 43.

20 Grigor'ev, *Skital'chestva*, 21.

21 Ibid, 22.

22 Fedorov, 'Novye materialy,' 373.

23 Grigor'ev, *Skital'chestva*, 25-6.

24 Ibid, 31–4.

25 Ibid, 33.

26 Ibid, 15.

27 *Materialy*, 218.

28 Grigor'ev, *Skital'chestva*, 29.

29 Ibid, 18

30 Alexander Herzen, *My Past and Thoughts: The Memoirs of Alexander Herzen* (Berkeley, Los Angeles, and London 1982), 22–34.

31 Grigor'ev, *Skital'chestva*, 33.

32 Letter to E.S. Protopopova (26 Jan. 1859), *Materialy*, 240.

33 A.A. Grigor'ev, 'Ofeliia. Odno iz vospominanii Vitalina. Prodolzhenie rasskaza bez nachala, bez kontsa i v osobennosti bez morali,' in Grigor'ev, *Vospominaniia*, 150–1.

34 Grigor'ev, *Skital'chestva*, 32–3.

35 In December 1825, army officers, almost all scions of the leading noble families, organized in two secret societies, staged a revolt in an attempt to establish a constitutional regime. The revolt was suppressed, and several of the ringleaders were hanged.

36 Grigor'ev, *Skital'chestva*, 39.

37 Fet, *Rannie gody*, 148.

38 *Materialy*, 318.

39 Fet, *Rannie gody*, 146.

40 Ia.P. Polonskii, 'Moi studencheskiia vospominaniia,' *Niva. Ezhemesiachnyia literaturnyia prilozheniia*, no. 12 (Dec. 1898), 659. Polonskii, contrary to other testimony, claimed that Grigor'ev played badly.

41 For a detailed discussion of the Law Faculty of Moscow University in the years immediately following Grigor'ev's graduation see A.N. Afanas'ev, 'Moskovskii Universitet v vospominaniakh A.N. Afanas'eva,' *Russkaia starina* (Aug. 1886), 363–74.

42 Fet, *Rannie gody*, 156.

43 *Materialy*, 320.

44 Grigor'ev, *Skital'chestva*, 6.

45 *Materialy*, 311.

46 N.M. Orlov, 'Zapiski N.M. Orlova,' in M. Gershenzon, ed, *Russkie propilei*, 1 (Moscow 1915), 210–15.

47 Fet, *Rannie gody*, 154.

48 Ibid.

49 Aleksandr Blok, 'Sud'ba Apollona Grigor'eva,' *Sobranie sochinenii*, v, *Proza, 1903–1917* (Moscow and Leningrad 1962), 493.

50 Fet, *Rannie gody*, 152. In an autobiographical story written in 1844, Grigor'ev spoke as well of Fet's psychological sadism. His friend convinced Apollon that he was without either heart or character. But Grigor'ev was never jealous of Fet's great talent and continued to transcribe his poems faithfully for as long as they remained together. In the same story, Grigor'ev described himself as nurse, mistress, and handmaiden to Fet and claimed to have saved him from suicide by convincing him to live not for himself but for his talent. Grigor'ev, 'Ofeliia,' 153–4.

51 A.A. Grigor'ev, 'Odin iz mnogikh, *Vospominaniia*, 233–7.

52 Fet, *Rannie gody*, 150.

53 Polonskii, 'Moi studencheskiia vospominaniia,' 659.

54 Fet, *Rannie gody*, 153.

55 Grigor'ev, *Skital'chestva*, 76–82.

56 Fet, *Rannie gody*, 192–3.

57 E.G. Kholodov, ed, *Istoriia russkogo dramaticheskogo teatra*, III, *1826–1845* (Moscow 1978), 229–307.

58 A.A. Fet, 'Student,' *Polnoe sobranie stikhotvorenii* (Leningrad 1959), 590.

59 Grigor'ev told the story in his autobiographical tale 'Ofeliia,' 158–66; it was also the subject of his poems 'E.S.R.' and 'No, I cannot be silent for you,' *Sochineniia v dvukh tomakh*, I, 29–30. Fet recounted the same story in his poem 'Student,' *Polnoe sobranie stikhotvorenii*, 589–600.

60 Grigor'ev, 'Ofeliia,', 155.

61 Ia.P. Polonskii, 'Moi studencheskiia vospominaniia,' 662.

62 R. Whittaker, 'Neopublikovannye pis'ma Apollona Grigor'eva,' *Vestnik Moskovskogo Universiteta*, no. 2 (1971), 67–8.

63 Fet, *Rannie gody*, 226; Nikolai Barsukov, *Zhizn' i trudy M.P. Pogodina*, bk. VIII (St Petersburg 1894), 36.

64 Grigor'ev, *Skital'chestva*, 59.

CHAPTER TWO: Thinking and Feeling (1842–1847)

1 Vl. Kniazhnin, ed, *Materialy dlia biografii Apollona Grigor'eva* (hereafter *Materialy*) (Petrograd 1917), 322–3.

2 A.A. Grigor'ev, 'Listki iz rukopisi skitaiushchegosia sofista,' in *Vospominaniia* (Leningrad 1980), 83–94. The tale in the 'Pages' is fictionalized in his short story of 1845, 'Moe znakomstvo s Vitalinym,' in *Vospominaniia*, 128–42. Ibid. It also appears in his long poem of 1845, 'Olimpii Radin.' Apollon Grigor'ev, *Sochineniia v dvukh tomakh*, I (Moscow 1990), 136–67.

3 Grigor'ev, Letter to his father, 23 July 1846, in *Vospominaniia*, 298.

4 Grigor'ev, 'Listki,' 89.

5 Once, in order to assert himself, he picked a quarrel with Kavelin about the immortality of the soul. Kavelin calmly pointed out how changeable Grigor'ev's opinions were. Still worse, Antonina chided him for his exaggerated religious views. 'God knows what you want from life,' she complained. Ibid, 90.

6 Grigor'ev, Letter to his father, 23 July 1846, in *Vospominaniia*, 299.

7 A.A. Fet, *Rannie gody moei zhizni* (Moscow 1893), 226–7.

8 *Materialy*, 330–4.

9 Grigor'ev, Letter to M.P. Pogodin, Oct. 1845, in ibid, 101.

10 Ibid, 102.

11 [Apollon Grigor'ev], 'Bezvykhodnoe polozhenie (Iz zapisok nenuzhnogo cheloveka), *Iakor'*, no. 1 (1863), 2.

12 Cited in P.P. Gromov, 'Apollon Grigor'ev,' in A. Grigor'ev, *Izbrannye proiz-vedeniia* (Moscow 1959), 8.

13 Grigor'ev, Letter to Pogodin, of Oct. 1845, in *Materialy*, 101. The novel was a loosely connected series of short stories called 'Rasskaz bez nachala i bez kontsa, a v osobennosti bez morali.' The drama in verse was 'Dva egoizma.'

14 Quoted in A. Ashevskii, 'Apollon Aleksandrovich Grigor'ev (k piatidesiatiletiu so dnia smerti),' *Golos minuvshego* (Sept. 1914), 13.

15 A.Ia. Panaeva, *Vospominaniia* (Moscow 1948), 115–16. Panaeva's memoirs are malicious and notoriously inaccurate. In her version of events, Grigor'ev helped Mezhevich to establish *Repertuar i Panteon* in 1839 – that is, five years before Grigor'ev arrived in St Petersburg. Ibid, 115. But her recollections about Grigor'ev's relations with Mme Mezhevich are confirmed in *Perepiska Ia.K. Grota s P.A. Pletnevym*, II (St Petersburg 1896), 763.

16 Nikolai Barsukov, *Zhizn' i trudy M.P. Pogodina*, VIII (St Petersburg 1894), 41.

17 V.P. Zotov, 'Peterburg v sorokovykh godakh. Vyderzhki iz avto-biograficheskikh zametok,' *Istoricheskii vestnik* (Feb.–March 1890), 337.

18 Grigor'ev, Letter to his father, 23 July 1846, *Vospominaniia*, 297.

19 Ibid.

20 On Milanovskii and his relationship with Grigor'ev, see Grigor'ev, *Vospominaniia*, 412–13.

21 Cited in V.I. Semevskii, 'M.V. Butashevich-Petrashevskii. Biograficheskii ocherk, preimushchestvenno po neizdannym materialam,' *Golos minuvshego* (Jan. 1913), 28–9.

22 Grigor'ev, Letter to his father, 23 July 1846, in *Vospominaniia*, 297–8. Grigor'ev spoke to Fet on several occasions about joining the Masons, though some of his friends suspected that it was only bravado. On the eve of his flight to St Petersburg, however, he told Fet that he had received money for the trip from a Masonic lodge. Fet, *Rannie gody*, 226.

23 A. Ia. Al'tshuller, *Teatr proslavlennykh masterov. Ocherki Aleksandrinskoi stseny* (Leningrad 1968), 63. Also see Zotov, 'Peterburg,' 567–8.

24 Grigor'ev, Letter to his father, 23 July 1846, in *Vospominaniia*, 299.

25 Grigor'ev, *Sochineniia v dvukh tomakh*, I, 67.

26 K.D. Kavelin, 'A Letter to F.M. Dostoevsky,' in Marc Raeff, ed, *Russian Intellectual History: An Anthology* (New York 1966), 302.

27 R. Whittaker, 'Neopublikovannye pis'ma Apollona Grigor'eva,' *Vestnik Moskovskogo Universiteta*, no. 2 (1971), 68.

28 Grigor'ev, *Sochineniia v dvukh tomakh*, I, 29.

29 Ibid, 32.

30 Ibid, 31.

31 [V.I. Belinskii], 'Russkaia literatura. Stikhotvoreniia Apollona Grigor'eva,' *Otechestvennyia zapiski* (April 1846), sec. VI, 55.

32 Grigor'ev, *Sochineniia v dvukh tomakh*, I, 35.

33 Ibid, 36.

34 Ibid, 35–6.

35 Ibid, 61.

36 Ibid, 53.

37 Ibid, 188–204.

38 In 'Olimpii Radin,' he discussed the Korsh family, with its half-Russian, half-German background. Ibid, 139–40.

39 Whittaker, 'Neopublikovannye pis'ma Apollona Grigor'eva,' 69.

40 Grigor'ev, *Sochineniia v dvukh tomakh*, I, 135–49.

41 A.A. Grigor'ev, 'Dva egoizma,' *Izbrannye proizvedeniia* (Moscow 1959), 193–4.

42 Grigor'ev, *Sochineniia v dvukh tomakh*, I, 150–3.

43 Ibid, 44–6.

44 Ibid, 332–419. Grigor'ev made it clear in the story that lack of moral equality transformed all relationships into patterns of domination and subordination.

45 Grigor'ev, 'Dva egoizma,' 183–268.

46 Whittaker, 'Neopublikovannye pis'ma Apollona Grigor'eva,' 70.

47 Grigor'ev, *Sochineniia v dvukh tomakh*, I, 283–303.

48 Ibid, 154–67.

49 The Petrashevskii circle was primarily a socialist talking shop rather than an organized conspiracy against the authorities. One group within the circle did, however, possess an illegal printing press, on which it planned to print seditious calls for peasant revolution. Fedor Dostoevskii had contacts with that group. In the wake of the revolutions of 1848 in western Europe, the government cracked down on Russian intellectuals. A number of the *Petrashevtsy* were arrested, among them Dostoevskii, who was condemned to be shot, taken to the place of execution, reprieved at the last moment, and sent to hard labour and military service in Siberia.

50 R. Ivanov-Razumnik, 'Apollon Grigor'ev (Vmesto poslesloviia),' in Grigor'ev, *Vospominaniia* (Moscow and Leningrad 1930), 608. Blok maintained that in his St Petersburg period 'Grigor'ev' was just a 'pseudonym' for a whole 'discordant company' that jostled inside the young man: a dreamy romantic lost in German philosophy; a shy lad, not knowing how to please a woman; a hack abusing the Russian language; a prototype of the future nihilists; an *intelligent*; and a drunk. Aleksandr Blok, 'Sud'ba Apollona Grigor'eva,' *Sobranie sochinenii*, V, *Proza 1903–1917* (Moscow and Leningrad 1962), 498.

51 Grigor'ev, *Sochineniia v dvukh tomakh*, I, 50.

52 Ibid, 39.

53 Ibid, 43–4.

54 Ibid, 62–3.

55 Ibid, 63–4.

56 Ibid, 67.

57 Ibid, 32.

58 'Smes',' *Finskii vestnik*, 9 (1846), 46–7.

59 [P.A. Pletnev], 'Novyia sochineniia,' *Sovremennik* (April 1846), sec. I, 229.

60 Ia.Ia.Ia., 'Russkaia literatura. Stikhotvoreniia Apollona Grigor'eva,' *Severnaia pchela*, no. 114 (1846), 455.

61 [V.I. Belinskii], 'Russkaia literatura. Stikhotvoreniia Apollona Grigor'eva,' *Otechestvennyia zapiski* (April 1846), sec. VI, 52–8.

62 V.G. Belinskii, 'Vzgliad na russkuiu literaturu 1846 goda,' *Sovremennik* (Jan. 1847), sec. III, 31.

63 Vl. Kniazhnin, 'Apollon Grigor'ev – poet,' *Russkaia mysl'* (May 1916), 130–35.

64 B.Ia. Bukhshtab, '"Gimny"Apollona Grigor'eva,' *Bibliograficheskie razyskaniia po russkoi literature XIX veka* (Moscow 1966), 38–41.

65 Letter of A.N. Pleshcheev to S.F. Durov, 26 March 1849, in V.E. Evgrafov, ed, *Sotsial'no politicheskie i filosofskie vzgliady Petrashevtsev* (Moscow 1956), 724.

66 Grigor'ev, *Sochineniia v dvukh tomakh*, I, 135–49.

67 Ibid, 420–511.

68 Grigor'ev, Letter to S.M. Solov'ev of Jan. or Feb. 1847, in *Materialy*, 105.

69 [A.A. Grigor'ev], 'Peterburgskii sbornik,' *Finskii vestnik*, 9 (1846), 5–7. On Grigor'ev's authorship of this article, see V.S. Spiridonov, 'A.A. Grigor'ev i A.N. Ostrovskii,' in *Ezhegodnik petrogradskikh gosudarstvennykh teatrov. Sezon 1918–1919* (Petrograd 1920), 168–9, and B.F. Egorov, 'Apollon Grigor'ev – kritik,' in *Uchenye zapiski Tartuskogo gos. universiteta*, vyp. 98 (1960), 218–19.

CHAPTER THREE: A Way Out of Despair (1847–1849)

1 Quoted in B.F. Egorov, 'Khudozhestvennaia proza Ap. Grigor'eva,' in *Vospominaniia* (Leningrad 1980), 342. Vl. Kniazhnin, the compiler of Grigor'ev's letters and other materials about his life, remarked that he had found not a single good testimonial to Lidiia Fedorovna. Vl. Kniazhnin, *Materialy dlia biografii Apollona Grigor'eva* (hereafter *Materialy*) (Petrograd 1917), 13.

2 A.D. Galakhov, 'Sorokovye gody,' *Istoricheskii vestnik* (Jan.–Feb. 1892), 409.

3 R. Ivanov-Razumnik, 'Apollon Grigor'ev (Vmesto poslesloviia),' in *Vospominaniia* (Moscow and Leningrad 1930), 623.

4 Grigor'ev distinguished between Slavophilism and Slavism throughout his career. Slavophilism was a theory espoused by a number of cultural, religious,

and social theorists. Slavism was a cultural principle and force that separated the Slavs spiritually from western Europeans.

5 For a family view of the marriage see A.A. Grigor'ev, Jr, 'Odinokii kritik,' *Knizhki nedeli* (Aug. 1895), 61–2. Alexander was the third son of the marriage; the first survived only a few weeks. He points out that his mother was an impressionable person who wanted to be a free woman in the sense of a Georges Sand heroine.

6 Grigor'ev, Letters to Pogodin, Dec. 1847 and Jan. 1848, in *Materialy*, 108–10.

7 P. Iudin 'K biografii A.A. Grigor'eva,' *Istoricheskii vestnik* (Dec. 1894), 780.

8 Grigor'ev, Letters to A.A. Kraevskii, Feb. and May 1849, in *Materialy*, 119–21.

9 Grigor'ev, Letters to F.A. Koni, March and April 1850, *Materialy*, 124–5.

10 Grigor'ev, Letter to M.P. Pogodin, 7 June 1847, in ibid, 106. That Grigor'ev was asking for a loan in this letter no doubt influenced his expressed concern to reform. In a letter of November 1849 to Pogodin, however, he described this period of his life as one of 'profound intellectual and moral dilemmas.' Grigor'ev, Letter to M.P. Pogodin, 22 Nov. 1849, in ibid, 121.

11 Apollon Grigor'ev, 'Gogol' i ego "Perepiska s druz'iami,' *Sochineniia*, I, *Kritika* (Villanova, Penn., 1970), 19.

12 Ibid, 22.

13 Grigor'ev, Letter to Gogol' of 14 Oct. 1848, in *Materialy*, 111.

14 Ibid, 112.

15 Ibid, 113.

16 Grigor'ev, Letter to Gogol' of 17 Nov. 1848, in *Materialy*, 113.

17 Ibid, 114.

18 Ibid, 115.

19 Grigor'ev, Letter to Gogol', Nov.–Dec. 1848, in ibid, 116–19.

20 See for example Grigor'ev's 'Velikii tragik,' published in 1859. *Sochineniia v dvukh tomakh*, vol. 1, 512–52.

21 For the history of Russian theatre and acting from the 1820s into the 1860s, see E.G. Kholodov, ed, *Istoriia russkogo dramaticheskogo teatra*, III and IV (Moscow 1978–9); V.F. Fedorova, *Russkii teatr XIXogo veka* (Moscow 1983); and Marc Slonim, *Russian Theatre: From the Empire to the Soviets* (Cleveland and New York 1961).

22 The best summary of Russian theatre criticism is A.Ia. Al'tshuller, ed, *Ocherki istorii russkoi teatral'noi kritiki*, I and II (Leningrad 1975 and 1976).

23 A. Grigor'ev, 'Ob elementakh dramy v nyneshnem russkom obshchestve,' *Teatral'naia letopis'*, nos. 4 and 8 (1845), 22–6 and 18–23, respectively.

24 A. Grigor'ev, 'Aleksandrinskii teatr,' in *Teatral'naia kritika* (Leningrad 1982), 49–50.

25 A. Grigor'ev, 'Zametki o Moskovskom teatre,' in ibid, 52–3.

26 Ibid, 70–2.

27 G.-T. Rotscher, *Die Kunst der dramatischen Darstellung* (Berlin 1841).

28 A.A. Grigor'ev, 'Letopis' Moskovskogo teatra,' in *Teatral'naia kritika* (Leningrad, 1985), 77.

29 Ibid.

30 A.A. Grigor'ev, 'Letopis' Moskovskogo teatra. G–n Poltavtsev v roliakh Gamleta, Giugo Bidermana i Chatskogo,' in ibid, 100–7.

31 Grigor'ev, Letter to M.P. Pogodin, 22 Nov. 1849, in *Materialy*, 122. The drama critic A.D. Galakhov, who had invited Grigor'ev to take part in *Otechestvennye zapiski*, remembered him as 'for Europeanism' at the time but as soon changing to a Slavophile position. A.D. Galakhov, 'Sorokovye gody,' *Istoricheskii vestnik* (Jan.–Feb., 1892), 411.

CHAPTER FOUR: The Leading Young Editor (1849–1855)

1   Isaiah Berlin chronicled this change in 'Russia and 1848,' in his *Russian Thinkers* (London 1979), 1–21.

2   A. Grigor'ev, Letter to M.P. Pogodin, of 26 Nov. 1851, in Vl. Kniazhnin, ed, *Materialy dlia biografii Apollona Grigor'eva* (hereafter *Materialy*) (Petrograd 1917), 131.

3   Grigor'ev, Letter to M.P. Pogodin, end of 1851 or beginning of 1852, in ibid, 132–3.

4   For a discussion of this incident, see B.F. Egorov, 'Poeziia Apollona Grigor'eva,' in A. Grigor'ev, *Stikhotvoreniia i poemy* (Moscow 1978), 15.

5   Ivan Turgenev, *A Nest of Gentlefolk* (London 1970), 72–4.

6   Ibid, 76.

7   A.V. Druzhinin recorded an evening in June 1856 when Grigor'ev and his wife, along with Edel'son and another gentleman, showed him the Moscow of the black arts (*chernoknizhnaia*) – an entertainment that included a number of taverns and beer cellars. A.V. Druzhinin, *Povesti. Dnevnik* (Moscow 1986), 393.

8   I.M. Sechenov, *Avtobiograficheskie zapiski* (Moscow 1952), 73–4, 90–1.

9   *Materialy*, xxi.

10 Sechenov, *Avtobiograficheskie zapiski*, 91.

11 Grigor'ev, Letter to E.S. Protopopova, 6 Jan. 1858, *Materialy*, 207.

12 Grigor'ev, Letter to E.S. Protopopova, 24 Nov. 1857, in *Materialy*, 193.

13 See V.P. Zotov, 'Peterburg v sorokovykh godakh. Vyderzhki iz avtobiograficheskikh zametok,' *Istoricheskii vestnik* (Feb.–March 1890), 337.

14 Fet recounted Grigor'ev's fascination with gypsy music and his skill on the guitar in a short story. A. Fet, 'Kaktus. Rasskaz,' *Russkii vestnik* (Nov. 1881), 230–8.

15 S.V. Maksimov, 'Aleksandr Nikolaevich Ostrovskii (Po moim vospominani-iam),' in his *A.N. Ostrovskii v vospominaniiakh sovremennikov* (Moscow 1966), 69.
16 Sechenov, *Avtobiograficheskie zapiski*, 90–1. Maksimov in his memoirs of Ostrovskii discussed in detail the penchant of the young editors for Russian national songs and incidentally the drinking establishments where the songs were performed. Maksimov, 'Ostrovskii,' 69–73.
17 Cf. A. Fet, *Moi vospominaniia, 1848–1889*, pt 1 (Moscow 1890), 193–4; and A. Fet, 'Kaktus. Rasskaz,' 235–6.
18 Fet, *Moi vospominaniia*, 193.
19 Apollon Grigor'ev, *Sochineniia v dvukh tomakh*, 1 (Moscow 1990), 95–117. In 1857 Grigor'ev also wrote another cycle of poems (reproduced in ibid, 118–20) inspired by Leonida Vizard; entitled 'Titania,' it appeared as the dedication to his translation of *A Midsummer Night's Dream*, which was published in *Biblioteka dlia chteniia* in August 1857. The seven-sonnet cycle explores the capriciousness and purity that Grigor'ev, with some scepticism, saw as the two poles of a woman's soul. The last sonnet declared:

> Titania! Forgive me always. I believe,
> I stubbornly want to believe, that you –
> Are a mixture of capriciousness and purity,
> And I know he bears in his heart
> An irredeemable loss; his dreams have been excised,
> Last dreams – and the gates of paradise
> Are forever locked for the wanderer-friend.
> I will not even attempt to plumb
>
> The full abyss of his grief. But he prays
> An ardent prayer, that your bright image
> Shine like a star, dimmed by nothing,
> That even a thought about him in the sleepless silence
>
> Cannot disturb the sanctuary of a heart,
> That God bestowed on someone else.

20 P. Iudin, 'K biografii A.A. Grigor'eva,' *Istoricheskii vestnik* (Dec. 1894), 780.
21 Grigor'ev, Letter to M.P. Pogodin, March 1855, in *Materialy*, 145.
22 Fet, *Moi vospominaniia*, 189.
23 A.A. Nil'skii, 'Vospominaniia A.A. Nil'skago,' *Istoricheskii vestnik* (Sept. 1894), 689–92.

24 A.A. Grigor'ev, *Moi literaturnyia i nravstvennyia skital'chestva. Avtobiografiia* (Moscow 1915), 51.

25 On *Moskvitianin*, see my *Dostoevsky, Grigor'ev, and Native Soil Conservatism* (Toronto 1982), 28–32.

26 N.V. Berg, 'Salon E. Rostopchinoi,' in N.L. Brodskii, ed, *Literaturnye salony i kruzhki. Pervaia polovina XIX veka* (Moscow 1930), 414.

27 The Rostopchins' living arrangements were the model for Chernyshevskii's ideal of household organization in *What Is to Be Done?* N.G. Chernyshevsky, *What Is to Be Done?* (New York 1961), 135–7.

28 For the formation of the 'young editors' group, see N.V. Berg, 'Posmertnyia zapiski Nikolaia Vasil'evicha Berga,' *Russkaia starina* (Feb. 1891), 252–3; N. Barsukov, *Zhizn' i trudy M.P. Pogodina*, bk. xi (St Petersburg 1897), 59–71 passim; and S. Vengerov, 'Molodaia redaktsiia *Moskvitianina*,' *Vestnik Evropy*, i no. 6 (1886), 581–612.

29 Barsukov, *Zhizn' i trudy*, bk. xi, 88. It is illustrative that when in 1853 Shevyrev organized a party in honour of the actor M.S. Shchepkin, whom Grigor'ev knew well, Pogodin, who added several names to the proposed list of guests, did not add Grigor'ev's name. Later, when Edel'son suggested that Grigor'ev be included, Pogodin gave no indication that he intended to do so, and there is no evidence that Grigor'ev attended the party. Ibid, bk. xii, 465–66.

30 Ibid, bk. xi, 88.

31 *Materialy*, xvii. Also see I.F. Gorbunov, 'Kruzhok "molodoi redaktsii *Moskvitianina*,"' in N.L. Brodskii, ed., *Literaturnye salony i kruzhki. Pervaia polovina XIX veka* (Moscow 1930), 405–7.

32 Ibid, 385–6.

33 P.V. Annenkov, *Literaturnye vospominaniia. Khudozhniki i prostoi chelovek. Iz vospominanii ob A. F. Pisemskom* (Moscow 1960), 491. On the 'young editors,' including their differences from the Slavophiles, see my *Dostoevsky, Grigor'ev, and Native Soil Conservatism*, chap. 2.

34 E. Edel'son, 'Kritika,' *Moskvitianin* (March 1854), 2. The young editors' emphasis on the centrality of the merchant class in Russian cultural development was part of a larger movement supported by Pogodin and Slavophiles such as Ivan Aksakov. The movement generated a newspaper, *Vestnik promyshlennosti* (The Industrial Messenger), and a merchant lobby that pressed for higher tariffs and for less reliance on foreign capital in Russia's economic development. For this phenomenon, see Alfred J. Rieber, 'The Moscow Entrepreneurial Group: The Emergence of a New Form in Autocratic Politics,' *Jahrbücher für Geschichte Osteuropas*, 25 (1977), 1–20 and 174–99.

35 A.N. O[strovskii], '"Oshibka", povest' G-zhi Tur,' *Moskvitianin* (April 1850),

88–9. 'Evgeniia Tur' was the pseudonym of Elizaveta Vasil'evna Salias-de-Turnemir, a minor Russian novelist.

36 [A.A. Grigor'ev], 'Kritika i bibliografiia,' *Moskvitianin* (Sept. 1850), 21–34.

37 A.A. Grigor'ev, 'Kritika i bibliografiia,' *Moskvitianin* (May 1851), 169.

38 A.A. Grigor'ev, 'Russkaia literatura v 1851 godu,' in *Sochineniia*, I, *Kritika* (Villanova, Penn., 1970), 27–8.

39 Ibid, 29.

40 Ibid, 35.

41 Ibid, 39-40.

42 Ibid, 58-62.

43 Ibid, 65-6.

44 N.L. Brodskii, ed, *V.P. Botkin i I.S. Turgenev. Neizdannaia perepiska, 1851–1869* (Moscow and Leningrad 1930), 26.

45 D.V. Grigorovich, 'Literaturnyia vospominaniia,' *Russkaia mysl'* (Feb. 1893), 56–7. Grigorovich was particularly bitter about Grigor'ev. The latter singled out the former on many occasions as a writer who understood nothing about Russian peasants but merely copied the French fashion of peasant writing. The reason, said Grigor'ev, was that because Grigorovich's mother was French he could know nothing of the spirit of the Russian people and his novels could have nothing Russian in them. Ibid, 57–8.

46 A.D. Galakhov, 'Sorokovye gody,' *Istoricheskii vestnik* (Jan.–Feb. 1892), 410.

47 Annenkov, *Literaturnye vospominaniia*, 494. At a gathering of Westerners at the home of V.P. Botkin, Granovskii, when chided by his friends for reading the latest issue of *Moskvitianin*, said that he intended to read on because 'this is so stupid it actually gets interesting.' But Turgenev, who was present, when asked what he thought of one of Grigor'ev's articles, said, 'I like it,' causing general laughter, at which Turgenev became embarrassed. Galakhov, 'Sorokovye gody,' 410–11. Others felt the same way as Turgenev, however. In 1852 G.P. Danilevskii, a writer, reported to Pogodin from St Petersburg that though he had recently heard Turgenev and Goncharov joking at a gathering about the direction of *Moskvitianin*, everyone there, except for the critic A.V. Druzhinin, commended the noble tone and sincerity of Grigor'ev's articles. Later he commented on the favourable impression that Grigor'ev's work was making on the editorial board of *Sovremennik*. Barsukov, *Zhizn' i trudy*, bk. XII, 221.

48 A.F. Koni, *Vospominaniia o pisateliakh* (Moscow 1965), 98–9. Annenkov also commented that for years *Otechestvennye zapiski* held stubbornly to the view that Ostrovskii was a representative of retrograde tendencies and Grigor'ev was his principal panygerist. Annenkov, *Literaturnye vospominaniia*, 495.

49 [Anon.], 'Zhurnalistiki,' *Otechestvennyia zapiski* (April 1854), 96–8.

50 Grigor'ev, *Sochineniia v dvukh tomakh*, I, 88–94.

51 [Anon.], *Sovremennik*, 3 (March 1854), 25, and 4 (April 1854), 52.

52 N.G. Chernyshevskii, 'Bednost'' ne porok. Komediia A. Ostrovskogo. Moskva. 1854,' in *Polnoe sobranie sochinenii*, 11 (Moscow 1949), 232–40.

53 A.A. Grigor'ev, 'O komediakh Ostrovskogo i ikh znachenii v literature i na stsene,' *Sochineniia Apollona Grigor'eva*, 1 (St Petersburg 1876), 110.

54 Ibid, 119.

55 Ibid, 119–20.

56 Ibid, 120–1. Belinskii had similarly distinguished between *natsional'nost'* (*nationalité*) and '*narodnost'* (*popularité*) in 1841. For him, *natsional'nost'* meant the life of the 'conglomerate body of all social estates,' and *narodnost'*, the life of the lower strata of the people. *Narodnost'* was the initial manifestation of *national'nost'*, and *natsional'nost'* the actualization of *narodnost'*. V.G. Belinskii, *Izbrannye filosofskie sochineniia*, 1 (Moscow 1948), 343.

57 [Anon.], 'Russkaia literatura v 1852 godu. Stat'ia pervaia,' *Otechestvennyia zapiski* (Jan. 1853), 49.

58 [Anon.], 'Zhurnalistiki,' *Otechestvennyia zapiski* (May 1855), 58–63. Ivan Pososhkov was the pre-eminent economic thinker of the time of Peter the Great and *Moskvitianin* had lionized him earlier.

59 [Anon.], 'Sovremennye zametki,' *Sovremennik* (July 1855), 105–18.

60 A.A. Grigor'ev, 'Zamechaniia ob otnoshenii sovremennoi kritiki k iskusstvu,' in *Sochineniia*, 1, *Kritika*, 77–126.

61 For a discussion of the publication of Annenkov's edition of Pushkin's poetry and its reception, see Charles A. Moser, *Esthetics as Nightmare: Russian Literary Theory, 1855–1870* (Princeton, NJ, 1989), 14-18 and passim.

CHAPTER FIVE: In the Light of the Ideal (1855–1857)

1 A.A. Grigor'ev, 'Kratkii posluzhnoi spisok,' in Vl. Kniazhnin, ed, *Materialy dlia biografii Apollona Grigor'eva* (hereafter *Materialy*) (Petrograd 1917), 305. In summer 1851, for example, Grigor'ev recommended to Pogodin that *Moskvitianin* purchase a piece by Ia.P. Polonskii. In December, Polonskii was still awaiting an answer. Barsukov, *Zhizn' i trudy M.P. Pogodina*, bk. xi (St Petersburg 1897), 417.

2 Barsukov, *Zhizn' i trudy*, bk. xi, 438 and 440.

3 Ibid, 410.

4 A useful guide to the conflicts and negotiations regarding the running of *Moskvitianin* is L.P. Kogan, *Letopis' zhizni i tvorchestva A.N. Ostrovskogo* (Moscow 1953), 27–85 passim.

5 A. Grigor'ev, Letter to M.P. Pogodin, Oct. 1851, in *Materialy*, 130–1. Though it is not known what the nature of Ostrovskii's changes were, it is likely that he

was trying to soften Grigor'ev's harsh criticisms of the actress. As it was, the Director of the Moscow Theatres, A.M. Gedeonov, objected to the tone of Grigor'ev's article. Barsukov, *Zhizn' i trudy*, bk. XI, 400.

6 Barsukov, *Zhizn' i trudy*, bk. XII, 221.

7 Grigor'ev, Letter to M.P. Pogodin, 23 Feb. 1853, in *Materialy*, 137.

8 Barsukov, *Zhizn' i trudy*, bk. XII, 295.

9 Grigor'ev, Letter to M.P. Pogdin, Jan. 1853, in *Materialy*, 143.

10 Barsukov, *Zhizn' i trudy*, bk. XIV, 240–1.

11 Grigor'ev, Letter to M.P. Pogodin, 18 Jan. 1856, in *Materialy*, 147–8.

12 Reproduced in full in B.F. Egorov, 'Apollon Grigor'ev – kritik,' *Uchenye zapiski Tartuskogo gos. universiteta, vyp.* 98 (1960), 227–9.

13 Grigor'ev, Letter to M.P. Pogodin, 18 Jan. 1856, in *Materialy*, 147–9.

14 Grigor'ev, Letter to M.P. Pogodin, Jan. 1856, in ibid, 143.

15 For the circumstances of the marriage, see I.M. Sechenov, *Avtobiograficheskie zapiski Ivana Mikhailovicha Sechenova* (Moscow 1945), 65.

16 Grigor'ev, Letter to M.P. Pogodin, 18 Jan. 1856, in *Materialy*, 147–9 passim.

17 Barsukov, *Zhizn' i trudy*, bk. XIV, 369.

18 The agreement and Grigor'ev's program announcement were published in full in *Materialy*, 312–14. In 1857 *Moskvitianin* was to be a historical and critical journal, without a literature section, because it could not compete financially with other journals for quality manuscripts.

19 On 2 October 1855 Granovskii reported to Kavelin that Grigor'ev was to be the literary critic for *Russkaia beseda*. Barsukov, *Zhizn' i trudy*, bk. XIV, 319.

20 Grigor'ev, Letter to A.I. Koshelev, 25 March 1856, in *Materialy*, 150–2.

21 Barsukov, *Zhizn' i trudy*, bk. XIV, 368.

22 V. Evgen'ev, 'N.A. Nekrasov i liudi 40 gg. IV, Pis'ma V.P. Botkina,' *Golos minuvshego* (Oct. 1916), 92–3.

23 I.S. Turgenev, *Polnoe sobranie sochinenii i pisem. Pis'ma*, II, *1851–1856* (Moscow and Leningrad 1961), 345.

24 S. Melgunov, 'Ap. Grigor'ev i *Sovremennik*,' *Golos minuvshego*, I (1922), 130–4.

25 Ibid, 135–6.

26 Turgenev, *Polnoe sobranie*, 347.

27 On 2 May 1855 he wrote in his diary, 'Acquaintance with Apollon Grigor'ev. An invitation.' On 8 May he visited Grigor'ev, accompanied by Grigorovich. A.V. Druzhinin, *Povesti. Dnevnik* (Moscow 1986), 335–6.

28 Ibid, 391–4.

29 Melgunov, 'Ap. Grigor'ev,' 136.

30 Grigor'ev, Letter to A.V. Druzhinin, July 1856, in *Materialy*, 154–6.

31 M.D. Prygunov, Iu. A. Bakhrushin, and N.A. Brodskii, eds, *Neizdannye pis'ma k A.N. Ostrovskomu* (Moscow and Leningrad 1932), 322, 324–6, 329, 331.

32 I.S. Turgenev, *Polnoe sobranie sochinenii i pisem. Pis'ma*, III, *1856–1859* (Moscow and Leningrad 1961), 39.

33 N.A. Nekrasov, *Sobranie sochinenii, Tom sedmoi. Kritika i publitsistika, 1841–1866* (Moscow 1967), 320.

34 P.V. Annenkov, *Literaturnye vospominaniia. Khudozhnik i prostoi chelovek. Iz vospominanii ob A.F. Pisemskom* (Moscow 1960), 494.

35 A.A. Grigor'ev, 'O pravde i iskrennosti v iskusstve. Po povodu odnogo esteticheskago voprosa. Pis'mo k A.S. Khomiakovu,' *Sochineniia Apollona Grigor'eva*, I (St Petersburg 1876), 129–30.

36 For a detailed and excellent discussion of this debate, see Charles A. Moser, *Esthetics as Nightmare: Russian Literary Theory, 1855–1870* (Princeton, NJ, 1989).

37 Grigor'ev, 'O pravde,' 134.

38 Ibid, 142.

39 Ibid.

40 Ibid, 135–6.

41 Ibid, 178.

42 Ibid, 177.

43 Ibid, 189.

44 Grigor'ev, Letter to A.V. Druzhinin, July 1856, in *Materialy*, 155.

45 N.L. Brodskii, ed, *V.P. Botkin i I.S. Turgenev. Neizdannaia perepiska, 1851–1869* (Moscow and Leningrad 1930), 92.

46 A.D. Galakhov, 'Sorokovye gody,' *Istoricheskii vestnik* (Jan. 1892), 138–9.

47 A. Fet, *Moi vospominaniia,1848-1889*, pt. I (Moscow 1890), 357.

48 Grigor'ev, Letters to E.N. Edel'son and A.V. Druzhinin, July 1856, in *Materialy*, 152–3 and 155–6, respectively. Grigor'ev wrote about going to Tver' to get the necessary court order. In April he had even arranged to meet Ostrovskii there, but when the playwright arrived at the station to meet him, Grigor'ev was not on the train. Kogan, *Letopis' zhizni*, 69.

49 Grigor'ev, Letter to A.V. Druzhinin, Aug. 1856, in *Materialy*, 157.

50 Grigor'ev, Letters to A.V. Druzhinin, 12 Dec. 1856 and 5 Jan. 1857, in ibid, 160–2.

51 A.A. Grigor'ev, 'Pis'mo k A.V. Druzhininu, po povodu komedii Shekspira: 'son v letniuiu noch'' i ego perevod,' *Biblioteka dlia chteniia* (Aug. 1857), 482–94.

52 Brodskii, ed, *Botkin i Turgenev*, 92.

53 A.D. Galakhov, 'Literaturnaia kofeina v Moskve,' *Russkaia starina* (April 1886), 181–98. See also A.A. Stakhovich, 'Klochki vospominanii,' *Russkaia mysl'* (Feb. 1898), 96.

54 Galakhov, 'Sorokovye gody,' 411. In using *zane* in place of *ibo*, Galakhov was poking fun at Grigor'ev's use of archaic words in his poetry.

55 Grigor'ev, Letter to E.S. Protopopova, 26 Jan. 1858, in *Materialy*, 218.
56 Grigor'ev, Letter to E.N. Edel'son, 13 Nov. 1857, in ibid, 185.
57 Grigor'ev, Letter to E.N. Edel'son, 5 Dec. 1857, in ibid, 197.
58 Prygunov, Bakhrushin, and Brodskii, eds, *Neizdannye pis'ma k A.N. Ostrov-skomu*, 117.
59 Ibid, 120.
60 *Materialy*, 334–5.

CHAPTER SIX: Western Perspective (1857–1858)

1 A. Grigor'ev, Letter to M.P. Pogodin, 10 Aug. 1857, in Vl. Kniazhnin, ed, *Mate-rialy dlia biografii Apollona Grigor'eva* (hereafter *Materialy*) (Petrograd 1917), 165.
2 M.D. Prygunov, Iu.A. Bakhrushin, and N.A. Brodskii, eds, *Neizdannye pis'ma k A.N. Ostovskomu* (Moscow and Leningrad, 1932), 14.
3 Grigor'ev, Letter to M.P. Pogodin, 10 Aug. 1857 (n.s.), in *Materialy*, 165.
4 Grigor'ev, Letter to E.S. Protopopova, 1 Sept. 1857 (n.s.), in ibid, 169.
5 Grigor'ev, Letter to E.S. Protopopova, 20 Oct. 1857 (n.s.), in ibid, 176.
6 Grigor'ev, Letter to E.N. Edel'son, 11 Sept. 1857 (n.s.), in ibid, 171.
7 Grigor'ev, Letter to M.P. Pogodin, 26 Aug. 1857 (n.s.), in ibid, p.166.
8 Grigor'ev, Letter to E.S. Protopopova, 27 April 1858 (n.s.), in ibid, 234.
9 Grigor'ev, Letter to M.P. Pogodin, 26 Aug.–5 Oct. 1859, in ibid, 248.
10 Grigor'ev, 'Kratkii posluzhnoi spisok,' in ibid, 306. The 'Record' was written in September 1864 as a pastime in debtors' prison.
11 Grigor'ev, Letter to E.S. Protopopova, 1 Sept. 1857 (n.s.), in ibid, 170.
12 Grigor'ev, Letter to A.A. Fet, 4 Jan. 1858 (n.s.), in ibid, 206.
13 Grigor'ev, Letter to E.S. Protopopova 20 Oct. 1857 (n.s.), in ibid, 177.
14 Grigor'ev, Letter to E.N. Edel'son 11 Sept. 1857 (n.s.), in ibid, 172.
15 Grigor'ev, Letter to E.S. Protopopova 15 Jan. 1858 (n.s.), in ibid, 204.
16 Grigor'ev, Letter to A.N. Maikov, 21 Jan. 1858 (n.s.), in ibid, 216.
17 Grigor'ev, Letter to M.P. Pogodin, 18 Nov. 1857 (n.s.), in ibid, 192.
18 Grigor'ev, Letter to E.N. Edel'son, 11 Sept. 1857 (n.s.), in ibid, 171.
19 Grigor'ev, Letter to M.P. Pogodin, 26 Jan. 1858 (n.s.), in ibid, 221.
20 Grigor'ev, Letter to E.N. Edel'son, 1 Dec. 1857 (n.s.), in ibid, 196.
21 Grigor'ev, Letter to E.N. Edel'son, 5 Dec. 1857 (n.s.), in ibid, 196–7.
22 Elsewhere Grigor'ev had written with regard to a letter of Georges Sand's that it 'represents an awesome exposure of a way of life in which ideas like love and fraternity have to be *invented*, in which the *universal* can attain the sub-mission of the particular, the individual only by force and despotism.' He added that such a way of life produced two extremes: 'the despotic absorption

of "personality" by "papism," whether Roman papism or (at root it is all the same) Fourierist and Saint-Simonian popery; and the exaggerated protest of the individual, a protest expressed in the thought of Max Stirner as the constant deification of the individual.' A. Grigor'ev, *Sochineniia*, I (St Petersburg 1876), 175–6. Grigor'ev's frequent references to people of the West as 'ants' and his association of Catholicism and socialism anticipated Dostoevskii's later views.

23 Alexander Herzen, *From the Other Shore* (London 1956), 36–7, 50, 67, and 96.

24 Grigor'ev, Letter to M.P. Pogodin, 8 Nov. 1857 (n.s.), in *Materialy*, 181.

25 Grigor'ev, Letter to M.P. Pogodin, 27 Sept. 1857 (n.s.), in ibid, 179–80.

26 Grigor'ev, Letter to E.N. Edel'son, 25 Dec. 1857 (n.s.), in ibid, 200.

27 Grigor'ev, Letters to M.P. Pogodin, 7 March 1858 (n.s.), and to E.N. Edel'son, 16 Nov. (n.s.) and 25 Dec. 1857 (n.s.), in ibid, 226, 188, and 201, respectively.

28 Grigor'ev, Letter to A.N. Maikov, 21 Jan. 1858 (n.s.), in ibid, 216.

29 Grigor'ev, Letter to M.P. Pogodin, 8 Nov. 1857 (n.s.), in ibid, 181.

30 Grigor'ev, Letter to E.N. Edel'son, 13 Nov. 1857 (n.s.), in ibid, 184.

31 Grigor'ev, Letter to M.P. Pogodin, 26 Aug.–5 Oct. 1859, in ibid, 246–7.

32 Grigor'ev, Letter to E.S. Protopopova, 15 Jan. 1858 (n.s.), in ibid, 204.

33 Grigor'ev, Letter to M.P. Pogodin, 27 Sept. 1857 (n.s.), in ibid, 179.

34 Grigor'ev, Letter to M.P. Pogodin, 8 Nov. 1857 (n.s.), in ibid, 181.

35 Grigor'ev, Letter to A.N. Maikov, 21 Jan. 1858 (n.s.), in ibid, 215–17.

36 Grigor'ev, Letters to M.P. Pogodin, 8 Nov. 1857 (n.s.), and to E.N. Edel'son of 13 Nov. 1857 (n.s.), in ibid, 181 and 185, respectively.

37 Grigor'ev, Letter to M.P. Pogodin, 8 Nov. 1857 (n.s.), in ibid, 182.

38 Grigor'ev, Letter to A.N. Maikov, 21 Jan. 1858 (n.s.), in ibid, 215–17.

39 Grigor'ev, Letter to M.P. Pogodin, 8 Nov. 1857 (n.s.), in ibid, 182.

40 Grigor'ev, Letter to A.N. Maikov, 21 Jan. 1858 (n.s.), in ibid, 216–17.

41 Grigor'ev, Letter to E.N. Edel'son, 9 Jan. 1858, in ibid, 212–13.

42 Grigor'ev, Letter to M.P. Pogodin, 7 March 1858 (n.s.), in ibid, 226–7.

43 Grigor'ev, Letter to A. Druzhinin, 10 Aug. 1857 (n.s.), in ibid, 164.

44 Grigor'ev, Letter to M.P. Pogodin, 26 Jan. 1858 (n.s.), in ibid, 222.

45 A.A. Grigor'ev, 'Kriticheskii vzgliad na osnovy, znachenie i priemy sovremennoi kritiki iskusstva,' in B.F. Egorov, ed, *Literaturnaia kritika* (Moscow 1967), 145.

46 Ibid, 130.

47 Ibid, 131. Herzen wrote, 'What does it mean to love humanity? What is humanity itself? It all sounds to me like the old Christian virtues, *réchauffés* in a philosophical oven. People like their fellow citizens – that is understandable. But what the love is that embraces everything that has ceased to be a monkey, from the Eskimo and the Hottentot to the Dalai-Lama and the Pope – that I don't

quite grasp, it's a little too wide.' Alexander Herzen, *From the Other Shore* (London 1956), 96.

48 Grigor'ev, 'Kriticheskii vzgliad,' 134.

49 Ibid.

50 Ibid, 125.

51 Ibid, 126.

52 Ibid, 126–7.

53 Alexander Herzen, *My Past and Thoughts* (Los Angeles and London 1982), 247

54 Grigor'ev, Kriticheskii vzgliad,' 115.

55 Ibid, 127–9.

56 Ibid, 138.

57 Ibid, 137.

58 Grigov'ev, Letter to E.S. Protopopova, 25 Sept. 1857 (n.s.), in *Materialy*, 174.

59 Grigov'ev, Letter to E.S. Protopopova, 1 Sept. 1857 (n.s.), in ibid, 169.

60 Grigov'ev, Letter to A.A. Fet, 4 Jan. 1858, in ibid, 206.

61 Grigov'ev, Letter to E.S. Protopopova, 1 Sept. 1857 (n.s.), in ibid, 169.

62 Grigov'ev, Letter to M.P. Pogodin, 10 March 1858 (n.s.), in ibid, 227–8.

63 A.A. Fet, *Moi vospominaniia*, 1 (Moscow 1890), 236.

64 A. Grigor'ev, *Sochineniia v dvukh tomakh*, 1 (Moscow 1990), p. 127–8.

65 Ibid, 228.

66 A. Grigor'ev, *Izbrannye proizvedeniia* (Moscow 1959), 566.

67 Grigor'ev, *Sochineniia v dvukh tomakh*, 1, 205–23.

68 Grigor'ev, *Vospominaniia* (Leningrad 1980), 300. Kniazhnin omitted the reference to the cleaning woman. Grigor'ev's chronic longing for a 'pure' woman to enter his life and 'clean up' his soul rendered this remark both ironic and supremely offensive.

69 Grigor'ev, Letter to E.S. Protopopova, 22 March 1858 (n.s.), in *Materialy*, 230.

70 Grigor'ev, Letter to E.S. Protopopova, 6 Jan. 1858 (n.s.), in ibid, 207.

71 Grigor'ev, Letter to E.S. Protopopova, 27 April 1858 (n.s.), in ibid, 233.

72 Grigor'ev, Letter to E.S. Protopopova, 6 Jan. 1858 (n.s.), in ibid, 211.

73 Grigor'ev, Letter to E.S. Protopopova, 20 Oct. 1857 (n.s.), in ibid, 175.

74 Ibid, 175–6.

75 Ibid, 176.

76 Grigor'ev, *Sochineniia v dvukh tomakh*, 1, 123–7.

77 Grigor'ev, Letter to M.P. Pogodin, 27 Sept. 1857 (n.s.), in *Materialy*, 178–9.

78 Grigor'ev, Letter to M.P. Pogodin, 9 Feb. 1858 (n.s.), in ibid, 223.

79 Ibid.

80 He described his days in Paris in a series of letters to Pogodin. Grigor'ev, Letters to M.P. Pogodin, 26 Aug.–5 Oct. 1859, in ibid, 246–55.

81 Grigor'ev, *Sochineniia v dvukh tomakh*, 1, 131.

82 N.A. Potekhin, 'Nashi v Parizhe,' in his *Nashi bezobrazniki* (St Petersburg 1864), 298–425.

83 Grigor'ev, Letter to M.P. Pogodin, 15 April 1858, in *Materialy*, 231.

84 Ibid., and Letter to I.S. Turgenev of 11 May 1858 (n.s.), in ibid, 236a.

85 Kniazhnin omitted the reference to the prostitute. She was restored to his bed by Soviet editors of the letter. Apollon Grigor'ev, *Vospominaniia*, 307.

CHAPTER SEVEN: True Realism (1858–1860)

1 A.A. Grigor'ev, 'Kratkii posluzhnoi spisok,' Vl. Kniazhnin, ed, *Materialy dlia biografii Apollona Grigor'eva* (hereafter *Materialy*) (Petrograd 1917), 306.

2 Grigor'ev, Letter to E.S. Protopopova, 27 Oct. 1858, in *Materialy*, 237.

3 M.D. Prygunov, Iu.A. Bakhrushin, and N.A. Brodskii, eds, *Neizdannye pis'ma k A.N. Ostrovskomu* (Moscow and Leningrad 1932), 140.

4 Ibid, 142.

5 Grigor'ev, 'Kratkii posluzhnoi spisok,' in *Materialy*, 306.

6 Quoted in L.E. Varustin, *Zhurnal 'Russkoe Slovo,' 1859–1866* (Leningrad 1966), 10.

7 I.S. Turgenev, *Polnoe sobranie sochinenii i pisem. Pis'ma*, III, *1856–1859* (Moscow and Leningrad 1961), 265–6.

8 Mikh. Lemke, *Politicheskie protsessy v Rossii 1860kh gg. (po arkhivnym dokumentam)* (Moscow and Petrograd 1923), 621.

9 G.P. Prokhorov, 'G.E. Blagosvetlov, Ia.P. Polonskii, G.A.Kushelev-Bezborodko. Pis'ma i dokumenty,' *Zven'ia*, I (Moscow and Leningrad 1932), 331–2.

10 Prygunov, Bakhrushin, and Brodskii, eds, *Neizdannye pis'ma k A.N. Ostrovskomu*, 455. Grigor'ev has sometimes been credited with writing the revolutionary song in question. Soviet researchers maintained plausibly that V. Kurochkin was the author though a few support a certain university student, from Kazan', Uvarov. Polonskii's suggestion – that Grigor'ev merely set the song to music – seems more probable than that he wrote its words. Ibid, 716.

11 Grigor'ev, Letter to E.S. Protopopova, 26 Jan. 1859, in *Materialy*, 240.

12 Turgenev, *Polnoe sobranie*, III, 268.

13 P.D. Boborykin, *Vospominaniia v dvukh tomakh*, I, *Za polveka* (Leningrad 1965), 233 and 280.

14 Grigor'ev, Letter to E.S. Protopopova, 26 Jan. 1859, in *Materialy*, 239.

15 A. Grigor'ev, *Sochineniia v dvukh tomakh*, I (Moscow 1990), 224–42.

16 Grigor'ev, Letter to E.S. Protopopova, 26 Jan. 1859, in *Materialy*, 240. One student who knew Grigor'ev during his days at *Russkoe slovo* was P.P. Chubinskii, later an ethnographer and statistician, who was to be one of the stu-

dents exiled in the university disturbances of 1861. Boborykin, *Vospominaniia*, 230.

17 Grigor'ev, Letter to N.N. Strakhov, 20 March 1862, in *Materialy*, 296.
18 Ibid.
19 Grigor'ev, Letter to M.P. Pogodin, 16 Sept. 1861, in ibid, 276–7.
20 Prygnnov, Bakhrushin, and Brodskii, eds, *Neizdannye pis'ma k A.N. Ostrovskomu*, 634.
21 P.L. Lavrov, 'Pis'ma P.L. Lavrova,' in *Shestidesiatye gody. Materialy po istorii literatury i obshchestvennomu dvizheniiu* (Moscow and Leningrad 1940), 285.
22 A. Marchik, 'Neizvestnye pis'ma Ap. Grigor'eva,' *Voprosy literatury*, no. 7 (July 1965), 254.
23 A.A. Grigor'ev, 'Besedy s Ivanom Ivanovichem o sovremennoi nashei slovesnosti i o mnogikh drugikh vyzyvaiushchikh na razmyshlenie predmetakh,' in R.V. Ivanov-Razumnik, ed, *Vospominaniia* (Moscow and Leningrad 1930), 292.
24 Grigor'ev, Letter to the Committee of the Literary Fund, 1 May 1860, in *Materialy*, 258–9. T.I. Ornatskaia, 'Deiatel'nost' Dostoevskogo v "Obshchestve dlia posobiia nuzhdaiushchimsia literatoram i uchenym" (1859–1866),' in G.M. Fridlender, ed, *Dostoevskii. Materialy i issledovaniia*, VII (Leningrad 1987), 247 n37.
25 Grigor'ev, 'Kratkii posluzhnoi spisok,' in *Materialy*, 307.
26 Turgenev, *Polnoe sobranie sochinenii i pisem*, IV, B.N. Eikhenbaum, ed (Moscow and Leningrad 1961), 159 and 518.
27 Grigor'ev, Letters to M.P. Pogodin, 26 Aug.–5 Oct., 1859, *Materialy*, 251.
28 N.N. Strakhov, 'Vospominaniia ob A.A. Grigor'eve,' *Epokha*, no. 9 (Sept. 1864), 4.
29 Grigor'ev, Letters to M.P. Pogodin, 26 Aug.–5 Oct. 1859, in *Materialy*, 248.
30 Grigor'ev, Letter to M.P. Pogodin, March or April 1860, in ibid, 258.
31 Grigor'ev, Letter to M.P. Pogodin, 4 Aug. 1859, in ibid, 245.
32 Ibid.
33 Marchik, 'Neizvestnye pis'ma Ap. Grigor'eva,' 254–6.
34 Nikolai Barsukov, *Zhizn' i trudy M.P. Pogodina*, bk. XVIII (St Petersburg 1904), 453–4.
35 Marchik, 'Neizvestnye pis'ma Ap. Grigor'eva,' 256.
36 A.A. Grigor'ev, 'Vzgliad na istoriiu Rossii. Soch. S. Solov'eva,' *Russkoe slovo*, no. 1 (Jan. 1859), 'Kritiki,' 1–48.
37 A.A. Grigor'ev, 'I.S. Turgenev i ego deiatel'nost'. Po povodu romana "Dvorianskoe gnezdo,"' in B.F. Egorov, ed, *Literaturnaia kritika* (Moscow 1967), 324.
38 A.A. Grigor'ev, 'Vzgliad na russkuiu literaturu so smerti Pushkina, 1, Pushkin – Griboedov – Gogol' – Lermontov,' in B.F. Egorov, ed, *Literaturnaia kritika* (Moscow 1967), 187.

39 A.A. Grigor'ev, 'Neskol'ko slov o zakonakh i terminakh organicheskoi kritiki, II,' in *Sochineniia*, I, *Kritika*, V.S. Krupitsch, ed (Villanova, Penn., 1970), 230.

40 A.A. Grigor'ev, 'Neskol'ko slov o zakonakh i terminakh organicheskoi kritiki, I,' in ibid, 212.

41 Ibid, 207–13.

42 N.N. Strakhov, 'Vospominaniia ob A.A. Grigor'eve,' *Epokha*, no. 9 (1864), 11.

43 A.A. Grigor'ev, 'Vzgliad na russkuiu literaturu so smerti Pushkina, II, Roman-tizm – Otnoshenie kriticheskogo sozdaniia k romantizmu – Gegelizm (1834–1840),' in B.F. Egorov, ed, *Literaturnaia kritika* (Moscow 1967), 236.

44 Grigor'ev, Vzgliad na russkuiu literaturu, I,' 166–7.

45 Ibid, 172.

46 N.M. Karamzin, 'Love of Country and National Pride,' in Marc Raeff, ed and trans, *Russian Intellectual History: An Anthology* (New York 1966), 110.

47 V.G. Belinskii, 'Vzgliad na russkuiu literaturu v 1846 g.,' in N.K. Gei, ed, *Sobranie sochinenii*, VIII (Moscow 1982), 195–6.

48 Alexander Herzen, *My Past and Thoughts* (Los Angeles and London 1982), 303.

49 Grigor'ev, 'Vzgliad na russkuiu literaturu,' 167.

50 N.V. Gogol', 'Neskol'ko slov o Pushkine,' in S.I. Mashinskii and M.B. Khrapchenko, eds, *Sobranie sochinenii v semi tomakh*, VI, *Stat'i* (Moscow 1986), 56.

51 Grigor'ev, 'Vzgliad na russkuiu literaturu,' 169 and 197.

52 Grigor'ev, 'I.S. Turgenev i ego deiatel'nost',' 245–6.

53 Ibid, 297.

54 Ibid, 298.

55 Ibid, 363–4.

56 Ibid, 364–5.

57 N.A. Dobroliubov, 'Temnoe tsarstvo,' *Izbrannoe* (Moscow 1970), 43–178.

58 A.A. Grigor'ev, 'Posle "Grozy" Ostrovskogo. Pis'ma k I.S. Turgenevu, I. Neizbezhnye voprosy,' in N.N. Strakhov, ed, *Sochineniia*, I (St Petersburg 1876), 454.

59 Ibid, 464.

60 Ibid, 474.

61 Ibid, 478–80. K.N. Leont'ev later recalled that Grigor'ev's view was supported by many: 'It had still not entered the heads of all of us lovers of Ostrovskii's plays until Dobroliubov's article that the author was exposing everything gross and hard in the way of life of the old merchantry. We, admiring these comedies in the theatre, imagined, on the contrary, that Mr. Ostrovskii was depicting *the Russian poetry of the merchant way of life* with love ... Apollon Grigor'ev was only a spokesman for this sentiment in society.' K. Leont'ev, *Sobranie sochinenii* (Moscow 1912), VIII, 101–2.

62 Grigor'ev, 'Posle "Grozy,"' 458.

63 A.A. Grigor'ev, 'Iskusstvo i nravstvennost'. Novye Grubeleien po povodu starogo voprosa,' in B.F. Egorov, ed, *Literaturnaia kritika* (Moscow 1967), 407.

64 Ibid, 421.

65 Apollon Grigor'ev, 'Realizm i idealizm v nashei literature. Po povodu novogo izdaniia sochinenii Pisemskogo i Turgeneva,' *Sochineniia v dvukh tomakh*, B.F. Egorov and A.L. Ospovat, eds, II, 261–79.

66 A.P. Miliukov, *Literaturnye vstrechi i znakomstva* (St Petersburg 1890), 255.

CHAPTER EIGHT: Native Soil and Self-Exile (1860–1862)

1 A. Grigor'ev, Letter to M.P. Pogodin, 13 Feb. 1861, in Vl. Kniazhnin, ed, *Materialy dlia biografii Apollona Grigor'eva* (hereafter *Materialy*) (Petrograd 1917), 264–5.

2 S. Zil'bershtein, 'Apollon Grigor'ev i popytka vozrodit' *"Moskvitiainin"* (nakanune sotrudnichestva v zhurnale *"Vremia"*,' *Literaturnoe nasledstvo*, 86 (Moscow 1973), 575–6.

3 N.N. Strakhov, 'Vospominaniia o Fedore Mikhailoviche Dostoevskom,' in O. Miller and N. Strakhov, eds, *Biografiia, pis'ma i zametki iz zapisnoi knizhki F.M. Dostoevskogo* (St Petersburg 1883), 202. For Strakhov's claim concerning *Russkii vestnik*, see N.N. Strakhov, 'Vospominaniia ob A.A. Grigor'eve,' *Epokha*, no. 9 (Sept. 1864), 5.

4 A.N. Pleshcheev to F.M. Dostoevskii, April 1859, in A.S. Dolinin, ed. *F.M. Dostoevskii. Materialy i issledovaniia* (Leningrad 1935), 444.

5 Ibid, 454. Grigor'ev did not return Pleshcheev's high regard, calling him a 'fool' and a 'milksop' sniveller in his 'Short Service Record.' Grigor'ev, 'Kratkii posluzhnoi spisok,' *Materialy*, 307.

6 Strakhov, 'Vospominaniia o Dostoevskom,' 202.

7 A.P. Miliukov, 'A.A. Grigor'ev i L.A. Mei,' *Istoricheskii vestnik* (Jan. 1883), 100.

8 Ibid, 101. In 1861, Grigor'ev wrote an article in *Severnaia pchela* (The Northern Bee) on the reform of the debtors' prison. Since, he argued, the purpose of the institution was neither punitive nor corrective but merely to ensure that a debtor did not flee his or her creditor, the incarcerated debtor ought to enjoy full civil and human rights. In Russia, however, detainees were deprived of many of their rights, including that of seeing family and friends at will and in privacy. They were deprived of personal effects and even forbidden to smoke or to play cards. Though enlightened local administrators often ignored these restrictions, they were answerable for their enforcement. He urged the government to reform the prisons along English lines. 'To emulate in this instance is no sin,' he

concluded. Apollon Grigor'ev, 'Neskol'ko zamechanii o znachenii i ustroistve dolgovykh otdelenii,' *Severnaia pchela*, no. 92 (1861), 1–2.

9 *Materialy*, 337.

10 P.V. Bykov, *Siluety dalekogo proshlogo* (Moscow and Leningrad 1930), 143 and 51.

11 Strakhov, 'Vospominaniia o Dostoevskom,' 223–4.

12 Studies of *pochvennichestvo* include Wayne Dowler, *Dostoevsky, Grigor'ev, and Native Soil Conservatism* (Toronto 1982); V.S. Nechaeva, *Zhurnal M.M. i F.M. Dostoevskikh 'Vremia', 1861–1863* (Moscow 1972); and V.S. Nechaeva, *Zhurnal M.M. i F.M. Dostoevskikh 'Epokha', 1864–1865* (Moscow 1975). The best assessment of Dostoevskii's contribution to and role in *pochvennichestvo* is in Joseph Frank, *Dostoevsky: The Stir of Liberation, 1860–1865* (Princeton, NJ, 1986).

13 From the manifesto of *Vremia* for 1861, reproduced in Miller and Strakhov, eds, *Biografiia Dostoevskogo*, 177.

14 F.M. Dostoevskii, 'Riad statei o russkoi literature. Poslednie literaturnye iavleniia. Gazeta *Den'*,' *Vremia* (Nov. 1861), sec. II, 71.

15 Anon. [F.M. Dostoevskii], 'N.A. Dobroliubov,' *Vremia* (March 1862), sec. II, 46.

16 F.M. Dostoevskii, 'Neizdannyi Dostoevskii,' *Literaturnoe nasledstvo*, 83 (Moscow 1971), 186.

17 N. Kositsa [N.N. Strakhov], 'Primer apatii,' *Vremia* (Jan.–Feb. 1862), sec. II, 65.

18 N.K. [Strakhov], 'Nechto o polemike,' *Vremia* (Aug. 1861), sec. II, 147–8.

19 Dostoevskii, 'Riad statei o russkoi literature. Vvedenie,' *Vremia* (Jan., 1861), 15.

20 From the manifesto of *Vremia* for 1861, in Miller and Strakhov, eds, *Biografiia Dostoevskogo*, 179–80.

21 Ibid, 45.

22 Ibid, 179.

23 F.M. Dostoevskii, 'Riad statei o russkoi literature. Knizhnost' i gramotnost',' *Vremia* (July 1861), sec. II, 50.

24 From the manifesto for *Vremia* for 1862 in Miller and Strakhov, eds, *Biografiia, Dostoevskogo*, 32.

25 From the manifesto of *Vremia* for 1861, in ibid, 180–1.

26 Dostoevskii, 'Riad statei, Vvedenie,' 33–4.

27 F.M. Dostoevskii, 'Riad statei o russkoi literature. g. – bov i vopros ob iskusstve,' *Vremia* (Feb. 1861), 173–4.

28 Ibid, 193.

29 Ibid, 202.

30 Anon. [F.M. Dostoevskii], '*Svistok* i *Russkii vestnik*,' *Vremia* (March 1861), sec. IV, 76.

31 A.A. Grigor'ev, 'Narodnost' i literatura,' *Vremia*, no. 2 (1861), 93.

32 Ibid, 94.

33 Ibid, 103.

34 Ibid, 111.

35 A.A. Grigor'ev, 'Zapadnichestvo v russkoi literature,' *Vremia*, no. 3 (1861), 9–14.

36 [A.A. Grigor'ev], 'Kniaz' Serebrianyi,' *Vremia*, no. 12 (1862), 46–52.

37 Grigor'ev, 'Zapadnichestvo v russkoi literature,' 27–30.

38 Ibid, 34.

39 Grigor'ev, Letter to M.P. Pogodin, 16 Sept. 1861, *Materialy*, 279.

40 A.A. Grigor'ev, 'Belinskii i otritsatel'nyi vzgliad v literature,' *Vremia*, no. 4 (1861), 185.

41 Ibid, 203.

42 Ibid, 215.

43 Ibid, 209–13.

44 A.A. Grigor'ev, 'Taras Shevchenko,' *Vremia*, no. 4 (1861), 634–40.

45 A.A. Grigor'ev, 'Severno-russkie narodopravstva vo vremena udel'no-vechevogo uklada,' *Vremia*, no. 1 (1863), 92–140.

46 A.A. Grigor'ev, 'Nashi literaturnyia napravleniia s 1848 goda,' *Vremia*, no. 2 (1863), 5.

47 Grigor'ev, 'Narodnost' i literatura,' 84.

48 Ibid, 88.

49 [A.A. Grigor'ev], 'Vzgliad na knigi i zhurnal'nye stat'i,' *Vremia*, no. 4 (1861), 175.

50 A.A. Grigor'ev, 'Stikhotvoreniia N. Nekrasova,' *Vremia*, no. 7 (1862), 26.

51 A.A. Grigor'ev, 'Oppozitsiia zastoia. Cherty iz istorii mrakobesiia,' *Vremia*, no. 5 (1861), 1–36.

52 Ibid, 19–25.

53 A.A. Grigor'ev, 'Lermontov i ego napravlenie. Krainiia grani razvitiia otritsatel'nago vzgliada, I,' *Vremia*, no. 10 (1862), 21.

54 A.A. Grigor'ev, 'Lermontov i ego napravlenie. Krainiia grani razvitiia otritsatel'nago vzgliada, II,' *Vremia*, no. 11 (1862), 63.

55 Ibid, 73.

56 Ibid, 72.

57 A.A. Grigor'ev, 'Graf Tolstoi i ego sochineniia, I,' *Vremia*, no. 1 (1862), 1–30.

58 A.A. Grigor'ev, 'Iavleniia sovremennoi literatury. Graf L. Tolstoi i ego sochineniia, II,' *Vremia*, no. 9 (1862), 17.

59 Ibid, 26–7.

60 Grigor'ev, 'Stikhotvoreniia N. Nekrasova,' 20.

61 Ibid, 9.

62 Ibid, 3.

63 Grigor'ev, 'Graf L. Tolstoi, I,' 10.

64 Ibid, 21–2.

65 [A.A. Grigor'ev], 'Stikhotvoreniia A.S. Khomiakova,' *Vremia*, no. 5 (1861), 46–58.

66 Grigor'ev, 'Graf L. Tolstoi, I,' 27.

67 Grigor'ev, 'Stikhotvoreniia N. Nekrasova,' 23–4.

68 Grigor'ev, 'Nashi literaturnyia napravleniia s 1848 goda,' 1–38.

69 Ibid, 35.

70 Odin iz mnogikh nenuzhnykh liudei, 'O postepennom no bystrom i povsemes-tnom rasprostranenii nevezhestva i bezgramotnosti v rossiiskoi slovesnosti,' *Vremia*, no. 3 (1861), 40.

71 Ibid, 48.

72 A.A. Grigor'ev, 'Russkii teatr. Sovremennoe sostoianie dramaturgii i stseny,' *Vremia*, no. 2 (1863), 149–82.

73 Grigor'ev, Letter to N.N. Strakhov, 23 Sept. 1861, in *Materialy*, 281.

74 A.A. Grigor'ev, 'Po povodu novago izdaniia staroi veshchi. Gore ot uma,' *Vremia*, no. 8 (1862), 35–50.

75 Strakhov, 'Vospominaniia ob A.A. Grigor'eve,' 6.

76 Ibid, 11.

77 Grigor'ev, Letter to N.N. Strakhov, 12 Aug. 1861, in *Materialy*, 273.

78 Grigor'ev, Letter to N.N. Strakhov, 18 June 1861, in ibid, 266–7.

79 Grigor'ev, Letter to N.N. Strakhov, 12 Dec. 1861, in ibid, 285.

80 F.M. Dostoevskii, *Pis'ma*, I (Moscow and Leningrad 1928), 312–13.

81 Grigor'ev, Letter to N.N. Strakhov, 18 July 1861, in *Materialy*, 270. In another letter to Strakhov, 19 Jan. 1862, Grigor'ev wrote: 'Openness [glasnost'] and freedom are in essence only words for me ..., nonsensical and contentless words.' How, he went on to ask, could anyone believe in freedom for *Russkii vestnik* or the theoreticians? Ibid, 293.

82 Grigor'ev, Letter to N.N. Strakhov, 12 Dec. 1861, in ibid, 286.

83 Grigor'ev, Letter to M.P. Pogodin, 16 Sept. 1861, in ibid, 278.

84 Grigor'ev, Letter to N.N. Strakhov, 23 Sept. 1861, in ibid, 281–2.

85 Much of what is known about Grigor'ev's stay in Orenburg comes from Iudin, on whose account the following is based. Iudin, 'K biografii A.A. Grigor'eva,' *Istoricheskii vestnik* (Dec. 1894), 779–86.

86 Grigor'ev, Letter to N.N. Strakhov, 18 July 1861, in *Materialy*, ibid, 268. In reporting to Strakhov the failed visit to Father Fedor, Grigor'ev criticized the Holy Synod by placing an exclamation mark after Holy.

87 Grigor'ev, Letter to M.P. Pogodin, 16 Sept. 1861, in ibid, 278.

88 B.F. Egorov, 'Materialy ob Ap. Grigor'eve iz arkhiva N.N. Strakhova,' *Uchenye zapiski Tartuskogo gosudarstvennogo universiteta*, vyp. 139 (1963), 349.

89 Grigor'ev, Letter to N.N. Strakhov, 21 Aug. 1861, in *Materialy*, 274. Razin was a collaborator in *Vremia* whose liberal articles had already provoked Grigor'ev to complain about him to Dostoevskii.

90 Strakhov, 'Vospominaniia ob A. Grigor'eve,' 19.

91 Grigor'ev, Letter to N.N. Strakhov, 21 Aug. 1861, in *Materialy*, 275.

92 Iudin, 'K biografii A.A. Grigor'eva,' 783.

93 Grigor'ev, Letter to N.N. Strakhov, 20 March 1862, in *Materialy*, 297.

94 Iudin, 'K biografii A.A. Grigor'eva,' 784.

95 Grigor'ev, Letter to N.N. Strakhov, 19 Jan. 1862, in *Materialy*, 291–2.

96 Grigor'ev, Letter to N.N. Strakhov, 23 Sept. 1861, in ibid, 282.

97 Egorov, *Materialy ob Ap. Grigor'eve*, 350.

98 Grigor'ev, Letter to N.N. Strakhov, 20 March 1862, in *Materialy*, 294–5.

99 Egorov, *Materialy ob Ap. Grigor'eve*, 348.

100 Grigor'ev, Letter to Strakhov, 20 March 1862, in *Materialy*, 295–6.

101 Ibid, 293.

102 Iudin, 'K biografii A.A. Grigor'eva,' 784–5.

103 Ibid, 785–6. Kniazhnin recorded incorrectly that Grigor'ev submitted the medical report of 27 July to the Orenburg Cadet Corps on 19 August. *Materialy*, 350.

104 F.M. Dostoevskii, *Polnoe sobranie sochinenii v tridtsati tomakh*, XXIV (Leningrad 1982), 228, 232, 235.

105 Apollon Grigor'ev, *Sobranie sochinenii v dvukh tomakh*, I (Moscow 1990), 224–42.

106 B.F. Egorov, ed, 'Perepiska Ap. Grigor'eva s N.N. Strakovym,' *Uchenye zapiski Tartuskogo universiteta*, vyp. 167 (1965), 167.

107 Strakhov, 'Vospominaniia ob Ap. Grigor'eve,' 40.

CHAPTER NINE: Beauty, Suffering, and Art (1862–1864)

1 N.N. Strakhov, 'Vospominaniia ob Ap. Grigor'eve,' *Epokha*, no. 9 (Sept. 1864), 41.

2 B.F. Egorov, 'Materialy ob Ap. Grigor'eve iz arkhiva N.N. Strakhova,' *Uchenye zapiski Tartuskogo gosudarstvennogo universiteta*, vyp. 139 (1963), 348.

3 Vl. Kniazhnin, 'Materialy po istorii russkoi literatury i kultury. Neizvestnaia stat'ia K.N. Leont'eva: "Neskol'ko vospominanii i mysli o pokoinom Ap. Grigor'eve,"' *Russkaia mysl'* (Sept. 1915), 114–15. Iudin's archival researches showed that in order to collect the debt owed by Grigor'ev to the Cadet Corps the police called on his apartment in May to seize his furniture and found it already bare. Iudin, 'K biografii A.A. Grigor'eva,' *Istoricheskii vestnik* (Dec. 1894), 786.

4 P.V. Bykov, *Siluety dalekogo proshlogo* (Moscow and Leningrad 1930), 145.

5 [A.A. Grigor'ev], 'Vstupitel'noe slovo o fal'shivykh notakh v pechati i zhizni,' *Iakor'*, no. 1 (1863), 1.

6 [A.A. Grigor'ev], 'Nasha pristan',' *Iakor'*, no. 3 (1863), 41.

7 Ibid.

8 Ibid.

9 [A.A. Grigor'ev], 'Teoriia i zhizn',' *Iakor'*, no. 7 (1863), 117–18.

10 A.A. Grigor'ev, 'Zhurnal'nyi mir i ego iavleniia, I. Vzliad na sud'bu russkoi zhurnalistiki,' *Iakor'*, no. 6 (1863), 101–2.

11 A.A. Grigor'ev, 'Zhurnal'nyi mir i ego iavleniia, II. Temnyia stremleniia,' *Iakor'*, no. 10 (1863), 183.

12 Grigor'ev, 'Zhurnal'nyi mir, I,' 102.

13 A.A. Grigor'ev, 'Zhurnal'nyi mir i ego iavleniia, III. Sudorogi mrakobesiia,' *Iakor'*, no. 14 (1863), 264–5.

14 [Grigor'ev], 'Na poldoroge,' 565–6.

15 [Grigor'ev], 'Vstupitel'noe slovo,' 1.

16 [Grigor'ev], 'Na poldoroge,' 565–6.

17 Ibid, 565. Poking fun at the radicals, Grigor'ev wrote, 'The title "leading" can hardly in our age entice mature people; a "leading hare" is not a particularly enviable title.' 'Leading hare' was a pun on *zaiats* ('hare'; colloq. 'stowaway'). V.A. Zaitsev was one of the 'leading theoreticians' of *Russkoe slovo*.

18 Ralph Waldo Emerson, 'The Conservative,' in John Gross, ed, *The Oxford Book of Essays* (Oxford, 1991), 171–86.

19 [Grigor'ev], 'Na poldoroge,' 565.

20 [A.A. Grigor'ev], 'Veter peremenilsia,' *Iakor'*, no. 2 (1863), 1.

21 [A.A. Grigor'ev], 'Vopros o natsional'nostiakh,' *Iakor'*, no. 5 (1863), 81.

22 Anon., 'Evrei i odesskii klub,' *Iakor'*, no. 3 (1863), 59.

23 [A.A. Grigor'ev], 'Bezvykhodnoe polozhenie (Iz zapisok nenuzhnogo cheloveka,' *Iakor'*, no. 1 (1863), 2.

24 Grigor'ev, in *Vospominaniia*, R.V. Ivanov-Razumnik, ed (Moscow 1930), 344–73.

25 A. Grigor'ev, 'Russkie narodnye pesni,' *Moskvitianin*, no. 15 (1854), 107.

26 Ibid, 98.

27 Ibid, 104.

28 Ibid, 105.

29 Ibid, 121.

30 Ibid, 123.

31 A.A. Grigor'ev, 'Russkie narodnye pesni s ikh poeticheskoi i muzykal'noi storony,' *Otechestvennyia zapiski*, nos. 4 and 5 (1860), 574–93 and 207–22, respectively.

32 See Robert C. Ridenour, *Nationalism, Modernism, and Personal Rivalry in Nineteenth-Century Russian Music* (Ann Arbor, Mich., 1981), for a discussion of the Rubenshteins and the early years of Russian music.

33 This account of Grigor'ev's and Serov's friendship is based on the memoirs of Serov's wife. V.S. Serova, *Vospominaniia V.S. Serovoi* (St Petersburg 1914).

34 Ibid, 47.

35 K.I. Zvantsov, 'Aleksandr Nikolaevich Serov v 1857–1871 gg. Vospominaniia o nem i ego pis'ma,' *Russkaia starina* (Sept. 1888), 658.

36 Ibid, 661.

37 Serova, *Vospominaniia*, 86.

38 Ibid, 87. Dm. Averkiev, a youthful disciple of Grigor'ev's in his last years, later noted that the critic had more followers than he knew. He recalled a comment made by Grigor'ev to a young naturalist, who deeply admired him – while he did not believe that everyone reviled him or that everyone was taken in by the new wisdom of the 'five little books,' so beloved as the source of all knowledge by the nihilists, he did not expect anyone to take up his cause or to understand his articles. Dm. Averkiev, 'Apollon Aleksandrovich Grigor'ev,' *Epokha* (Aug. 1864), 11.

39 Serova, *Vospominaniia*, 86.

40 [A.A. Grigor'ev], 'Russkaia opernaia truppa. Neskol'ko slov o eia nostoiash-chem i budushchem,' *Iakor'*, no. 23 (1863), 447–8.

41 [A.A. Grigor'ev], '"Iudif" opera v piati aktakh A.N. Serova,' *Iakor'*, no. 12 (1863), 222–3.

42 A. Grigor'ev, 'Russkii teatr, I. Po vozobnovlenii v pervyi raz,' *Epokha* (Jan.–Feb. 1864), 423.

43 Ibid, 433.

44 See for example [A.A. Grigor'ev], 'Russkaia opernaia truppa,' *Iakor'*, nos. 23 and 24 (1863), 3–4 and 2–3, respectively.

45 P.D. Boborykin, *Vospominaniia v dvukh tomakh, I. Za polveka* (Moscow 1965), 392–3.

46 A.A. Grigor'ev, 'Po povodu spektaklia 10 maia "Bednost' ne porok" Ostrov-skogo,' reprinted in A.A. Grigor'ev, *Teatral'naia kritika*, E.S. Alekseeva and M.A. Venskaia, eds (Leningrad 1985), 369.

47 See his 'Nasha dramaticheskaia truppa,' in ibid, 274–87.

48 Ibid, 278.

49 F.M. Dostoevskii, *Polnoe sobranie sochinenii v tridtsati tomakh*, XXVIII, pt. 2, *Pis'ma, 1860–68* (Leningrad 1985), 104.

50 A. Grigor'ev, 'Russkii teatr v Peterburge, II,' *Epokha* (March 1864), 234.

51 Ibid, 235–7.

52 [A.A. Grigor'ev], 'O Pisemskom i ego znachenii v nashei literature,' *Iakor'*, no. 18 (1863), 341–5.

53 A.A. Grigor'ev, 'Otzhivaiushchiia v literature iavleniia,' *Epokha* (July 1864), 1–26.

54 A.A. Grigor'ev, 'Paradoksy organicheskoi kritiki, 1. Organicheskii vzgliad i ego osnovnoi printsip,' *Epokha* (May 1864), 259.

55 Ibid, 266. In 1868 Dostoevskii wrote to A.N. Maikov that he disagreed with Grigor'ev's view that Belinskii, had he lived longer, would have become a Slavophile. F.M. Dostoevskii, *Pis'ma*, 1860–68, 228. In 1876 he had changed his mind and suggested that Grigor'ev had been correct. See V.A. Tunimanov, 'Ap. Grigor'ev v pis'makh i "Dnevnik Pisatel'ia" Dostoevskogo,' *Dostoevskii. Materialy i issledovaniia*, VII (Leningrad 1987), 34. Evidently, Dostoevskii did not understand the passage in Grigor'ev's article, since the latter argued that had Belinskii lived he would have adopted the 'organic view,' which, in his mind, was distinct from Slavophilism but not exclusive of it.

56 Grigor'ev, 'Paradoksy,' 265–6.

57 Ibid, 268.

58 A.A. Grigor'ev, 'Paradoksy organicheskoi kritiki. Pis'mo vtoroe,' *Epokha* (June 1864), 274–5. Heidegger later called the idea of 'final reason' the philosophy of mastery.

59 Herzen had written: 'It is true that the laws of historical development are not opposed to the laws of logic, but their paths do not coincide with those of thought, just as nothing in nature coincides with the abstract norms constructed by pure reason.' Alexander Herzen, *From the Other Shore* (London 1956), 76.

60 Grigor'ev, 'Paradoksy, II,' 274.

61 Grigor'ev, 'Paradoksy, I,' 258.

62 Ibid.

63 N.N. Strakhov, 'Vospominaniia o Fedore Mikhailoviche Dostoevskom,' in Strakhov, *Biografiia, pis'ma i zametki iz zapisnoi knizhki F.M. Dostoevskogo* (St Petersburg 1883), 274.

64 Boborykin, *Vospominaniia*, 394.

65 A. Grigor'ev, 'Kratkii posluznoi spisok,' in Vl. Kniazhnin, ed, *Materialy dlia biografii Apollona Grigor'eva* (hereafter *Materialy*) (Petrograd 1917), 307.

66 V.S. Serova, 'Aleksandr Nikolaevich Serov. Prazdniki i budni v nashei sovmestnoi zhizni,' *Russkaia mysl'* (March 1913), 28.

67 Grigor'ev, Letter to F.M. Dostoevskii, 22 Aug. 1864, in *Materialy*, 301.

68 Grigor'ev, Letter to F.M. Dostoevskii, late August or early September 1864, in ibid, 301.

69 Strakhov, 'Vospominaniia ob Ap. Grigor'eve,' 44.

70 Ibid, 43.

71 Boborykin, *Vospominaniia*, 395.

72 Egorov, 'Materialy ob Ap. Grigor'eve,' 348.

73 Boborykin, *Vospominaniia*, 395.
74 P.D. Boborykin, 'Dolgo li? ...' *Otechestvennye zapiski* (Oct. 1875), 411–19.
75 Egorov, 'Materialy ob Ap. Grigor'eve,' 348–9.
76 Ibid, 349.

EPILOGUE

1 M.D. Prygunov, Iu.A. Bakhrushin, and N.D. Brodskii, eds, *Neizdannye pis'ma k A.N. Ostrovskomu* (Moscow and Leningrad 1932), 7.
2 K.I. Zvantsov, 'Aleksandr Nikolaevich Serov v 1857–1871 gg. Vospominaniia o nem i ego pis'ma,' *Russkaia starina* (Sept. 1888), 663.
3 V.S. Serova, *Vospominaniia V.S. Serovoi* (St Petersburg 1914), 114.
4 F.M. Dostoevskii, *Polnoe sobranie sochinenii v tridtsati tomakh*, XXIV (Leningrad 1982), 235.
5 D.I. Pisarev, *Sochineniia*, III (Moscow 1956), 253.
6 Anon., 'A.A. Grigor'ev,' *Otechestvennye zapiski* (Sept. 1864), 511–12.
7 Editor, 'Nekrolog,' *Den'* (3 Oct. 1864), 20.
8 Anon., 'Vospominaniia ob Apollone Grigor'eve,' *Sovremennik* (Nov.–Dec. 1864), 101–14.
9 F.M. Dostoevskii, *Polnoe sobranie khudozhestvennykh proizvedenii*, XIII (Moscow and Leningrad 1930), 351.
10 Ibid, 578.
11 Letopisets [N.N. Strakhov], 'Zametka letopistsa,' *Epokha* (Dec. 1864), 25. Strakhov's Slavophile preferences were always much stronger than Grigor'ev's or Dostoevskii's. Later he wrote, 'As *pochvenniki*, Apollon Grigor'ev and Dostoevskii constantly asserted that they were not Westernizers and not Slavophiles ... I decided that it was necessary to identify myself directly as a Slavophile.' Cited in N. Piksanov and O. Tsekhnovitser, eds, *Shestidesiatie gody* (Moscow 1940), 256.
12 Dostoevskii, *Polnoe sobranie khudozhestvennykh proizvedenii*, XIII, 353. Blok agreed that there was 'something Hamlet-like' about Grigor'ev: he betrayed nothing and no one and did not harm anyone, poisoning only his own life. Aleksandr Blok, 'Sud'ba Apollona Grigor'eva,' in V.N. Orlov et al, eds, *Sobranie sochinenii*, V, *Proza, 1903–1917* (Moscow and Leningrad 1962), 512.
13 F.M. Dostoevskii, 'Neizdannyi Dostoevskii,' *Literaturnoe nasledstvo*, LXXXIII (Moscow 1971), 244.
14 Aileen Kelly has explored the tension between irony and utopia in Herzen and Dostoevskii. She pointed out that the ironist Herzen, with his belief that freedom lay in accepting contingency, gave ammunition to the ironist side of Dostoevskii's character and posed a threat to its Orthodox-utopian side. Conse-

quently, he misrepresented Herzen's views in order to quell his own ironist leanings. Aileen Kelly, 'Irony and Utopia in Herzen and Dostoevsky: *From the Other Shore* and *Diary of a Writer*,' *Russian Review* (Oct. 1991), 397–416. Grigor'ev's strong ironist side prevented him from confusing his Orthodox faith with utopianism, a confusion to which Dostoevskii increasingly gave himself up.

15 Marc Raeff, ed, *Russian Intellectual History. An Anthology* (New York 1966), 300.

16 V.A. Tunimanov, 'Ap. Grigor'ev v pis'makh i "Dnevnik Pisatel'ia" Dostoevskogo,' in G.M. Fridlender, ed, *Dostoevskii. Materialy i issledovaniia*, VII (Leningrad 1987), 28.

17 See for example Dostoevskii, *Polnoe sobranie sochinenii*, XXIV, 228, 232, and 235.

18 V.G. Selitrennikova and I.G. Iakushkin, 'Apollon Grigor'ev i Mitia Karamazov,' *Filologicheskie nauki*, no. 1 (1969), 13–24.

19 A.A. Grigor'ev, *Sochineniia Apollona Grigor'eva*, I, N. Strakhov, ed. (St Petersburg 1876).

20 For the similarities of Grigor'ev's and Leont'ev's thinking, see my 'Two Conservative Views of Nationality and Personality: A.A. Grigor'ev and K.N. Leont'ev,' *Studies in Soviet Thought*, 41 (1991), 19–32.

21 Vlad. Kniazhnin, 'Materialy po istorii russkoi literatury i kultury. Neizvestnaia stat'ia K.N. Leont'eva: "Neskol'ko vospominanii i myslei o pokoinom Ap. Grigor'eve,"' *Russkaia mysl'* (Sept. 1915), 124. The article was intended for publication in *Zaria*, but for some reason the editor, N.N. Strakhov, decided not to print it.

22 V.G. A[vseenko], 'Bluzhdaniia russkoi mysli,' *Russkii vestnik* (Oct. 1876), 872–5.

23 Nikolai Shelgunov, *Literaturnaia kritika* (Leningrad 1974), 366.

24 S. Vengerov, 'Molodaia redaktsiia *Moskvitianina*,' *Vestnik Evropy*, I, no. 2 (1886), 581–612.

25 A. Skabichevskii, 'Ocherki literaturnago dvizheniia posle Belinskago i Gogolia,' *Russkaia mysl'* (May 1888), 15.

26 N.N. Strakhov, 'Pominki po Apollone Grigor'eve (1822–1864),' 251–2.

27 'Na mogile Apollona Grigor'eva,' *Novoe vremia* (26 Sept.–8 Oct. 1889), 3.

28 Grigor'ev's son Alexander wrote to *Novoe vremia* to announce the subscription. Apparently charges were being made that the family was neglecting the grave, charges that Alexander wished to dispell. A.A. Grigor'ev [fils], 'Pis'mo v redaktsiiu,' *Novoe vremia*, 11 no. 23 (May 1889), 3.

29 S. Vengerov, 'Apollon Grigor'ev,' *Entsiklopedicheskii slovar'*, IX (St Petersburg 1893), 721–3.

30 V. Rozanov, 'O trekh fazisakh v razvitii nashei kritiki,' *Russkoe obozrenie* (Aug. 1892), 583–4, 591; Iu. Nikolaev [Iu.N. Govorukh-Otrok], 'A.A. Grigor'ev (Po

povodu ispolnivshagosia 30 letiia so dnia ego smerti),' *Moskovskiia vedomosti* (28 Sept. 1894), 2.

31 A.L. Volynskii, *Russkie kritiki. Literaturnye ocherki* (St Petersburg 1896), 639–84.

32 A.K., 'Liberal'nyia pominki Apollona Grigor'eva,' *Moskovskiia vedomosti* (11 Oct. 1899), 4

33 P. Morozov, 'Iz zhizni i literatury. Po povodu dvukh literaturnykh pominok,' *Obrazovanie* (Nov. 1899), 41; Iv. Ivanov, *Istoriia russkoi kritiki*, pts. 3 and 4 (St Petersburg 1900), 437.

34 V. Rozanov, 'K 50-letiu konchiny Ap. A. Grigor'eva,' *Novoe vremia* (26 Sept.–9 Oct. 1914), 5.

35 V.V. Rozanov, 'N.N. Strakhov. Ego lichnost' i deiatel'nost',' in V.V. Rozanov, ed, *Literaturnye izgnanniki*, Vol. 1 (St Petersburg 1913), 56.

36 Leonid Grossman, 'Apollon Grigor'ev (K piatidesiatiletiu smerti), 1. Osnovatel' novoi kritiki,' *Russkaia mysl'* (Nov. 1914), 1–19. The article was later republished in Leonid Grossman, *Tri sovremennika (Dostoevskii, Tiutchev, Grigor'ev)* (Moscow 1922), 39–62.

37 Ibid, 2–3 and 10.

38 A.A. Grigor'ev, *Sobranie sochinenii*, 14 vols., V. Savodnik, ed. (Moscow 1915–16).

39 V. Rozanov, 'Dorogaia knizhnaia novinka,' *Novoe vremia* (23 April–6 May 1915), 5.

40 A.A. Grigor'ev, *Polnoe sobranie sochinenii i pisem*, 1, V.S. Spiridonov, ed. (Petrograd 1918).

41 A.A. Grigor'ev, *Stikhotvoreniia*, A. Blok, ed. (Moscow 1916). Blok's grandmother, E.G. Beketova, had known Grigor'ev personally and possessed a copy of his 1846 collection of poems of which only fifty had been published. D. Blagoi, 'Blok i Apollon Grigor'ev,' *Tri veka iz istorii russkoi poezii, XVIII, XIX, XX vv.* (Moscow 1933), 269.

42 Blok, 'Sud'ba' 487–520.

43 Ibid, 513. In a letter of 28 January 1916 to A.A. Izmailov, Blok wrote, 'In Grigor'ev, you know, are heaped up the embers of a mighty culture, which are literally fading out these days under the ashes of polemics and indifference.' V.N. Orlov et al, eds, *Sobranie sochinenii*, VIII, *Pis'ma 1898–1921* (Moscow and Leningrad 1963), 456.

44 Blok, 'Sud'ba,' 499–500.

45 Ibid, 513.

46 Ibid, 488.

47 Iu. Aikhenval'd, *Slova o slovakh. Kriticheskie stati* (Petrograd, 1916), 63.

48 Ibid, 65.

49 Iv. Rozanov, 'Stikhotvoreniia Apollona Grigor'eva,' *Golos minuvshego* (May–June 1916), 431.

50 N.M. Mendel'son, 'Sobranie sochinenii Apollona Grigor'eva pod redaktsiei V.F. Savodnika,' *Golos minuvshego* (Dec. 1916), 242.

51 Cited in B. Kostelianets, 'Poezia Apollona Grigor'eva,' in Apollon Grigor'ev, *Stikhotvoreniia i poemy* (Moscow and Leningrad 1966), 83.

52 S. Ashevskii, 'Apollon Aleksandrovich Grigor'ev (k piatidesiatiletiu so dnia smerti),' *Golos minuvshego* (Sept. 1914), 5–38. Another early study was D. Mikhailov, *Apollon Grigor'ev, zhizn' v sviazi s kharakterom literaturnoi deiatel'nosti ego* (St Petersburg 1900).

53 A.A. Fet, *Moi vospominaniia*, 2 vols. (Moscow 1890). Other memoirs included N.V. Berg, 'Moskovskie vospominaniia Nikolaia Vasilevicha Berga,' *Russkaia starina* (Oct. 1884), 53–71; A.A. Grigor'ev [fils], 'Odinokii kritik,' *Knizhki nedeli* (Aug. 1895), 5–23; P. Iudin, 'K biografii A.A. Grigor'eva,' *Istoricheskii vestnik* (Dec. 1894), 779–86; and Ia.P. Polonskii, 'Moi studencheskie vospominaniia,' *Niva* (Dec. 1898), 642–87. In many others, Grigor'ev received brief mention.

54 Vl. Kniazhnin, ed, *Materialy dlia biografii A. Grigor'eva* (Petrograd 1917).

55 M.D. Beliaev and V.S. Spiridonov, *Apollon Grigor'ev. Biografiia i putovoditel' po vystavke v zalakh Pushkinskogo Doma* (Petrograd 1922).

56 P. Sakulin, *Russkaia literatura i sotsializm, I. Rannii russkii sotsializm* (Moscow 1924), 406–29.

57 V. Friche, 'Apollon A. Grigor'ev,' in A. Lunacharskii and Val. Polianskii, eds, *Ocherki po istorii russkoi kritiki*, I (Moscow and Leningrad, 1929), 305–20.

58 N.L. Rubinshtein, 'Apollon Grigor'ev,' *Literatura i marksizm – Zhurnal teorii i istorii literatury*, bk. 2 (Moscow 1929), 95–121. That Grigor'ev was a bourgeois nationalist became the orthodox view. In 1936, for example, G. Berliner called him a 'bourgeois nationalist' and the 'most original of the ideologues of the young Russian bourgeoisie.' G. Berliner, 'Literaturnye protivniki N.A. Dobroliubova,' *Literaturnoe nasledstvo*, xxv and xxvi (Moscow 1936), 50.

59 R.V. Ivanov-Razumnik, ed, *A.A. Grigor'ev. Vospominaniia* (Moscow and Leningrad, 1930), pp. 608–30.

60 Ef. Meierovich, 'Apollon Grigor'ev-kritik Ostrovskogo,' *Teatr*, no. 10 (1940), 148 and 150.

61 B.P. Gorodetskii et al, eds, *Istoriia russkoi kritiki*, I (Moscow and Leningrad 1958), 475–6.

62 Ibid, 472.

63 A. Ianov, S. Pokrovskii, and B. Egorov, 'Literaturnaia kritika rannikh slavianofilov,' *Voprosy literatury* (May 1969), 90–135.

64 Apollon Grigor'ev, *Izbrannye proizvedeniia*, B.O. Kostelianets, ed (Moscow 1959); Apollon Grigor'ev, *Stikhotvoreniia i poemy*, B.F. Egorov, ed (Moscow

and Leningrad 1966); and Apollon Grigor'ev, *Stikhotvoreniia i poemy*, B.F. Egorov, ed (Moscow 1978).

65 'Stranitsy russkoi poezii XVIII–XX v.v. Ia.P. Polonskii, A.A. Grigor'ev,' *Melodiia* (1982).

66 A.A. Grigor'ev, *Literaturnaia kritika*, B.F. Egorov, ed (Moscow 1967); A.A. Grigor'ev, *Teatral'naia kritika*, E.S. Alekseeva and M.A. Venskaia, eds (Leningrad 1985); A.A. Grigor'ev, *Estetika i kritika*, M.F. Ovsiannikov, ed (Moscow 1980); and A.A. Grigor'ev, *Nravstvennost' i literatura*, F.F. Kuznetsov et al, eds (Moscow 1986).

67 A.A. Grigor'ev, *Vospominaniia* (Leningrad 1980), and Apollon Grigor'ev, *Odisseia poslednego romantika*, A.L. Ospovat, ed (Moscow 1988).

68 B.F. Egorov, ed, 'Apollon Grigor'ev – kritik,' *Uchenye zapski Tartuskogo gos. universiteta*, XCVIII (1960), 194–246; B.F. Egorov, ed, 'Materialy ob Ap. Grigor'eve iz arkhiva N.N. Strakhova,' ibid, CXXXIX (1963), 343–50; B.F. Egorov, ed, 'Publikatsiia i soobshcheniia perepiska Ap. Grigor'eva so N.N. Strakhovym,' Ibid, CLXVII (1965), 163–73; and R. Vitaker, 'Neopublikovannye pis'ma Apollona Grigor'eva,' *Vestnik Moskovskogo universiteta*, no. 2 (1971), 66–73.

69 Apollon Grigor'ev, *Sochineniia v dvukh tomakh*, B.F. Egorov, ed (Moscow 1990).

70 P.P. Gromov, 'Apollon Grigor'ev,' in Grigor'ev, *Izbrannye proizvedeniia*, 5. Recognition of the complexity of the intellectual influences on Grigor'ev opened up new avenues for Soviet scholars to explore. Egorov, for example, pointed out his strong affinity with Herzen during the emancipation period. B.F. Egorov, 'Khudozhestvennaia proza Ap. Grigor'eva,' in Grigor'ev, *Vospominaniia* (Leningrad 1980), 356–7.

71 V. Rakov, *Apollon Grigor'ev – Literaturnyi kritik* (Ivanovo 1980), 3–4 and 9.

72 V.Ia. Kirpotin, *Dostoevskii v shestidesiatye gody* (Moscow 1966), especially 164–70; I.Z. Serman, 'Dostoevskii i Ap. Grigor'ev,' in B.G. Bazanov and G.M. Friedlender, eds, *Dostoevskii i ego vremia* (Leningrad 1971), 130–42; G.M. Friedlender, 'U istokov "pochvennichestva" (F.M. Dostoevskii i zhurnal *Svetoch*),' *Izvestiia Akademmii nauk SSSR. Otdelenie literatury i iazyka*, 30 (Sept.–Oct. 1971), sec. v, 400–10; U.A. Gural'nik, 'Dostoevskii, slavianofily i "pochvennichestvo,"' in K. N. Lomunov, ed, *Dostoevskii-Khudozhnik i myslitel'. Sbornik statei* (Moscow 1972); A.L. Ospovat, 'K izucheniiu pochvennichestva (Dostoevskii i Ap. Grigor'ev),' *Dostoevskii. Materialy i issledovaniia*, III (Leningrad 1978); V.A. Tunimanov, 'Ap. Grigor'ev v pis'makh i "Dnevnike Pisatelia" Dostoevskogo,' in *Dostoevskii. Materialy i issledovaniia*, VII (Leningrad 1987), 22–34.

73 A.L. Ospovat, 'Zametki o pochvennichestve,' in *Dostoevskii. Materialy i issledovaniia*, IV (Leningrad 1980), 168–9 and 172. The idea that Grigor'ev's theory was

'objectively reactionary' and oriented to the past, however, remains in recent Soviet Russian scholarship. S. Vaiman remarks that Grigor'ev saw Russia's salvation in social involution, a return to patriarchal forms of community. S. Vaiman, '"K serdtsu serdtsem ..." (Ob "organicheskoi kritike" Apollona Grigor'eva),' *Voprosy literatury*, II (Feb. 1988), 151.

74 S.N. Nosov, *Apollon Grigor'ev: Sud'ba i tvorchestvo* (Moscow 1990).

75 Alexandre Koyré, *La philosophie et le problème national en Russie au début du XIX siècle* (Paris 1929); T.G. Masaryk, *Russland und Europa* (Prague 1919), Czech translation in 1930; D.I. Chizhevskii, *Gegel' v Rossii* (Paris 1939); Ettore Lo Gatto, *L'estetika e la poetica in Russia* (Florence 1947).

76 W. Giusti, 'Annotazioni su A.A. Grigor'ev,' *Annali* (Istituto Universitario Orientale, sezione Slava), I (1958).

77 Laura Satta Boschian, *Il regno oscuro. Vita e opere di A.A. Grigor'ev* (Naples 1969).

78 Jurgen Lehmann, *Der Einfluss der Philosophie des deutschen Idealismus in der russischen Literaturkritik des 19. Jahrhundert. Die 'organische Kritik' Apollon A. Grigor'evs* (Heidelberg 1975); an American attempt to make a sampling of Grigor'ev's work available in the West was A.A. Grigor'ev, *Sochineniia*, I, *Kritika*, V.S. Krupitsch, ed. (Villanova, Penn., 1970); another was an English translation of Grigor'ev's autobiography: Apollon Grigoryev, *My Literary and Moral Wanderings*, Ralph Matlaw, trans (New York 1962).

79 T.G. Masaryk, *The Spirit of Russia*, 3 vols. (London 1955); V.V. Zenkovskii, *A History of Russian Philosophy*, 2 vols. (London 1953).

80 René Wellek, *A History of Modern Criticism, 1750–1950*, 4 vols. (New Haven, Conn., 1965).

81 Examples of the former are a pioneering chapter on Grigor'ev in Edward C. Thaden, *Conservative Nationalism in Nineteenth-Century Russia* (Seattle 1964); Robert C. Williams, 'The Russian Soul: A Study in European Thought and Non-European Nationalism,' *Journal of the History of Ideas*, 31, no. 4 (1970), 573–88; E.B. Chances, 'The Ideology of "Pochvennichestvo" in Dostoevsky's Journals *Vremia* and *Epokha*,' PhD dissertation, Princeton University, 1973; Andrzej Walicki, *The Slavophile Controversy: History of a Conservative Utopia in Nineteenth-Century Russian Thought* (Oxford 1975). Walicki shared the Soviet view that thinkers such as Grigor'ev and K.N. Leont'ev were 'objectively reactionary.' Wayne Dowler, *Dostoevsky, Grigor'ev, and Native Soil Conservatism* (Toronto 1982). Examples of the latter are frequent references to Grigor'ev in Victor Terras, *Belinskij and Russian Literary Criticism: The Heritage of Organic Aesthetics* (Madison, Wis., 1974), and G.C. Jerkovich, 'A. Grigor'ev as a Literary Critic,' PhD dissertation, University of Kansas, 1970.

82 Victor Terras pointed to Grigor'ev's affinity for Carlyle and others in his 'Apollon Grigor'ev's Organic Criticism and Its Western Sources,' in Anthony Milkotin, ed, *Western Philosophical Systems in Russian Literature* (Los Angeles 1979), 71–88.

83 Charles Moser argued that among Russian critics 'Belinsky exerted the most direct and profound influence on [Grigor'ev].' Charles A. Moser, *Esthetics as Nightmare: Russian Literary Theory, 1855–1870* (Princeton, NJ, 1989), 21. Victor Terras also emphasized Belinskii as a source for Grigor'ev. Terras, *Belinskij*, 214–22. In my view, that influence, though powerful, was far less direct and more subtle than has previously been supposed.

84 See my 'Two Conservative Views,' 19–32.

85 See my *Dostoevsky, Grigor'ev, and Native Soil Conservatism*, 174–5.

Grigor'ev's Writings

'Apollon Grigor'ev – kritik.' B.F. Egorov, ed., *Uchenye zapiski Tartuskogo gos. universiteta*. XCVIII (1960), 194–246. It includes previously unpublished letters of Grigor'ev and a complete listing of his non-fictional prose writings.

Estetika i kritika. M.F. Ovsiannikov, ed. Moscow 1980

Izbrannye proizvedeniia. D.O. Kostelianets, ed. Moscow 1959

Literaturnaia kritika. B.F. Egorov, ed. Moscow 1967

Materialy dlia biografii A. Grigor'eva. Vl. Kniazhnin, ed. Petrograd 1917. It incorporates the largest extant collection of Grigor'ev's letters.

'Materialy ob Ap. Grigor'eve iz arkhiva N.N. Strakhov,' B.F. Egorov, ed. *Uchenye zapiski Tartuskogo gos. universiteta*. 139 (1963), 343–50

My Literary and Moral Wanderings. Ralph Matlaw, ed and trans. New York 1962

'Neopublikovannye pis'ma Apollona Grigor'eva.' R. Vitaker [R. Whittaker], ed, *Vestnik Moskovskogo universiteta*, no. 2 (1971), 66–73

'Neizvestnye pis'ma A. Grigor'eva.' A. Marchik, ed, *Voprosy literatury*, no. 7 (1965), 254–6

'Novye pis'ma A.A. Grigor'eva.' N.N. Strakhov, ed, *Epokha* (Feb. 1865), 152–82

Nravstvennost' i literatura. F.F. Kuznetsov et al, eds. Moscow 1986

Odisseia poslednego romantika. A.L. Ospovat, ed. Moscow 1988

Polnoe sobranie sochinenii i pisem, I. V.S. Spiridonov, ed. Petrograd 1918. Only one volume was published.

'Publikatsiia i soobshcheniia perepiska Ap. Grigor'eva s N.N. Strakhovym.' B.F. Egorov, ed, *Uchenye zapiski Tartuskogo gos. universiteta*, 167 (1965), 163–73

Sobranie sochinenii, i–xiv. V. Savodnik, ed. Moscow 1915–16

Sochineniia Apollona Grigor'eva. I. N. Strakhov, ed. St Petersburg 1876

Sochineniia. I. Kritika. V.S. Krupitsch, ed. Villanova, Penn., 1970

Sochineniia v dvukh tomakh. B.F. Egorov and A.L. Ospovat, eds. Moscow 1990

Stikhotvoreniia. A. Blok, ed. Moscow 1916

Stikhotvoreniia i poemy. B.F. Egorov, ed. Moscow and Leningrad 1966
Stikhotvoreniia i poemy. B.F. Egorov, ed. Moscow 1978
Teatral'naia kritika. E.S. Alekseeva and M.A. Venskaia, eds. Leningrad 1985
Vospominaniia. R.V. Ivanov-Razumnik, ed. Moscow and Leningrad 1930. It
  includes Grigor'ev's memoirs and memoirs about him.
Vospominaniia. B.F. Egorov, ed. Leningrad 1980

Index